Why Fiction?

Why

STAGES

Series Editors

General Editor: Gerald Prince
University of Pennsylvania

Michael Holquist
Yale University

Warren Motte
University of Colorado at Boulder

Patricia Meyer Spacks
University of Virginia

Fiction?

POURQUOI LA FICTION?

Jean-Marie Schaeffer

TRANSLATED BY DORRIT COHN

University of Nebraska Press :: *Lincoln and London*

Cet ouvrage, publié dans le cadre d'un programme
d'aide à la publication, bénéficie du soutien du
Ministère des Affaires étrangères et du Service
Culturel de l'Ambassade de France aux États-Unis.

This work, published as part of a program of aid
for publication, received support from the French
Ministry of Foreign Affairs and the Cultural Service
of the French Embassy in the United States.

Publication of this book
was assisted by a grant from the
National Endowment for the Arts.

"A Great Nation Deserves Great Art"

NATIONAL
ENDOWMENT
FOR THE ARTS

Library of Congress Cataloging-in-Publication Data
Schaeffer, Jean-Marie.
[Pourquoi la fiction? English]
Why fiction? / Jean-Marie Schaeffer; translated
[from the French] by Dorrit Cohn.
p. cm.
Includes bibliographical references and index.
ISBN 978-0-8032-1758-4 (cloth : alk. paper)
1. Mimesis in literature. 2. Imitation in literature.
3. Fiction—History and criticism. 4. Fiction—
Technique. I. Cohn, Dorrit. II. Title.
PN56.M536S3313 2010
809.3—dc22   2009048485

Designed by Nathan Putens.

Contents

Introduction

The demands of summertime information being what they are, the daily newspaper *Libération,* dated July 26–27, 1996, attracted the customer thanks to the charms of a creature named Lara Croft. Next to a reproduction of the young woman — "armed with an Uzi, in a bikini signed Gucci" — and under the title "A Virtual Star Is Born," one could read: "Well turned out, intrepid, wily, Lara Croft turns the head of millions of earthlings. A sexual myth undressed on a multitude of Internet sites, she is not in danger of aging: Lara Croft is the heroine of an immensely successful video game, *Tomb Raider*: more than two million copies sold in the world, of which 300,000 in France alone. Beyond the enormous economic stakes, this creature of bits and pixels, and the fascination she creates, are the symptoms of a new culture." According to the statements, two pages farther on, of a manager of a firm specializing in digital effects for the cinema, this new culture — "cyberculture" — would be "an evolution comparable to the Renaissance."

What was striking in this otherwise excellent report was to see a video game—thus, it would seem, an interactive fictional universe—raised to the status of a symptom of "cyberculture," that is, of the whole of cultural practices linked to digital media. It is I, of course, who use the expression "fictional universe." In "cybercultural" circles one would rather speak of "virtual reality" with a view to distinguishing between digital universes and "traditional" fictions. The articles in *Libération* suggested in any case the idea of an essential link between the technical revolution of the digital and a parallel revolution that would concern the human imagination. We are actually witnessing the birth of a new modality of being, the "virtual reality"—different at the same time from "true" reality and from traditional products of the human imagination, that is, fictions. In qualifying Lara Croft as a "star," in according her the status of a virtual actress rather than that of a "simple" fictional character, the newspaper made this postulate its own again.

This conception of the digital revolution is not new: we have found it all over the place for at least the last ten years. But it gives rise to two different interpretations. The record devoted to Lara Croft is typical of the euphoric interpretation. It is opposed by a radically dysphoric variant, it too presented more than once in the same newspaper. Its starting point is the same: the digital revolution will make humanity enter a new era, an era of "virtual realities." But it draws from this an entirely different conclusion: this revolution announces the end of "true" reality. "Cyberculture" will end with the victory of imitation over reality, or at least with a lack of differentiation between the two: we will enter an era characterized by the end of the ontological division between (authentic) being and (illusory) appearance.

The fact that these two positions sum up the essential of the opinions exchanged in public on the subject of "cybernetic" revolution is revealing; obviously, it is difficult for us to speak of digital simulation other than in extreme terms, whether it is in the enthusiastic perspective of a conquest of infinite virtual spaces or in the opposed one of an eschatology of a humanity condemned to live in the semblance and manipulated by the structures of totalitarian power á la Orwell. But the important point is elsewhere: although the two versions oppose each other when it comes to the consequences of "cyberculture" for the future of humanity, they are in accord where their premises are concerned. Both maintain that the realities created thanks to digital techniques have a radically new status, irreducible to anything humanity has known to this point. Yet these premises result in crossed equivoques. The euphoric vision of digital revolution, illustrated by the record devoted to Lara Croft, raises a banal fictional game to the level of a supposedly new ontological modality, that of "virtual reality." The rival vision denounces this same "virtual reality" as an "imitation" and as a "semblance"—all terms traditionally used to condemn . . . fiction. This is strange, to say the least.

Far be it from me to want to underestimate the profound upheavals that the digital revolution—and in this case "revolution" does not seem to me too strong a term—will lead to (already leads to) in the domain of sciences, technology, information, and communication. This transformative power of the digital is intimately linked to the fact that it is a generalist tool, because, as Claude Cadoz emphasizes, "the information technology has this that is exclusive to it, that it intervenes alone in the three domains, that of action, that of observation and of knowledge of the real, and that of communication."[1] On the other hand, there is no doubt that the utilization of digital techniques opens up new possibilities for fiction. These new forms of fiction will perhaps rearrange to a certain degree the traditional relations between fiction and the other forms of interactions with reality. But nothing of all this justifies the implicit presuppositions of the two existing theses or the historical scenarios they develop.

The catastrophic scenario is especially unconvincing. First, the very idea of a possible victory of imitations over reality seems to me absurd. Suppose for a moment that humanity "decides" no longer to distinguish between the true and the false, or that the technological evolution leads it one day to confuse the real and the imaginary (e.g., real copulation with "cybersex"): if such a thing happened, it would not result in a totally insane society but, more prosaically, in the rapid disappearance of our invading species. Furthermore, happily (or unhappily from the point of view of most of the other species), the numerical revolution has strictly nothing to do with some victory of imitation over reality or over true representation. Though digital techniques surely give birth to "virtual realities," "virtualization" of the world is not the same thing as its fictionalization: the virtual as such opposes the actual, not reality.[2] Only fiction can be said to oppose reality (even though, when one says this, one has said nothing at all). Finally, contrary to what the eulogists as much as the Cassandras of the digital revolution presuppose, virtualization is by no means an invention of the digital era. The "virtual realities" are born with biological systems of representation: *every* mental representation is a virtual reality.[3] There is thus definitely a link between the virtual and fiction; being a particular modality of representation, fiction is at the same time a specific form of the virtual. But as a specific form it is precisely irreducible to the general definition of the virtual.

The thesis according to which the digital revolution would mark the birth of a new modality of the human imagination, statutorily different from traditional fictions, rests on the same confusion. This is perfectly illustrated by the article from *Libération* when it transfigures the fictional character Lara Croft into a "virtual star." Because, if (at least provisionally) one leaves aside the fact that Lara Croft is a character in a game rather than a character in a story (a difference that points effectively toward an interesting aspect of digital fictions), she distinguishes herself from her nondigital ancestors only in that she is "generated" by a digital code, whereas those were — and still are — created by language (like Julien Sorel), by a filmic print (like Indiana Jones), or graphically (like Droopy). At the level of her ontological status Lara Croft is neither more nor less "virtual" than any other imaginary character. The fact that she is a fictional character in a digital simulation of filmic sequences does not influence her status — which shows that digital fiction does not disrupt the logical status of fiction (in relation to "reality") but merely puts at our disposal new ways of fabricating and receiving fictions (which is not too bad, after all).

BUT WHY INTRODUCE A BOOK THAT MEANS TO TREAT fiction by observations devoted to video games and to "cyberculture"? Is this not to give oneself a futile and unsuitable starting point? It seems to me that this double objection asks for a double response. First of all, I don't know if the realities in question go back to a futile domain. After all, the division between the serious and the futile does not pass in the same place for everyone, as is proved by the fact that even literary fiction, though it is unanimously celebrated today, has often in the past been accused of being futile. Second, and this is in reality the only thing that matters, even if the diagnostic of futility were accepted, we would have to say that today the question of fiction is *also* the one of video games and of "cyberculture."

First, it is undeniable that video games are in the process of taking a larger and larger place in the imagination — and thus in the fictional culture — of our children and grandchildren, as is notably proven by the fact that their ordinary ludic form is more and more often the starting point for fictional *representations* in the canonical sense of the term, for example, films or television series. This would already justify their being taken into account by anyone who asks himself the question of fiction. But there is a more profound reason why one must not ignore them. I am convinced that one cannot understand what fiction is if one does not take as a starting point the fundamental mechanisms of "doing-as-if" — of ludic feint — and of imaginative simulation, of which the genesis is observed in the games of role-playing and the daydreaming of early childhood. Now, video games develop the same aptitudes: to be able to play a digital game, one must be capable of entering a universe ruled by ludic feint. They thus constitute one of the possible entrances for the more general question of the relations between fictional *games* and fiction in the canonical sense of the term.

So far as "cyberculture" in general is concerned, if the discussions it occasions do not teach us much about digital revolution, they inform us (involuntarily) on what concerns the question of fiction at this end of the twentieth century. As I indicated, the "digital revolution" has, in itself, no interesting link with the question of "semblance" and thus with fiction. I do not want to suggest by this that the worry that some people feel when faced with the development of digital media is without a cause. Men have in all periods put technological progress in the service of the most diverse ends in such a way that the consequences have been in general mixed. One would have to be naive to think that it could be otherwise with digital techniques. But these risks, whatever they are, cannot explain the virulence and the often eschatological character of the polemics or their polarization on a supposed hegemony of "imitation." The situation is enlightened as soon as one becomes conscious of the fact that the argumentation on which the dysphoric vision of the "cybernetic" future rests is largely borrowed from the traditional accusations formulated against fiction. In other words, the ancient problem of fiction is simply hiding under the outside of a warning against the dangers of the digital revolution. The present debate is thus only the avatar of a questioning that has recurred in Occidental culture since ancient Greece. It explains why it does not help us to evaluate the eventual dangers of the digital revolution but teaches us, on the other hand, a lot about the ambivalent attitude that we continue to hold toward fictional creation. In fact, it demonstrates that, so far as our attitude toward fiction is concerned, we are still the contemporaries of Plato.

THE CONTEXT THAT I HAVE JUST SKETCHED OBVERSELY delimits the aim of this book. It will be a matter of developing an analysis of fiction that would be capable of making us understand its central role in human culture and that at the same time explains the anthropological importance of mimetic arts, inasmuch as these arts are also — certainly in variable proportions and according to multiple modalities — arts of fiction. This perspective will lead me to give (again) a central place to the notion of mimesis. Imitation, resemblance, feint, illusion, and so on are terms that, at least as of now, have a bad reputation: the facts they designate are often decreed to be incompatible with every "true" art; and the analytic notions that correspond to them are supposedly deprived of all pertinence in the domain of artistic reflection on the arts. I hope to show not only that these are indispensable categories but also that they designate technical procedures for effects that play a central role in innumerable artistic activities. In doing this I do not pretend to propose innovative work: the way I will take has been opened by other works to which I shall have occasion to refer in the course of these pages.

It is nonetheless advisable not to misunderstand the function that I will grant to the question of mimesis. Not all arts are representational; thus, the category cannot constitute the foundation of a general theory of the arts. It would be quite as improper to identify the arts of representation with the mimetic mechanisms that they employ. For one thing, the fact of representing something can never be restricted to the fact of imitating something, even in the case where the representation uses mimetic mechanisms. For another thing, fiction is an "emerging" reality, that is to say that it is a matter of a specific intentional fact that is irreducible to the simple addition of its basic mechanisms. On the other hand, I propose to reaffirm the (real but too often forgotten) links between "daily" mimetic activities and fiction (and thus also the mimetic arts). For it is the importance of (ludic *and* serious) mimeticism in the lives of human beings that permits us to understand why the arts of representation so often (but not always) tend to an exacerbation of the mimetic effect. Only an adequate comprehension of the anthropological foundations of mimetic *activities* can enlighten us on the common bedrock of mimetic *arts* and indicate to us the primary source of the attraction that since ancient times it has not ceased to have on human beings.

This at least is the ideal horizon of this book. But to propose a general framework is one thing, to fill it is another. In this case the path surpasses by far the limits of a book and, I'm afraid, of my competence. My real plan will therefore be much less ambitious. Among the multiple aspects of the problem I will retain only five. Though they are far from exhausting the question, they seem to me nonetheless likely to capture some essential points of it:

1. The discussion around the "digital revolution" shows that, if one wants to arrive at a *positive* understanding of mimesis and more specifically of fiction, it is suitable first to defuse the antimimetic argumentation. The latter is in fact so profoundly anchored in our cultural tradition that it sometimes brands even the theories of the defenders of fiction. I use the term "defuse" purposefully: it will not be a matter of "refuting" the position of Plato (and of his disciples). But one can show on which (sometimes implicit) presuppositions it rests, one can

try to understand the worries that motivated it. The presuppositions of the antimimetic position are linked to a profound incomprehension of mimetic activities, as proved notably by the (insidious) mixture between fiction and false illusion. At the same time, fiction is caught in the debate between the philosopher and the sophist, where it can only occupy a losing place: who would assume the place of the "nasty" sophist? It will nonetheless be necessary to try to understand the motives for worry underlying the polemics, because its virulence is probably not reducible to the competition between two discursive devices, that of the philosopher and that of the sophist. My hypothesis will be that these worries have partly a more "obscure" foundation linked to a particular conception of the genealogy of feinting activities. But this conception is likely to teach us important things — if not on what fiction is, at least on what it is not.

2. The notion of *fiction* immediately brings up that of *imitation*, of *feint*, of *simulation*, of *semblance*, of *representation*, of *resemblance*, and so on. But while all these notions play an important role in our ways of speaking of fiction, they are rarely used in a manner that is unambiguous. It is not astonishing, therefore, that the notion of "fiction" itself remains elusive — hence the importance of a conceptual clarification. It should allow one to replace fiction in the global context of our manner of representing the world and of interacting with it. My reader will have understood that this analysis will be a key point of this work in the sense that all later considerations will depend directly on it.

3. Many species of animals have developed mimetic capacities, and many are able to put mimetic mechanisms at the service of acts of (serious) feint. In addition, many species of mammals are capable of uncoupling certain motor activities from their first function and produce ludic imitations: it is enough to observe

kittens or puppies brawling with each other or with their parents. But the human species seems to be the only one to have developed an aptitude to produce and to "consume" fictions in the canonical sense of the term, that is, fictional *representations*. Aristotle had already noted that man was the imitating animal par excellence and that it was this natural disposition that was basic to the invention of fiction: "Imitation is natural to man from childhood, one of its advantages over the lower animals being this, that he is the most imitative creature in the world, and learns at first by imitation."[4] That fiction was born only at so late a stage in the evolution of life need not surprise us. Fictional competence necessitates the learning of a set of intentional attitudes of great complexity (so great it surpasses, it would seem, even the aptitude of our cousins, the large apes). In other words, the division between the fictive and the factual is a human conquest on the phylogenetic plane as well as on the ontogenetic plane. But it is a matter of a human conquest as such and not of a particular culture: all human communities know activities of fiction, even if it is only in the form of the ludic feint (of children). If there are good analyses of *verbal* fiction and of its relationship with ludic feint and, to a lesser degree, some other particular fictional forms (e.g., the theater or the cinema), the general question of fiction—which is fundamentally that of fictional competence—is paradoxically less explored.[5]

4. Fiction can take multiple forms. A "good" description must be valid, if not for all these forms (no one is obliged to perform the impossible . . .), then at least for the most important ones. It must particularly take account of fictional games as much as of fictions in the canonical sense of the term. And in the latter it must be valid for the theater, graphic representations (pictures, comic strips . . .), and the cinema quite as much as for (verbal) stories. But at the same time it must take into account the differ-

ent modalities according to which fictionality combines in these different activities and artistic forms. A particular problem is that of the status of visual representations (painting, photography). In Plato the notion of *mimēsis* treats in the same way literary fiction and pictorial representation, both being considered of the same rank in the domain of "semblance." According to this conception, which has been very influential, a figurative picture would be a fiction by the simple fact that it is an imitation (an analogical representation) of reality rather than a perception of this reality and not because—or insofar as—it would rest on a ludic feint. I think that under this nonsubtle form the thesis cannot be maintained, but it will force us to take the entire measure of the complexity of the question of fiction in the domain of visual representation.

5. Why do human beings devote themselves to fictional activities, and why do they consume with so much eagerness the fictions created by their fellow creatures? Causal inquests in the domain of cultural facts (and more widely of facts of intentionality) are in general difficult to carry out. For that reason I will limit myself in what will be the concluding chapter of this book to a few reasonable reflections. The question—is it necessary to recall it?—had already been approached by Aristotle in his *Poetics*. Since then we have surely made some progress in the knowledge, for example, of the anthropological predisposition of (serious and ludic) imitation, of the links between imitation and modelization, and more globally of the functioning of fiction. But concerning the essential, this new knowledge confirms his hypotheses and corroborates the general framework of his analysis. The manner in which I will approach (without great pretensions) the question of the functions of fiction will thus also be a (timid) tribute to him who has known, more than any other, how to give this eminently pleasant and profitable human practice the place it deserves.

MY READER WILL HAVE UNDERSTOOD THAT THE AMBITION of this book is not to develop a theory of mimetic arts or a theory of fiction as an artistic form. In the fourth chapter I will indeed be led to turn my attention to some mimetic arts, but it will essentially be a matter of evaluating the concrete pertinence (or absence of pertinence . . .) of the conception of fiction that I have here proposed. My work takes its place on a more elementary level: it is a matter of understanding the anthropological foundations of fiction. Whence the importance that I will grant to the question of mental attitudes, of intentional competences, of psychological mechanisms, of pragmatic presuppositions, and so on, that allow us to create (and to understand) fictions. Whence also the taking into account of the question of the functions of the fictional device — because only these functions are capable of explaining why we create fictions, why they interest us, why they give us pleasure. For all these reasons this book will interest itself more in what the "doing-as-if" of children or the fictional games of the *Tomb Raider* kind (and its heroine, Lara Croft) have in common with the great literary, theatrical, and cinematographic fictions than in what (ultimately) distinguishes them. In other words, according to the perspective presented here, the universes of "great" art and of "futile" games do not oppose themselves as two incompatible worlds. On the contrary: in the absence of the second, the first would not exist. It is only because at an early age we have acquired the competence of the ludic feint that we are able later to appreciate artistic fictions that are more complex. It is not a matter of choosing between *Tomb Raider* and *Le Cid*, between Lara Croft and Chimene: they do not compete in the same category. It is a matter of appreciating them all, each in its own manner.

1
Who Is Afraid of Imitation?

1. From the Imitator Wolf to the Virtual Wolf

It is the story of two little girls — Delphine and Marinette — and of their meeting with the wolf. Even though their parents made them promise never to let the beast get near them, the children, curious and greedy for adventures, profit from their parents' momentary absence to open the door to him. The wolf, as may be expected, is all gentleness and civility. The slanders of which he is the object due to a few sins of his youth — among them the regrettable incident of Little Red Riding-Hood emphasized by petty souls — depress him. The times are distant when the wolf was a wolf for human beings. The putting under guardianship and the encirclement of the last vestiges of savage life have inverted the roles: from now on it is man who is a wolf for the wolf. In his cordiality our friend asks only to show himself innocent, and he is the first to regret his dissolute behavior of the past that earned him his general disgrace. He is no longer the one whose eyes shine in the night; he is the companion of games — the consenting victim, rather — who lends himself to the children's whims.

The first visit passes wonderfully, and the accomplice is received as an old friend on the occasion of a renewed absence of the parents. The children and the wolf kiss each other, they tell the news of the week, they play—a horse game first. Then: "Wolf, what if we played wolf?" The wolf doesn't know this game, and the little ones must explain it to him. It is understood that it is he who will play the wolf. Choked with laughter, he begins to play the beast. To ritual questions he gives no less ritual answers. He willingly mimes the gestures of the big bad wolf: he puts on his underpants, his pants, his braces, his collar, his vest. In short, they have a great time. But, little by little, our wolf stops laughing. He becomes serious and plays his role with more conviction. Then a strange agitation seizes him: at the sight of the little girls' legs, which pass and pass again in front of the table under which he is hidden, he starts trembling and his chops start to wrinkle. Finally, the poor beast can hold back no longer: no sooner have the children asked the ritual questions for the third time—"Wolf, are you there? Do you hear me? What are you doing?"—than he belches with a foaming mouth "I'm on a horse and I'm leaving the woods," emerges from under the table, throws himself on his playmates, tears them into pieces, and devours them.[1]

This little story by Marcel Aymé, a parodic variation on a classic theme, produces certain essential notions that we spontaneously associate with fiction and more generally with the arts said to be mimetic: the resemblance (here raised to ontological identity between character and actor), the imitation (here somewhat special, since it is a matter of an imitation of oneself), the ludic feint (the "true" wolf is meant to be only "for make-believe," the big bad wolf of fairy tales). But it illustrates primarily in an eloquent manner the ambivalent attitude—a mixture of fascination and distrust—that is ours when we are faced with mimetic activities. Fascination, since we actively look for limitations of all sorts, and nothing pleases us more than being (made to be) caught up in the game: like the spectators of the Elizabethan period who — at least according to a persistent legend — fled the theater when the Devil appeared on the scene, like the child who cries when one tells him the story of the death of the little match seller in the tale by Andersen, like (almost) anyone of us immersed in some *Indiana Jones* or some *Batman* and moving back instinctively when the Bad Man appears . . . Distrust is born when the charm is broken: isn't there something worrisome in the fact that we can be overwhelmed in this way by shams? Their power seems irresistible: even if we knew, at the moment we exposed ourselves to their charm, that they were shams (it was precisely this knowledge that had primarily motivated us to expose ourselves), we let ourselves be taken. Doesn't this capacity that semblances have to neutralize our instances of "rational control" constitute a more than sufficient reason to distrust all imitation, even an artistic one? Or at least, should we not in the arts that, for one reason or another, have recourse to it thwart its efficacity by procedures of ironic distance, by a rupture of the effect of the real, by a deconstruction of the mechanisms of alienation that it puts to work?

In Occidental culture this distrust has been in existence since Greek antiquity. It is of course Plato who expressed it with greatest force, to the point where all the subsequent antimimetic polemics did no more than embellish the argument developed in the *Republic*. For the reactivations of the antimimetic attitude have been innumerable: one finds it again, for example, in medieval (Byzantine) iconoclasm; it reappeared in the Jansenist warning against theater and figurative painting; it guided at least in part the reflection of Jena romanticism on poetry; some decades later it tended to disqualify photography; in the twentieth century it belonged to the program of the inventors of abstract art (Kandinsky and Mondrian), and it was utilized as a criterion of disqualification in a (large) part of criticism in the domain of the plastic arts; it is the foundation of the epic theater of Brecht and nourished the majority of "antirealist" and "antinaturalist" polemics in the domain of literary fiction (through the criticism of "reality effect" and of "verisimilitude"); finally, in the most immediate present, it still founds a large part of the reluctances triggered by the development of digital media (and notably of images of synthesis and devices of virtual reality).

Since the mimetic procedures have a constituent function for certain arts, for example, figurative painting and verbal fiction as well as photography, the cinema, and, nowadays, the digital arts, the most radical form of the antimimetic attitude consists in condemning these arts as such. Thus, in the domain of the plastic arts the enemy of mimeticism accepts solely nonfigurative art (abstract painting, conceptual art . . .) and treats the mimetic practices (figurative painting, photography, cinema, multimedia . . .) as simple symptoms of an endemic iconolatry. In the literary domain it saves only poetry (preferably nonnarrative) and despises fiction in all its forms. A less radical attitude consists in distinguishing between essential (or pure) practices and adventitious (or impure) practices. This is how certain critics of art maintain that figurative painting certainly is part of pictorial art but that only abstract painting has discovered its essence. The discovery of the latter, they add, from now on allows us to see figurative art according to its true essence, that is, neutralizing those adventitious elements, since we have become conscious of the fact that the mimetic relation does not concern the artistic status of works but only their representational function. The same attitude is sometimes found in the domain of literature: it is then poetry as a pure linguistic game that is meant to realize the essence of verbal art; in fiction the artistic element would begin only once we go beyond the mimetic constituent.

This second form of the antimimetic attitude, nowadays the

most widespread, therefore aims in its essence at neutralizing the pertinence of the mimetic function in the inside itself of the arts of representation. From the point of view of aesthetic values it results in a support brought to works that "subvert" their mimetic basis and in a condemnation of the ones that, instead, develop imitative techniques (resemblance, naturalism, reality effect, trompe l'oeil) and by that reinforce the mimetic "illusion." This position has the advantage of "saving" the mimetic arts, but to do so it has to defend them against themselves. The essential objection against it is that, if it were right, the very existence of mimetic artistic practices would be a mystery: in fact, if, as it affirms, the mimetic aspects concern the infra-artistic, one does not understand why men have developed precisely arts based on these aspects. Why have they not been content to develop artistic practices without a mimetic constituent? This intrinsic weakness of the "sophisticated" antimimetic position paradoxically does not affect the more radical position that takes on mimetic arts in themselves: it condemns them, it is precisely because it recognizes their power of attraction that it distrusts them.

The crusade against shams presents itself often at the same time as a moral struggle and as a defense of artistic excellence, since the mimetic drive is said to be at the same time dangerous (it alienates us) and easy (it obeys "prescriptions"). So the antimimetic discourse is first the discourse of a pedagogue: it is always Marinette and Delphine—the inhabitants of the Cave induced to error by the shades, the iconological pagans, the children who live in a naive immediacy not yet mediatized by the exercise of reason, the oppressed ones incapable of discovering on their own the mechanisms of social alienation that the mimetic identification serves to reproduce and reinforce, the "great public" manipulated by "Hollywood cinema," the "postmodern subjects" lobotomized by digital technologies—whom it is suitable to enlighten and to lead (or lead again) to reason. It is then a denunciatory discourse: if there are victims, there must be a wolf. The latter, to be sure, takes on diverse forms according to the times: at present it is the merchant, for example, the "Hollywood" producer or the "techno-capitalist of Silicon Valley"; in other eras it was the dramatic actor; or else, as in Plato, it was the tragic poet and the painter. But no matter what clothes he puts on, the imitator-wolf always pursues the same end: to corrupt hearts and to alienate reason. Since the mimetic effects are said to be "easy" or even "vulgar," the antimimetic discourse is also a distinguished discourse. It allows us to trace a line of demarcation between art in the noble sense of the term and a whole set of more or less doubtful practices that, if we were not on our guard, would tend to throw us off the trail, because, alas, a part of the noble art is based on the same techniques, the one of imitation precisely. In the same way, in the domain of reception it allows us to disqualify as not pertinent every mode of reception that constructs the works as mimetic models, that is, that treats fictions as representations, when it would be suitable to part with all "referential illusion" in order to have access to the artistic purity of works.

I deliberately exaggerated the traits and caricatured somewhat the antimimetic positions presently defended: they are sometimes more complex and sophisticated. But at bottom they all reduce to the few theses that I have just sketched. We will find them further on in Plato: it is because they have not budged since this first formulation — which, be it said in passing, does not rejuvenate us. Only the target of the polemic has changed in the course of history. Thus, nowadays, and thanks to the ad hoc thesis of the infra-artistic status of mimetic elements, pictorial art and literary fiction escape the debate. It must be said that, through this auxiliary hypothesis (which was naturally not present in Plato), the antimimetic position also saves itself: the original targets of the antimimetic argumentation — painting as well as dramatic and narrative literature — have long since acquired a canonical status in our culture, a status that would no doubt risk rendering any revival of the Platonic grievances in respect to them ineffective. The result is a displacement of the attack toward the mimetic arts, whose birth is more recent. These are targets all the more vulnerable because they are technological arts. They depend in part on a divided know-how and necessitate sometimes a collective execution in several planned phases; finally, they often need important financial aid and cannot escape the question of economic profitability. They thus permit the antimimetic argument to lean on segregationist (art against technique) and antieconomic (art against the industry of the media) ideals that command in great part the manner in which we at present think of the relations between art and society.

Consequently, contrary to the classical Platonic argument, the "new manner" antimimetic position is always constructed around a thesis of a profound rupture between the "technological" practices that it condemns and the "traditional" mimetic arts. This rupture is said to correspond to a difference in status: art on one side, industry (and commerce) on the other. The first manifestation of this modern variant of the antimimetic polemic can be found in the hostile reactions provoked by the birth of photography, the first artistic medium issued directly from modern technology (in this case from chemistry and from optics). We find it afterward in the attacks against "commercial" cinema and, more recently, against television. And it still delivers a large part of the ammunition to the present-day denunciation of digital techniques (with the wolf Bill Gates as Big Brother). This last debate is worth staying with a little longer than I did in my introduction, for if, as I have noted, it does not teach us much about digital media, it reveals the persistence of an ambivalent attitude toward fiction.

The thesis of the rupture goes back to maintain that the digital media abolish the distinction between the true and the *false in itself* and that through this they escape the "traditional" distinction between fiction and referential truthfulness. There are thus two aspects. On the one hand, the digital media are techniques of "irrealization" of the real: everything they do is transformed into semblance. On the other hand, because of this intrinsic characteristic of the digital tool, the traditional distinction between fiction and the "factual" is no longer applicable: the digital goes back to sham; that is, it replaces reality (in which humanity lived up till now) by a monstrous proliferation of semblances. Both affirmations seem to me false. I think that, in the domain of the digital, the question of the distinction between the true and the false continues to be posed in exactly the same terms as in the predigital representations. On the other hand, when one replaces the development of digital fictions, or, rather, the utilization of the digital tool for fictional ends, in its historical context, what is presented as a rupture reveals itself to be a simple phase of a development that lasts several centuries.

The first point calls for a simple answer. Since the thesis opposes digital media to other semiotic supports, it is enough to ask oneself if the characteristics by which the digital support distinguishes itself from the "traditional" support effectively abolishes the distinction between the "true" and the "false." Yet one must first identify these specific characteristics.[2] It seems to me that the specificity of the digital code is in fact double.

First, it is a matter of a universal semiotic support: any signal can be digitized. This signifies that the translation of any information into the binary language of the computer can correspond to quite different transformations according to the information of departure concerned. It can be a matter of the transformation of a mimetic information into a digital information: this happens when a picture is digitalized. It is suitable to note that the fact of whether or not it is a matter of a mimetic information is completely indifferent at the level of digital transcoding itself (this is precisely where its universal character resides): a scanner treats in exactly the same manner a photograph and a page of writing. It is only at a second stage, thanks to a program of alphabetic knowledge, that the pixelated marks, extracted from the page of text, will be re-encoded with a view to being treated as linguistic signs. The point of departure can of course also be an already digitized signal. This is what happens each time I enter letters or numbers on the keyboard: each letter or number (and, more generally, every digital symbol on the keyboard) corresponds to a given binary combination (e.g., 0010111010). In this case, the binary code functions in relation to alphabetical writing as the latter functions in relation to oral language; that is, it is a matter of a digital metacode of an already digital code.

In a general manner a large part of computer code is in fact a metacode of informations already treated, whether mimetically (images) or digitally (texts, digital information). Contrary to appearances, computerized photography — to be distinguished from the computerization of images created graphically or photographically — has, for example, the status of a metacode. In fact, the pixelation effected on the level of the electronic sensor bears on an information already treated with a view to its exploitation as a mimetic figuration, since the flux of the photons has been centered by the objective and the sensor constitutes the plan of the project ion of this centered flux. Even in the images of synthesis there is in general a residual level that takes over from metacode, since our starting point is very often the mimetic modeling of objects to be presented. It is at a second moment that these modelings will be transformed into a set of coordinates of surface points from which the program will construct the polygons, those polygons constituting the departing data of the work of evaluation of the synthetic image itself.

The second essential characteristic of the digital code is its reversibility: it is capable not only of transcoding any information but, moreover, of restituting it then in its original form. Here again there is a kinship with the system of writing in the domain of languages; the writing can always be retranslated into an oral discourse. The difference is that, contrary to the transcode of the systems of writing, digital transcode is not limited to a single type of entrance signal. More fundamentally, when one compares the digital code no longer with the metacode of the written but with the linguistic code itself, the crucial difference resides in the fact that the latter is *not* reversible. It has been said that everything that can be thought can be said, and Wittgenstein went so far as to say that the limits of one's world are the limits of what one can say. Suppose this thesis is valid, that is, suppose that the field of informations that can be treated by a human being is reduced to those that can be represented linguistically, languages are in any case incapable of restituting transcoded information in its original form.[3] For example, suppose that the information contained in an image can be translated into a verbal description, it is in any case impossible to retranslate it afterward in visual form in such a way that it keeps the homological links with the mimetic form it started out from. On the other hand, the binary calculator is not only capable of transcoding an image into a set of binary signs, but it can also at each moment retranslate this information into graphic information, be it in the form of an exit from the screen or a printing exit, and this in such a fashion that the mimetic signs of entry and exit are linked by a local or global relationship of homology.

If these two characteristics are in effect the principal traits through which the digital code distinguishes itself from other supports of information, then the response to our question is not in doubt, since neither of the two indicates the least elective affinity between digital media and fiction. In fact, where the question of the relationships between "truth" and "semblance" is concerned, the digital support is in the exact same situation as the other semiotic supports. A digital factual text remains a factual text, just as a digital fictional text remains a fiction. This is also true for the domain of visual representations, with which the essence of the polemic raised by digital media is concerned. One often hears that the digital image is an image "without origin and without model" and that this would explain its intrinsically fictional status. But a synthetic image is not more without origin and without model than a painting. Both are produced intentionally by human beings (the computerized program does nothing more than to execute the calculations that the computer graphics designer orders it to do in accord with the results he wants to obtain) and both are, depending on the case, fictional modelings or mimetic signs that have a "denotative" function.

In this way, nothing forbids us from using synthetic techniques of images to realize the portrait of a real person: the semiotic status of this portrait will be exactly the same as that of a pictured portrait; that is, it will be a matter of an iconic sign representing a real person. In the same way, a digital photograph has the same status as a "traditional" photograph: it is a matter of iconic indices caused by what the photograph represents, even if incidentally the photons act not on a chemical agent but on an electronic sensor. One sometimes says that the specificity of the digital photograph is in the fact that one can transform practically all the parameters of the electronic imprint with the help of a treatment of the image, that one can encrust the elements coming from other images, and so forth. But here again it is not a matter of a rupture but simply of an adaptation and perfection of methods of touching up an image utilized already in the silver-planted photography. In short, like any other semiotic support, digital techniques are capable of fulfilling various functions. Among these functions fiction is far from being the most important, and, in any case, it is not linked to the support itself.

Let us come to the second problem, that of the relation of digital fictions with "traditional" fictions. At this stage of the inquiry I evidently don't have at my disposal yet the elements that would allow me to answer this question directly, since the notion of "fiction" itself remains to be clarified. But I can at least show that another explicative hypothesis exists, more satisfying than the one of rupture. To do this we have to start from the fact that contemporary culture produces and consumes an enormous quantity of fictions under the most diverse forms. Nonetheless, contrary to what one hears from present-day polemics, the invention of *digital* fictions, far from being the origin of this mimetic bulimia, is only its (provisional) outcome. In fact, in the Christian world, which is (still) our own, the rise in power of mimetic arts—or, to be more precise, the perfecting of the mimetic techniques in the arts of representation—began during the Renaissance. The first milestones of it were the reactivation of pictorial naturalism (in the sense Ernst Gombrich gives to that term) starting in the sixteenth century, the development of theater starting in the sixteenth century, and the blossoming of fictional literature since, roughly, the seventeenth century. The evolution acquired a superior speed with the invention of photography and then, above all, the cinema. Even though the majority of the employments of photography are not fictional, its invention was a qualitative leap from the point of view of visual "fidelity." That makes of it a very powerful fictional vector each time it inscribes itself effectively in such a design (which happens sometimes).

For cinema (in which I include fictional television) the case is understood: the place of synthesis of visual naturalism and of novelistic narration, it has become over the last few decades the essential vehicle of contemporary fiction. The speed with which it imposed itself everywhere proves its capacity to answer in an (for the moment) optimal manner our need for fictional universes. It is enough to place the questions of digital fictions in this historic frame for the impression of rupture to diminish and for them to appear instead as the most recent phase of a development that has lasted several centuries. In the same way the polemic to which it gives rise is not new in the least: each of the marked phases of the development of mimetic techniques has given rise to reactions of the same type as those provoked in our own day by the devices of "virtual reality." The only thing that has changed is, as I already indicated, that the polemic has displaced itself in the course of time from mimesis as such toward the technological mimetic devices.

This does not signify that the birth of digital fictions is not an important stage in the history of mimetic techniques. It is an important stage, and for several different reasons. For one thing, the quasi instantaneity of the transmission as well as the infinite reproducibility of the transmitted signs make the modes of circulation of digital fictions, in principle at least, much more flexible than "traditional" fictions. Therefore, there has been an extraordinary multiplication of fictional worlds "in circulation" and their dimension of entry into the transcultural game: whether we want them to or not, video games have inaugurated the period of games of planetary roles. On the other hand, the digital phase of the development of the mimetic ideal allows to reunite on a unique communicative support the set of fictional techniques that up until now had been linked to media different from each other. Finally, as we will have occasion to see, the digital fictional devices effectively transform certain modalities of fiction as we have known it to this day. But none of these developments involves the distinction between fiction and referential truthfulness, between sham and reality, between illusory appearance and being, and so forth. Digital fictions correspond to specific usages of the digital tool that do increase the mixture of the distinction between "sham" and "reality" more than verbal fiction puts into question the distinction between what is said "for make-believe" and what is said "for real." In both cases — digital fiction and verbal fiction — the very efficacity of the imaginative devices, far from putting these distinctions in danger, presupposes their validity.

In sum, to redramatize the present-day debates concerning the cybernetic revolution, it is enough to take a little historical remove. We can even remove ourselves further than I did until now. In fact, the present historical situation strangely resembles the one that saw the birth of the original argument directed against fiction, that is, the Platonic conception. In fact, contrary to what the analysis sketched above could imply, the cycle of development of mimetic techniques inaugurated by the Renaissance is not the first episode of this type in Western history. There was at least one precedent in classical antiquity. Starting roughly in the middle of the fifth century, there was in Greece a veritable rise in mimetic fever in the theater as much as in painting: development of the realist drama of Euripides (480–406 BC), invention of the linear perspective and creation of illusionist theatrical scenes, invention of shading by Apollodorus of Athens (about 420), Zeuxis's naturalist painting, Parrhasius's expressive psychologism, and so on.[4] Now this precedent corresponds precisely to the period of Plato. What is valid for the denunciation of "cyberculture" can thus also be applied to this case: one would not be able to understand the virulence of Plato's offensive if one did not place it in the framework of the development of mimetic techniques in the philosopher's own period. Since, moreover, the values promoted by Platonic philosophy are the essential base of the vision of the world of Christian Occidental culture, it is hardly surprising that his worries have been recycled ceaselessly and that today we use them still to denounce digital media. In short, if under the diversity of his historical masks the wolf is always the same, the "parents," worried about the well-being of their children, have not changed either. There remains the question if they are not abusive parents, a question to which the analysis of the Platonic conception could give us the beginning of an answer.

2. Plato I: From "Making" to "Making as if"

The Platonic conception of *mimēsis* as it is developed in the *Republic* is complex, that is, plural. This is first of all due to the fact that Plato uses two different approaches. In some passages he proposes simply to limit (in a drastic manner, to be sure) the types of behaviors (or persons) that it would be permissible to imitate. This position seems to accord a certain positive function to imitation, providing that the choice of object is favorable. But in other passages he suggests that it is imitation *as such* — the mimetic *relation* independent of the choice of object — that is harmful. On the other hand, he uses the notion of mimesis at the same time when he approaches the problem of fiction (and thus of feint) and when he analyzes the mimetic *representation* (and thus of imitation). The situation is made even more complex by the fact that, even as he condemns fiction, he accepts the usage of lying tales when they are at the service of the politics of the Wise. Finally, his principal critique of artistic *mimēsis* does not prevent him from maintaining a theory of knowledge that is itself a theory of reflection — of resemblance — and thus, it seems, of imitation. I will not be able here to take account of all the issues linked to these multiple uses of the same notion, and as a consequence my analysis simplifies in an improper manner the Platonic conceptions. On the other hand, I believe that it retains what the antimimetic tradition that inspires them retains. In other words, the Plato of which we will speak in the following pages will be uniquely the one of the antimimetic tradition.

The first reproach that Plato addresses to the mimetic arts is close to the conclusion suggested by Aymé's tale insofar as, after all, the misadventure of the two children testifies not as much against imitation itself as against a bad choice of object. If a bad choice of object can be dangerous, it is because real behaviors risk being polluted by the reprehensible behavior that is imitated. Speaking of those who devote themselves to ludic imitations of reprehensible behavior, Plato notes that, if these imitations are to be proscribed, it is "to avoid that the contagion of that imitation reaches the reality of their being": "Or have you not observed that imitations, if continued from youth far into life, settle down into habits and [second] nature in the body, the speech, and the thought?"[5] It is this (supposed) danger that Aymé's tale dramatizes: the catastrophic issue of the game is due to the fact that the imitator becomes what he imitates, the "for make-*believe*" (as children say) transforming itself into the "for real." This is effectively a possibility: it happens that ludic jousts between children (or adults) end in serious fistfights; in the same way as in the "role-playing" of adolescents, some of the "actors" push their identification with the incarnated character to the loss of their own identity. (Have we not been told that the reading of *Werther* pushed a certain number of young people to suicide out of mimeticism of Goethe's hero?) The worry thus seems justified. The real meaning of the argument remains to be examined.

As I have said, from the point of view of the explicit strategy adopted by Plato it is not a matter of an argument on principle against imitation but of a warning against certain choices of object (of imitation): the danger of the effect of training depends uniquely on the status of the imitated object and does not question the act of imitation itself. It would suffice therefore to choose a good model for imitation, to feign a laudable behavior, for the eventuality of a passage from "for make-believe" to "for real" not only to harbor no danger but, on the contrary, to be desirable. This is what Plato in fact proposes: given that mimetic activities have a modeling function, imitation is acceptable if it refers to morally irreproachable behavior, susceptible to constituting examples to be followed. It is this principle that he makes into a rule for choosing mimetic activities acceptable for the education of the guardians of the ideal City: "If they imitate they should from childhood up imitate what is appropriate to them — men, that is, who are brave, sober, pious, free, and all things of that kind; but things unbecoming the free man they should neither do nor be clever at imitating, nor yet any other shameful thing, lest from the imitation they imbibe the reality."[6] What seems, according to this passage, to be only a reluctant concession, maybe because the eradication of the mimetic impulse in itself would risk being too difficult to realize, presents itself elsewhere in a resolutely positive form. It is because the wise person himself, in his political work, would be unable to do without not only fictions but even lies (serious feints).

We perhaps remember the passage in book 2 of the *Republic* where, after declaring that a lie is *in itself* hateful, Plato admits a few exceptions. It is thus permissible to lie to our enemies; we even have the right to lie to our friends when it is for their own good, that is, "when it happens to one of them, under the influence of a delirium or some other madness, to intend to undertake some bad action." The lie then serves as a derivative, "in the way a remedy serves."[7] He comes back to it in the third book, when he is concerned with the education of the guardians. The exception he admits here has weightier consequences, since it is a matter of elaborating a true myth of origins — an etiological tale — susceptible of justifying a social hierarchy (the three classes) of the ideal City. This is a myth that it is suitable to instill in children from their earliest age — before they are capable of exercising their reason . . . and eventually their skepticism. We will in fact see that for Plato the mode of action in fiction is that of contagion and not of rational knowledge: it will thus be efficacious the more the instance of rational control is little developed, as is the case (we are told) with children. But if only the inoculation from the earliest age is susceptible of guaranteeing the efficacity of the *serious* mythomimetic operation, how are we not to suspect Plato of excessively dramatizing the contagious effect of *ludic* imitations (e.g., of the theater) that denounce themselves as fictive? Or, to formulate it differently, it is, to say the least, spicy to see the alarmed refusal of ludic imitation (the theater, epic poetry, painting) to be accompanied by a benevolent tolerance with regard to lying (since myth is here explicitly conceived as an impostor that knows itself to be false but wants to be accepted as true) as soon as it is known to be useful for the Good as conceived by the wise person.

This first phase of the Platonic analysis is at least as interesting because of its omissions and because of the distortions that it inflicts on the reality of the mimetic relationship as because of the theses explicitly assumed. I will limit myself here to indicating two problems that all tentative comprehension of mimetic activity must take into account but that the Platonic polemic presents under a unilateral light (when it does not ignore it completely).

At first sight the effect of contagion, that is, the effect of training induced by the mimetic activities, seems to have to concern only the fabricator of fictions, since it is the fact of imitating x that is meant to induce the dispositions to do x. There would thus be danger on the part of the children who devote themselves to role-playing and on the part of the actor without this allowing us to conclude anything about the effects of the fiction on the public. But, in reality, for Plato as for the antimimetic tradition he inaugurates, the worry that there might be an effect of training concerns the public — when a public exists, which is the case with artistic variants of mimetic activity — as much as, if not more than, the fabricator of fiction: all risk taking fictional worlds as a model. Perhaps we could go further than that and establish three implicit poles: the person who imitates ludically for his own profit (his own loss) and that of his companions in the game; the actor who imitates for the sake of the game but for the benefit (the loss) of the public; and finally this public itself, which — as public — does not imitate but which, lending a complacent attention to the behaviors ludically imitated by the actor, risks imitating them seriously later, in real life.

In the first case, the effect of training is due to the contagion of real behavior by mimetic behavior; in the second case, what is involved is instead the capacity of manipulation of the public by the actor (but also by the mythological philosopher of the ideal City . . .), even though the question of knowing to what degree the manipulator risks manipulating himself as well cannot be excluded, as the story of the wolf imitating himself shows us; in the third case, the effect of training resides again in a contagion of real behavior by mimetic behavior, but, contrary to what happens in the first case, it is not a matter of self-information of behavior habits (habits transgressing the frontier between the ludic and the serious) but an effect of modeling. The player who feigns to do x reinforces his disposition to do x in reality, since (because of the postulated inefficacity of the frontier between the ludic and the serious) feigning to do x has practically the same effect as doing x; the public, on the other hand, which contemplates the actor feigning to do x, takes this action as an example of the actor's own serious future actions (here again because the frontier between fiction and reality is supposed to be receptive to the contagious effect). In the Platonic argumentation these different effects are never clearly distinguished, which seems to signify that for the actor they all obey the same logic.

Yet I believe that when one asks the question of the eventual effects of fiction on "real life" (whether it be that of the player, that of the actor, or that of the public), it is necessary to distinguish between two very different problems: that of immersion (thus of the permeability of the frontiers between fiction and reality) and that of the effect of training (thus of the modeling of reality by fiction). The eventuality of a complete immersion in the sham, an immersion that would lead us to take fiction for reality, does not hide at all the one of transition of fictional worlds in reality, a transformation that would lead us to copy exactly our ulterior behavior from that of fictional characters. I can be the victim of a "referential illusion" in the face of a fiction without later imitating fictional behaviors. Inversely, I can take fictional behavior as a model of a fictional universe knowing full well that it is a matter of a fiction. The identification by immersion and the identification in the sense of the modeling projection are even two psychological activities that exclude each other (in the sense that they presuppose that the individual finds himself in different relations to the world): the first is a variant of cognitive attention, whereas the second comes from the regulation of our actions. Yet only the first is specific to mimetic activities and can thus be considered as posing a problem of legitimacy that would be particular to these activities.

The effect of training, on the other hand, is found as much on the side of "serious" activities as on the side of mimetic activities: any activity, and, notably, real reprehensible behavior as much as the imitation (ludic or not) of such a behavior, is susceptible to inducing a serious imitation. One should even go further than that: if the feigned behavior can have an effect of training, it is only because in life as such our performing behavioral competence and our ethical norms owe their existence in large part to activities of imitation (by repetition and identifying introjection) of "serious" behavior observed in our fellow creatures. It is because a large part of our behavior is acquired by a formative imitation of habits, because a large part of our ethical values is endorsed by an idealizing identification, that the mimetic representation of these behaviors

and values can itself possibly induce transpositions by modelization. If this is the case, it is natural that the effect of training of
fictions will always be much weaker than the one of "real reality."[8]
Besides, the fictional behaviors that do not find a real guarantor
in reality have only very marginal training effects: we have rarely
seen people imitate the sportive feats of Superman or Batman. It
certainly happens that life imitates (mimetic) art, but it imitates
only what in the latter (already) imitates life—which does not
cease to imitate itself.

From the point of view of the question of the status of fiction,
it is understood that the antimimetic argument has different consequences according to whether it is imitation itself—the fact of
modeling one's behavior on that of another—that is concerned
or, on the contrary, immersion. Thus, the Augustinian concept
according to which we must force people to believe (i.e., in fact we
must force them to feign to believe) is at the root of the effect of
immersion: thanks to this effect, feigned belief is meant to change
in due time to true belief.[9] In the Platonic argument against the
imitation of reprehensible actions but also in his defense of untrue
myths, what is put in the foreground is, on the contrary, the capacity
of imitation to form habits and thus the effect of training.

The second problematic element of this first antimimetic argument developed by Plato is in the manner with which he approaches
the question of the permeability of the frontier between feint and
reality, between a mimed and a "serious" action. For Plato, mimetic
activities appear essentially in the horizon of the lie, thus of serious
feint, as shown in an exemplary manner by the fact that nowhere
does he treat the (enormous) difference between the ludic feint of
mimetic arts and the serious feint of the philosopher-mythologist of
the ideal city. This way ludic feint appears only as a debased remainder of serious feint and is never considered as a specific relationship.
The fear of immersion, like the fear of the effect of training, seems

to be proportional to this reduction of ludic mimetic activities to a weakened form of serious feint and to an absence of notional distinction between imitation as reiteration and imitation as feint (doing as if). What is involved in this first antimimetic argument is finally the refusal (or the incapacity) to recognize the autonomy of the imaginative capacity as specific mental activity and thus also the autonomy of ludic mimetic processes.[10] Yet only the recognition of this autonomy permits an adequate comprehension of fiction. We will have occasion to see later on that what developmental psychology teaches us about this subject in fact goes directly against the Platonic conception of mimesis, notably in what concerns the relation between the exercise of fictional capacity and the risk of training: the danger of passage to act does not originate, as Plato and those who take up his theses again believe, from a too well nourished imaginative life but, to the contrary, from a too little developed imaginative capacity. Opposing the exercise of imaginative capacities, far from limiting the risks of a passage from "for make-believe" to "for real," augments them.[11]

3. Plato II: To Imitate and to Know

The antimimetic argument that I have just summed up is not the last word of Plato—far from it. In fact, while in the first moment he seemed to involve only choices of reprehensible objects, the second argument he developed is directed against the mimetic relationship as such. It is not a matter only of avoiding the simulation of reprehensible activities but avoiding mimetic activities as such. The reason he invokes is due to the mode of action of imitation. Beginning again with the imitation of reprehensible actions, he says: "For a while knowledge they must have both of mad and bad men and women, they must do and imitate nothing of this kind."[12] There are thus in fact three terms that are present:

action (in this instance the imitated referent), knowledge, and imitation. It is legitimate and without a doubt even necessary to know reprehensible behaviors; it is evidently not a question of devoting oneself to them, since that would mean behaving in an unjust manner, but one must not imitate them either (understood in a ludic perspective, since an imitation-reiteration would make us fall again in the second category). Why must we not imitate them? The answer is simple: according to Plato, imitation is not knowledge. And this has value indifferently for its genesis and for its mode of operation on the public. The elaboration of an imitation does not result from knowledge of what is limited, as Socrates does not fail to show with biting irony at the expense of the rhapsode Ion.[13] Instead, it distinguishes itself from serious action, which, when it is rational, is based on knowledge (e.g., on the knowledge of good and evil). Nor does the contemplation of an imitation produce more knowledge: if this were the case, Plato would not condemn it when it is related to reprehensible behavior, since the knowledge of what is reprehensible is a good thing (according to him).

If mimesis does not result from knowledge or produce knowledge, it is because it acts — as we already know from the first argument — by affective contamination and not by rational persuasion. It is of course the effect of immersion that is nabbed: "I think you know that the very best of us, when we hear Homer or some other of the makers of tragedy imitating one of the heroes who is in grief, and is delivering a long tirade in his lamentations or chanting and beating his breast, feel pleasure, and abandon ourselves and accompany the representation with sympathy and eagerness."[14] Badly chosen, the imitation is thus dangerous, indistinctly for him who practices it or for the public. Corrupted himself by the model he imitates, the imitator will also corrupt his public, up to "the best among us," that is, up to the wise person "with the exception of a few of small number."[15] The result is the necessity for a severe police, for, according to Plato, the imitating artists have spontaneously the tendency to choose objects of imitation that are *not* decent, not only because the reasonable temperament is more difficult to imitate than the irritable temperament but also because, even if it is well imitated, it is more difficult to understand than the imitation of an irritable temperament and thus does not interest the public of feasts.[16]

At first sight this argument also would seem to concern only the choice of the object of imitation. In fact, contrary to the first one, it is in reality directed against imitation itself, all questions of the choice of models to imitate put aside. In fact, in the frame of Platonic rationalism we see badly how the mode of action by contagion — inasmuch as it opposes rational persuasion operated through a dialectic approach — could escape condemnation of principle. That is, what is involved in the second angle of attack is no longer as much the moral question as the problematic of knowledge: through the construction of an opposition of the mode of action of mimesis and the mode of action of knowledge, Plato slides toward a gnoseological problematic, for it is because of its cognitive deficit that mimesis as such is reprehensible. To say it differently, what is concerned in this second antimimetic argument is not only a problematic of feint but just as much a problematic of mimesis as a re-presentation insofar as it is opposed to the presentation of Ideas.[17] Whence also repeated passage from theatrical mimesis (fiction in the strict sense of the term) to pictorial figuration (analogical representation).

This passage of mimesis as feint to mimesis as analogical representation (imitation) appears clearly in the famous comparison of the three beds (book 10) and the ontological hierarchy that it involves: from the idea of bed (the being of bed such as it is present in the divine soul but also as it is present in philosophical knowledge) we pass to the material bed (the bed as appearance), which is an imitation of it, and then to the pictorial representation of the material bed, which is only the imitation of an imitation. This hierarchy, as I indicated before, poses a problem for the antimimetic polemic to the extent it indicates that the theory of Platonic knowledge is itself a theory of reflection, a mimetic theory; true knowledge is also an imitation.[18] We could thus ask, Have we not found ourselves in the paradoxical situation of a condemnation of mimesis in the name of a gnoseological conception that is itself mimological? Or, at least, doesn't what at the start seems to be a qualitative opposition risk finally reducing to a simple difference in degree, that is, a progressive loss of the isomorphism between the represented and its representation? The more distant we are from the Idea, the more the isomorphism weakens itself, to the point where, when we arrive at the level of pictorial representation, most of the original proportions are lost.

But in fact this hierarchy of knowledge itself imitates a hierarchy of objects of knowledge. It is this last hierarchy that reintroduces discontinuity: by virtue of the principle that says that from what is confused we can have only confused knowledge, the elaboration of an imitation of an imitation — the pictorial representation of a material bed — could only be the implementation of a fundamentally degraded knowledge because the object on which it bears is itself a degraded mode of being. But the different modalities of being define discontinuous (and opposed) ontological domains and not continuous passages. The descending hierarchy that leads us from rational knowledge (rational knowledge is possible for Ideas) to opinion (the *doxa* that rules our cognitive relationship to the world of appearances, which imitates ideas) and finally to mimesis thus limits also three discontinuous ties of relation to truth. In this instance the level of the mimesis is the one where the relation to truth is not even that of a simple not-knowing but that of a feint of a relation to truth—which reestablishes the link with the first antimimetic argument. In the *Sophist* the painter sees himself accused of creating only "a sort of artificial dream for those who remain awake."[19] In the *Republic* the imitator dupes the spectator to the point where he has the illusion of having to do with a total sage; this of course is not the case.[20] It is the same for verbal imitation: "The mimetic poet sets up in each individual soul a vicious constitution by fashioning phantoms far removed from reality and by currying favor with the senseless element that cannot distinguish the greater from the less, but calls the same thing now one, now the other."[21] In brief, the imitative artist is a sorcerer who perverts the human soul by helping himself with magic (*thaumatopoia*).[22] It thus becomes the issue of a fight between the imitator and the sage: the first pulls the soul toward the bottom (and this by an affective contagion), whereas the sage wants to raise it toward the contemplation of Ideas (and this by rational persuasion). Similarly, as there can be no compromise between the true and the false, there would be no compromise between the sage and the imitator.

What shall we think of this second antimimetic argument? It seems to me that it in fact includes two aspects that we must carefully distinguish. First, there is the epidemiological conception of the action of mimesis. Second, there are the conclusions that Plato draws from this conception.

The epidemiological conception has the advantage of permitting Plato to think of the fact that fiction acts differently and on another level from philosophical discourse. It acts differently not by abstraction of general concepts but by mimetic interiorization. It acts at a different level, not at the level of reflexive formation of beliefs but at that of interiorized schemas in the form of global gestalts. In this the Platonic conception puts its finger on what is effectively a deep functional divergence between the domain of fiction and that of the "referential" relationship to reality, between modeling exemplification and conceptual analysis.

Let us take the case of literary fiction. As it shares with analytic reflection the same semiotic support (language), it manifests the more clearly this function difference: the fictional exemplification of behavioral situations and behavioral sequences possesses a modeling function (i.e., it puts at our disposition schemas of situations, scenarios of action, emotive and ethical constellations, etc., that are susceptible to be interiorized by immersion and possibly reactivated in an associative manner), whereas analytic reflection ends in abstract knowledge of which the possible application necessitates the passage by a rational calculation guided by explicit rules. We will have occasion later on to see this distinction, formulated here in a somewhat abrupt and simplifying manner, cover up facts that have nothing mysterious and of which we have a daily experience. For the moment it is a matter simply of indicating by an example that the epidemiological conception of the action of fiction that Plato develops in the *Republic* must be seen as a way of recognizing the specificity of the mode of action of mimesis.

That Plato has so well seen this specificity can be explained in different ways. The most banal explanation is clearly found in the extraordinary acuteness that he shows here as elsewhere. But one has also to take into account the fact that he was an important actor in a major historical transformation of belief systems, or, rather, of the modes of legitimation of beliefs: the passage from a society founded on "mythical" exemplification toward a new constellation, one of philosophy, mathematics, and empirical knowledge.[23] In this new constellation the legitimation of beliefs is no longer based on the transmission of a social knowledge but on individual learning founded on universalizing conceptual abstraction, hence the theory of ideas. This does not mean that there was no longer a transmission of social knowledge but simply that it was no longer a criterion of legitimation of knowledge, hence the decline of social knowledge in doxa, in "opinion" (as opposed from now on to rational knowledge), indeed in "forgeries of the ancients."[24] This fundamental change was accompanied by the will, on the part of the philosophers, to take their distances from the "mythic" etiologies of Being. But these explications of the origin of things were surely tales, thus modelizing exemplifications, and not conceptual exemplifications, and not conceptual explanations. The self-clarification of the philosophical approach thus required that one would try to understand what distinguished it from the cognitive functioning of "myths."

Despite the acuity of the epidemiological thesis, Plato's analysis seems to me nonetheless faulty. In the first place, the position he adopts in the face of mimesis does not take account of the fact that this passage from "myth" to philosophy (as mode of epistemic legitimation) is contemporary with another transformation that takes place in the interior itself of the sphere of narrative exemplification: it is a matter of the dissociation of the "mythic" modelization into two types of narration with very different pragmatic status, namely, historiography on one side, narrative fiction (i.e., ludic verbal imitation) on the other. (I leave aside the questions of theatrical fiction and figurative representation, which do not enter into this historical frame.)

It is no doubt the epic that is the place of this passage, at least if we are right to admit that in the classical period it passes progressively from "mythical" status to the status of an imitation that is no longer valid "for real"; the fact that in the *Poetics* of Aristotle it is treated equally with dramatic poetry, of which the fictional "nature" was already clearly recognized, seems to me revealing of this new status that will make of it the matrix of originary legitimation of novelistic fictions to come (as early as the Hellenistic epoch). What is certain is that the term "passage" does not really fit, since the proper cognitive function of the "myth" does not disappear: no society can reproduce itself outside of a transmission of social knowledge (i.e., of beliefs internalized as a whole and not acquired by individual apprenticeship), and in this sense every society reproduces itself partially by "mythic" modeling. Nevertheless, this conjoined birth of historiography and the notion of narrative fiction is a part of the same movement as that which brings philosophy, and, more globally, "rational" knowledge, to extricate itself from "myth."

I do not want to suggest by this that fiction itself, in other words, the capacity to devote ourselves to ludic feints, is born at this very moment: as far as we know, this capacity is much older. The birth is the one of a new *art* in a specific cultural sphere (our own), that is, that of a symbolic practice delivered to public aesthetic appreciation. Still, it must be said that this new art is no doubt first an art defined attentionally (that we accord an aesthetic function to a practice of which the original status had been, we may suppose, different) before being a new specific literary *practice*, that is, an art in the intentional sense of the term.[25] The birth of narrative fiction corresponds first to a reorientation of the receptive attitude in the face of narrations of epic tradition; as far as we know, it is only later, perhaps only from the second or first century BC, that this attentional art will move to become a new literary genre, the one of novelistic fiction.[26] There is no doubt in any case that at the time of Plato this change in the mode of reception of epic was already in process. Insofar as his analysis does not take this evolution into account, it is not astonishing that he never distinguishes clearly between lie and ludic feint—which leads him to accuse mimetic representation of being a lie.

The second limit of his analysis—and this limit is without a doubt the basis of his polemical attitude toward mimesis—is his incapacity to recognize that mimetic "contagion" *is* a type of knowledge and even in a way a type of knowledge that is more fundamental than that of dialectical reason and rational persuasion. That is, even as he recognizes the mode of specific action of mimesis, he does not see—or he refuses to accept—that this mode of action is of a cognitive order. This crucial question will be treated in the next chapter, which is devoted to the analysis of mimetic behaviors. In fact, in all its generality the problem of the cognitive status of mimesis is situated on this side of the problematic of fiction if one admits that this last is a specific modality of the first. But at the same time the answer that one brings to it is of crucial importance for the conception of fiction. In fact, if, as Plato pretends, mimesis is not a mode of knowledge acquisition, then, a fortiori, fiction would not be one either. If by contrast one can show that mimetic relation is a cognitive relation, and if fiction is a specific usage of this relation, then it is also a cognitive vehicle, the specificity of which evidently must still be described.

4. The Two Genealogies of Ludic Imitation

The question of the status of the ludic feint, which is at the center of all adequate comprehension of fiction, is found again at the level of the problem of its genealogy, phylogenetic as well as ontogenetic. There essentially exist two genealogical models. The first, of which the best-known formulation is no doubt the one found in *The Birth of Tragedy from the Spirit of Music* by Nietzsche, explains the genesis of the ludic mimetic representation, starting with a religious frame: fiction would be born from the fact of the progressive weakening of the serious belief in magical incarnation. The second, illustrated in an exemplary manner by the Aristotelian theory of mimesis, sees in the ludic mimetic activities a relation to the world irreducible to any other, that is, illustrating a basic anthropological behavior possessing a proper function that could not be filled by any other relation in the world. According to whether we privilege one or the other of these genealogies, we end up at a quite different conception of ludic feint and of mimetic activities.

According to the first genealogy, the first mimetic activities (from the phylogenetic point of view) are not activities of apprenticeship but come from the sphere of religious rituals and magic, that is, incarnations with serious performative functions: to imitate someone is to become the one imitated. Thus, the origin of fiction would be in the rituals of possession. The mimetic activity was of course not lived as the production of a sham but as the taking possession of the officiant by the spirit, the gestures and words of the first producing the signs of identity socially acknowledged by the spirit taking possession of him. The total immersion of the officiant in the mimetic activity was thus not feared but wished for: the aim was to dismantle one's own person in order to become the receptacle of a supernatural identity. "To become another" was not a risk but a chance. In the reverse the actual ambivalence of our attitude toward the mimetic arts would be explained by the fact that, from the instant that humanity would have bypassed this "magic" stage for the advantage of a "rational" mastery of the world, everything that would recall these experiences of immersion (and thus of loss of self) would be a generator of anguish. This anguish would translate in a way our attitude of "rationally emancipated" subjects to the extent that fiction would give rise in us to the fear of a "regression" toward magical and thus "irrational" behavior.

According to this hypothesis, which is also that of Marcel Aymé, our worry about fiction and mimetic arts would come from the fact that they make us run the risk of relapsing into a "prelogical" attitude: imitation, which is with us at the service of ludic shams and is therefore recognized *as* shams, would always risk nonetheless becoming again the instrument of an alienation of our rational identity. The ludic mimetic activities would at the same time be a first witness of the passage of magic thought to logical thought, a passage that can be, according to our preferences, either a progress (Lévy-Bruhl) or, on the contrary, a sign of decadence (Nietzsche). The birth of ludic mimeticism would thus correspond to the replacement of the hallucinatory belief in a real incarnation by two "new" mental attitudes: bad faith (linked to a provoked and no longer spontaneous immersion) and manipulating lie (inasmuch as it profits consciously from the effect of training). This genealogical hypotheses permits us to understand the moralizing polemic recurring in the Western world and inaugurated by the Platonic argument that we have just looked at: the contagious character of fiction would testify to the fundamentally irrational status of ludic feint. It is clear that in such a genealogy the mimetic activity could not have its own positive function. It is only an unstable remainder, trace of the passage between the true and the false. Because of that, it is always dangerous.

This explanation of the relations between living and (seriously or playfully) simulated possession does not seem to me convincing. In fact, many of the works devoted to the rituals of possession show that the change of identity, far from being a given at the beginning of mimetic activity, is its result. What ends by being "for real" begins, on the contrary, in general as a "for make-believe," that is, inasmuch as it is an imitation lived *as* an imitation. It is through the process of immersion that this feint transforms itself little by little into a "for real," into a taking of possession of the imitator by the one he imitates. It is the trance or ecstasy induced by mimetic activity itself that makes it swing onto the side of serious incarnation. Besides, from the point of view of the officiant it does not concern a regime of belief but a living state. Voluntary imitation is an inductor of immersion: in other words, the rites of possession, far from preceding the birth of imitation conceived *as* imitation, presuppose the capacity to absorb themselves in a conscious manner in such an activity. What happens in the rites of possession is thus of the same order as the total immersions that swing certain adolescent role games onto the side of "serious" identification, which, as we may note in passing, shows that the mechanism of the game is not in any sense linked to some allegedly primitive stage of humanity.

This complex relation between the stage of conscious imitation (the stage where the officiant is an actor in the theatrical sense of the term) and the stage of lived incarnation often poses problems to the external witnesses (the ethnologists), tossed between what seems to them indices of bad faith (on the part of the officiant as of his public) and what on the contrary seems to indicate the existence of a real transformation of identity (by hallucinatory illusion). One finds an interesting illustration of this hesitation in the work of Michel Leiris in the journal he wrote during the Dakar-Djibouti mission (1931–33) and in his essay "La possession et ses aspects théatraux chez les Éthiopiens de Gondar."[27] In the journal entries we see him permanently oscillate between the belief that what he observes turns up from the undergone possession and the somewhat irritated observation that all these people are simulators and dissimulators.[28] In the essay he tries to find an intermediary concept that would allow him to realize the two aspects of the lived possession and of the conscious imitation without necessitating a recourse to the unconvincing hypothesis of the generalized dissimulation. The notion he chooses, namely, that of "lived theater," is very suggestive. He opposes it at the same time to the "played theater," where the "lie . . . appears preponderant," since the possession is "simulated deliberately," and to "possession that one could say is authentic (be it spontaneous, be it provoked but undergone in good faith, in a magic-religious perspective where the trance would depend on no conscious decision on the part of the patient)."[29]

The very convincing manner—except for one point that I will discuss later in the text—with which he describes this eminently unstable state (at the same time for the actor and for the spectators-participants), which is the "lived theater," tallies again with what we know of the functioning of the games of roles and mainly tends to show that the triad "serious" possession–lived theater–played theater does not define an evolutionary series but three different mimetic dynamics in permanent interaction. In other words, the idea according to which the passage from possession to fiction would be the historical passage from the faith in a real presence toward the idea of a representation identified as a representation simplifies in an improper manner relations that are of a synchronic much more than a diachronic order—and this includes the case of fiction instituted as such. In rites of possession there exist points of passage between conscious and lived imitation, and in fiction there exist points of passage between mimetic immersion and the effect of lure.

The second genealogy, in contrast to the first, does not explain the birth of the mimetic representation in the frame of a gnoseological model, for it is on all counts to such a model that the opposition between "magic" and "rational" thought reduces. Its perspective is rather pragmatic. In general, it supposed that the public ludic mimetic activity is born as a ritualization of real conflicts. It is in sum the Aristotelian model, if we are willing to admit that, according to the theory of catharsis, the function of theatrical mimesis is to displace real conflicts toward a purely representational level and to resolve them on this level. The question that interests me here is not that of the validity of the catharsis theory but solely that of the genealogical conception of fiction, which it supposes implicitly.[30] According to it, far from being a fallen form of the magic incarnation, fiction is founded on a cultural competence and specific psychology not derivable from another relationship to the world. This does not signify that it is not a cultural and psychological *conquest* corresponding to a specific moment of human evolution, even if we will no doubt never know when and how this evolution took place at the phylogenetic level. All that we can say is that our closest relatives, the primates, don't seem to have developed the competence in question but that it is a part of the cultural repertory of all present human societies, whatever their degree of material development. In any case, the analysis of most societies shows us the importance of this ludic ritualization of conflictual situations. According to this perspective, mimetic practices would not be the ultimate stage of the loss of legitimacy of magical beliefs but would answer a proper positive need, that of a pacification of human relationships by way of a ludic distanciation of conflicts.

We are less disarmed at the ontological level than at the phylogenetic level to study the birth of fictional competence. Every child must in fact learn to make the distinction between what is "for real" and what is "for make-believe." He must notably learn to identify the contexts adapted to the two attitudes and to recognize the indices (pragmatic, syntactic, semantic, inflexions of the voice, etc.) of one and the other. Now, it seems that practically all children develop this aptitude, and this quite early in their lives, essentially by way of games of feint with adults. I will have occasion to return later to this question of the placing of fictional competence, which seems to me to confirm the accuracy of the thesis that I somewhat imprudently advanced at the beginning of this book, namely, that the capacity to understand artistic fictions presupposes the development of a specific psychological aptitude of which the acquisition goes back to the games of early childhood.[31]

Whatever it may be, if we compare it to the Nietzschean genealogy, this second genealogy proposes a considerably different vision from ludic feint: instead of focusing on the risk of retraversing the frontier between the fictive and the real, it invites us to take the whole measure of the very important stage constituted by the instauration of a domain of ludic feint in the humanization of social relations. To say it in different terms, the second genealogy invites us to recognize the autonomy of the imaginative faculty and the importance of its role in the mental life of human beings and in cultural development.

5. Plato in Spite of It All

The analysis of the Platonic conception strengthens the hypothesis according to which the antimimetic polemic misjudges in a profound manner the nature of fictional activity. It would evidently be absurd to criticize Plato for not having considered present knowledge in the domain of developmental psychology. On the other hand, the present antimimetic polemics, whether they object to cinematographic and televised fiction or to the digital media, no longer have this excuse. It was thus important to try to show that, insofar as they limit themselves to reactivate the Platonic argument and notably the suspicion of a contagion of reality by shams, they are based on a conception of mimesis that we would not be able to uphold any longer.

It appears notably that, contrary to what Plato maintained, mimesis is a cognitive operation in the double sense that it is the production of a knowledge and the source of knowledge. That it was not recognized as such and that, except for rare exceptions, philosophy even opposed it to thought is no doubt due to multiple reasons. We have met with some of these. There is first the fact that philosophy in general defends very restrictive modalities of human knowledge and, notably, underestimates the nonreflective access to the world that is made possible by the mimetic exemplification. There is also the simplistic opposition between truth and falseness, that is, the incapacity of recognizing the diversity of modalities of belief and the diversity of registers between which each of us does not, however, cease to alternate. There is then our naive conception of mental life, which makes us blind to the irreducible formative role of mental *simulation* and *modeling* (notably, in our relations with our fellow creatures). There is, moreover, the reluctance in the face of the ludic functionality of mimesis, or, rather, the idea according to which there would be incompatibility between knowledge and the pleasure of immersion. There is, finally, our conception of personal identity conceived as self-sufficient presence-to-oneself that, misjudging the plurality of personae thanks to which we succeed in flowing in different social molds and to adopt existential modes irreducible one to the other, cannot think of incarnation and mimetic identification except in the mode of inauthenticity.

It is nonetheless important to qualify the unilateral character of the analysis that I have proposed. We would be wrong not to take into account, if not the Platonic polemic, at least the problematic on which it nourishes itself, namely, that of the feint. This problematic is in fact mostly absent from the Aristotelian vision, which proposes a very peaceful image of fiction. For Aristotle, what characterizes fiction is the specific representational structure of a narration that represents facts, whether they are necessary, likely, or possible. In all cases it appears as though separated from factual discourse by a stable categorical barrier, the one that distinguishes a mode of representation that constructs a modeling with a generalizing value from a mode of representation that remains confined to the particular and the contingent. The eventual proximity between the "furniture" (i.e., the entities) of the fictional and the historical universe is of little importance, then. Aristotle thus remarks that it is of little importance that the tragic poet invents characters or that on the contrary he gives them "known names," that is, tells traditional stories, putting on the stage characters whose being is transcendent to the fictional universe. Even if it works with real persons or at least persons acknowledged by tradition, he will remain no less a mimetic poet and does not risk being regarded as a historian; in fact, he stays always the *poiētēs* of a mimetic structure that is a generalizing modeling and thus would not be confused with a factual report.

Aristotle goes even further, since he affirms that "if he should come back to a subject from actual history, he is none the less a poet for that, since some historic occurrences may very well be in the probable and the possible order of things; and it is in that aspect of them that he is their poet."[32] In other words, Aristotle has an absolute confidence in the reciprocal immunization of the world of fiction and of the world of historical reality. Also, his conception of mimesis is not that of imitation as lure but that of imitation as modeling. In fact, in elaborating his fable along the lines of the possible, of the necessary, or of the probable, the poet elaborates a cognitive model of which the validity exceeds the reality he imitates in the sense in which he abstracts from it the profound actional structure susceptible of giving rise to multiple empirical incarnations and variables according to the contexts. It is interesting to note that if Aristotle accepts the possibility of a fictionalization of real events, he faces on the contrary at no moment the inverse possibility, that is, the situation where the poet, far from transfiguring the real through a modeling that makes emerge from it the underlying structure of action, attempts on the contrary to make his fictional invention descend into the arena of the real. We will later meet an example of this second type of possibility, which risks precisely putting in danger the categorically stable frontier that the author of the *Poetics* establishes between the two discursive and more largely representational wholes.[33] Yet, to find a taking of consciousness of this particular possibility, we must turn toward the Platonic theory of mimesis. For what worries Plato, as we have seen, is precisely the situation of a possible contamination of reality by imitation, by feint.

It seems to me, therefore, that to really understand fiction as well as the ambivalent attitude that Occidental culture has not ceased having toward fiction it is necessary one way or another to integrate the Platonic point of view (imitation as feint) into the Aristotelian model (imitation as cognitive modelization). Only this double perspective permits us to understand in what sense fiction is a cultural conquest of humanity. This conquest draws profit from the transformation of a mental device that, from the point of view of phylogenesis, is far more ancient than fictional activity, since it already exists in the animal kingdom, namely, the feint. This does not mean that we have to endorse the genealogical thesis that attempts to explain the birth of fiction from a stage of magic identification, since what is concerned here is not the relation of fiction with magic identification but rather with the ruse, as much as a lure can go back to a ruse (thus to a mental attitude that is wholly opposed in everything to that of magic identification). We will then have to try to understand in what sense fiction, even as it serves different degrees of this device of lure, can only be a fiction if it at the same time limits the effects of this device, thus the degree of immersion induced by it—hence the importance of "blockages" of all sorts that are meant to prevent the immersion extending itself up to the global pragmatic frame that establishes the work as a fiction. One finds such mechanisms of blockage in all mimetic activities, whether role-playing games, daydreaming, or artistic representations. As Plato had well seen, imitation conceived as production of an appearance has its own proper dynamic determined solely by the degree of isomorphism between imitation and what is imitated and thus by the degree of immersion it permits.

When that isomorphism surpasses a certain threshold, the lure operates in full, whatever the intention that ruled at its production: we pass from the partial immersion that characterizes fiction to the total immersion that characterizes the lure, proving precisely the importance of a study of the ontological genesis of fictional competence conceived as psychological competence, an importance that is the greater the more the reconstruction of the phylogenetic genesis risks remaining forever largely hypothetical. And if the Platonic theory is in a certain manner the worrisome echo of this phylogenetic genesis of fiction, it is not astonishing that one finds worries of the same kind in children who don't stop asking the Platonic question: "Is it for real, or is it for make-believe?" The difficulty is evidently not to remain confined to this question: we must try, insofar as it is possible, to reconstruct the passage from this unstable stage between fiction and feint toward the psychologically and culturally stable state of fiction, that is, toward the Aristotelian problematic.

2
Mimesis: To Imitate, to Feign, to Represent, and to Know

1. Of a Secular Imbroglio

The analysis of the antimimetic position will have shown at least one thing: even though fiction is a current notion, it remains singularly opaque. The misunderstandings to which it gives rise are so multiple that the analysis of the antimimetic polemic risked at every moment getting lost in them in its turn. This opacity of the notion has been linked for more than two centuries to that of the term *mimesis*." Both Plato and Aristotle, as we have seen, proposed analyses of it that differed greatly. Their translation into Latin and into different modern European languages only intensified this drift, since the notion was drawn into semantic fields that were far from coinciding from one language to another and from one linguistic state to another. Its application to different arts (e.g., the theater, the narrative, and painting) did not put things in order. This multiplicity of historical and contextual sedimentations as well as the semantic instability that came out of it would no doubt deserve a detailed lexicological study.[1] But whatever the historical incidents of the term, the present consequences of this evolution are simple: the notion of mimesis has become a true carry-all.

In fact, if we were asked to enumerate some examples of what we associate with the mimetic relation in the artistic domain, we could, according to the contexts, cite the most diverse enunciations; for example: "The novel imitates life," "Photography faithfully reproduces its object," "An abstract picture is a nonrepresentational painting," "The image resembles reality," "Virtual imagery abolishes reality and replaces it with its imitation," "Fiction feigns reality," and many more. At one or another moment of Western history, in one context or another, the majority of the verbal notions entering these sentences ("imitate," "reproduce," "represent," "resemble," "feign") as well as most nouns (notably, "fiction," "imitation," "image") have functioned as synonyms of mimesis. That is not all. To the extent that these different terms are in transit for multiple contexts, we could easily distribute them in a different way and say, for instance, "The novel reproduces life" instead of "The novel imitates life," "The novel represents life" instead of "Fiction feigns reality," or else "Photography faithfully imitates its object" instead of "Photography faithfully reproduces its object" — so many substitutions that seem to indicate that to reproduce is the same thing as to imitate, that to feign is the same thing as to reproduce, and so forth.

Yet an elementary analysis makes it appear that many of these relations that are supposedly interchangeable are in reality irreducible one to another, even incompatible — as are the notions of "sham" and "imitation." One understands better in this way why many of the debates around mimetic arts or, nowadays, around virtual realities are falsified and why the bitter ideological debates concerning their social function and their possible effect on the public are founded largely on doubtful presuppositions. If thus, in the reverse, we want to render justice to fiction and understand its central function in human culture, we must first try to make for ourselves a more coherent idea of the pertinent differentiations.

It is this question that I want to pose in this chapter. The question of fiction will thus not be asked in it yet; instead, the activities and attitudes from which it results will be examined, it being understood that each of these activities or attitudes can inaugurate many other human conducts and put themselves at the service of aims that have nothing to do with those that fictional creation pursues.

How do we proceed with a view of bringing out the pertinent elements? The lesson that I for my part draw from the discussion of antimimetic polemics is that in the domain of the arts the notion of mimesis is used in such an incoherent manner that it seems improbable that we can succeed in clarifying it by internal analysis. Rather than trying to clear up this confused tangle from the inside, it seemed to me preferable to approach the question from the outside. It happens in effect that the facts around which the notion of mimesis gravitates are to be found not only in artistic practice but also in a large number of other domains, where they are taken up by various disciplines, notably, ethology, developmental psychology, theories of learning, the psychology of knowledge, and artificial intelligence. It is true that each of these disciplines treats specific phenomena. But because of this the elements that the artistic conception of mimesis has a tendency to confuse present themselves on the contrary with all the desired clarity.

The detour via the nonartistic mimetic facts does not obey only heuristic and didactic reasons. To me it has a still more profound justification that results from the framework in which I approach the question of fiction here. This framework, as I may remind the reader, rests on the conviction that artistic fiction is an institutionally marked and culturally "evolved" form of a group of practices of which the most fundamental examples have an integral part in our everyday lives (projective activities, fictional games, games of parts, dreams, daydreams, imagination, etc.). Now these practices themselves—and thus, a fortiori, artistic fiction—result from the combination of a group of cognitive aptitudes, mental attitudes, or more elementary psychic activities. It is precisely these elementary constituents of fiction that I would like to isolate in this chapter. To do this I will have to sometimes introduce technical terms and develop considerations that may seem abstract to certain readers. For all that, I will try to avoid all unnecessary jargon, and I will attempt to give concrete examples to show that the facts in question are a part of common reality and that the complexity of certain distinctions that I will be led to introduce is only the reflection of the complexity of common reality. In addition, some of the phenomena analyzed could seem at first sight very far removed from the question of fiction. I am thus obliged to ask the reader to show a little patience: it will appear in the course of the analysis that the nebulous and apparent dissimilarity of mimetic facts constitutes in reality the phylogenetic background without which we would not be able to understand the birth of fictional competence.

2. Mimetisms

When we try to show the significations of the notion of *imitation* as it is used in the various works dealing with mimetic relations, we discover that it defines at least five types of different phenomena that are distinguished in their functions and in their complexity. I will regroup them here, taking as my main theme their complexity; that is, I will start with the most elementary phenomena and those that are most widely spread in the living field, and I will end with the most complex and the most specific to the human species:

a) When biologists and ethologists utilize the term *imitation*, they refer essentially to the facts of mimeticism with a function of lure (*mimicry*). Lures are widespread among plants and in the animal kingdom, including, of course, human beings. Their effects are the same everywhere: in the relations between species they favor the imitating organism, whether it is in relation to predators or to prey. In the relations internal to the species they favor the imitating animal (or the imitating group) with respect to its fellow creatures, the aim being here too either aggressive or defensive. It must be recalled that the most "primitive" lures are not behavioral facts but phenotypical characteristics selected in the course of the evolution of a species. This is the case, for instance, with the designs in the form of an eye of a bird of prey that decorate the wings of certain kinds of butterflies and defend them from possible predators, that is, birds that are at the same time natural predators of butterflies *and* natural prey of the birds whose eye the butterfly wings imitate. It is the same thing with the passive homeochromy of the zebra in respect to its ecological niche, the grasses of the steppe. Other lures correspond to reactional mechanisms that release themselves in interaction with the environment. The best-known example is the active homeochromy of chameleons and turbots, two species whose coloration varies according to the environment in which the animals find themselves.[2] Finally, the most complex lures are those that invest the level of behaviors in the strict sense of the term: in producing a behavioral lure, the animal selectively imitates the specific behavior of another animal, in general with the end of inducing an error in its potential predator or prey. There thus exist nonpoisonous serpents that, when they are attacked, imitate the postures of a poisonous species "in order to" deceive their predator.

Among all the known species of animals, the human species is the one that has developed the widest register of behavioral lures both in its relations with other species and in its connections with other humans. This evolution was facilitated by at least two factors. For one thing, with human beings the fan of compartmental lures is not genetically fixed, in contrast to what happens, for example, with the serpent that adopts "automatically" the same mimetic behavior when it is placed in identical circumstances. The mimetic repertory can thus be indefinitely enriched by social and individual apprenticeship. On the other hand, human beings dispose of a larger number of registers of interaction with their environment (human or not) than other species, and they possess the mental competences necessary to use *any* of these registers for the sake of producing lures. In the relations that human beings entertain with their fellow creatures, the register that is richest in lures is without a doubt the one of the symbolic systems and in the first place the one of language. The lie — one of the ineradicable usages of language — is in fact nothing else than a linguistic lure, since to lie comes back to emit an act of language that imitates a sincere report without being one, the aim being to deceive the auditor (or the reader).

We see that the distance between the two extremes of the spectrum of lures is enormous, since at one pole they are realized phenotypically and genetically selected, whereas at the other extreme they are produced by a conscious individual strategy and selected by cultural evolution and the psychological maturation of the individual. Despite these differences, their function is everywhere the same: it is always a matter of inducing an error in the one to whom the mimeme is addressed. And if we except the cases, rare and ambiguous, when we lie to someone "for his own good" (e.g., because we think the truth would make him suffer to much or because we have reason to think that he "wants" us to lie to him), the lie and the other human behavior lures have exactly the same effect as the phenotypical mimeticisms of the most primitive beings: insofar as they succeed, they constitute an advantage for him who produces them. In this they distinguish themselves fundamentally from fiction, which, as we will see, is not based on an agonistic relation but in contrast on a principle of cooperation.

b) The second type of phenomena that one generally describes with the help of the term *imitation* is situated at the frontier of ethology and psychology. It is a matter of the reproduction "in a mirror" of elementary motor behavior, a reproduction founded on what one calls mechanisms of innate relate (Niko Tinbergen). This type of behavior is observed, for example, in babies: from the first hours of their lives, they reproduce certain facial movements of the person facing them, for instance, the opening of the mouth, the stretching out of the tongue, the advancement of the lips.[3] According to the most commonly accepted explication, the launching of this neonatal behavior results from a motor "contagion" of the same type that throughout our lives operates in the case of yawning, for example.[4] It is necessary to add that here, in contrast to the first type of mimetic activity, the resemblance between the reproduced act and the reproducing act does not have the function of "lure."

This having been said, the interpretation of these facts in terms of *mimetic causality* is controversial. We long thought that they testified to the existence, from the neonatal period on, of "imitative" capacities in the intentionalist sense of the term, which would presuppose that the human baby disposes from its birth of a capacity to elaborate a mental representation of the mimics of others. More recent research, however, tends to show that the reinstantiations in question are not selective; for example, when the person in front of the infant pushes a pencil forward or backward in front of his mouth, the baby also reacts by stretching out her tongue. This absence of selective link between the induced act (the stretching out of the tongue) and the inducing act has favored an interpretation in terms of a response reflected to a stimulus poorly differentiated. The plausibility of this explanation is still reinforced by the fact that the stretching out of the tongue disappears after two months, at the same time as the neonatal motor reflexes (e.g., automatic marching).[5] If this explanation is correct, we would not be able to speak of mimetic activity in the technical sense of the term, since the reproduced behavior is not the sufficient cause of the reproducing behavior.

At first sight this detail does not seem to have the least pertinence for the question of artistic mimesis. In fact, it will turn out to be of great utility when we study the relations between the mimetic activity (imitation) and the relation of resemblance (similitude). In the innate launching mechanisms we are in the presence of a relationship of resemblance between different stimuli but without this relation being causally introduced by the starting stimulus (since a different stimulus — the movement of a pencil — produces the same reaction). We would thus not be able to conclude automatically from a relation of resemblance to a relation of imitation: y can resemble x without, however, imitating it. I am a little ashamed to announce such an obvious truth, but in the discussions dealing with the question of imitation it often happens that one forgets it.

c) Another field in which we use the notion of imitation is the one of the ethological study of the phenomena called *observational priming*. This term designates the group of situations in which the direct or indirect observation of the behavior of a fellow creature or a group of fellow creatures induces in the one who observes an activity of the same type. Contrary to the facts resting on the innate launching mechanisms, the phenomena of observational priming are eminently selective. They are thus mimetic facts in the strict sense of the term. On the other hand, they inscribe themselves in a probabilistic logic and are thus no doubt linked to motivations and volitions rather than to a purely reactional behavioral loop (as is the case of innate launching mechanisms). Thus, a monkey who sees another monkey bursting a coconut will *have a tendency* to engage in the same behavioral sequence but will not necessarily engage in it. It is not a matter, therefore, of simple motor contagion but of a behavior motivated mimetically.

We explain the functioning of this mimeticism in the following manner: the observation of a fellow creature devoting himself to any activity induces in the one observing a tendency to devote himself to the same activity because the activity of the fellow creature raises the differential pregnance of certain stimuli, pregnance that augments the probability that the observing ape will choose in his turn the sequence of actions "normally" induced in him by the same stimuli.[6] We observe acts of the same type in humans: when we find ourselves in the middle of a group of persons engaged in a type of given behavior, we have a tendency to adopt the same behavior rather than a behavior that would be different from it. Observational priming designates precisely the role of beginning that the behavior of another plays for our own behavior. Of course, the role of beginning may be played not only by the behavior itself but also by its effects, thus, a child who discovers that a fellow is rewarded when he succeeds in attaining a given end. The reward raises the pregnance of the aim in question, pregnance that in its turn induces a mechanism of emulation.

I will not enter into the detail of these launching mechanisms, which play an important role notably at the level of the production of social conformisms, that is, of mechanisms that augment the homogeneity of motivations in social groups and thus their coherence. What matters to me is their common characteristic, namely, the fact that it is a matter of situations in which they reproduced behavior that is always *already* a part of the behavioral repertory of the person who imitates. Said in a different way, the observation of the behavior of another does not end in the production of imitation of a novel comportment (in the person who observes). This having been said, we must distinguish between two types of observational priming. In the first type the observation of the behavior of the fellow creature is limited to augment the probability of occurrence of the observed behavior, compared to the other behaviors that have a part in the behavioral repertory of the observing individual. The observation of the behavior of another thus has no causal effect on the development of the "reproducing" behavior; instead, it is limited to releasing it: the development of the reproducing act does *not* rest on an activity of imitation but develops according to a purely internal regulation. Thus, when I see my neighbor in the process of ridding his garden of weeds, I might be inspired to devote myself to the same task; but the manner in which I do it (i.e., by erratic hoeing, since I am reluctant to get rid of flowering vegetables, which makes my hoeing particularly inefficient) obeys a scenario that is my own and that rests on a very lax interpretation of the principle that the better is the enemy of the good (this does not have much to do with the scenario, devilishly efficient, inspired by Attila and developed by Monsanto that my neighbor applies, the so well named Roundup). But there exists a second type of observational priming when the observed behavior does not limit itself to releasing an activity of the same type but when the development itself of the induced behavior imitates the one that has function at the beginning. There is thus an age when children have a tendency not only to devote themselves to the same activities they observe in their peers but also to imitate the whole of their peers' behavioral sequence (e.g., to give food to a doll) during the observed behavior, even though they dispose in their behavioral repertory of alternate scenarios to those they imitate (facts of the same type evidently also play a role in adult life).

In contrast to what happens in the mechanisms of innate beginnings, where the link between the two activities is not sufficiently selective for us to speak of a process of imitation, in the two types of observational priming that I have just distinguished the behavior that the induced activity resembles plays a causal role (the link between the two activities is selective). But in the first type this causal role of the inducing activity does not determine the development of the induced activity: even if the *development* of the induced activity possibly resembles the inducing activity, it is not caused by an imitation of it. In the second type, in contrast, causality performs also at the level of the resemblances between behavioral sequences: if the induced behavior resembles the beginning, it is because it imitates the behavioral sequence of this beginning.

d) In the domain of cognitive psychology the term *imitation* designates the phenomena of observational learning and social learning.[7] The term *observational learning* is perhaps not a very happy one, since in most learning observational processes intervene, whereas the term in question designates mimetic learning, that is, learning by reactivating immersion of the aptitude to acquire. It is the type of learning that constitutes the implicit referent of Plato when he denies all cognitive impact to the act of imitation. On the other hand, if the manner in which I understand passage 48b of the *Poetics* — "imitating is natural to man and manifests itself since his childhood (man differs from the other animals in that he is very much inclined to imitation and it is by way of it that he acquires his first knowledge" — is correct, this signifies that Aristotle refers to the same phenomenon, except, contrary to Plato, he attributes to it a positive cognitive impact.[8] As for imitation-feint, although for different reasons, the facts of learning by imitation risk thus to be at the heart of our problem.

For us to be able to speak of observational learning two conditions have to be fulfilled. First, the reproduced behavior must not be limited to set off a type of behavior already acquired but must end with the acquisition of an activity that was not yet a part of the repertory of the individual who imitates. Second, it is necessary that the acquisition be caused by the observation of the reproduced behavior. The causal function of the latter must thus not be reduced to the simple role of beginning at the level of behavioral choice or ending at the imitation of a behavior of which the general structure already has a part in the repertory of the one who imitates.

The fact that acquisition must be caused by imitation does not signify that the latter is necessarily the unique cause: it is possible that it activates an innate capacity — thus virtually preexistent — but can only develop by way of the intermediary of observational learning. The best-known example of such an innate aptitude that develops only by way of a process of learning by imitation is linguistic competence. It seems in effect established that linguistic learning is based on innate aptitudes. This is notably the case at the level of phonetic discrimination. The works of Jacques Mehler have thus demonstrated that as early as the neonatal period babies show a capacity to discriminate between phonemes.[9] The team of Pierre-Marie Baudonnière did experiments that suggest that from the age of one month babies are capable not only discriminating between phonemes but of limiting them selectively.[10] If a baby is not exposed to language, however, he will *not* learn to speak by himself. Learning by observation, that is, selective imitation, seems thus to be a necessary condition for the innate linguistic aptitudes to be activated.

The domain where the advantages of observational learning are most visible is without contest that of technical aptitudes. In an already ancient study (1962) Neal Miller and John Dollard demonstrated the specific advantages in this domain: "A technician is someone who has organized a large number of connections between specific stimuli and responses into complex habits. For him who wants to acquire the same competence, it is much easier to make copying units intervene with an end of establishing the correct connections between responses and stimuli, rather than to try to discover them by way of uncertain behavior."[11] One could be tempted to say that these aptitudes acquired by mimetism turn up "only" from practical expertise and are not "true" knowledge: they do not tell me how things are but limit themselves to showing me how to comport myself with them. But such an objection has meaning only if we identify (abusively) knowledge itself with reflexive or "abstract" knowledge. In reality, all practical expertise implies knowledge that concerns the "how" of things. Simply, this knowledge is inserted in the expertise instead of being detached from it, as is the case for reflexive knowledge. Thus, to be able to drive a nail correctly I must—or, rather, the representational structure that modelizes the sensorimotor program of my hand must—integrate a great number of informations concerning the weight of the hammer, the rigidity of the nail, its length and its diameter, the density of the material in which it is to be sunk, and so forth. That this knowledge need not be thematized explicitly and that I would be incapable of formulating most of these details should not mislead us: to drive in a nail correctly, my assessment of the pertinent physical parameters must be as adequate, all things being otherwise equal, as the one I need to resolve an equation of the second degree. Simply, it does not take the same form in the two cases because it is not treated by the same mental modules or the same neurological functions: the practical knowledge remains mounted in a sensorimotor program, whereas the algebraic knowledge takes the form of explicitly formulated rules and is accessible by way of an effort of conscious rememorization.

The learning by mimemes exists in two different forms. The copy can in effect deal either with the surface form of behavior or with its organizational structure. In the first case it concerns a detailed linear specification of sequential acts. In the second case it deals with the hierarchical organization of a global behavioral program (generally intentional).[12] Richard Byrne and Anne Russon, who introduced this distinction, have drawn attention to the fact that imitations with cognitive function (in human beings as well as in the great apes) bear practically always on the behavioral *structures*; that is, what is copied is the organization of a complex intentional process, including a sequential structure (the regulated sequence of actions of which the global activity composes itself), different modules of actantial routine (one same type of action is susceptible of intervening several times in the global activity), and schemas of motor coordination (a complex motor program corresponds to each elementary action).[13] Such an imitation evidently presupposes that he who imitates disposes of a capacity of hierarchical organization of behaviors, a capacity that demands a highly complexified central nervous system (according to Byrne and Russon, the gorilla would be capable only of an organization of hierarchical actions at two levels). Richard Dawkins, notably, has drawn attention to the fact that a hierarchical organization of behaviors is far more effective than a purely linear behavioral organization: for one thing, it can be repaired more easily in case of failure, and, for another, it is more economical, since multiple behavioral sequences can share the same structural routine. It would thus essentially be reasons of efficacity and of (mental) economy that would explain why imitative learning bears in general on the hierarchical structure of a behavior rather than on the sequence of its phenomenological exteriorization.

When there is imitation of the sequential phenomenological manifestation, it aims for the essentials at a mimetic approximation at the perceptive level: it tries thus to reproduce the perceptually most pregnant details of the imitated behavior, what Byrne and Russon call its "style."[14] I will come back later to the notion of actantial "style," since it seems doubtful to me that we can bring it into a relation with a surface imitation. Whatever it may be, the two authors insist on the fact that this type of imitation has largely a social function. Though they do not say more about it, we can suppose that surface mimeticism ends at a homogenization of behavioral signals and that the latter is susceptible to ease relations between human beings: by standardizing the form of the communication, the surface mimeticism diminishes the relational anguish and at the same time certain types of aggressivity.[15]

For my purpose, the most important aspect of this distinction between two mimetic levels resides in the fact that it shows that imitation does not translate necessarily into a surface isomorphism.

The acquisition by imitation of a given behavioral structure is compatible with a great variability in the sequential implementation of this structure and thus with its phenomenological manifestation: "Imitation allows the assembly of novel sequences of units by observation, but, given the possibility of several degrees of hierarchical embedding, imitation might occur at many different levels, with radically different consequences for what we would observe."[16] The efficacity of learning by imitation rests precisely on this variability, which permits that learning to remain operative in multiple situational contexts that never coincide in a strict manner.

Byrne and Russon also remark that we only very rarely find purely sequential processes of imitation: the simple cutting up of the global behavior in sequential mimemes seems already to show a hierarchical imitation, since we must dispose of a global model in order to be able to decompose it into sequential units. It seems to me nevertheless that the distinction between surface sequential imitation and hierarchical imitation has to be maintained. For example, when I imitate the sounds of a foreign language without wanting to learn that language, I do not construct a model of competence of its phonemes, and in this sense, compared to what happens in a true linguistic learning by imitation, it is a matter of a surface imitation. In the same way, when I imitate the gestures of a person, my attempt to stick as closely as possible to their directly perceived characteristics rather than to the gestural model of which they are a concretization is a surface rather than a generalizing imitation. We will have occasion to return later to this question, which permits us notably to understand the distinction between "real" imitation (the one that is implemented in observational learning) and feint. In effect, the fact that Byrne and Russon have discovered only a few examples of surface imitation seems to me directly tied to the type of imitation they have studied: the imitation reinstantiation rather than the imitation semblance. This is a distinction that, as we shall see, plays an important role in fiction, since it permits us to make the division between what concerns fictional modeling (the created universe) and what concerns the level of ludic feint.

e) The last domain in which the problematic of imitation plays a large role is that of artificial intelligence and, more precisely, that of simulation. The term *simulation* is, unfortunately, a source of misunderstandings. This is due to the fact that its traditional semantic field is that of semblances of shams, of lures, although in the frame of artificial intelligence it is utilized to designate the creation of cognitive models; thus, it is an activity from which every intention of lure and every component of sham (in the sense of illusion) are absent.[17] A simulation in the cognitive sense of the term reproduces "the structural properties required and the operatory principles of the entity that one wants to simulate."[18] It is homologous to the real entity, which results in our being able to substitute it for the latter for the realization of virtual experiences (of which the ultimate sanction remains, however, the ultimate reproducibility in reality itself).[19] In our own days, when we use the term *simulation*, we think in general of numerical or mathematical modeling (e.g., the modeling of the genetics of populations by the theory of games) and thus of what we could call nomological models (in the sense that the model represents the modelized "object" in the form of abstract rules of engenderment). But in reality the procedures of modelizing simulation are not at all linked in a specific manner to computer sequence or to mathematics.[20]

There exists, as a matter of fact, a second type of modeling that is not nomological but mimetic. It is clearly this type that interests us particularly here. A mimetic model is a model that establishes the homological relation — which corresponds to its cognitive finality — by way of a relationship of resemblance. Civil or naval engineers, for example, often construct reduced models of their projects to submit them to predictive tests. A reduced model of a bridge or a skyscraper permits a civil engineer to study the wind resistance of the considered construction; a reduced model of a ship allows a naval engineer to test the hydrodynamic resistance of the ship's streamlined shell. Similarly, to simulate the electrical activity of neurons, one has the choice between nomological and mimetic models. Nomological models, in this case digital, represent the activity of neurons with the help of differential equations of which the variables are, among others, the transmembranate electrical potential of the neurons and the kinetic parameters of opening and closing the ionic canals of the synapses (the neurons interact by way of ionic exchanges). But one can also construct analogical models in which the neurons, the groups of neurons, and their interactions are simulated by electronic circuits: the mimetic adequation of these models is from now on such that we are able to connect them directly on biological neurons and thus construct hybrid neuronic networks.[21]

What are the essential characteristics of modeling? In spreading somewhat the analysis of the numerical simulation proposed by Claude Cadoz, we can retain four traits:

1) Modeling constitutes in itself a cognitive gain, since it realizes the passage of the observation of a concrete reality to a reconstruction of its structure and underlying processes: it "is a means of passing from the realized, perceived, or measured phenomenon to a more fundamental, more unified, more universal entity: its cause, its origin, its deep reason."[22] We must note that this structural reduction intervenes also in the mimetic models, as we have seen with the presentation of the facts of mimetic learning that do not limit themselves to reproducing the phenomenological traits of the surface of a behavior but accede to its intentional structure and its hierarchical organization. How can we not think here of the Aristotelian distinction between history and fiction? It is in fact exactly of the same type in that it affirms that the cognitive force of a representation with a singular denotation—which represents what

really happened—is less than that of a mimetic modeling—which represents facts according to more general modalities of the possible or the necessary.

2) It ends with an economy in terms of representational investment, since by relationship to the perceptive information it realizes a reduction in the number of parameters that have to be taken into account for describing and mastering reality.

3) The virtual reality elaborated by the simulation can be manipulated cognitively (including at the experimental level) in place of the entity or the simulated process. Concretely, by making the parameters of the entity or the virtual process vary and by "observing" the consequences of these variations, one can make oneself an idea of the consequences of an effective possible manipulation without having to undergo the immediate sanction of real experience.

4) We can use simulation not only to construct a model of entities existing with a view to mastering these entities better but also to elaborate, thanks to the combination of mimemes issued from different real contexts, a representation of purely virtual objects in the sense in which no original preexists them. Subsequently, these virtual objects can possibly serve to create real objects; that is, they can function as models in the usual sense of the term—this is how human inventions are born. This prospective usage of simulations of objects that don't preexist modeling implies an inversion of the relationship between model and reality that controls the cognitive simulation of existing entities: whereas in the canonical cognitive simulation the virtual represents reality, in what one could call projective simulation it is, as Cadoz has noted, "reality which represents the fictive," since one assists at an inversion of the causal relation between actuality and virtuality.[23] In many ways this distinction between the two functionalities of simulation rejoins the traditional one between knowledge and (intentional) action. What is action if not the result of an intentional causality, that is, a real effect *caused* by the previous mental representation—the mental model—of this

same effect?[24] This having been said, it is necessary to recall that the virtually elaborated object must not necessarily change into a prescriptive model for the realization of a real entity: it can quite as well keep its status of purely virtual reality, even if it enters into a relationship with other modeling of the same type.

I said already that computerized and mathematical modelings were not the only domains of cognitive simulation. They are not their original domains either. In fact, the modelizing virtualization (the creation of simulation being able to be treated in certain respects as the reality that the modelings replace, whether downstream or upstream) is no doubt one of the essential competences of human consciousness. In effect, one of the adaptive values of consciousness — conceived as a faculty that has mental representations — resides in the fact that it permits beings who dispose of it to simulate scenarios of interaction (with the world or with their fellow creatures) and to test their probable consequences without running the risk of a direct experimental sanction. Daniel Dennett has noted that the evolution of consciousness (as a specific mental capacity) creates the possibilities for a larger temporal unhooking between perception of stimuli and motor reaction; this latent time between the reception of stimuli and the reaction is utilized essentially to travel mentally through different contemplatable reactional scenarios and to test their probable consequences, given the characteristics of the entering stimuli.[25] The same idea is the basis of the popular adage that it is better to think before speaking, an adage that is nothing but a specific application of a more general precept that says it is better to think before acting (since speaking is a form of action). And "to think" signifies in this case "to give oneself a mental representation of the action to be undertaken and of its probable consequences," which in its turn can be translated as "to simulate mentally the action to be undertaken."

We were able to note that the field of mimetic facts is extremely large and diversified. But it is precisely this diversity that allows us to distinguish the multiple and sometimes incompatible meanings of the notion of mimesis in the artistic domain. It seems to me that the reviewed facts can be regrouped into three types of relationships. First, there is mimesis as imitation in the technical sense of the term, that is, a production of something that resembles something else and that copies that thing in the sense in which the imitating action is a reinstantiation (total or partial) of the imitated action. Observational learning is the canonical example of this variant of the mimetic relation. Second, there is mimesis as feint, that is, a production of a thing that is taken for the thing it imitates and thus that it resembles, even though it is *not* a reinstantiation of that thing. Among the mimetic facts summarized the phenomena of *mimicry* represent this relationship most clearly. Finally, there is mimesis as representation, that is, a production of a mental or symbolic model founded on an isomorphous cartography of the reality to be known, thus by virtue of a relation of (direct or indirect) resemblance between the two. We have met this type of mimetic fact in the form of mimetic modeling, but it also intervenes in observational learning, since the latter comports always the production of an isomorphous mental model of the behavior to be imitated.

Even though the question of the (mental *or* symbolic) representation by imitation and that of the cognitive function of the mimetic relation are intimately linked, I will approach them separately because they ask questions that are somewhat different. The three types of mimetic facts that we have just brought out thus give rise to four types of problems: imitation in the technical sense of the term; feint; representation by imitation; and the cognitive function of the mimetic relation. In addition, it is not hard to see that, despite their irreducible differences, the mimetic facts summarized have one common denominator: all benefit from the relation of resemblance and from a process of selective imitation, whether it is to produce a copy (or a reinstantiation) of what is imitated, to create a semblance, to give a representation of it, or to develop a modelizing simulation of it. Thus, we would not be able to approach the first problem, that of imitation, without at the same time asking the more general question of the status of the relation of similarity.

3. From Resemblance to Imitation

If in our day imitation is so often badly thought of, it is essentially because we suppose that it is founded on the notion of *resemblance*. The supposition is correct: all imitation implies a relation of relative similarity between what imitates and what is imitated. In addition, if fiction implies mimetic processes, then it also implements relations of similarity. It is thus important that we arrive at making for ourselves a precise idea of this notion and especially of its validity. In fact, for complex historical reasons that need not retain us here, the notion of resemblance is often judged to be of little appeal both from the artistic point of view (thus as an ideal of creation) and from the philosophical point of view (thus as a notion). What will retain me here is uniquely the notion and its cognitive validity, not the question of the "value" of the imitation as an artistic practice. It must be added that in general the explicit target of those who criticize the "mimetic illusion" is the representation by imitation (sometimes still called "analogical representation") and not the relation of similarity as such. But the arguments that they advance to negate the possibility of a representation that would be mimetic presuppose that the notion of resemblance itself is without a veritable object.

This is quite a surprising idea if only because in everyday life we do not cease to have recourse to judgments of similarity, as shown by the frequency of enunciation of the kind "Today I met someone who resembles what's-his-name" or "Oh, this noise reminds me of something… Damn it, it's the sink that's overflowing!" or else "This photograph is truly not a good likeness." In fact, the aptitude to recognize as similar or dissimilar external stimuli that are digitally distinct is a condition of survival not only for human beings but for the majority of the animal species. All movements of avoidance (e.g., to find nourishment) imply the capacity to recognize that stimulus y is of the same type (or of a different type) as stimulus x met earlier. In short, all classification of a perceptive nature is founded on a more fundamental aptitude that is the capacity to recognize a similarity between different stimuli. And what is valid for classifications (categorizations) is valid also for judgments of singular identification, that is, for the aptitude to recognize that a given stimulus, met with at a given moment, is the same as the one met at an anterior moment. In fact, to be able to *re*cognize an individual, for example, we must be capable of recognizing a formal resemblance (a similarity) between a group of actual stimuli and the mnemonic representation of another group of stimuli given earlier.[26]

It is thus not surprising that the capacity to recognize similarities plays an absolutely fundamental role in all the processes of learning. This is the case in the most elementary learning, such as the identification of colors, forms, odors, or tastes, but also, as Willard Quine recalled, in more complex learning, like that of language:

> One learns by ostension what presentations to call yellow; that is, one learns by hearing the word applied to samples. All he has to go on, of course, is the similarity of further cases to the samples. Similarity being a matter of degree, one has to learn by trial and error how reddish or brownish or greenish a thing can be and still be counted as yellow. When he finds he has applied the word too far out, he can use the false cases as samples to the contrary, and then he can proceed to guess whether further

cases are yellow or not by considering whether they are more similar to the in-group or the out-group. What one thus uses, even at this primitive stage of learning, is a fully functioning sense of similarity.[27]

Still, it is advisable to specify the mode of functioning of the relation of similarity.

In the first place — as Quine and many others recall — we would never be able to speak of absolute similarity but only of relative similarity. To decide that y is part of class a because it resembles "in the absolute" x, which is a sample received from class a, would amount to exposing oneself to the most disagreeable disappointments. If we were to apply such a criterion of absolute similarity, that is, founded on a dyadic relation, we would find ourselves quickly reduced to having to choose between two extremities, both unattractive. We could count every trait of similarity between two objects as sufficient to pour them into the same class and then find ourselves with a single class containing all the objects that resemble each other in one way or another, that is, a class that would be coextensive to the whole of the thematized world, since, in some respects, everything resembles everything. Or we could decide that, to be similar, two things must have in common all their properties, and then we would have as many classes as objects, since there are no two objects that have in common all of each other's properties — they distinguish themselves at least by their spatial and temporal coordinates or else by their numerical identity. In both cases the classification would be of no cognitive or pragmatic utility. The salmon that concludes that the large menacing fish approaching it is not a shark since it does not share *all* its properties with the shark from which the salmon escaped yesterday would not survive long; but the one that systematically chooses a behavior of avoidance as soon as it meets a herring since it resembles the large menacing fish that narrowly missed eating the salmon yesterday would not be better off. The first would end up being eaten by the shark, and the second would die of starvation.[28] Briefly, if the norms of similarity were absolute norms, there would no longer be any salmon. And in this respect we are all in the same situation as the salmon, since, as Quine notes, "creatures that would grow old with mistaken inductions have pathetically and praiseworthily the propension to stop being before their species reproduces itself."[29] The only cognitively efficacious similarity in everyday life is relative similarity: to say that y belongs to class a to which x already belongs does not signify that in the absolute y is similar to x but rather that y is more similar to x than to a third term, q, of which we know that it does *not* belong to class a. Quine gives the following example: a child has learned by ostentation that a yellow ball and a yellow cube count as yellow; he has also learned that a red ball and a red cube don't count as yellow. When he must decide whether a yellow garment enters into the first or the second class, we may suppose that he would include it in the first because he will find the garment more similar to the yellow ball and cube than to the red ball and cube. We can represent the situation in the form of a graphic:

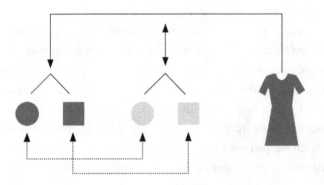

But we can also complicate the situation imagined by Quine. In his example the two beginning classes are based on the criterion of color. Suppose that they have been defined by forms; that is, suppose the child had learned to put together the balls on one side and the cubes on the other rather than the yellow objects on one side and the red objects on the other. In this case he would be fairly disadvantaged faced with the yellow garment, since he has not learned to treat color as a pertinent criterion of classification. In such a situation the child would have to either invent a new class resting not on form but, for instance, on function (in this instance the function of covering the human body) or redistribute at the outset the (already classified) objects into new classes resting not on form but on color, which would imply a permutation of elements. We would thus have the following situation:

The example is elementary, but it already shows clearly that our classifications, and thus our judgments of similarity, are not independent of each other. They form a network that has its history in such a manner that one same object can find itself in very different classes of resemblance according to the network of similarities already admitted, that is, already existing at the moment when one

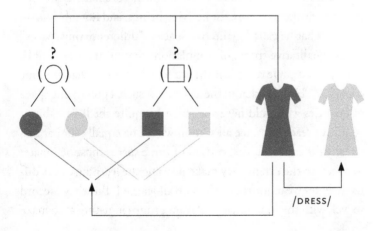

/DRESS/

has to classify it. In this sense, "to recognize" similarities is not a passive process but an active one. Whereas judgments of similarity put into relation effective object properties, they are nonetheless human constructions, since the objects of the world don't bear labels that we can decode or arrows that point to other objects that in one way or another are similar to them. Every similarity asserted between two or several things results from an attentional hierarchy that makes us privilege—display—certain properties instead of others. To recognize the central cognitive function of the relation of resemblance is therefore not at all incompatible with a constructivist epistemology (e.g., of the Goodman type), with the condition that the constructivist admits that our construction of networks of similarities is sanctioned by the world in that only those that are operative can maintain themselves. We thus seem "condemned" to reconcile the realist point of view (i.e., the idea that the judgments of similarity are forced by reality) with the constructivist point of view (i.e., the idea that relations of similarity are not found "in" nature but are chosen by human beings and no doubt more generally by every living being endowed with a central nervous system).

Quine recalls on this subject that judgments of similarity are only possible insofar as there exist in living beings, and notably human beings, what he calls "qualitative spaces," "differentiating spaces," or else qualitative spaces of stimulations that mean, for example, that "the red circle resembles the scarlet ellipse more than the blue triangle."[30] He adds that in the absence of such a preexisting space of qualities we would never be able to acquire the least habit of cognitive reaction, since all stimuli would be equally similar and equally different. At least certain of these spaces must be innate: in effect, to the extent they make possible the learning of the difference, they cannot themselves be all learned. But they "accord so well with the functionally relevant groups in nature as to make our inductions tend to come out right."[31] How can this accord be guaranteed, since these spaces are mental (or neurological) properties and not realities in the world, and, in addition, the world does not bear labels? If one refuses to have recourse to the deus ex machina of preestablished harmony or to the transcendental apriority (of which we don't see how it could be legitimized), the only possible explanation seems to me to be the one proposed by evolution. Natural selection results in the progressive domination of the spaces of quality that accord themselves with the functionally pertinent groups in nature. As for the nonconcordant spaces, they have disappeared little by little because of the extinction of their bearers, the latter reproducing themselves less than the bearers of adequate spaces because of behavioral inefficiency. Like all human knowledge, judgments of similarity are born from the interaction between human beings and the world. They testify jointly to the constraints of the real and to those of the human brain in its biological as well as cultural determinations. Or, to cite Quine one last time: "A man's judgements of similarity do and should depend on his theory, on his beliefs; but similarity itself, what the man's judgements purports to be judgements of, purports to be an objective relation in the world. It belongs in the subject matter not of our theory of theorizing about the world, but of our theory of the world itself."[32] The capacity of human beings to apprehend and to structure the world in terms of similarities thus appears as an absolutely fundamental given. It is, moreover, correlative to the one that permits us to recognize dissimilarities and thus differences between objects. The two types of discrimination are two faces of the same reality and can thus be conceived only in concert. Said differently and in contrast to the received idea, which says that the notion of resemblance is more problematic than the notion of difference, the two have meaning only with respect to each other, something that is forgotten by those who think they can revoke the validity of the first by exalting the second. In addition, from the moment when the notion of resemblance in itself finds its place, which it has every right to in the explanation of the manner in which we construct the world in which we live, the argument directed against imitation in the artistic domain loses much of its bite, since it can no longer take advantage of the nonvalidity of the basic relationship that founds the mimetic processes (artistic or not). Of course, this is not enough to invalidate the antimimetic argument in the domain of representation. The fact that different inner-worldly objects can be linked by relationships of resemblance, that is, the fact that we are able to orient ourselves in the world by serving ourselves of a capacity to recognize similarity between objects, does not prove that such a relationship can also be established (in certain cases) between a symbolic representation and what it represents. But at least it forces the antimimetic crossbreeds to circumscribe in a more precise manner the field of the possible validity of its argument.

Let us return to the problem that occupies us for the moment: the question of the connections between the relation of similarity and imitation. If resemblance is a condition that is necessary for there to be imitation, it is evidently not a sufficient condition. The fact that a thing resembles another thing does not in any sense mean that it imitates it: the profile of a rock can resemble the profile of a face without this signifying that the first imitates the second. Said differently, the constraints that govern imitation are stronger than those of a simple relation of similarity. During the presentation of the mechanisms of innate launching we have seen that for us to be able to speak of imitation, the relation of resemblance needs to be selective. Taking up again the conclusion of the discussion devoted to the phenomena of observational priming, one can express the same thing in another way. For one to be able to say that traits x', y', and z', which resemble traits x, y, and z, imitate traits x, y, and *z*, the latter must be the cause (or, rather, one of the causes) of the existence of traits *x'*, *y'*, and *z'*. Or for one to be able to say that object *a'* — endowed with properties *x'*, *y'*, and *z'*, similar to properties *x*, *y*, and *z* of object *a* — imitates object *a*, it is necessary that *a'* be similar to *a* because it possesses properties *x*, *y*, and *z*. One will say more simply that an imitation is the production of a relation of resemblance that did not exist in the world before the mimetic act and the existence of which is caused by this act.

The pertinent causal relation can take at least two forms: the "functional" mimetic causality and the intentional mimetic causality. The first is illustrated by the facts of *mimicry* incarnated phenotypically and mimeticisms genetically programmed, the second by feigned behavior, observational learning, representation by imitation, and modelizing simulation. The "functional" mimetic causality does not directly interest us here, since it does not intervene in the domain of fiction, the production of which concerns an intentional mimeses.[33] We will limit ourselves to noting the fundamental difference that separates the two forms. In the functional causality the relation of resemblance changes a posteriori in relation to imitation (because of the fact of the pressure of natural selection, which regulates the differential reproduction of the traits of resemblance born "fortuitously" by a process of mutation).[34] On the other hand, in the intentional mimetic causality the resemblance is produced from the beginning in a mimetic finality. In the first case the selectivity is posterior to the coming into being of the relation of resemblance (it is natural selection that "chooses" the functional similarities a posteriori), whereas in the second case it orients the production of the mimeme.[35]

In sum, to feign that one is sad when one is indifferent, to learn to speak a foreign language by repeating the sounds emitted by the speakers of that language, to elaborate a perceptive or graphic schema that allows us to know "in an instant" if a given cactus belongs or not to the genus *Mammillaria*, to design a tree, to take a photograph, and to write a journal-novel are so many activities that, despite the differences that separate them otherwise, all have in common the fact that their realization contains as a nontrivial condition the production of a mimeme, that is, a relation of selective resemblance. All are thus founded on the same elementary competence, the one that consists in benefiting from a relation of similarity. Certainly, it is fitting not to confuse the aptitude to recognize similarities (which is a cognitive aptitude) with the aptitude to create similarities (which corresponds to the mimetic activity); to recognize resemblances between objects of the world is not a mimetic activity but a cognitive act.

But this distinction implies no incompatibility between the cognitive usage and the "poietic" usage of the relation of resemblance — far from it. For one thing, as we have seen, there exists a knowledge by imitation, that is, there exist cognitive processes (thus processes founded on the capacity to recognize similarities and dissimilarities) that realize themselves by way of mimetic activity (thus by way of the production of a relation of similitude): when I learn to drive in a nail correctly by imitating my father's gestures, it is by imitation that I acquire the whole knowledge necessary to realize correctly the motor action in question. On the other hand, when I construct a mimeme, I reach at the same time a knowledge of what I imitate: to the extent the construction of an imitation is selective with respect to the properties of the imitated thing, it is, ipso facto, a tool of intelligence of this imitated thing. If the existence of learning by imitation is of crucial importance for appreciating the veritable range of mimetic arts, it is because they show us that, contrary to what Plato maintained, the construction of an imitation *is* always a way of knowing the imitated thing. Imitation is never a (passive) reflection of the imitated thing but the construction of a model of that thing, a model founded on a selective network of similarities between imitation and thing imitated. We find again here, at the level of the activity of imitation, a new example of the fact that the relation between representation and reality is a relation of interaction: even though the mimeme is constrained by the properties of what is imitated, it is only by way of its elaboration that we discover the object properties that constrain it.

4. From Imitation to Feint

Just as every imitation implies a relation of similarity but is not implied by it, every feint implies an imitation (and thus a relation of resemblance) without being implied by it. When I copy my behavior (in real life) from that of another person, I elaborate a certain number of mimemes, that is, I imitate this person or his behavior. That does not mean that I feign to be that person or that I feign the behavior that I imitate. In this way the believer who imitates a saint or Jesus Christ does not feign to be a saint and still less to be Jesus Christ (which would be a blasphemous act). He proposes uniquely to lead a life that *resembles* those of these august personages, and *he takes them as a model*. It is a matter of fact of social mimetism that concerns learning by imitation: I take the imitated person as a model, and I make the imitated behaviors my own.

We find the same distinction again in the artistic domain. Imitating a painting is not equivalent to making a counterfeit, that is, wanting to make the imitation pass for what is imitated, even if making a counterfeit implies an act of imitation. The activity of apprentice-painters who copy the pictures of masters does not concern making counterfeits but learning by imitation. In the same way, the Chinese calligrapher who copies the work of a great master does not want to make a counterfeit but wants to interiorize the human qualities of the work he imitates.[36] And this distinction remains applicable even when the imitation ends up in an indiscernible copy, when it functions de facto as a sham of the original. Even in the domain of behavioral imitation the possible will of identification with the model (in view of properties on which the imitation focuses) must be distinguished from feint. It is possible that the Christian who imitates Saint Francis wants not only to resemble the saint in taking him as a model but in addition, by way of this imitation, to arrive himself at the status of a saint, thus become what he imitates, without this implying the least feint on his part: the imitation in question concerns reinstantiation.[37]

These distinctions are elementary and easy to understand. If we had them always in our minds, we would escape many false problems. Thus, most of the passionate debates that surround the development of digital techniques are founded on the absence of distinction between imitation and semblance, which permits upholding the confusion between the notion of *simulation* — which designates the (virtual) modeling of an actual situation — and the one of *sham* — which designates a semblance that passes for real. The (virtual) simulation of actual situations with a view to making of them a simplified representation but susceptible of generating predictions applicable to this situation is indeed one of the major usages of digital calculators. Thus, they fabricate without contest virtual realities. But despite the common etymology, such cognitive simulations are *not* shams (in the sense that they would take the place of them whose place they take) or feints (in that their aim would be to induce the erroneous belief according to which they would effectively be that of which in reality they are only a representation). On the contrary, it is because the virtual model remains distinct from the modelized situation that it is susceptible to take its place and to apply to it (with more or less success).

The situation is quite different with the sham. To the extent that it is taken *for* reality, it takes its place (at least in the head of the person who is its victim, consenting or not) and thus short-circuits the relation between representation and reality. Certainly, the two phenomena are based on the same operation, which is the elaboration of a group of mimemes. There thus exists a link between imitation on one side and cognitive simulation and sham on the other, but it is the one that exists between a tool (the imitation) and two of its multiple usages and epistemic statutes. Imitation is a technique, whereas modeling simulation and sham define two different usages of this technique. These two usages give rise to distinct epistemic statutes founded on different relations between mimemes and the imitated reality: a relation of representation in the first case, a relation of substitution in the second. This implies, a fortiori, that there can be no identity between "virtual reality" and feint. Virtual reality — representation by imitation, be it mental or artifactual — is a "generalist tool" that can be put to service in the most diverse usages.[38]

The distinction between imitation and feint allows one also to understand that an imitation is not necessarily better the more difficult it is to distinguish it from the thing it imitates, because in that case the functional ideal of every good imitation would be the lure. The fact is that the lure is equivalent to the collapse of the relation of imitation in the sense that what imitates substitutes for what is imitated. At least this is the case for the receiver, because the notion of *lure* approaches the question of imitation from the angle of its reception and not from that of its ontological status: a lure is an imitation, but an imitation that is not regarded as such. The impossibility of distinguishing imitation from what is imitated must therefore be distinguished from the question of knowing if in fact it is a matter of an imitation or not.

We know the famous test of Alan Turing, according to which one can say that a computer thinks, starting from the moment when it beats its human adversary regularly in an imitation game.[39] The rules of the game are the following: both the computer and his human adversary are hidden from the view of a (human) arbiter but can communicate with him with the help of two terminal computers. By sending messages to the arbiter's screen, the human player tries to convince the arbiter that he, the player, is a human being; the computer on its side "tries" to succeed in the same thing. According to Turing's test, if the judge is incapable of saying which of the two adversaries is the human being and which is the imitator, then the computer is capable of thinking, since its operational power is (at least) equal to that of the human brain. It seems to me that the essential default of this test is that it presupposes that from the moment an imitation cannot be distinguished from the imitated activity, there is no longer a pertinent difference between the two. Now, the fact that we are incapable of distinguishing two facts does not at all imply that there is identity between them.[40] Likewise, the fact that we are incapable of distinguishing between an imitation and what it imitates does not transform the relation of imitation into a relation of identity. Certainly, a lure is efficacious only in that one cannot distinguish it from what it imitates, but this efficacity *is that of a semblance*: if the butterfly were a bird of prey, it would not need to be taken for a bird of prey; it would, on the contrary, have an interest in *not* being taken for a bird of prey.

When one applies Turing's test to the human activities of imitation and feint, it ends in any case at conclusions difficult to accept. Suppose that in lieu of the machine and the human being there were two humans behind the curtain, a person who has lost someone close to him and an actor imitating a person who has lost someone close to him. We can even drop the intermediary of the screen. It is easy to conceive a situation in which the judge would be unable to decide who is the person really sad and who is the actor feigning sadness. Strictly, this would change nothing of the fact that the person who has lost someone dear to him *is* sad and that the actor limits himself to feigning sadness. In brief, the fact that we are incapable of distinguishing between reality and semblance changes nothing of the fact that from one side there is reality and from the other semblance. It is necessary to add that the replacement of the computer by a real intentional system (a person) is not a trivial change. It implies in fact a transformation in the ontological status of the mimetic relation, the one that precisely distinguishes the functional lure from the intentional feint: the mimetic computer is a functional lure and not an intentional system that would devote itself to a feinted behavior.[41]

The existence of a sham, of a semblance that passes for the real that it resembles, thus does not necessarily signify that there had been a feint: it can be a simple functional lure. Let us note in passing that the analysis of the semblance or the imitation in terms of nonbeing is not pertinent. The semblance created by the feint is quite as real as the reality for which it is taken; simply, among its properties there is the functional (lure) or intentional (feint) property to be taken for another thing than what it really is and, more precisely, to be taken for what it resembles. A hallucination is not a nonbeing but a reality taken not for what it is effectively (i.e., an endogenous representation) but for another thing (i.e., a perception).

The fact that we use the same term, *imitation*, to designate the two types of mimetic relation—the imitation reinstantiation and the feint—is the source of misunderstandings. The terminological identity leads us to think that it is at bottom the same activity and that the two relations are distinguished only by their functional orientation. However, the difference between imitating a behavior to reinstantiate it (e.g., in a process of learning) and to imitate it to produce a sham or a semblance cannot be reduced to a simple functional difference of an activity that in itself would remain fundamentally the same. When I "really" imitate, I produce a thing of the same type as the one I imitate; when I imitate to feign, I pretend to produce a thing of the same type as the one I imitate when in reality I serve myself of imitation as a means to accomplish something else.[42] In this way, when Jean de La Fontaine imitates Aesop or Phaedrus, he accomplishes a thing of the same type as the models he imitates: he writes fables; that is, he realizes a reinstantiation of the literary form he imitates.[43] But when Aesop, Phaedrus, or La Fontaine imitates the mode of presentation of the factual anecdote, he pretends (ludically) to accomplish referential elocutionary acts when in reality he helps himself to processes of imitation in order to do another thing, in this instance, to elaborate a fictional universe.

The difference touches the imitative process itself. To reinstantiate a behavior that one imitates is to produce mimemes of which the sum (or the integration into a hierarchized actantial sequence) ends at a behavior that inscribes itself in the same ontological class as the behavior imitated. The apprentice hunter who imitates the gestures of the experienced hunter devotes himself to the same activity as his model, he pursues the same goals, his action will have the same types of effects, and so on. On the other hand, to feign a behavior that we imitate is to produce mimemes of which the sum ends in a behavior that inscribes itself in a different ontological class from the one of the imitated behavior. The actor who feigns being Hamlet-who-kills-Polonius does not devote himself to the same activity as his (fictional) model: he does not pursue the same goals, his actions will not have the same effects, and so on. And what applies to the ludic feint applies also to the serious feint: the hypocrite who feigns being sad does not devote himself to the same activity as the (really sad) model whom he imitates.

To say that in imitation-reinstantiation the imitating one and the imitated one belong to the same ontological class while in feint they belong to different classes implies that, related to the same model, the mimemes cannot be the same in the two cases. We can show this by taking up again the example of the apprentice hunter and comparing his mimemes to those selected by the local mime, who, on a feast day, incarnates the most gifted hunter. The mime will imitate the apparent signs that permit us to identify the most gifted hunter (his gait, his gestures, his facial expression, his way of bending his bow, his satisfied look when he has reached his target, the pout he makes when he has missed his prey, etc.), but he will not engage himself in the intentional sequence of the hunt, of which these apparent signs are manifestly public: he will not bring his booty back to the village. In the reverse, as we have seen, the apprentice hunter will reinstantiate the hierarchical structure of the actantial sequence and thus its real finality. His aim is not to reproduce the apparent signs of the actantial sequence "hunt" but to accede, thanks to these signs, to the underlying hierarchical behavioral structure, which, he hopes, will allow him to bring back booty from his expedition.

Since in feint the mimetic activity is a means in the service of the production of something that is ontologically different from what is imitated, the chosen mimemes must in fact fill a double condition: (1) they must function as nonequivocal signs of the imitated thing; (2) they must *not* really reinstantiate the imitated thing. The importance of the evocatory signals explains why in feint the mimemes often accent the traits of what is imitated up to the point of ending at what in ethology one call "hypernormal lures" but that one had without a doubt better call "hypernormal mimemes," since the notion of "lure" characterizes a mode of functioning of mimemes (in this case the mode in which the mimeme takes the place of what it imitates) rather than a type of mimeme. Dolls, for instance, are generally hypernormal mimemes with respect to traits of identification of the childish silhouette that they imitate.[44]

The real imitation, on the other hand, should reinstantiate what is imitated, and here the pertinent mimemes are those that permit this reinstantiation and not those that function as identifying signals. We cannot miss being struck by the kinship that exists between this distinction and the one, met earlier, between the surface imitation and the imitation of hierarchical behavior structure. The imitation-reinstantiation always implies an imitation of the hierarchical actantial structure, and the surface imitation plays only an adventitious role there. The imitation-semblance, on the other hand, is a surface imitation that excludes the imitation of the effective intentional structure. The opposition is thus not totally symmetrical, since the imitation-reinstantiation can also include a surface imitation, on the condition that it is the translation of pertinent mimemes from the point of view of global intentional activity or at least is not incompatible with them, whereas imitation-semblance must, on the contrary, withhold from reinstantiating the imitated activity.

As an example of fables showed, the same object can be the conjoined place of two types of operations. This allows the better to make the differences stand out. We may thus ask ourselves in what way the mimetic process by which La Fontaine imitates Aesop and Phaedrus is different from the mimetic process by which Aesop, Phaedrus, and La Fontaine imitate the illocutory traits of the factual anecdote. The analysis that precedes should allow us to answer that question.

When La Fontaine imitates Aesop and Phaedrus, the situation is the one of imitation-reinstantiation. This intervenes at multiple levels, but I will limit myself here to take into account that of stylistic imitation. As Gérard Genette has noted, stylistic imitation always implies the establishment of a matrix of competence: "Between the imitated corpus . . . and the imitative text itself a matrix of imitation is inevitably interposed that is the model of competence or, if one prefers, the idiolect of the imitated corpus destined also to become that of the mimotext. . . . For to imitate a particular text in its particularity first means that one should establish that text's idiolect (i.e., identify its specific stylistic and thematic features) and then *generalize* them (i.e., constitute them as a matrix of imitation, or a network of mimeticisms, that can serve indefinitely)."[45] We thus find again here the two typical traits of learning by imitation: imitation bears on a hierarchical structure ("a network of mimeticisms"), and it ends at a model that can be reinstantiated at will ("to imitate is to generalize").[46] And what is valid for the style of a text is valid also for the style of a person. This is why it seems to me that Byrne and Russon are wrong in identifying the surface imitation (of a person) with the imitation of his "style." The surface imitation of a person is rather to imitate his mannerisms, that is, the whole of the pregnant signals that permit us to identify him perceptually. On the other hand, when we propose to ourselves to imitate the style of a person, we would not limit ourselves to imitating some mannerisms.

In a more general way, it is not a matter of reproducing (such as they are) "public" behavioral sequences of the imitated person, which would demand the logic of surface imitation, but to accede to the "personality," which induces these behaviors. One can note besides that artistic imitation (in the sense of stylistic imitation) can be a means for imitating the "style" of the person. This seems in any case to be the function of imitation in Chinese calligraphy: it is a matter of stylistic imitation whose true aim is the imitation of the moral qualities of the artist whose artistic style is being imitated (the implicit presupposed being surely that the style expresses the moral qualities of the person). Yolaine Escande notes that for the calligrapher who imitates a classical model, it is not a matter "of imitating forms externally, which would have no meaning, because it is necessary to relive internally the creative gesture": it is not the external similitude — the "formal resemblance" — that is important but the reactivation of the spirit of the imitated artist.[47] In other words, the imitation must end in an immersion in the moral style of the imitated artist (through the imitation of his work), since calligraphy is essentially worthy of an expression of ethical qualities, and the imitation aims at appropriating these qualities.

Let us go back to our fables. The pertinent mimetic relation in the stylistic imitation undertaken by La Fontaine—in this case a reinstantiation of the model of imitated stylistic competence—is very different from the one that intervenes when Aesop, Phaedrus, or La Fontaine imitates the illocutory traits of the factual anecdote. We have already seen that in this last case the function of imitation is of the order of feint: the illocutory intention of the three authors, that is, the function they accord to their statements, is not referential; they feign to make referential assertions, that is, that they have recourse to the illocutory frame of the factual anecdote in order to create a fictional universe. The imitation-semblance is thus utilized as an inductor of a fictional universe and not as an end in itself, in contrast to the stylistic imitation-reinstantiation. According to Genette, this instrumental status of imitation-semblance is valid for the whole of heterodiegetic narrative fiction (narration in the third person): "In feigning to make assertions [on fictional beings], the novelist does something else, which is to create a work of fiction."[48] The diagnostic applies also to homodiegetic fiction (narration in the first person) and, more generally, to the dramatic mode (theater)—with the condition that one replaces the expression "in feigning to make assertions" with "in feigning to be someone other than himself." In this way, when Aymé's wolf feigns being the big bad wolf, his feint is at the service of the creation of the fictional universe of "the-wolf-pursuing-and-devouring-the-children."

The distinction between imitation-reinstantiation and imitation-semblance is nonetheless not sufficient to clarify the relations between feint and fiction. It applies in fact equally to the activities of serous feint: when I lie, the fact that I feign to think (or to know) that x is real has an instrumental function with respect to a different aim, which is, in this case, the desire to draw profit from the credibility of the other. And yet the big bad wolf who feigns to be the grandmother of Little Red Riding-Hood does something that is profoundly different from what the companion of Delphine and Marinette does when he feigns being the big bad wolf. All conception of fiction that limits itself to defining it in terms of semblance, of sham, is thus incapable of accounting for the fundamental difference that exists between lying and inventing a fable, between usurping the identity of another person and incarnating a person, between doctoring a press photography and elaborating a photomontage, between creating Potemkin villages and painting a theatrical trompe l'oeil, in short, between a manipulating feint and a "shared feint."[49] Yet, to the extent that this problem concerns not as much the study of mimetic procedures as the definition of the fictional device, it seems to me preferable to postpone its analysis to the next chapter.

5. From Representation to Mimetic Representation

In their translation of the *Poetics* Roselyne Dupont-Roc and Jean Lallot underline that in Aristotle the notion of mimesis designates according to the contexts either a relation of imitation or a relation of representation. In the first case, mimesis would be conceived as a copy, whereas as a synonym of the relation of representation it would, on the contrary, be defined as a proper semiotic object that does not send us backward toward its origin (the imitated original) but forward toward its effects (notably, pragmatic). It seems to me indisputable that the notion of mimesis — not only in Aristotle but in the majority of authors — includes such a duality. On the other hand, contrary to what Dupont-Roc and Lallot think, the two conceptions are not at all incompatible, for the quite simple reason that a representation can operate by imitation.[50] It is advisable to specify that the question of representation by imitation does not concern fiction in a specific manner. Simply, whoever is interested in fiction would not be able to make of it an abstraction, for it intervenes by two means: for one thing, certain forms of fiction (e.g., the one that concerns depiction) incarnate themselves in symbolic systems that in addition exploit a relation of similarity (direct or indirect) between the sign and what it represents; for another thing, to the extent that *all* fiction implies a device of ludic feint, it contains elements of "formal mimesis" (Michal Glowinski) susceptible to induce the representational posture of its relation to the world with respect to which it functions as a feint.[51]

It being given that there exists a large consensus to consider that the notion of "representation *by* imitation" is an inconsistent notion, my essential task will be to try to show that it corresponds in reality to one of the major usages of the mimetic relation, even as it is at the same time irreducible to imitation by reinstantiation and to imitation-semblance. But if fiction includes mechanisms of representation by imitation, it presupposes a fortiori that it concerns the more general field of representations: all fictions, whether they are fictional games or fictions in the canonical sense of the term, are representations in the sense that it is a matter of events about other events, to which they refer, which they denote, which they depict, which they give us to see, and so on. Before harnessing ourselves to the question of representation by imitation, it is thus advisable to try to circumscribe the more general field of representation itself, of which the mimetic representation is only a specific form.

The term *representation* is used to describe at least three types of facts. It designates first of all the manner in which human beings relate to reality: we know reality by way of "mental representations" of this reality, representations induced by perceptive experiences but also by the interiorization "as a whole" (or *holistic*, to use a technical term) of a vast amount of social knowledge already elaborated under the form of symbolic representations that are publicly accessible. It is used thereafter to describe a relationship between two inner-world entities: in specific contexts the first holds the place of the second without, however, its mode of existence being constitutively that of a sign. This is how the ambassador represents his country or how the actor personifies (fictively) his character. We could utilize the terms of "incarnation" or of "personification" to designate this type of relation, though the entities treated as such signs ad hoc are not necessarily living beings. Finally, the term is utilized to define the means of representation publicly accessible, invented by human beings *as* means of representation. This is how one says of an image that it represents an object or of a proposition that it represents a state of fact. We are herein the domain of true "semiotic devices," in the first place language but also the multiple groups of graphic conventions elaborated for figurative visual representation. The frontier between the second and the third types of facts is no doubt porous. In any case, the only frontier that matters to me is the one between mental and symbolic representation in the large sense of the term, that is, the group of means of representation publicly accessible and divisible developed by human beings. Whatever it be, beyond their differences, the three (or two) types of facts share one same function: it is a matter of "intentional" entities in the sense that they are not valid in themselves but are "regarding" another thing. Before approaching the specific question of representation by imitation, it is thus fitting first to clarify the general notion of representational device, of which it is only a specific form.

Simplifying grossly, one can say that from the point of view of human evolution, representational devices have two essential functions. In the first place, they allow humans to communicate the contents (and the modalities) of their mental representations and by this means to act upon each other. The representational devices are thus always also inductors of mental representations, since the transmission of a message is successful only to the extent that it induces in the receiver a mental representation that, all other things being equal, is equivalent to the one that the transmitter has encoded in his message. To this a second, altogether as important, function is added: since the invention of nonvolatile material stock (graphic arts, writing), human beings have the possibility of safeguarding mental elaborations independently of individual biological memories.

The development of nonvolatile representational supports has thus played a central role in the acceleration of the cultural evolution of the human race not because the nonvolatility of the symbolic elaborations would be its condition of possibility (culture exists as soon as supports of public representation exist, whatever their state, volatile or no) but because it permits us to thwart (in a large measure) the phenomena of drift, which are inseparable from the stockage of informations in the individual human memory. Now, the stability of the memorized traces is one of the conditions for the cumulative effect of the experiences made by humanity in the stretch of time to be able to unfold fully. If this effect is particularly evident in the domain of abstract knowledge, it is not less important in other domains, whether it concerns social institutions or artistic practices.[52] The assimilation of nonvolatile semiotic supports by practically all the human communities existing today thus explains the exponential development of the cultural world (irreducible at the same time to the physical world and to that of the individual mental representation), which is one of the most characteristic traits of the end of our millennium.

Whether their supports are volatile or not, the existence of "symbolic commodities" (to adapt the title of a book by Vincent Descombes) is one of the characteristics that distinguishes humanity most strongly from the other forms of life existing on our planet.[53] Whereas many animal species have representational capacities, humanity alone has secreted in a substantial manner (almost even a frenetic manner) representational devices publicly incarnated.[54] The relation between this "third world" and mental representations is double. On one side, it depends on it radically, for cultural facts exist only as exteriorizations of mental representations, and they only act if they are interpreted by human beings.[55] But on the other side, it is an inductor of representations of which the potential is infinitely superior to that of any individual group of mental representations and even to the sum of mental representations of all the individuals living at a given moment. Thus, even though from a causal point of view the very existence of the cultural world depends on mental representation, it evolves according to a dynamic that de facto circumscribes in large part the mental representations that a given individual may entertain at a given moment in a given society. To say it differently: if the genesis of culture and its existence depend radically on the fact that human beings possess the neurological capacity to develop mental representations, its evolution has acquired a largely autotelic dynamic in the sense that human beings treat it as a domain meriting to be developed for itself. This applies also to canonical fictions, which are one of the essential devices of this cultural world. In fact, if mimetic arts are emerging realities with respect to the mimetic devices that we are in the process of studying for the moment, it is precisely because they develop according to the double dynamic — dependency and autotelism — proper to cultural facts.

One of the difficulties the notion of "representation" poses — notably in the field of fiction — is due to the fact that we have a tendency to think spontaneously in terms of truth and falsity and to reduce this last question to the problem of the referential value. In brief, rather than to conceive the mental representation as a psychological fact and the representational devices invented by humans as symbolic facts, we bring back the notion of representation as such to the representation in the logical sense of the term, that is, we measure all our representations at the worth of the verificational ideal, thus of a very specific usage of the representational faculties.[56] This double reduction explains without doubt why the question of the referential value — or rather of the absence of that value — is in general at the center of the philosophical discussions devoted to fiction, whether we approach it in the frame of a classical verifunctional theory or in that of modal logic.[57] The question of the relations between fiction and referential truth will only be considered in the next chapter, but, since every theory or reference or, more generally, every theory of truth presupposes explicitly or implicitly a conception of representation, it is indispensable that I explain briefly my perspective here.

To say it simply, neither the reduction of modalities of the presentation to the distinction between true and false representations nor the reduction of the question of truth to the one of referential truth seems to me legitimate. Certainly, it is indisputable that the mental and symbolic presentations are "semantic structures" in the logical sense of that expression; that is, they are always "on the subject of something." But this does not signify that the question of their truth or of their falsity is at the center of their functioning. In fact, the relation of dismissal is immanent to the very nature of representation (whether it is mental or symbolic), independently of the question of knowing if to the object to which it relates by the very fact that it *is* a representation corresponds effectively a transcendent object in such and such a universe of reference. Said in a different way, even before the question of truth and, a fortiori, that of referential truth in the logical sense of the term participates, representation has always already stated the object (to which it refers) *as* represented object. This structure is common to all representations whatever their conditions of satisfaction.

This explains why the idea according to which there exists a modality of representation that would be specifically fictional and that would distinguish itself from a factual modality seems to me incorrect. There exists only one representational modality, because the representational capacity has been fashioned by natural selection as an interface between our central nervous system on one side and the external environment and our own internal states on the other. Besides, there exist numerous indices that show this oneness of functioning of the representational mechanism. Thus, from the psychological point of view there are no differences between the representational operations induced by the reading of a historical tale and those induced by the reading of a fictional tale. We will see in the next chapter that this does not signify that there is no difference between the two experiences but that these differences are located elsewhere than at the level of the status of induced representations. In addition, researches in cognitive psychology have shown that there is a troubling parallelism between the attitude that we adopt faced with perceptions and the one we adopt faced with statements that are addressed to us. Our general attitude faced with our perceptions is that of naive belief, which is entirely normal to the degree where in most conditions this naive perceptive confidence *is* justified. Ruth Millikan notes that the same thing is true for what we learn by way of speech: "It is traditional to assume that gathering information by being told things is a radically different form of process from gathering information directly through perception. There is reason to think, however, that the difference has been greatly exaggerated — that uncritically believing what one hears said is surprisingly like uncritically believing what one sees. For example, there is experimental evidence that what one is told directly generates a belief, unless cognitive work is done to prevent this, just as with what one perceives through other media."[58]

It seems to me that there are two reasons for this parallelism. On the one hand, our perceptive experiences and our linguistic access to the world do not form separate islands but are, on the contrary, totally interconnected. The second reason, more general, holds precisely to the fact that *every* representation poses a representational content, whether it is a matter of representations induced by perceptions or statements or endogenous representations issued by our "imagination." The difficulty is not to make us believe that our representations have "real" objects that correspond to them but, on the contrary, to keep us from bringing a spontaneous belief to everything that we see, hear, or imagine. That this goes for imaginations as much as for perceptions, dreams are there to show: if we live them in the mode of reality when it is a matter of pure fictions concocted in an endogenous manner (even if, by the way, like all fictions they reutilize "referential" representational materials), this is due simply to the fact that, for reasons that are linked with the state of sleep, the whole of the mechanisms of control that in waking life permit us to do the part between exogenous and endogenous representations is neutralized. Certain philosophers insist strongly on the failed members of this spontaneous belief in the adequation or the veracity of our representations. It is understood that these failed members exist, but if we had to submit to a rigorous criticism the whole of the beliefs that we have acquired (and that we continue to acquire) through "what we have seen" or through "what we have heard" and "what we have read," we would have to abandon innumerable beliefs that are indispensable to us to guide the most necessary daily behaviors to our survival (biological *and* social).

One last precision is essential: we must not confuse the fact that every representation has conditions of satisfaction with the thesis according to which every representation can be judged in terms of truth and falsity. Truth is a specific condition that is satisfied when representation "corresponds" to things, that is, when they are like the representation "says" or "shows" that they are. But this condition is pertinent only for the representations that have a descriptive function. The fact is that our representations carry out many other functions that all have their conditions of satisfaction, irreducible to the question of truth and of falsity. Thus, the representations that express willful states do not have as their function to be conformist to the world: in their case, on the contrary, it is a matter of adapting the world to the representation. On the other hand, often the descriptive relation is inserted in other functions; that is, the success of the description should not be measured with respect to its adequation to the world but uniquely with respect to its capacity to induce a belief whose force of conviction is susceptible to transmit itself to the argumentation that it serves. The most studied functional insertion is the one that endows the descriptive representation with a persuasive function (this is the object of study of rhetoric). But other functional insertions are quite as important, for example, the model insertion. One finds it, among other places, in fables: the function of etiological narrations with respect to the general rule they "found" is the one of a concretizing modeling of the rule. One has here the example of an indubitably cognitive functioning of a narrative device in which the question of the referential truth has not even to be asked because the narrative has not any other function except to exemplify the general rule through a sort of (narrative) "thought experience."

It is in the light of this somewhat cavalier sketch of the general question of representation that it is advisable to examine the more particular problem of representation by imitation. Among the representational means developed by man, there exist in fact some that rest on mimetic relations in the sense that they function by exploiting relations of similarity between the sign and what it represents. Certain forms of incarnation concern this representation by imitation. This is the case of the play of the actor, for example, who imitates him whom in addition he represents (even if the person he imitates has himself only a fictional existence). By contrast, this is not the case with the ambassador: he incarnates the country of which he is a representative without this function of representation implying the least mimetic relations.

Contrary to a persistent belief, the idea that there might exist symbolic devices functioning through relations of similarity, thus as representations by imitation, does not pose a particular problem. In fact, from the time that we are capable of knowing similarities between objects of the world, we do not see why we would be incapable of fabricating entities that would resemble other entities and of helping ourselves to the first in order to transmit information concerning the second in such a way that the transmitted information is inserted in the relationship of resemblance, that is, that the sign informs us of the thing to which it sends us back *thanks* to the relation of resemblance that links them.[59] Said differently, to exploit mimetic signs in an efficacious manner, humanity has no need of a special capacity that would add itself to the general aptitude that allows it to recognize similar objects. The only difference that separates a simple identification of the similarity between objects of the world from the recognition of a representation by imitation rests on the fact that in the second case we must interpret the factual relation of similarity as being the vehicle of a relation of representation between the mimetic entity and the imitated object.[60] But this condition applies to all types of signs, since a sign functions as a sign only if it is recognized *as* a sign.

The idea according to which representation by imitation would pose a particular problem is explained, it seems to me, by the fact that when we speak of mimetic representation we often think that analogy must play directly between the representing and the represented.[61] Certainly, there are cases in which this is so. In this way the actantial incarnation is found on a direct link of resemblance between the representation (the play of the actor) and what is represented (e.g., Hamlet killing Polonius). This does not signify that in situations of this kind the relation of resemblance is itself already a relation of representation. For it to transform itself into a relation of representation there must exist a social stipulation that endows it with this function. The play of the actor does not represent the action of Hamlet *because* it resembles this action. In fact, the relation of similarity is not the cause of the representative relation but its means, its instrument.

But another point is much more important: in the domain in which the question of resemblance and analogy is most passionately discussed, namely, that of visual signs, the relation of resemblance pertinent for the representation by imitation is *not* a direct relation between the sign and what it represents. It links the sign to the perceptive modalities of taking into knowledge of what is represented. A figurative representation of two dimensions or a photograph does not directly resemble the object it represents but the modalities of visual perception through which we have direct access to the object in question.[62] The conviction according to which "iconic representation imitates reality" — a conviction that acts as an easy foil to the conventional positions — thus presupposes that we identify the perceived object with the object itself. This identification, which is the one of "robust realism," is wrong if we take it literally or if we adopt a rigoristic epistemological point of view. It is, on the other hand, entirely legitimate from the point of view of its predictive and pragmatic value. It is in fact adapted to the particular "cognitive niche," which is that of humanity: apart from exceptions, to treat analogical images as though they imitated reality, it produces cognitive results that are correct.[63] In any case, whether it is legitimate or not, it is constituent of our relation to reality. This being the case, we can consider that the idea according to which there is a direct resemblance between the representation (graphic or photographic) and the represented object, although technically incorrect, is in the end only an innocent shortcut, justified by the fact that, from the point of view of the natural constraints in the frame of which humanity has evolved, it has turned out to be that in a normal situation the perceived object and the object itself can be identified.

The question of the similarity between graphic representation and visual perception must also be distinguished from the thesis (going back to Aristotle) according to which the *perception* of an object would resemble the perceived object and, more generally, according to which our ideas would represent the exterior objects by a relationship of resemblance or of isomorphism between the two. To admit the existence of symbolic systems based on the relationship of similarity does not imply that we must defend a mimetic theory of knowledge or of perception. In fact, it seems to me that the question of knowing if the visual perception resembles the perceived object is simply without meaning. What one can say is that, in order to construct a coherent model of the real, visual (the same as auditory) perception draws profit from our capacity to recognize similarities between objects; on the other hand, the idea according to which there would be a relation of similarity between the vision and the object seen is, strictly speaking, not understandable, for it presupposes the existence of a third instance that would be able to compare the object "itself" and the vision of the object.[64] It is the more important to distinguish this thesis from the problem of the isomorphism of a symbolic representation — for example, a two-dimensional (photo)graphic project of an object — with the perception of the same object.

When we pose the question of similarity at the level of the relation between a symbolic representation of an object of the world and a perceptive modality of the same object, we find ourselves in fact in a situation that has three terms: the symbolic representation, the seen object, and human consciousness, which, drawing profit from its capacities of discrimination of similarities, can measure the resemblance between the seen object and the painted or photographed object, since the painting or the photograph is itself an object of vision.[65] No need here of a "superconscience" or a "divine eye" that would have an absolute access to the real and that would escape from there to the intrinsic aspectuality of the (human) representation.[66] One must not forget, moreover, that our competence in the domain of interpretation of relations of similarity by visual projection does not date from the invention of the first representational devices: under the form of shadows and reflections, nature has, at all times, confronted humanity with such devices. And we know to what point these natural images have fascinated human beings, precisely because of their mimetic power: Narcissus drowns himself wanting to embrace his reflection, Li Po suffers the same fate wanting to catch with his hands the reflection of the moon in the water of the lake. It is therefore possible that they have served as cognitive models to us when it was a matter of imagining and creating the first artifactual devices of visual representation, since they share the essential characteristic with it, namely, the indirect isomorphism between representation and object represented.

We often object to the idea of representation by imitation that it is impossible to limit the field of constraints of pertinent isomorphism in order to distinguish it from other types of representation.[67] We must note first of all that in all its generality the problem of constraints of isomorphism is not particular to the representation by imitation but concerns the relation of similarity as such. It thus poses itself as much, for example, in the domain of perceptive classifications, or of the identification, from one instance to the next of the same object, the same person, and so on but also in the recognition of the same type through multiple examples, an aptitude we need in order to be able to identify, for example, the phonemes of a language.[68] On the other hand, it poses itself exactly in the same manner in all these domains for the simple reason that the cognitive mechanism is the same everywhere. The works conducted in the domain of perception and, notably, in perceptive categorization tend to show that the mechanisms of perceptive identification (of the same object from one occurrence to the other, or the same type through multiple occurrences) are endogenous and "cognitively not penetrable"; that is, they are *constituents* of the perception and operate in an automatic manner.[69] And insofar as every mechanism of perceptive identification is based on a mechanism of recognition of similarities, what is valid for the first is necessarily valid for this last. It is thus futile to want to look for (epistemological) *criteria* of similarity, since criteria have meaning only with respect to processes that are cognitively penetrable. The truly pertinent questions are those of knowing how the mechanisms of recognition by similarity have developed, in what empirical conditions they are activated, and how they function. And these questions concern the biology of evolution, neuropathology, and psychology rather than logic or philosophy.

Two points still merit to hold our attention. The first is that if representations by imitation function thanks to capacities that are at least in part cognitively not penetrable (the ones of recognition of perceptive similarities), we have to expect their ontogenetic acquisition (in the frame of the maturating of the individual) to rest on processes of learning different from those that are necessary for the acquisition of the other symbolic competences. Now the acquisition, for example, of the capacity to identify correctly objects represented graphically, photographically, or filmically is in fact a simple visual extension of the capacity of visual representation and necessitates no specific learning (a one-year-old child already has no problem identifying correctly graphic or photographic representations).

The second point is the facility of transcultural generalization of the devices of symbolic representation founded on the representation by imitation. Since the beginning of the twentieth century, historians of art have continued to accumulate proofs that show that the schemas of visual isomorphism retained by the different pictorial traditions do not coincide and that the differences from one culture to the other are sometimes very great. Nevertheless, whatever our cultural background, we establish spontaneously equivalences between our own representational schemes and those of other cultures. Thanks to these equivalences, we approach, for example, an Egyptian or a Chinese visual representation in the same manner as we do a graphic image from our own culture and with the aid of analogical capabilities of recognition acquired in the frame of the latter. This shows that graphic schemas, though different from one culture to the other, are nonetheless compatible among themselves. All thus obey common minimal constraints that are without a doubt those imposed by the limits of functioning (in our species) of the mechanisms of recognition by similarity.

6. Mimesis as a Means of Knowledge

The recognition of the cognitive function of the mimetic processes has met (and still meets) multiple resistances. They are due essentially to the fact that more than two millennia of philosophical rationalism have had the tendency to remove all legitimacy from the processes of learning by imitation and by immersion. According to this rationalist vision, human knowledge would all be elaborated through processes of individual learning causing founded beliefs, that is, susceptible to be justified for reasons that can be explicated and enumerated. This idea has a corollary: any belief that we are unable to found on reasons of this type would not be a knowledge but at most an opinion. Yet mimetic learning has characteristics that run counter to this rationalistic model. The knowledge acquired by mimemes is interiorized as a whole by immersion, outside of all immediate control exercised by the environmental context or by the instance of rational calculation. In the same way, mimemes are undertaken spontaneously (i.e., still here without the intervention of a rational calculation) when the pertinent situational context presents itself.[70]

This fact had, moreover, been displayed by Plato when he reproached the actor Ion for not having a rational knowledge of his mimemes. In addition, although the behaviors that they model have a regulated appearance, the mental processes that end with the constitution of models of mimetic competence comprise in fact no elaboration of rules that would be abstract by induction starting from individual cases: they proceed by holistic assimilation of mimed exemplifications at the motor or imaginative level.[71] Finally, the competences acquired mimetically comprise routines of which certain ones are cognitively not penetrable in the sense that they cannot be detached from the mimeme that exemplifies them.[72] This does not signify that the processes of learning by imitation are an unconscious process or that they are induced by subliminal stimuli: they necessitate, on the contrary, very complex attentional processes; simply, these processes cannot be exploited by reflected activities of abstraction of rules and reasonings. By all these traits the attitudes and the knowledge acquired by mimetic immersion violate the epistemological criteria established by rationalism, and it is thus entirely understandable that it does not acknowledge for them any true cognitive dignity.

But reality is stubborn, and if the analyses presented here are correct at least in their broad outlines, then a large part of the learning that regulates our relation to reality is interiorized by imitation of exemplifying models, thus by immersion, which means that they are *not* acquired by an individual investigation founded on insightful planning.[73] Mimetic learning, far from being a secondary or marginal phenomenon, constitutes in fact one of the four canonical types of learning, next to the cultural transmission of explicit knowledge, individual learning by trial and error, and rational calculation. And in the domain of the first learning of the child it constitutes even the most widespread type. Studies in cognitive psychology have in fact shown in a concordant way that in the child most fundamental learning is not individual learning by trial and error (contrary to what Rousseauistic pedagogy would want) or learning based on rational choices (contrary to what philosophical rationalism would want) but social learning by imitation. Children immerse themselves mimetically in exemplifying models: these models, once assimilated in the form of units of imitation, of mimemes, can be reactivated at will later.[74] Paradoxically, the part of social learning is much more important in the human being than in the other animals; therefore, from the cognitive point of view, individualism does not find itself where we would tend to situate it. And it is precisely because we are cognitively much less individualistic than other "evolved" animals that (for the moment at least) we have succeeded in getting the better of most of the other earthly species. Social learning entails in fact an enormous selective advantage over individual learning. It permits the limitation of the exploratory part by trial and error, which is a modality of learning that is particularly expensive (and dangerous): thanks to social learning, we profit directly from the successes (and mainly from the errors) of our fellow creatures who preceded us.

To say it differently, together with the explicit transmission of knowledge rendered possible by the intervention of symbolic devices, social learning by imitation allows us to make "heritable" some traits (behavioral and other) that are not susceptible to be transmitted at the level of genetic heritage.[75] It is only because most of our cognitive baggage is thus transmitted by direct cultural heritage that we dispose in addition of enough free time to devote ourselves to very complex individual learning, long lasting, and without immediate benefit (scientific activities, philosophical reflection, artistic creation, etc.). Richard Dawkins goes so far as to maintain that human culture as such can be understood basically in terms of differential replication of memes submitted to the same constraints as genes (and notably to a process of natural selection), which leads him to see in learning by imitation the supreme evolutionary principle of cultures.[76] Even if this conception is no doubt founded on a too simplistic analogy between the genetic code and mental categorizations and does not take into account the complexity of cultural facts, it has the not negligible merit of reminding us of the central place of mimetic facts in the construction of human cognitive identity.[77] I would like to draw attention more particularly to four points susceptible of showing the efficacity of learning by imitation at the same time as their irreducible specificity.

In the first place, we must insist on the profound link between the cognitive function of imitation and mimetic modeling. In fact, mimetic modeling is the central stage of all learning by observation: all mimemes that concern the level of hierarchical or structural imitation (insofar as they are opposed to the surface imitation of behaviors) are acquired thanks to an activity of modeling the operating principles of the imitated activity. Let us take the example of a Chinese or Japanese apprentice potter who proposes to learn his art by inspiring himself from the manner of proceeding of his master. To do this he must elaborate a mental representation of the pertinent manual gestures; that is, the model of competence that he elaborates must be homologous to the one that guides the hand of the master. To elaborate this mental (thus virtual) model he will not lean on the explicit instructions (or the rules) furnished by the master (in the artistic craft industry of the extreme Orient the master generally refuses to give instructions) but will initiate a process of mimetic immersion. This process will no doubt be double. For one thing, the apprentice will really reproduce the gestures of his master in order to assimilate the sensorimotor program commanding the hands and fingers of his master. We must note that it is essentially the resemblance between the result of his own actions and those of his master that will serve him as a yardstick to evaluate the success of this assimilation, since there is no reflexive access to the process of assimilation itself, which is cognitively "silent." On the other hand, he will no doubt complete the imitation-reinstantiation by virtual imitations, that is, by purely mental mimetic simulations (he will imagine pertinent gestures, he will execute them imaginatively).

Since the practices carried out in the 1960s and fully confirmed since, we know in fact that imaginative simulation is a very powerful cognitive operator, and that in a specific manner in the domain of sensorimotor learning; thus, the imaginative repetition of a gesture is as effective as its real repetition for the learning of that gesture. Concretely, when we ask a group of subjects to *imagine* in a repeated manner in which they execute the gesture that they are to learn and of another group to learn it by *really executing* it in a repeated manner, and we then compare their performances after a certain number of repetitions, we notice an almost perfect similarity of progress of the two groups (compared to a witness group, which devoted itself to no exercise, either real or mental). The mimetic model assimilated by these two routes will fulfill essentially two functions, intimately linked: the apprentice will be able to reinstantiate it in the real — realize it — by individualizing in a differential manner according to the exigencies of such and such a concrete situation; on the other hand, he will be able to reactivate it in a purely endogenous manner in order to realize mental simulations that, when he will be confronted with a concrete technical problem, will permit him to choose between several possible actualizations. It is only because mimetic models have a hierarchical organization, including a sequential structure, different modules of actantial routines, and schemas of motor coordination able to be combined in diverse fashions, that they are susceptible to give rise to variable reinstantiations according to the contexts as well as to mental simulations with multiple choices.

A second important remark concerns the specificity of the mental processes at issue in mimetic cognition. If the mechanisms of acquisition and of reactivation of mimemes are relatively inaccessible to conscious control, it is because from the point of view of biological evolution (but also from the point of view of ontogenesis) they activate modules of cognitive treatment more "ancient" and more "basic" than rational calculation. We must add that, contrarily to what is understood by the Platonic thesis, the existence of complex competences that are inaccessible to a ratiocinating decomposition is by no means limited to mimemes. Our perceptive relation to the world (with the complex structurations it implies) is the drama of extremely important and continuous cognitive processes; nonetheless, it effectuates itself generally outside all rational calculation. In fact, contrarily to what the "phenomenological illusion" endorsed by so many philosophers would make us believe, when we perceive the world, we do not need to interpret our sensations in order to abstract from them the real causes; we see (or hear) directly the objects that have caused the perceptions.[78]

It is, by the way, for this reason that we would be very embarrassed if someone asked us to justify rationally our most fundamental perceptive certitudes. Suppose that you say, "I have just perceived a deer in the corner of the woods," and someone objects, "How do you know that it is a deer that you saw?" What else could you answer him if not "Because I saw it"? The most fundamental visual structurations, like the translation of the "plane image" formed on the retina in three-dimensional stimulus laid out in depth or the behavioral mechanisms canceling the effects of distance or illumination, are even cognitively not penetrable.[79] Perceptive illusions show this in their way: when we are victims of a visual illusion, the fact that we know (on a conscious level) that it is a matter of an illusion does not prevent it from being active, quite simply because the level of cognitive treatment where the erroneous interpretation has effected itself is inaccessible to every conscious correction.[80] We will have occasion to see that fictional mimemes also draw profit from this cognitively not penetrable character of the foundational characteristics of our representations to induce the posture of mimetic immersion that gives birth to the fictional universe.[81]

A third remarkable point of learning by mimemes resides in its economic character, a trait it shares with the learning by explicit transmission (essentially verbal but also iconic) of knowledge already organized: it allows us in record time to internalize and stock efficiently large cultural repertories. From this fact a mental organization directly engaged in learning by imitation has a certain advantage of adaptation (in Darwinian terms) over mental systems that can proceed only by trial and error.[82] This fact has been underlined notably by Bandura: "It is hard to imagine a process of social transmission in which language, styles of life, and institutional practices of a culture would be instilled to each member by a selective reinforcement of chance behaviors, without the intervention of models that exemplify the cultural structures."[83]

We have to add that only species of which individuals possess complex repertories of interaction can draw full profit from the potential advantages of mimetic learning. To illustrate the advantages of this type of learning, M. V. Flinn and R. D. Alexander have taken as an example the transmission of the hunting competence in a society of hunters. According to them, the best manner (in terms of economics of time and of efficacity) for an individual to learn to hunt well does not consist in engaging himself in a process of individual trial and error but in imitating the behavior of the most efficient hunter of the group.[84] They add that the imitation will tend to be global (or holistic), since the one who imitates does not know in advance which of the multiple behaviors of the imitated hunter are causally linked to his successes. Of course, in doing this the apprentice risks imitating the elements that, from the point of view of pure hunting efficacity, are informational commotion. For example, perhaps the most gifted hunter has the habit of preparing for the expedition by devoting himself to certain "superstitious," purely personal behaviors without causal link to the hunting efficacity itself, even if they can be linked causally to his *individual* success (maybe because they diminish an anguish linked to his personal history).[85] But this (possible) price in terms of informational commotion is much inferior to the one that an individual learning by trial and error would demand. We may note parenthetically that this also speaks in favor of the pertinence of the distinction between surface and hierarchical imitation, since the apprentice hunter is incapable, at least at the beginning of the learning process, to sort out what is pertinent in terms of the deep actantial structure and what does not belong to it: it is for this reason that he risks imitating surface facts that are in reality inert from the point of view of actantial efficacity.

The example of learning the art of hunting should not lead us to conclude that learning by imitation is limited to the domain of physical and technical aptitudes. This leads me to the fourth important remark: learning by imitation plays a central role in the learning of social aptitudes and norms. The acculturation of children is realized for the major part thanks to learning by imitation and not thanks to an explicit transmission of norms: the child imitates the behaviors of adults and at the same time interiorizes the implicit norms inserted in these behaviors. The extreme visibility of scholarly transmission of knowledge in contemporary society often makes us blind to this fact. But even now the essentials of social and moral learning (including school learning) continues to rest on mimetic assimilation rather than on the explicit learning of norms and rules. This last only comes along with the learning by mimemes, which explains its lack of efficacity when for different reasons it has failed. In the moral domain this fact is particularly striking, as shown by the pathetic inefficiency of scholarly civic education each time it cannot found itself on norms of sociability already set in the daily behaviors of children or young people. The reason for this fact is hardly mysterious: like many other fundamental competences, social intelligence and moral interdictions are certainly learned behaviors, but they lend themselves very badly to being taught.

The question that poses itself is clearly to know if what concerns learning by imitation and cognitive simulation can be applied to the domain of fiction, since it is generally admitted that the latter concerns semblance and not imitation conceived as reinstantiation or exemplification. Therefore, even if the imitation-reinstantiation and the mental modeling it implies are cognitive tools, it is not evident that one can extend this hypothesis to fiction. In imitation-semblance the imitating behavior produces in fact only a semblance of what it imitates, whereas the mimemes that are concerned in social learning end in effective reinstantiations of what is imitated. We have seen, for instance, that the child who "mimes" the most experienced hunter of the tribe devotes himself to a very different activity from the one of the young man who (really) imitates this same hunter: the child imitates the identifying signs of the hunt without really hunting, whereas the young man internalizes the actantial structure of the real hunting activity.

Evidently, there cannot at this stage of the inquiry be an answer to the question of the cognitive functioning of fictions, if only because the idea according to which fiction would be reducible to the production of mimemes having a pure function of semblance will in fact reveal itself as false. I will thus simply limit myself to try to show that even if this were the case, it would be no less a cognitive vector. One can see it in taking up again one last time the example of the child who ludically mimes the activity of hunting adults (if the reader does not like this example, he or she can replace it with the one of a child who mimes the activity of his mother or his father in changing the diapers of his little brother or little sister). Even though the ludic limitation of the child is different from the effective imitation of the apprentice hunter in that it is not really concerned with hunting, it leads him nonetheless to really effectuate certain gestures of the hunter. It permits him, therefore, to acquire *a part* of the motor automatisms and of the actantial sequences that will be useful for him later on, when he will really have to learn to hunt by duplicating his effective behavior on that of the most efficacious hunter. Said differently, an imitation-semblance also always includes mimemes in the technical sense of the term, that is, real reinstantiations of certain aspects of the feigned behavior: even the simple phenomenological surface imitation implies mimemes that are homologous to what is imitated. Of course, the difference between the two types of imitation stays complete: the ludic reinstantiations do not bear on the actantial structure conceived as a complete intentional activity. But we see that it is in no way opposed to the fact that activities of ludic mimesis can be a part of a process of learning by imitation.

We must as a consequence widen the field of application of this last notion: mimetic learning is not limited to the domain of imitation-reinstantiation but also operates through the imitation-semblance of the ludic feint. From the point of view of biological evolution, it is moreover not impossible that the first manifestations of ludic feint have had a cognitive function. When the puppies, the kittens, or the young monkeys make-believe that they attack and bite each other, these games have as a function to allow them to acquire the motor automatisms and a part of the actantial sequence of the real predation. At the same time, there is no doubt that these games concern ludic feint. E. O. Wilson in fact remarks that they are always accompanied by "meta-communicational" signs that are addressed to the game's partner and signify to him that the undertaken gestures are only "for the game."[86] The fact had, moreover, already been noted by Darwin in 1872: "When my terrier bites my hand to play, often accompanying his bites with grunts, and I tell him: 'Gently, gently!', he continues biting but he answers me by some wriggling of the tail which seems to say: 'Don't worry, it's only a game!'"[87] The wriggling of the tail has a meta-communicational function to the degree that it transmits a message that changes the meaning of other transmitted signals, in this case, the fact of biting the hand of his master. The existence of this meta-communication illustrates the necessity in which all ludic feint finds itself to announce itself *as* feint.

The example of Darwin's terrier shows also that, even in animals, mimetic learning is without a doubt not the only function of games of feint. In fact, the terrier plays with his master throughout his life, and, generally, dogs and cats as well as horses and donkeys continue to devote themselves to activities of ludic feint even when they are adult, that is, even when the mimed activities are long since a part of their behavioral repertory. With domestic animals this persistence of ludic feint at an adult age is perhaps linked to their domestication, to the degree that the artificial selection practiced by humans generally privileged the phenomena of neoteny, that is, the retention of traits typical for the youthful animal—of which games of feint are a part.[88] In what concerns savage species this cause is evidently not operative. If one puts aside the eventuality of a purely hedonistic function (the autotelic pleasure of the motor discharge), most of the imitation-semblances in adults of savage species seem linked, whether it is to parental functions (e.g., parents playing with their little ones) or ritual functions (e.g., the ritualized predation that is observed with the ashen heron, which, when he courts the female, performs the motor movements of fishing) or ritualized flight (e.g., the females of numerous species mime a behavior of flight when faced with a male that wants to copulate with them).[89]

Whatever it may be, the human beings, many ludic feints inscribe themselves manifestly in a frame that concerns processes of learning, even if the immediate motivations that make us engage in such games are uniquely the pleasure we expect from them. This fact has been underlined notably by Iouri Lotman, according to whom ludic simulation has at least three functions: it permits us to learn a behavior without being submitted to the immediate sanction of reality; it teaches us to modelize situations susceptible to presenting themselves in the future; and, finally, it permits us to get used little by little to the dysphoric situations that we have to confront in real life (he gives the example of death).[90] One of the domains where the cognitive function of ludic simulation is the most apparent is the one of social learning. In this way, when the little girl (or the little boy) plays with her (his) dolls, she (he) interiorizes at the same time certain reactions that later will inform the maternal or paternal functions. In the same way, to the degree that martial conflicts imply body-to-body contacts, ludic battles between boys prepare them for real conflicts at an adult age. Or again, the experience in terms of social interaction that children acquire thanks to role-playing games forms them to adult social life, where we must not only change persona according to the context in which we find ourselves but also be able to put ourselves in another's place, that is, to see the world through his eyes, even if it is only to predict (and possibly to avoid) his reactions.

Yet this function of learning is not limited to childhood. It lasts, in fact, during our entire life. In fact, when adults of other species devote themselves hardly at all to games of feint (except in the particular situations that I gave account of: the parent-child relation, neoteny selected by humans, genetically fixed ritual ludic feints), human beings accord to them a large importance at every age. This seems to be linked to a difference in level of the individual maturation: in other species the aptitude for learning new behavioral repertories diminishes dramatically after sexual maturation, whereas in human beings this borderline is much less marked. The fact that our cognitive profile is of neotenic nature, that is, that our aptitude to have new learning experiences does not get lost with sexual maturation, renders us capable, throughout our lives, of adapting ourselves to environments that are very different from each other. It is thus not at all astonishing that ludic feints can fill important cognitive functions, including in the life of adult human beings. And what applies in general for ludic feints applies also in particular for artistic fictions (seen from the side of their creator). It is not a matter of affirming that this function of learning is *the* function of fictional games or of artistic fiction but only that these activities are, to the degree that they are founded on a relation of imitation-semblance, susceptible of being cognitive vectors.

We see nonetheless that what precedes is far from resolving our problem. For one thing, the facts that I have just presented only show that ludic mimesis can have a cognitive function for him who *creates* imitations. We have perhaps shown that Ion can acquire knowledge in devoting himself to mimetic practice, but we have not answered the other side of the Platonic objection, that is, the thesis according to which the public that assists at mimetic spectacles does not draw the least cognitive profit from it. Said differently, the analysis applies to fictional games where the creator and the receiver coincide but not to artistic fictions: the receivers produce no mimemes; they limit themselves to reactivating mimemes created by someone else. In addition, the analysis that precedes treats fiction as though it might be reduced to what in it concerns semblance and mimetic immersion. But when we are interested in fictions, it is not so much feint that concerns us as that which it gives us access to: the fictional universe. The same as, in learning by observation, mimetic immersion is only the means by which we assimilate the behavioral structure we want to master, in the fictional devices the semblance and the immersion are only the vectors that give us access to the fictional world. For fiction to be a mimetic mode of learning in the strong sense of the term, it is thus necessary for fictional modeling to have a cognitive range. How could this be, if fiction is engendered through a semblance and if, as seems to be established, the universe it projects has no existence outside of this act of projection itself? So many questions that come down to one: what is fiction?

3
Fiction

1. Imitation, Lure, Feint, and Fiction

In 1977 the German writer Wolfgang Hildesheimer published a biography of Mozart entitled quite simply *Mozart*. Although the book provoked numerous controversies at its publication, it ended by being regarded as one of the classical biographies of the musician. Four years later, in 1981, Hildesheimer published *Marbot. Eine Biographie*, the intellectual biography of English aesthetician and critic of art Sir Andrew Marbot (1801–30). Tireless voyager, he had the good fortune to meet the outstanding cultural figures of his period: Goethe, Byron, and Shelley, Leopardi and Schopenhauer, Turner and Delacroix (the last of whom, moreover, made a lithographic sketch of him). On everyone he met Marbot made the impression of a man of extreme intelligence combined with a strong soul but curiously detached from life. This was notably the judgment of Goethe, as we know from a letter he wrote to his friend Schutz and from a passage in his *Dialogues with Eckermann* that is cited by Hildesheimer. Marbot disappeared in 1830: even though his body was never found, numerous clues speak in favor of suicide. According to the letters and the papers found after his death, it appears beyond doubt that for several years he maintained an incestuous affair with his mother, Lady Catherine Marbot. Was his (likely) suicide linked to this incestuous relationship? According to his biographer, it would appear more likely that Marbot drew practical conclusions from a radically pessimistic vision of the world, reinforced by his meeting with Schopenhauer.

When the book came out, one part of German critics congratulated Hildesheimer for having saved from forgetfulness a fascinating historical figure not only on account of his tragic life but as much on account of his aesthetic theories. Two years later the work was translated into French under the title *Sir Andrew Marbot*. As far as I know, the French edition has been sold out for a long time, but in 1989 I had the good fortune of finding a copy for sale at the Fnac Forum des Halles in the section devoted to the criticism of art. I was looking for a different book, and I was a little taken aback to find *Marbot* there, for it would never have occurred to me to look for it in the art criticism section. In fact, in contrast to what the critics thought who congratulated the author for having drawn attention to a misunderstood thinker, in contrast also to what the worker for Fnac thought who had stored the book in the section reserved for the criticism of art, Sir Andrew Marbot has never existed except as a mental representation elaborated by Hildesheimer and reconstructed by each one of the readers of the book. In other words, despite the generic indication that decorates its cover, *Marbot* is an imaginary biography, a fictional text.

During a conference devoted to his book Hildesheimer expressed astonishment that numerous readers had been deceived:

> If so many readers and critics found themselves entrapped by my feint [*Täuschung*], all that I can answer is that it is not my fault. It is true that my intention had been to give life to Marbot,

but I wanted to abuse [*hintergehen,* "deceive," "dupe"] no one, even if I am conscious today that the revelation of his fictive character was perhaps too hidden and too weak. One finds it in the first place in the text of the flaps of the dust jacket, where it is said that Marbot is, so to speak, woven [*eingewoben*] in the cultural history of the nineteenth century—an explanation that no one seems to have read. One finds it thereafter in the index: it contains exclusively the names of persons who really existed and becomes, for this fact, the key of the book. It is consequently strange that even certain minute readers, endowed with *esprit de finesse,* did not notice it. Not only should they have concluded from the index that the historicity of the book is a problem, but they furthermore could have established the nonexistence of Marbot by consulting the *Encyclopedia Britannica,* the *Dialogues of Goethe with Eckermann,* the letters of Ottilie, or the journals of Platen and of Delacroix, the autobiography of Berlioz, the notes of Karl Blechen devoted to his voyage to Italy, or finally the minute journal of Crabb Robinson. That they did not do so testifies, all things considered, to the likelihood of the existence of Marbot.[1]

In a certain way this retrospective astonishment of the author can only astonish.[2] The two indices of fictionality to which he refers are so weak and so well hidden that it takes a detective-reader to discover them. In addition, they are more than counterbalanced by a multitude of massive indices that, on the contrary, push the reader to believe that he is faced with a real biography. There is no reason not to believe that he has been presented with a real biography. As Dorrit Cohn has noted: "It is a case of a brilliant disguise."[3] There is no reason not to believe Hildesheimer when he states that his aim was not to deceive the reader but simply to "give life" to his character—or, to use the notions brought out in the last chapter, that his aim was not to devote himself to a serious feint but only to maximize the mimetic component of his tale with a view to facilitating the fictional immersion of the reader in the imaginary universe.[4]

So is *Marbot* a fiction or a feint? Or is it a fiction and a feint? Or a fiction even though it functions as a feint? Or a feint even though the intention of the author had been to compose a fiction? Whatever the answers to these questions (and others linked to them), *Marbot*, in bringing them up, places us from the start at the very heart of the problem of fiction. In fact, if, according to the hypothesis proposed in the previous chapter, fiction results from the interaction of several more "elementary" components, each of which has its own dynamic, we can suppose that it finds its foundation in the manner it realizes the integration of these components. As these have in part divergent dynamics, we have, however, to expect this integration not to be structured once and for all but rather to be an integration of a dynamic balance, of a fluctuating and potentially unstable homeostasis. The fact that *Marbot* has failed — at least for a part of its readers — to realize this integration, the fact that it was received as a factual text when the intention of the author was fictional, should show us on the contrary what are the conditions that must be fulfilled for the fictional device to be able to function.

To understand the mode of reception of *Marbot* we have to analyze a little more closely the means employed by the author to convey the force of conviction of his fiction, since it is these same means that have ended, on the contrary, in the invisibility of the fictional status of the work. We can group them under four headings: the authorial context, the paratext, the "formal mimesis" (i.e., the stated imitation of the biographical genre), and the contamination of the (referential) historical universe by the fictional universe.[5]

a) The authorial context. I have already said that in the bibliography of Hildesheimer *Marbot* follows directly after *Mozart*. It is thus not astonishing that many readers had confidence in the generic indication of the subtitle, *Eine Biographie*. What is more, the two texts are very close from the point of view of their construction: in both cases the author designs the portrait of his character by thematic blocks that allow him to liberate himself in a certain way from the purely chronological order of traditional biographies. This mimetism between a real and a fictional biography operates even at the level of the visual presentation of the books. Thus, the author's acknowledgments are inserted in the same place, present themselves in the same words, and address in large part the same persons. Let us add that before the publication of *Marbot*, Hildesheimer had introduced his character "to the world." During a conference on music in 1980, one year before the appearance of his tale, Hildesheimer made this statement: "The English theoretician of art Andrew Marbot refused to speak about music with the young Berlioz. He said to him: 'Music is an untranslatable language: one can speak of its grammar, but for each one of us it has a different significance. If it meant the same thing to us, it would enlighten less the music than our spiritual affinities.'" It is true that toward the end of this conference Hildesheimer specified that we must not look for information concerning Marbot in some dictionary "because I have invented him."[6] But a repeal is not equivalent to a cancellation: the hardest challenge is not to make-believe the reality of fictional entities but to reduce to fictional status entities that have been introduced as real. In fact, the simple occurrence of a proper name induces in the receiver a thesis of existence: only an explicit stipulation of fictionality can, if not prevent this projection of dismissal that seems to me inseparable from the usage itself of proper names, at least circumscribe its field of pertinence in such a way that the proper name in question cannot get mixed up with those that designate persons of whom we suppose (rightly or wrongly) that they really exist.

b) The paratext. The most solid paratextual element in the service of the strategy of feint is of course the generic indication *A Biography.*[7] We might note that, contrary to *Marbot*, the biography devoted to Mozart did not include generic information. The difference is easily explained: the proper name Mozart being known to the reader as the designation of a historical personage, it was not necessary to state that a book having his name as the title was a biography.

The second important paratextual element is the iconography, beginning with the (supposed) portrait of Marbot that decorates the cover and associates a face with the name of the hero. Here also, the resemblance with the book on Mozart is almost total, with one small difference: when in the case of the musician no textual indication tells us that the portrait is that of Mozart, the fictive biography includes, on the reverse of the title page, an identification not only of the character but also of the artist supposed to have portrayed him. One can read there, in fact: "Cover page: Sir Andrew Marbot. Lithograph with pencil by Eugène Delacroix (1827). Paris, Bibliothèque nationale." This attribution is evidently made credible by the diegesis that records a meeting between the painter and Marbot. The book includes in addition, like the biography devoted to Mozart, a full central iconographic section. It is made up in part of paintings and drawings attributed to their real authors but decked out with a false referential component. This is the case with the (supposed) portraits of the mother and father of Marbot: the two portraits were painted by Henry Raeburn and are owned by the National Gallery of Scotland in Edinburgh. These portraits, with their diverted identification, are mixed with real portraits of historical personages such as Leopardi, Thomas De Quincey, and Henry Crabb Robinson. The existence of the latter reinforces of course the belief of the reader in the truthfulness of the diverted portraits. There are added photos meant to reproduce the family residences of the Marbots as well as reproductions of paintings that Marbot would have seen during his travels that he comments on in the text. The effect of the real induced by the reproduction of these paintings profits the ontological status of the hero himself: since the works commented on by the character are real paintings and since on top of it all the author displays them for the reader, how could the latter be prevented from endowing the hero himself with real existence?

Another important paratextual element is the presence of an index of names, little used in the domain of literary fiction except in critical editions such as those of Balzac's *La comédie humaine* and Proust's *À la recherche du temps perdu* included in Gallimard's Bibliothèque de la Pléiade series. The status of the index is contradictory. On the one hand, it functions as a mimetic element, since it mimes a usage that is normal for factual biographies. But on the other hand, Hildesheimer makes of it also an index of fictionality, since he includes in it only the names of historical persons—those who act in the tale and those who are merely mentioned—with the exclusion of the fictional characters. But since in *Marbot* the large majority of proper names designate historical persons, the book presents a heavy quantitative disequilibrium in favor of the latter in such a way that the absence in the index of a few rare names with a fictional denotation hardly risks being noticed. The index, therefore, can hardly fill its function. Moreover, the fact that the index treats in the same way the historical persons simply mentioned and those who act in the tale still reinforces the effect of the real: the latter play the role of hinge in the device of immersion, insofar as through them the fictional universe "contaminates" the historical universe.[8] The historical persons who interact with the fictional characters accomplish actions that they were not able to accomplish "in real life," since they put them into relation with invented persons. Because of that fact they are fictionalized. But while in addition their proper names remain attached to the real persons, they make up the stitch between the historical and the fictional universes.

c) The formal mimesis. Among the properly narrative mimetic traits that Hildesheimer implements to produce the perfect appearance of a real biography, there are first of all those that concern the enunciative posture. He adopts the posture of the biographer perfectly. He does everything to avoid having the narrator take the substance of an I-narrator (*Ich-Erzähler*), such as Serenus Zeitblom does in *Doktor Faustus* by Thomas Mann, since such a thickness of the narrator-subject as a character removes his figure from the real author and at the same time fictionalizes the tale. Also, we notice no rupture in the enunciative posture when we read, one after the other, *Mozart* and then *Marbot*. Moreover, Hildesheimer adopts systematically an external perspective and refrains from all internal focalization. Thus, whenever he describes the supposed mental states of Marbot, Hildesheimer presents his description as a psychological induction founded on publicly accessible materials.[9] He resorts frequently, for example, to quotations, the sources of which are always indicated, whether they are passages supposedly included in Marbot's notebooks and letters or statements attributed to real authors. In the "quotations" of Marbot's texts the original English words used by him are sometimes added in parentheses, a trait of erudition (or pedantry) that is a supplementary element of mimesis.

The quotations that are attributed to historical persons have diverse statuses. Certain quotations are simply truthful: this is the case of all those of which Marbot is not the direct referent. Of course, those that speak explicitly of Marbot are, to various degrees, forgeries. When the context permits it, the same quotation combines both sentences effectively borrowed from the cited author and forged sentences. This is the case, for example, of a quotation of Goethe dated December 1825 and attributed to *Dialogues with Eckermann*: the beginning of this quotation is effectively found in the *Dialogues*; in contrast, the final sentences, where Goethe refers to Marbot, are forged. Generally, Hildesheimer limits the extent of the forged passages, which renders their discovery the harder, even for a reader who knows the quoted passage from memory. This care to limit the quotational forgeries is part of a more global tactic that consists of fictionalizing the historical persons as little as possible in order to have them attract the fictional person into their orbit rather than the contrary.

From the point of view of the dynamics of reading, the generic frame of the factual biography and the quotations reinforce themselves mutually: the reader takes the quotations as cash because he thinks he is reading a real biography, but insofar as they refer to real authors known by him (Goethe, Platen, Berlioz, etc.), they reinforce in turn his conviction that he is reading a real biography. Said differently, the trap of the mimetic lure closes on him again thanks to a perverse variation of what is known as the hermeneutical circle.

d) The contamination of the historical world by the fictional world. The status of the quotations is only a local effect of what is, without doubt, besides the formal mimesis, the strongest operator of feint, namely, that Hildesheimer multiplies the meetings between Marbot and well-known historical persons. What is important to note is that the contamination of the two universes follows a direction that is diametrically opposed to the one that generally associates with fiction. When we pose the question of the relations between invention and referentiality in fictional texts, we think of the introduction of referential elements in a globally invented universe: the question is thus that of the incursion of reality into fiction. The strategy of contamination that most commonly serves the effect of the real — and that is realized in an exemplary manner by realist fiction — consists of introducing referential elements — historical as well as geographic, temporal, and so on — in the invented universe. In *Marbot*, on the contrary, one attends to the universe strategy: Hildesheimer introduces invented elements (persons and actions) into a globally referential universe. One can thus note that roughly 90 percent of the proper names that intervene in a direct or indirect manner in the diegesis belong to the ontological class of historical persons, which inverses the proportion observed in most of the realist fictions of the nineteenth and twentieth centuries. In the same manner, a great part of the events told or commented on are grafted into the real historical universe: descriptions and interpretations of paintings, reflections on music, references to historical events, and so on. It is advisable to add that the strategy in question diverges also from that of the historical novel. The genre of the historical novel in fact is a fictionalization of historical persons. Hildesheimer, on the contrary, not only has an invented hero but still limits as much as possible the procedures of fictionalization of historical persons. I have already noted these traits apropos of his use of the quotational device. This is attested also by the fact that, rather than extending the surface of interaction of historical persons with invented figures, he multiplies their number, which permits him to limit more for each of them their interaction with the fictional universe, it being understood that the surface of intersection is proportional to their fictionalization.

Finally, we must note with Dorrit Cohn that *Marbot* distinguishes itself also in a fundamental manner from what she calls fictional historical biography, as notably exemplified by Hermann Broch's *Der Tod des Vergil* (*The Death of Virgil*); in fact, at the level of narrative techniques, the refusal of all internal focalization on the subject of the hero makes *Marbot* the perfect inversion of this genre. In the fictional historical biography "the life of a historical person is told by a clearly fictional discourse. In *Marbot*, on the contrary, the life of a fictional figure is told by a clearly nonfictional (historical) discourse." Whence her conclusion: *Marbot* is the first example of a new genre, the "historicized fictional biography."[10] Hildesheimer himself has perfectly summed up the result of his approach in saying that Marbot and his family are woven (*eingewoben*) in the history of the nineteenth century: they are effectively inserted in real history, forming a fictional pocket in a universe solidly secured to cultural history. *Marbot* is an incursion of unreality (i.e., invention) in reality rather than an incursion of reality in unreality.

Hildesheimer's book, however, does not interest me here in itself but uniquely for the general education that we can draw from it for the functioning (or rather the dysfunctioning) of the fictional device. The vicissitudes of its reception show in the first place that if fiction is born from a specific intentional posture, it does not guarantee by itself the effective functioning of the developed device. And, in this case, what is involved in the case of *Marbot* is not the competence (or the lack thereof) of the reader but the lack of respect by the author of the necessary conditions in the absence of which this competence can only go unheeded. From fiction the tale has passed to lure in such a manner that it exemplifies the quite paradoxical situation of a (verbal) representation that, from the intentional point of view, is fictional (it is not a matter of a fake) but that, from the point of view of its public status, proves to be incapable of functioning as fiction. Manifestly, this failure is linked to the mimetic characteristics that we just looked at: having pushed the mimetic component "too far," Hildesheimer found himself with a tale that functioned as a factual tale. What remains to be discovered is the extra move in this mimetic escalation.

Cohn has strongly underlined the exceptional character of *Marbot* from the point of view of traditional fictional genres. According to her, let us remember, Hildesheimer has in fact invented a new genre, the historicized fictional biography. But she also thinks that *Marbot* risks greatly remaining forever the unique exemplification of the genre it inaugurates.[11] To judge by the work's radically unstable pragmatic status, this skepticism seems well-founded. The true interest of the book does not reside in the improbable genre it could give birth to but in the fact that it constitutes an experimental device permitting a study of the constraints that rule fiction. According to Cohn, the central aspect of the device lies in the formal mimesis, thus in the imitation of factual biography. Her diagnosis is founded on the thesis of Käte Hamburger, according to whom there would be a radical distinction in status between the feint of statements of reality — reserved for the nonfactual tale in the first person — and fiction properly speaking, concerning the nonfactual tale in the third person. *Marbot* denies this thesis strongly, since it is manifestly a matter of a nonfactual tale in the third person that concerns the feint of statements of reality. There is no doubt that, statistically speaking, Dorrit Cohn is right to underline the exceptional character of Hildesheimer's tale in view of the norms of modern fiction. On the other hand, it seems to me that this trait — the maximalization of formal mimesis — is hardly susceptible to explain the pragmatic dysfunctioning of the book. The self-destructive character of the fiction constructed by Hildesheimer is not due to the fact that it mimes statements of reality; it proceeds from the impossibility in which the reader finds himself to recognize — before he involves himself in the reading of the text — that he will read a fiction. The fact that the intention of the author is not sufficient to guarantee the correct functioning of the fictional device does not therefore imply that we must look for the decisive criterion at the level of the mimetic procedures in themselves. I do not want to suggest that formal mimesis played no role in the passage from fiction to lure. It is formal mimesis itself that permitted the tale to function as lure. On the other hand, it is not formal mimesis that prevented the book from functioning as fiction, or, rather, if it did so, it is not because of the rules proper to historicized fictional biography but because Hildesheimer spread mimesis up to the programmatic frame of the work.

Neither the formal mimesis, nor any other mimetic device internal to the tale, nor the fact that Hildesheimer has produced a "hyper-normal mimeme" of the genre of factual biography is therefore a decisive factor.[12] This role goes back to pragmatic mimesis, that is, to the fact that the whole of the editorial frame—the whole of the paratext—imitates that of the factual biography. If he had wanted to avoid having his book function as a lure, Hildesheimer would not have needed to change anything in the intratextual mimetic traits. A simple explicit paratextual indication would have sufficed to guarantee a reception in accord with his fictional intention. Or, to take up again a distinction introduced in the preceding chapter, when he should have limited the use of mimetic techniques to an imitation-semblance of the surface structure of factual biography, the fact that he extended the mimesis to the pragmatic frame of the work could only lead the uninitiated reader to believe himself to be faced with an imitation-reinstantiation of the deep structure of factual biography, that is, with an exemplification of factual biography endowed with its normal illocutionary force. By spreading the mimetic logic to the pragmatic frame that institutes the space of the fictional game, Hildesheimer, instead of exploring a new form of fiction, has enclosed his uninitiated readers in the (involuntary) trap of a lure.

2. The Phylogenesis of Fiction: Shared Ludic Feint

Marbot seems to justify the Platonic distrust toward fiction and to constitute a blatant counterexample to the Aristotelian hypothesis of a stability of frontiers between mimetic semblance and reality.

In effect, at least with some of the readers, the fictional universe has interfered with the system of "serious" beliefs concerning what "is the case" and what "is not the case." Thus, it would seem that there is a contamination of reality by fiction. In fact, at least if the analysis I proposed is correct, the situation is very different. Rather than having forced open the borderlines between the fictional and the factual, *Marbot* fell onto this side of fiction in the field of mimetic manipulation. Hildesheimer's tale is not a fiction that succeeded in destabilizing the frontiers of the real and the fictional but a narrative work that failed to accede to the status of fiction. Far from being an experimental proof of the dangers of immersion, it throws light to the contrary on the fundamental constitutive rule of all fiction: the institution of a pragmatic frame appropriate to fictional immersion. In fact, the manner in which readers, after reading the book, believe in the existence of Marbot is radically different from the attitude they would adopt faced with a fictional character: the universe of Hildesheimer's tale interferes with the repertory of their historical beliefs, which is what a fictional narrative does not do, and this precisely thanks to its pragmatic frame.

The appropriate pragmatic frame is evidently the one that we designate commonly by the term *ludic feint* or *shared feint*.[13] Both terms appear problematic. Don't they combine two paradoxical "imperatives"? Can one say of someone who feints ludically, thus "for false," that he feints? And how can a feint that is shared still be a feint? What is at issue is not only the intention of the creator but—as *Marbot* showed—the communicative status of the work: it is not enough that the inventor of a fiction has the intention to feint "for false," it is still necessary that the receiver recognize this intention and thus that the first of these gives him the means to do it. This is why the feint that rules the institution of public fiction needs to be not only ludic but also shared, because the ludic status concerns uniquely the intention of him who feints: for the fictional device to be able put itself into place, this intention must make room for a subjective accord.

The apparently paradoxical character of the two terms is the translation of a real difficulty: how do we think the relation between the activities of feint and the fictional situation?[14] The existence of such a relation is not in doubt, since — as *Marbot* taught us — a fiction that fails to impose itself as such functions at the same time as a feint. We also know already on which level this relation ties itself, namely, that of the means. Fiction and feint have recourse to the same means, the ones of imitation-semblance. But they do not have the same function: in the case of fiction the mimemes are supposed to make possible the accession to an imaginary universe identified as such, while in the case of feint they are supposed to deceive the person who exposes himself to them. The paradoxical aspect of the two terms in a certain way does nothing but translate this distinction between the means and the end. The means of fiction are the same as those of feint, but the end is different. It being given that, from the point of view of biological evolution, the activities of "serious" feint precede the development of ludic and shared feint, we are without a doubt allowed to go further and to uphold the hypothesis of a genealogical relation: the means of fiction are borrowed from feint. If this is so, the study of the specificity of the situation of shared ludic feint is thus susceptible to enlighten us regarding the phylogenetic genesis of fiction conceived as a cultural conquest of humanity. Or, at least, it can enlighten us on the birth of fiction as a shared public reality. It is in fact far from evident that the notion itself of "ludic feint" is still pertinent for describing "private" fictions, that is, fictions in which the creator and the receiver are one and the same person. But this is a problem that I will approach only in the next section. For the moment I will take into account only fiction as a shared public device.

In order to try to understand how shared ludic fiction functions, we can start from the banal statement already announced above. When I feign seriously, I have as my aim to deceive effectively the one I address. When I feign with a ludic intention, this is clearly not the case; on the contrary, I don't want to deceive him. The conditions that must be assembled for a ludic intersubjective feint to succeed are thus contrary to those demanded by a serious feint: a serious feint succeeds only if it is not shared, while a ludic feint succeeds only if it is shared. And, of course, the two situations must be distinguished from a third: the one where someone communicates to other people beliefs (and, more generally, representations) that are "false" but that he believes are real. Said differently, we must distinguish not only between lie and fiction but also between error (real or supposed) and fiction. The question of truth and falsity does not pose itself in the same way in the three cases. When I lie or feign "seriously," I present as true what I believe to be false. Certainly, I can deceive myself, that is, it can happen that what I believe to be false is in reality true. But that only demonstrates the complexity of the lie as intentional attitude with respect to truth or falsity as a relation of fact between a representation and what it represents. A lie can fail in two very different manners: it can fail either because the mimemes are not believed or because the liar maintains wrong beliefs about the mimemes' subject. In the case of error, the definitional conditions are the inverse of those of the lie: I must have a wrong belief (or a representation), but at the same time I must believe that it is true. In fiction the situation, as we will see, is still very different: in a certain manner (but in what manner?) the question itself of the truth or falsity of representations does not seem to be pertinent to it anymore.

These elementary distinctions permit us to see already that, counter to a recurrent tendency, we should not apply the notion of fiction either to "mythological" representations or to religious ones or in a more general manner to the beliefs of men who hold them to be true and those who do not hold them to be true.[15] In fact, whether it is from the point of view of their genesis or of the mental attitude of those who adhere to them (like those who refuse to adhere to them), these facts do not concern a shared ludic feint. It is true that the term *fiction* has often been applied to the religious domain, whether by zealots wanting to disqualify concurrent religions or by nonbelievers wanting to disqualify religion as a whole. The application of the same term to two orders of facts as distinct as religion and the devices of ludic feint is revealing for the importance of the antimimetic position in Occidental culture. But it should also be clear that in this usage, in which it functions as a synonym of falsity, the term has in fact not much to do with what interests us here. We might think that things are different in our own day, but, insofar as we continue to apply collective representations of a religious or "mythical" type, we do not do so to express a rejection. It is, rather, a sign of a reinterpretation of these representations from a point of view that is no longer concerned with them. The meaning thus seems to be closer to the one that interests us here. Of course, if it is used in the sense of the fictional devices, its application to the facts in question is the more out of place. It allows us certainly to show "tolerance" toward beliefs we don't adhere to, but it is a tolerance acquired at a low price, since it exempts us from conforming really to them, as we should do if we took them seriously as beliefs—which is what those do who adhere to them.[16] Graver for our purpose, the fact of spreading the term to beliefs and representations held to be true (by those who have developed or develop them) comes back to disregarding the specificity of the fictional device that resides for a large part in the fact that the representations to which it gives birth do not concern the regime of beliefs held to be true (or false).

It goes without saying that my objection concerns only the application of the term to cultural contexts in which the representations in question are effectively held to be true. To say that the *Epic of Gilgamesh* is a fiction is to express an untruth. On the other hand, it is no doubt true that in our culture it functions as a fiction: to the degree that we live in a society in which this tale does not find a hitching point with the beliefs that we generally take to be true or false, we spontaneously tend to read it in a fictional mode. For the believers who belong to one or another of the religions actually believed in, *Gilgamesh* would no longer rival the tales that they adhere to, since it belongs to a religion that has disappeared. For the nonbelievers it would no longer constitute a false belief, since there is no longer anyone who believes in it. It is nonetheless true that, doing this, the present use imposes the pragmatic frame of fiction onto a group of representations that were not concerned in their intentional context of origin. Gérard Genette speaks apropos of this of "an involuntary state of fiction" — an involuntary state because in the societies where they are valid, the beliefs called "mythic" don't function as fictions.[17]

From the moment these representations are reactivated in our own culture their fictionalization allows them to be recycled in support of aesthetic satisfaction and thus to continue to draw a profit in cognitive and affectionate terms. But we have to distinguish between the fact that we approach them as fictions and the pretension that we could have to define them as such. My objection concerns only the second approach, and this because it ends in a lack of understanding of the specificity of the situation of ludic feint — and thus of the fictional device — even in the societies that in addition have produced groups of serious beliefs that in our society function only as fictions. Because the idea according to which in so-called primitive societies the distinction between representations held to be true (or false) and fiction would not exist is due mainly to the lack of interest of classical anthropology for fiction: fictional games seem in any case to exist in all societies and in forms equivalent to those that we can observe in the children of our own society.[18] Thomas Pavel has very well marked the distinction between the two types of representation in reminding us that "the belief in the myths of the community is obligatory," whereas "the adhesion to fiction is free and clearly limited from the spatial and temporal point of view."[19] The two characteristics of fiction that he underlines — the free adhesion and the spatial and temporal boundary — are direct consequences of shared ludic feint: the adhesion is free because the fictional device is an exemplification of the mode of ludic interaction, which would only establish itself on a voluntary basis; and, like any game, fiction institutes its own rules, which implies a provisional (and partial) suspension of those that apply outside the ludic space. This is precisely the status that "mythological" representations — "myths" are clearly never only the beliefs of others — have acquired in our society in the frame of the "involuntary state of fiction."

The notion of myth, at least if it is not manipulated with precaution, has still another disadvantage, which is in some ways the inverse of the first: those mythologists who do not want to disqualify the beliefs of the societies they study have a tendency to minimize, if not to deny, the pertinence in the societies in question of the distinction between beliefs held to be true and imaginative fictions. At the same time, they are blind to the fact, however very interesting, that the narrative sceances from which they reconstruct the so-called myths can very well combine sequences "held to be true" by the narrator and his audience (e.g., genealogical tales) with sequences clearly put down as fictive. Laurence Goldman and Michael Emmison have thus shown that the narrative sceances (*bi te*) of the Hulis of Papua New Guinea are true pragmatic makeshifts that combine narrations to which the narrator and the audience adhere "seriously" with fictional inventions. And, exactly as in our own societies, it is the existence of conventional markers of fictionality (stereotyped introductory phrases, repertory of proper names specifically reserved for the fictional universes) that permits the auditors to know at each moment if the context is fictional or not.[20] In other words, the Hulis distinguish very clearly between fictive imagination and serious belief, even if some of the facts they believe seriously are not the same as those that we believe seriously.

But the crucial point in the distinction between fictional situation and "serious" beliefs is precisely not in the order of truth or "effective" falseness: many of our serious beliefs have such distant links with the knowledge that is indispensable for us to adapt to reality (physical and social) that, in practical terms, the fact that they are true or false is all the same. On the other hand, it is indispensable that we trace a frontier between the beliefs (true or false) to which we adhere and that concern the principle of reality (even if it can happen that they escape its approval de facto) and the imaginative constructions that do not concern this principle (or at least not in the same manner). Except in the case of very grave cognitive dysfunctioning systematically producing false beliefs, the frontier between what pretends to a status of truth and what does not pretend to such a status is more vital than the one between what is effectively true and what is effectively false.

But if we must distinguish between fiction and false beliefs or illusions, the problem still remains that, as soon as fiction operates through mimemes, it cannot operate through a mechanism that is the same as that of the lures. In fact, if the hypothesis proposed in the preceding chapter is correct, the general logic of the posture of representational attention is one: every representation poses its contents, and it does so because of the simple fact that it is a representation.[21] Every representation has a structure of return in the logical sense of the term, meaning that it "is on the subject of something," that it "has bearing on something." The existence of such a structure is immanent to the nature of representation. It defines representation as independent of the question of knowing whether it is an object of cross-reference (to which it adds the simple fact that it is a representation) and corresponds effectively to a transcendent object in one universe or another. We must thus abandon the idea according to which there would be two modalities of representation, one that would be fictional and the other that would be referential: there exists only one, namely, the referential modality, because the referential capacity is a neurological structure that has been fashioned in such a manner by natural selection that it functions as an interface between our central nervous system, on the one hand, and the external environment, like our own states and corporeal and mental acts, on the other. Thus, even if it aims for an nonexistent object, it cannot represent it as nonexistent, because to represent (oneself) something comes back to posing this thing as a representational content.[22]

In addition, fictional representations pose exactly the same classes of referents as those of common representation: external environment, corporeal and mental states and acts. And this is true for all representations, independently of their source, of their mode of access, or of their mode of existence. In this way, whatever the logical difference (from the denotational viewpoint) between the representation of a horse and the representation-of-a-unicorn, the horse and the unicorn are equivalent from the point of view of the content.[23] It is true that certain approaches are excluded in the case of the unicorn: I could (of course) never see a real unicorn; that is, none of my representations of a unicorn will be caused by a unicorn. In the same way, we have seen that it is vital that I make the difference directly between the representations caused by what they represent (i.e., perceptions) and those whose cause is not the represented object — which is the case (among other things) of the representations produced by mimetic self-stimulation. However, if I can't see a real unicorn, I can easily see one imaginatively. Here again, from the point of view of the manner in which I apprehend this image visually and from which I construct mentally the entity that it aims for, there is nothing to distinguish it from the image of a horse — that is, what applies to mental representations also applies to iconic representations. And if I have never seen a horse but have, on the other hand, a long experience of images of unicorns, the representation that I will form will be much richer and more complex in the second case than in the first.

These examples show that the existence or nonexistence of what we represent to ourselves makes no difference at the level of the internal constitution of the representations: this constitution differs much more according to the representational vehicles (perception, act of imagination, linguistic sign, analogical figuration, sound or tactile stimulus, etc.) than according to causal history of the representational contents. In other words, it is because fictional invention can only construct its universe by using the canonical representational structure (at the same time, it puts out of the circuit the question of the transcendental reference that is the functional correlative of the immanent relation of return) that it cannot include an element of the "as if" of feint. In fact, in the fictional invention these referents put down by the very nature of mental representation are not the causal source of the representation that constructs them — as is the case in the canonical cognitive representation — or become in their turn a causal force susceptible to produce the corresponding reality — as is the case in the representation insofar as it is an intentional cause of the production of an object. Representation is the result of a self-affection of the representational capacity, self-affection that is possible from the moment that a representational system gains access to reflexive processes, which is the case of the human representational capacity. The function of ludic feint is to create an imaginary universe and to lead the receiver to immerse himself in this universe. It is not to induce him to believe that this imaginary universe is the real universe. The situation of ludic feint thus distinguishes itself profoundly from that of serious feint. In this last case the function of mimemes is to deceive the beliefs, that is, the conscious instant that regulates our direct interactions with reality; in the fictional device their function is to engage the representational attitude (perceptive or linguistic-semantic), it being understood that shared feint implies that we know that it is a matter of mimemes, a knowledge that stimulates the specific usage that it is advisable to make of the universe generated by this representational attitude.

To try to understand a little better the relation between mimemes and shared ludic feint, it might be useful to start out from the question of lures. In the case of *Marbot*, the absence of a situation of shared feint made the tale function as a lure of factual biography, and at the same time the effect was the same as the one of a (successful) serious feint. One would thus think that there is incompatibility between shared ludic feint and the effects of lure. But in reality the relation is more complex. The reason for this is double: for one thing, and *Marbot* showed this, there can be lure in the absence of all intention of feint; for another, there is lure and lure, to the extent that lures can invest different mental modules and that consequences are not the same in each case.

Let us start out from the fact that there can be lure — that is, confusion or short circuit between the mimeme and the reality it imitates — in the absence of all intention of feint. We already know why: feint is an intentional fact, whereas lure is a functional fact. The mode of operation of a mimeme (or of a set of mimemes) has its own dynamic that is independent from the intentional attitude of the creator and determined fundamentally by the degree of isomorphism between imitation and what is imitated.[24] As soon as this isomorphism exceeds a certain threshold, the mimeme functions as lure, whatever the intention that ruled its production. In particular, any representation founded on an exploitation of analogical relations (i.e., any "representation by imitation") is susceptible, in "favorable" circumstances, to transform itself into a lure, and this in the absence of all intention of feint. In the reverse, even if there is intention of feint, as soon as the isomorphism is too weak, the lure does not operate: there are those who know how to lie, and there are the others. It is thus important to distinguish between the specific mimetic relation that is the production of a lure and the intention of (serious) feint.

This distinction is all the more important in that in fiction the situations of fictional immersion are linked to effects of lure when there is no intention of (serious) feint. Of all the devices of mimetic representation known to this day, cinema is the one that has the easiest time producing effects of this type. It is a matter in this case of perceptive lures.[25] The possibility of it is anchored in the cinematic device itself, that is, in its quasi-perceptive status of analogical representation. It is thus situated uphill from the distinction between fiction film and documentary film — a characteristic that singularly complicates the study of cinema as a whole and cinematographic fiction.[26] It nevertheless remains that it is basically the fiction cinema, and this from its origin, that has striven to draw profit from it. The principal motivation of all progress in the domain of cinematographic techniques seems in fact to have been — more than the care for "reproductive faithfulness" — the will to saturate films with hypernormal mimemes at the level of the image (exaggeration of luminous contracts, of radiance, or of contrasts of colors, etc.) as well as that of the sound (it is enough to think of digital Dolby, characterized by a systematic exaggeration of the effects of sound reverberation and the amplitude of low frequencies to provoke an effect of reality). As each cinematic spectator experiences from time to time, such hypernormal mimemes are punctually capable of functioning as perceptive illusions. The proof of it is that they induce short reactional loops that lead us, for example, to bend over, to throw back our head, or to close our eyes. Such reactional loops, reflexive in nature, are typical of preattentional perceptive treatments. It is thus the perceptive module that has been mistaken: the mimetic isomorphism has been sufficient to trigger the reaction that would have been adequate if in place of the mimeme there had been an imitated real stimulus. We have to note that the stimuli that induce the lure must, in a real situation, be treated in a preattentional mode to be treated efficaciously; thus, they do not reach our consciousness until our reaction is already engaged.[27] It is a matter of reactional loops genetically programmed, indispensable for our corporeal integrity (we throw our head back to avoid a blow, we lean over to escape a projectile, etc.) or psychological (we close our eyes to escape a traumatizing perceptive experience).

The preattentional character of these perceptive illusions is interesting for our purposes. In effect, all the hypernormal cinematographic mimemes are far from being reproductions of stimuli that normally activate short reactional loops of the reflexive type. Only the mimemes that reproduce such stimuli end in perceptive transfers. In order to appreciate the importance of this fact correctly in what concerns the comprehension of the relations between shared ludic feint and effects of lure, it must be completed by a supplementary precision: contrarily to the lure induced by *Marbot*, the perceptive illusions in question never have any consequence. In fact, as Christian Metz notes with great acuteness, the "perceptive transfers" and the motor reactions they induce are always of short duration. He adds, and it is for me the decisive point, that it is the very sketch of the motor reaction that makes the lure abort: comparing the state of the spectator during the perceptive transfer to a state of quasi sleep, he notes that "it is precisely this action [the motor reaction] that wakes him, that draws him from his brief fall into a sort of sleep, where it had its root."[28]

If we wanted to be still more precise, we would no doubt have to say that it is at the moment when the proprioceptive feedback of the sketched reflexive reaction accedes to consciousness that, jointly, the motor reaction is blocked and the perceptive lure defused. In other words, the decisive instant that hinders the lure from controlling the real behavior is that of conscious control, of attentional cognitive treatment: the consciousness of the spectator takes things back in hand, it reinstates the adequate perceptive and mental posture, the one of shared ludic feint — and thus of immersion in a semblance. In reverse, in the case of *Marbot* it is the conscious attention of readers that has been deceived, since the identification of the pragmatic status of a tale is a decision that concerns conscious attention. This is in agreement with the fact that, as we have seen, it is not the hypernormal lures of formal mimesis that were responsible for Hildesheimer's "failure" but a self-destructive pragmatic tactic.

The comparison between the two situations — the one of the cinematic perceptive transfer and the one of *Marbot* — is enlightening in at least two ways. In the first place, it shows that the situation of ludic feint is not incompatible with the existence of functional lures operating at a preattentional level. The most important aspect of the perceptive transfers studied by Metz is in the fact that, given the imitated stimulus, the treatment of the signal has taken place in the framework of a short reactional loop, not penetrable cognitively. What is at issue is thus not so much the existence of a preattentional lure as the fact that the instance of conscious control has been short-circuited, an effect that specifically depends on the type of mimeme concerned. It could very well happen that the hypernormal mimemes serving as a starting point for the fictional immersion always produce preattentional lures; it could even happen that this is their function in the frame of the fictional variant of the mimetic immersion. It could happen that the creator of fictions, though he has not at all the will to deceive us, can only lead us to adopt the attitude of mimetic immersion insofar as he succeeds in deceiving our preattentional representational module: in order to make us accede to the mental universe he creates, he must make us develop representations that assert that universe.

Such at least is the hypothesis that I shall contemplate to try to understand the situation of fictional immersion. For the moment I will limit myself to what the situation of perceptive transfer teaches us, even though it is a contrario, concerning the situation of shared ludic feint, namely, that in a "normal" situation the vision of a film is accompanied by a neutralization of the set of mental modules that command the reactions (motor and other) that would be appropriate if, instead of being faced by mimemes, we would find ourselves in the corresponding perceptive situation. The fact that there is production of hypernormal mimemes is therefore in no sense in contradiction to the situation of shared ludic feint, at least if we accept the hypothesis of a relative independence of the mental modules of preattentional treatment of representations (whether they are perceptive or linguistic) with respect to the center of conscious control that governs our beliefs and operates the integration of the representational data in specific epistemological frames.

Thus, the possibility of the coexistence of a dynamic founded on the efficacity of a lure with absence of deception and illusion explains itself as soon as we admit the relative independence of the representational mental modules with respect to the center of conscious control that rules our beliefs and realizes the epistemic interpretation of the representational data. The ludic feint realizes the functional decoupling of these two mental "modules" when in general they are coupled: in fact, in a normal situation, everything that is treated by the representational mechanisms (whether it is on the mode of perception or of linguistic denotation) enters into our holistic system of beliefs as an aspect of the "reality" in which we live. The situation of ludic feint demands on the contrary that we cut this link, which results in a permanent travel between the representational posture and the subsequent neutralization of the effects normally induced by this representation—hence the hypothesis that ludic feint realizes a decoupling between the representational mental modules (perceptive and linguistic) and the epistemic module of the beliefs. In a "normal" situation everything that is treated by representational modules (whether it is by the mode of perception or of linguistic denotation) is affected with an epistemic value (true, false, probable, possible, impossible, etc.) in order to be stocked thereafter in the long-term memory in the form of beliefs utilizable directly in our cognitive and practical interactions with the world in which we live. In contrast, the situation of ludic feint cuts this link, which demands a permanent travel between the representational posture and a neutralization of effects normally induced by this representation. Thus, a writer of novels, to the extent he imitates the signs of identification of the acts of referential language without reinstantiating the imitated acts, produces mimeme-semblances that, on the same basis as reality statements, will induce on the reader's part a mental representation of the narrated objects and events. But because of the fact of ludic feint, this treatment is blocked at the threshold of the mental module where the reader elaborates his beliefs concerning (whatever he means by it).

We can also express the difference in another way. Contrarily to a received idea, a fiction is not obliged to denounce itself as fiction.[29] On the other hand, it should be announced as fiction, the function of this announcement being to institute the pragmatic frame that limits the space of the game at the interior of which the semblance can operate without the representations induced by the mimemes being treated in the same manner as would be the "real" representations mimed by the fictional device. According to the cultural context and the type of fiction, this announcement is more or less explicit: in the case of a fictional tradition well anchored in a given society and of a work inscribing itself strongly in this tradition, the act instituting the fiction can at the limit be tacit, that is, take part in the implicit presuppositions of the situation of communication. For example, our implicit knowledge of the outstanding traits of cinematographic fiction means that when we turn on the television in the middle of a program we know right away if the images that succeed one another are part of a documentary or part of a fictional film — except in the case of a fiction film founded on the formal mimesis of the documentary genre (such as certain passages of *Zelig* by Woody Allen) or a documentary that borrows its construction from fiction (like *Nanook of the North* by Robert Flaherty).[30]

The forms that this announcement takes, when it is explicit, are in addition very diverse according to the types of fiction. In the case of oral literature, the role is generally filled by conventional introductory formulas. For verbal fiction in the regime of writing, it is usually the paratext that takes the responsibility for it, whether it is by explicit generic indications or in a more tacit manner by the type itself of the title retained — which evidently supposes a familiarity of the reader with the literary tradition in question.[31] In other forms of fiction the pragmatic contract materializes itself in the form of a veritable physical frame. This is the case of the theatrical scene — to measure its efficacity as a frame of fictionalization, it is enough to think in contrast of street theater and of the difficulties that can happen there to trace the limits between the game and the reality (which is understood to be one of the aims of street theater). It is the case also of the movie theater (and screen), although in the case of cinematographic fiction it is more a matter of fit-together frames.

The material framing is not enough, since a movie theater projects not only fiction films but also documentaries. Even though it is a relatively reliable indication, given the scarcity of documentary films projected in a theater, it must be confirmed by paratextual (or rather parafilmic) indications: title, names of the actors and of the director, possibly generic indications, and so on.

If the hypotheses that precede are generally correct, then in the situation of shared ludic feint it is not feint that operates as feint. The term *shared ludic feint* must not be taken literally: what the fictional device has in common with feint is the recourse to the same technique — the production of mimeme-pretenses. What we call *ludic feint* characterizes itself by a dissociation between the production of mimeme-semblances and the intentional attitude or the pragmatic function of the feint, resulting in the hypothesis — somewhat speculative, I agree — that from the phylogenetic point of view the ludic feint, and thus the fiction, would have been born from the cut between the productive operation of lures and the activity of feint with respect to which it had been selected in the frame of biological evolution. The very possibility of fiction, conceived as the cultural conquest of humanity, therefore rests on at least three conditions. If it demands a dissociation between mimetic procedures and conduct of *mimicry*, a dissociation of this kind must first be possible. It seems to me that this condition poses no problems, since we saw that the efficacity itself of the mimemes is independent of the function or the conduct they serve, which shows well that it is a matter of two facts irreducible one to the other. The second condition is evidently the existence of a complex mental organization that should possess at least two characteristics: an instance of conscious (or attentional) control susceptible of blocking the effects of preattentional lures at the level of beliefs as well as a sophisticated intentional organization susceptible of distinguishing between what is valid for real and what is valid make-believe. This implies a fortiori that fiction could be born only from the moment when the activities of mimicry had invested the intentional behaviors. The third condition is of a social nature: the situation of shared ludic feint is possible only in the frame of a social organization in which the part of reciprocal cooperation is larger than the one of conflictual relations. It demands in effect that the mimetic techniques stop being at the service of basically manipulating (predation or self-defense) relations and be recycled by an intentional attitude that rests, on the contrary, on a relation of communicative transparency and confidence between the one who produces the mimemes and the one who is invited to play.

3. The Ontogenesis of Fictional Competence: Mimetic Self-Stimulation

I just suggested that from the point of view of phylogenesis fiction implied a dissociation between the mimetic operators and the vital function that had been (and that, in other contexts, remains) that of mimeme-semblances conceived as instruments in the service of "serious" feint. The hypothesis is clearly speculative, but insofar as in biological evolution the facts of serious feint precede by far the genesis of ludic feint, it is at least plausible. Whatever it is, if we suppose that it is able to realize the birth of fiction as a shared social activity, we do not see very well how it might apply to the fictional device conceived as a "private" game. Fiction can be a solitary pleasure, and it often is, at least in our childhood: to play with a doll, with tiny cars, or with tin soldiers, to imagine oneself as a movie star or Superman comes back to elaborating "private" fictions. One does not see how the ontogenesis of this competence could explain itself by a dissociation between mimetic operators and serious feint. But if this is so, what then is the validity of the notion of shared feint of which I just made such a big case?

The question of the ontogenesis of fictional competence is a little less speculative than that of the phylogenesis of fiction as social activity. Nonetheless, we approach it often in a perspective that misjudges the real issue. We have actually a tendency to think spontaneously that fiction simply arises from the referential relationship to reality by neutralizing certain of the constraints that rule it. This supposition is intimately linked to a simplistic conception of the genesis of the relation between the individual and nonsubjective reality and more broadly of the cognitive and affective development (the two largely go hand in hand) of the little child. It presupposes in effect implicitly that the brain of the newborn functions like an empty sheet required to fill itself little by little with referential knowledge as the external reality imprints its marks on it, the whole under the control of a central epistemic instance that would be none other than the "self" of the baby. Against this way of seeing, it is advisable to recall some elementary facts that show not only that the birth of the fictional competence is a complex process but also that its acquisition is a very important factor in the process of mastering reality. In other words, far from being a parasitical outgrowth of a connection to the real that would be an originary given, the imaginary activity, thus the access to fictional competence, is an important factor in the establishment of a stable epistemic structure, that is, in the distinction between the self and reality.

There are two things that the psychology of development — beyond all the quarrels of the movement — has succeeded in establishing in a reasonably certain manner: it is wrong to believe that a baby disposes from birth on a structured self; it is also not true that at the same time his brain is originally blank of all prestructuration of the real. Far from being a blank slate, a baby's brain is endowed from birth with a certain number of structural organizations already functional from the epistemic point of view that, activated by appropriate exterior stimulations, will guide in an autonomous manner the first behaviors. These organizations, which are genetically "pre-cabled" (David Stern speaks of "preformed mental structures"), of which the best studied are those linked to visual perception, the acquisition of language, and the motor reflexes, operate on a preattentional plane and seem unable to be modified by attentional (i.e., conscious) factors.[32] It is thanks to this characteristic that they are already effective even if consciousness and its instances of attentional control are still in an inchoative state.

In effect, and here still contrary to the received idea, the child is not born with an already structured "self" capable of posing itself as distinct from its environment.[33] At the level of its lived states — states attached to the experience of the needs and of their satisfaction, to the sensibility to pleasure and to suffering, to the sensations produced by the degrees of muscular tone and loosening, as well as to sensorial stimulations that come from what we sometimes call the "zooconscience" — the newborn sees the surrounding world, including the persons who occupy themselves with him, as nothing but an unlimited extension of himself. The consciousness of being "himself" is still lacking in him, for one becomes "oneself" only in "secreting" a separatist membrane that gives birth simultaneously to the two universes, that of subjective interiority and that of objective exteriority. As the multiple failures, sometimes heavy in consequences, of this process illustrate to the contrary, the establishment of such a stable frontier between oneself and the world, between what is a part of our interiority and what is a part of the "outside," is an enterprise of which we cannot overestimate the complexity — or the frustrating character, since the small child loses with it at the same time his original feeling of all-powerfulness and has the experience of his dependency.

It would seem that from the cognitive point of view it is the disproportion between very complex preattentional aptitudes, capable of reacting in a differential manner to signs coming from various sources, and the still largely underdeveloped character of the integrated conscious organization to which the responsibility falls of the ulterior treatment of these signs (and notably their representational stockage and their categorization) that poses the greatest challenge to the little child. The preattentional instruments are already fully active, but the conscious control that is to take its turn is not yet able to fill its role in a reliable manner. Concretely, the baby is still incapable of dividing up in an adequate manner the stimuli that invest it from all sides between the different sources that cause them and thus to adapt its reactions (conscious, intentional) to them. As Jerome Singer notes (following numerous other psychologists), for the baby the crucial distinction between exogenous and endogenous signs is far from apparent: "As a matter of fact, it may not be an easy task for the child to determine which stimuli are basically internal in the form of reproductive imagery and snatches of past conversations that have been stored and which are the external stimuli currently in the immediate environment."[34] Insofar as, having left early childhood, we are capable — at least in the absence of preattentional sensorial illusions, of pathological states, or of too strong affective counterinvestments — of classifying with more or less success our mental contents according to the different source from which they stem and to adopt the mode of reaction that agrees with each type, our tendency is too large to underestimate the fact that the baby lives in a universe that has an ontological status undetermined in large part and that the epistemic relations it entertains with the stimuli of which it makes the experience are still fundamentally unstable.

This instability is all the larger because the intentional (or representational) mental activity is not a discontinuous phenomenon that would be released by the appearance of external stimuli (perceptive or of somatic origin) and that would cease in the absence of such exogenous information.[35] In fact, a large part of the mental activities are not dependent on stimuli but concern a phenomenon of self-stimulation and thus of a functioning in a closed loop. This functioning in a closed loop gives rise to new mental contents that result from a reprocessing (alteration, recombination, deletion, etc.) of exogenous informations (and the results of anterior self-stimulation) already stocked in memory. Among these self-stimulations the processes of mimetic modeling occupy a large place. But here again, in a first moment the baby is incapable of tracing a tidy frontier between two types. First, there is the homologous modeling, in which the structural relations of the model must be superposable according to a relation regulated with those of the modeling fact — a situation that prevails, for example, in the learning processes by imitation of which I recalled the important role they play in the acquisition of the first human aptitudes and notably in the frame of the activation of the genetically programmed structural organizations. Second, there is the fictional (or imaginative) modeling, conceived as a production of a representation in which the relation between the virtual model and the reality does not obey constraints of global and local homology but in which it is enough that a relationship of global analogy be maintained, the local correspondences, being able to be indifferently analogical or homological.[36]

It is the more vital for the little child who succeeds in establishing these distinctions that the self-stimulations are massively invested by his needs and drives and that he consequently has a natural tendency to use them as counterinvestments susceptible to be directed against disagreeable and painful stimuli. Said differently, everything pushes him to project his self-stimulations into disagreeable stimuli in order to recover them and replace them with representations that are more malleable and more in line with his desires. The result is the risk of a parasitage of the homologous modeling by the fictional modeling, which at the same time renders the first inefficacious and hinders the second from taking form as a specific mental attitude. A well-known example of such a dysfunctioning is mythomania: it is a current and normal manifestation with the little child, since the two types of modeling are still largely undifferentiated; on the other hand, if it subsists beyond a certain age, it becomes a cognitive (and social) handicap often weighty in consequences. The issue is thus sizable: it is a matter of establishing a frontier between fictional immersion and the facts of self-deception of a fantasmatic nature.[37]

The affective investment of self-stimulations must make us attend to another fact that I have neglected to this point: in contrast to what my description could suggest, the baby is not a cognitive machine but an organism moved by needs and drives. The adult is without a doubt not in a fundamentally different situation. But, compared to the baby, he is in a lesser incapacity to satisfy his needs and drives by his own means. The baby is in fact in a radical dependency with respect to adults, a real situation that contrasts singularly with the illusory sentiment of all-powerfulness that is given to him by the fact that, at least in the first period, they obey him regularly. It is thus not astonishing that the first stable elements of his world, the first constellations of stimuli that will crystallize themselves in permanent figures, are persons who provide the satisfaction of his vital needs: the mother (or the person who replaces her) and, more widely, the circle of "nourishing family." Insofar as these answer all his needs in an optimal manner, even though they manifest themselves to him as constituents of a perceptive field that is par excellence that of the stimuli that escape his control, namely, that these stimuli attack him (too strong a light, too loud a noise, resistance of material objects, etc.), these persons acquire an altogether singular status: by their reactions to the needs that the child externalizes, they are what "externally" (or rather among the groups of stimuli that will constitute themselves into an "exterior") resembles the most endogenous world that he rules. From this fact, they play a central role in the differentiation between the inside and the outside and in the acceptance of reality: they become in a sort of way the representative of the infantile "self" in the untreatable element that will crystallize into external reality.

The progressive distinction between internal subjectivity and external reality is thus not the result of a simple relation between the child and the world.[38] It is mediatized by the relations he entertains with the mother and more widely with the nourishing family, who play the role of plug, affective and cognitive, between the two worlds. For a long time they will play the role of cognitive protheses, of which the child will serve himself as soon as he can meet the difficulties of distinguishing between "what is" and "what is not." And we will see that their role is particularly crucial in that which concerns the resolution of the question of the status it is advisable to accord to their mimetic representations induced by self-stimulation and lived on the mode of immersion: for the little child, it is the adults who are the depositors of the distinction between "what is" and "what is not." Briefly, they are the guarantors of the cognitive stability of the universe in which he lives; at the same time they protect him from the anguish of epistemic destructiveness that lies in wait for him quite as much as existential lability.

Let us remember that what is important to understand at this stage of the analysis is the genesis of the ludic feint, of self-affection, as a reflexive intentional attitude, as a game played with oneself. The question is thus no longer the one of the relation between the ludic "doing as if" and the activities of "serious" feint but that of the genesis of a stable frontier between the fictional variant of the mimetic immersion on one side and the endogenous functional lures (e.g., hallucinations) and the facts of self-deception for self-manipulation (of which the rites of possession are a part) on the other. We might therefore think that we find here in part the problematic that underlies what I have called "the first genealogy of fiction," that is, the theory according to which fiction would find its origin in possessive states or self-manipulation.[39] In fact, there are no genealogical links between hallucinations, possessive states (possibly induced by self-manipulation), and fictional states: it is more a matter of different types of functioning of activities of mimetic self-stimulation. Yet it is advisable to distinguish carefully between the possessive states voluntarily induced in the frame of ritual sceances and hallucinations undergone involuntarily. These last ones are linked to mental dysfunctionings: they are veritable cognitive pathologies in that they interfere with the perceptive construction of the world of daily reality. Also they end generally at a grave social handicap, safe in the rare cases where they are elevated a posteriori by the social group to the status of visions, such as certain mystical experiences in the frame of the Christian tradition (still, it was necessary to have the chance to hallucinate some saintly character rather than the devil . . .). The states of possession themselves are from the start legitimized socially, they find their origin in a conscious self-manipulation, and they obey the rules of a ritual context. They are in fact always framed in such a manner that they cannot invade the profane time of social and individual life. By these two traits they approach fiction with this notable difference: their relation with the beliefs of everyday life is mediatized by the idea that reality is double and that there exist (socially sanctioned) points of passage between the two levels. Despite this difference, the relationship is strong enough for there to be the possibility of unstable states and of transitions between fictional immersion and ritual possession, such as the situations analyzed by Michel Leiris with the help of the notion of "lived theater."

Conscious self-stimulation is not the only mental activity confronted with the necessity of a frontier between the endogenous mimemes and the informations intervening in the loops of direct interaction with reality. Dreams are in a related situation. There is of course a large difference between dream and fiction: the latter is a conscious elaboration, whereas the first escapes all control by the conscious self.[40] Oneiric representations impose themselves on us in the manner of perceptions and in such a way that the oneiric state is lived as a "real" state, hence the belief, widespread in many societies, that human beings live in two realities, that they live two lives, that of waking life and that of the dream.[41] There is, moreover, a tight relationship between this belief and the one that postulates the existence of two planes of reality in order to conciliate the experiences of the states of possession with the profane experience: with many peoples, the oneiric reality and the one the possessed has access to are in fact one and the same. Whatever it may be, if one disregards the question of the modalities of production of the representations, the parallelism between dreams and fictions is striking. Like fiction, dreams consist of the activation of a system of endogenous stimulation that gives birth to representations in the absence of every (direct) perceptive source. In addition, like the conscious imaginative stimulations, oneiric representations are strongly invested by affects. And mainly, the problem that biological evolution had to "resolve" in the case of the dream is related to the one the baby must confront in what concerns imaginative self-stimulations: how do we avoid that the purely endogenous representations come to contaminate the reactional loops that rule the relations with the environment?[42] In the dream this risk exists because the oneiric representations there are always related to an endogenous activation not only of the sensorial systems (attested by the rapid eye movement, which is the index most easily observed of paradoxical sleep and thus of the dream) but also of the neurological zones that order motor movements.[43]

The oneiric scenes mime real scenes to such a point that they are correlated to the motor influxes that correspond to those of the mimed scenes. The immersion is thus not only representational but, at least potentially, actable. Also, it is vital that there be a countermechanism capable of making sure that the excitement of the motor systems that correspond to the dreamed "actions" do not translate into real motor activities; in fact, in the case of oneiric representations, one of the essential conditions of all successful motor activity, namely, the perceptive return, is lacking. And there exists effectively a very precise biological mechanism that acts as what Michel Jouvet calls a "motor brake": the brain of the dreamer produces inhibiting signs (i.e., chemical transmitters) that block the motor signals induced by the virtual behavioral sequences before they translate themselves in actual behavior. The most visible external sign of this blocking mechanism is the muscular lifelessness characteristic of paradoxical sleep (it does not exist during the phases of "normal" sleep).[44] The works of Jouvet have put into evidence in an experimental manner the crucial role of this "motor brake." It has appeared that if we hinder the action of the countermechanism in question, for example, by injection of a neurotoxin that destroys the neurological zone that orders the postural lifelessness, the animal in a phase of paradoxical sleep (thus involved in a dream) truly executes actantial sequences. It is a matter in general of stereotyped actantial sequences that correspond to basic activities of the animal. With the cat we observe in this fashion sequences of visual (in the absence of all real visual perception, since the perceptual accesses are inactive during sleep) and motorized exploration, predatory movements (e.g., the adoption of a blind posture), and grooming as well as reactions of fear and rage.[45] The flinching of the ears and the stirrings of cats (or the movements of the paws of dogs) that one observes during the phase of paradoxical sleep result from an incomplete motor blockage due perhaps to particularly powerful motor signals.[46] I ignore everything of the possible phylogenetic and neurological links between oneiric self-stimulation and the activities of conscious imaginative self-stimulation.

Thus, we must not be mistaken about the range of comparison: the two activities are linked to modalities of functioning of the brain that are different (sleep on one side, waking and conscious life on the other), and the mechanics of control are themselves very different. On the other hand, the fundamental givens of the problem are the same, in that the genesis of fictional competence implies also the putting in place of a "brake" that hinders the imaginative simulations from contaminating the cognitive representations controlling our direct interactions with reality.[47] The existence of such a "brake" is all the more important considering that imaginative self-stimulation is an irrepressible mental activity, as is testified eloquently by the fact that we devote ourselves extensively, independently of all finalized cognitive function, both during waking life (day dreaming) and during sleep (dream). Briefly, we have to save a space, a territory, where imaginative self-stimulation can train freely without the risk of contaminating the mechanisms of epistemic regulation — including cognitive modeling — that order the "basic" interactions with reality. To say it in other words: the child must learn to channel his activity of imaginative self-stimulation along ways that allow him to invest his desires, affects, and volitions without the risk of sinking into pathological states like self-deception, mythomania, and so on.

How is this space, this territory of fiction, established? All those who have studied the affective and cognitive development of the little child agree to recognize that the birth of fictional competence, of the "do as if," of the "for wrong," coincides with the one of ludic behaviors: fiction is born as the space of game; that is, it is born in that very particular portion of reality where the rules of reality are suspended. Access to fictional competence is thus characterized by the adoption of imaginative self-stimulations, called to deploy themselves from now on in that neutral territory that is the one of the game, territory where they can in a certain way be lived according to the mode of exteriority while continuing to profit from the status of endogenous realities, that is, while not being submitted to the sanctions of this exteriority. From the fact of the fundamentally relational nature of the construction of subjective identity, the delimitation of this territory is not the result of an autarkic maturation of the child but results from his interactions with adults and, more generally, others, because for the baby "the other is someone who regulates the self."[48]

It seems to me that it is Winnicott, through his model of transitional phenomena and objections (e.g., blankets, plush objects), who has proposed the most convincing hypothesis of the genesis of the accord from which the fictional territory is born: "The transitional object and the transitional phenomena bring from the start to every human being something that will always be important for him, namely a neutral area of experience that will not be contested. We are able to say about the transitional object, that there is an accord between us and the baby without which we would never ask the question: 'This thing, did you conceive it or did it come to you from outside?' The important point is that no decision is expected on this point. The question itself has not been formulated."[49] The facts induced by self-stimulation that are concerned with this contract are of course not only the objects in the proper sense of the term but quite as much the verbal activities and the motor activities (Winnicott speaks in a more general manner of transitional phenomena). The quoted passage's manner of describing the accord that establishes itself between the mother (or the adult who fills her function) and the child regarding the destiny of the exteriorizations of self-stimulations of the latter coincides in a significant manner with the contract of ludic feint as it operates in the domain of canonical fictions, a domain that is also instituted as "transitional space."[50] Whence the hypothesis—and I am not, of course, the first to propose it—that it is this accord concerning the first transitional events and objects that constitutes the place of (ontogenetic) birth of the state of fiction conceived as putting into brackets the question of truthfulness and the referentiality of representations proposed to verbal attention or to perceptive apprehension. As Winnicott still notes, this territory is neither the one, purely interior, of phantasms (and thus potentially that of self-deception) nor the one, purely external, of reality: "The transitional object is never, like the internal object, under magic control nor, like the real mother, out of control."[51] It is a matter of a "potential space" that gives birth to a world that can be shared publicly and lived in privately without being interrogated about its status.

It must be remarked that if it is the mother (or any other person who replaces her) who sedates the self-stimulations on the terrain of ludic activities, the material of the interactive dynamic stems from the baby. In fact, what will function as "transitional object" is originally a pure product of the endogenous self-stimulation of the child. But at the beginning the baby "ignores" that it is a matter of an exteriorization of an object of which the origin is interior: for him it is a matter of one of the multiple representational constellations invested by affects and that populate the still largely unstructured universe in which he gropes. This is why the role of the adult is so crucial: it is the manner in which he will react to this imaginative exteriorization that will decide the destiny of the self-stimulating activities and at the same time in large part the destiny of the child. If, for various reasons, he is incapable of reacting in an adequate manner, that is, by a "counter-game" susceptible of fixing—for the benefit of the child—the status of his externalized imaginations, it is in fact the aptitude of the latter to master reality himself that risks being compromised.[52] For it is only through this interaction between the childish game, which is still ignorant of itself as such, and the counter-game of the adult, in which the game of the child can make itself recognized as game, that the "solitary" imaginary activities (e.g., daydreams) will themselves accede to a definite status and take their nomadic dynamic.

Certainly, as the representations that will accede to the fictional status have an internal origin, the capacity to produce such representations—what we could call the imaginative invention—precedes the institution of the shared feint that organizes itself around transitional objects. But for the little child to be able to experiment with its endogenous representations induced by self-stimulation *like* imaginary inventions, it is necessary for someone to institute them for him in this status. And this happens in the interactive field that ends in the establishment of a territory of shared feint. This one precedes the private fictions in the sense that it establishes the conditions of categorical identification. One could say that fiction as private mental activity is the result of a reinteriorization of the projections of the endogenous self-stimulation in that they are from now on at the same time settled and legitimized by the accord of shared feint put into place by the counter-game of the adult. This interactive character of the genesis of fictional competence is one of the multiple indices of the fact that, as Nathalie Heinich notes, "the construction of identity is not a solitary action that would send the subject back to himself; it is an interaction that puts a subject in relation with other subjects, with groups, with institutions, with bodies, with objects, with words."[53]

Given the complexity of the intentional processes involved, it is hardly astonishing that the capacity to master foreign fictional worlds (i.e., works of fiction) develop themselves only after the active competence (i.e., after the capacity to construct and to pay attention to interactive and autogenous fictions). Even though the ontogenetic institution of the field of fiction rests, as we have seen, on a shared feint, the autogenous fictional universes precede the foreign fictional worlds. This priority of the active capacity over the receptive capacity translates itself notably by the fact that, though already at the age of four children are able to distinguish clearly, among the interactive activities that they participate in, between those that concern a real behavior and those that concern a ludic feint, they will continue when faced with a film or a tale to ask: "Is it real or is it unreal?" The reason for this discrepancy is already known to us: the assumption of endogenous mental stimulations as purely imaginative realities is done through an interiorization of behavioral feints that are "original" instituted by the interactive contract that gives birth to a territory of shared feint. It is the progressive interiorization of the mechanisms of this ludic "doing as if" that then gives birth to the capacity to restructure the fictional universes of the works of fiction, universes that are delivered to us so to speak with key in hand.

4. Fictional Immersion

Plato deserves credit for having shown that fictional immersion is at the heart of the fictional device. In order for a fiction to "work," we must see the (painted) landscape, be present at the (filmed) holdup, live (again) the (described) family scene. And the manner in which we describe the failure of a fiction — "It's impossible to get inside this film," "This story does not catch me," "This character does not exist," or "The portrait of this character does not live" — is just as revealing of this central role of immersion. But it is also the Achilles' heel of the cultural (notably, philosophical) honorability of fiction, since it links it indissolubly to the *semblance* and to what appears as a mode of "thoughtless" action. And Plato did not fail to show that this honorability is even more compromised, because the dynamic of immersion operates not only at the reception of works but also at their creation. We must insist on this symmetry, because, on account of a historical peculiarity, we have come to dissociate the two poles: we celebrate the imaginative power of the creator of fiction, but we devalue fictional immersion as a mode of reception. However, the distinction is a lexical illusion: the "imaginative power" is nothing but an alternate designation of the process of creative fictional immersion, thus of the active fictional competence. Yet active competence and receptive competence are two sides of the same reality. Indeed, if the ontogenetic foundation of fictional devices is in the interaction of the game of the child and the counter-game of the adult, then the access to fictional space consists in the development of an intentional competence that is in an indissociable manner the one of the imaginative production (the self-stimulation) and of the reactivation of the mimemes captured in the framework of the interaction of ludic feint. Thus, the "original psychological act called Reading" that Proust describes at the beginning of *Journées de lecture*, identifies a situation of reactive fictional immersion, not a creative one; nonetheless, we find the characteristics that he emphasizes again, for example, in the narrative production of creative immersion that Jean Giono develops in *Noé*. Also, it might be interesting to start out from an elementary description of the outstanding traits of the situation of fictional immersion in general. It seems to me that this phenomenology can be argued around four points:

— Fictional immersion is characterized by an inversion of hierarchical relations between inner-worldly perception (and, more generally, attention) and imaginative activity. Whereas in "normal" situations imaginative activity accompanies inner-worldly attention like a sort of background noise, the relationship is reversed in a situation of fictional immersion. The narrator of *Noé*, perched in his olive tree and accumulating one fiction after another while picking up olives, has completely forgotten the presence of his wife and of his daughter, who gather olives a few steps away. The inner-worldly attention is not abolished certainly; thus, in Proust the little boy does not fail to register the noises of the environment during his reading. But the threshold of alertness that gains access to consciousness is raised higher than in a "normal" situation in the same way as in the phase of paradoxical sleep; thus, during dreams the threshold of awakening is raised higher than during other phases.

Concerning cinema, Metz went so far as to compare the situation of the spectator with that of a subject who is asleep: "In the ordinary situations of projection, everyone could observe ... that the spectators at the exit, brutally rejected from the black belly of the auditorium into the bright and bad light of the hall, sometimes have the dazed (happy or unhappy) face of those who wake up. To leave a cinema is a little like getting up: not always easy (unless the film was really indifferent)."[54] The comparison is exaggerated from the point of view of mental (and neurological) realities that correspond to the two states, but it also has a certain heuristic function, which is the only value Metz wanted to accord it. Every cinema spectator can observe in himself that when he is in a situation of fictional immersion his threshold of attention to real perceptions is higher than in a "normal" situation. For example, the stimuli registered on the level of peripheral vision influence the dynamic of visual exploration much less strongly than is the case in a perceptive situation outside immersion. The same is true at the level of hearing: there is a partial neutralization of sonorous stimuli of which the spatial origin and the timbre do not correspond to the flow of the sound track (it is only when one assists at the projection of a film without being in a situation of immersion — e.g., because one does not get inside the story — that one becomes aware with astonishment that the level of the surrounding noise is often considerable). Also, the reestablishment of normal attentional hierarchies necessitates that one force oneself: called by the cook, the childish reader of Proust is obliged to "call back his voice from afar," to "make it come out," in order "to give the appearance of ordinary life, an intonation of response, which it had lost."[55]

— The divided attention ends with the coexistence of the two worlds, that of the real environment and that of the imagined world (even if it is imagined through perceptive acts, as in cinema, where visual perception itself seems to divide itself in two), each with its own references. At first sight the two worlds seem mutually exclusive. Proust thus distinguishes the real space, the room of the little reader, from the fictional space: to calm the "turmoil" that the reading has "aroused" in him, he starts to walk in the room, "his eyes still fixed at some point which one would vainly look for in the room or outside, for it was only situated at a distance of the soul, one of those distances which cannot be measured in meters or leagues, like the others."[56] But Giono describes a more complex situation, which is rather the one between background and figure or the one of a palimpsest. He thus shows in a very concrete way how the scenery and the characters in *Un roi sans divertissement* coexist in the consciousness of the author with the real space of his office, of his house, and of Manosque, because "the invented world has not effaced the real world: it superimposed itself. It is not transparent."[57] In fact, in *Noé* the two worlds interpenetrate each other to the point where the fictional characters borrow certain traits from characteristics of the real place where they have been pinned down and that sort of contaminated them: "In my West window I have installed . . . Mme Tim. . . . It is because this window is next to the map of Mexico with its Yucatán, Cuba, Florida, Jamaica, Haiti, Puerto Rico, and the Antilles of foliage and its big sky alternately azure and of boiling tar that Urbain Timothée made his fortune in Mexico and that Mme Tim is Creole and that she has three daughters of whom I said hardly anything."[58]

One might think that the difference between the two descriptions is due to the fact that Proust describes a reactivating situation of immersion, whereas with Giono it is a matter of a creative dynamic where immersion is much more broken up, and therefore the presence of the perceptive world is stronger. In reality, Proust himself shows that the two worlds, despite their ontological difference, remain intimately linked. He reminds us in fact that the remembrances we keep of our childish readings relate as much to the (real) circumstances of the readings as to their content.[59] It seems to me that this observation is valid for all the significant experiences of fictional immersion: the interpretation of the actual context and of the world of fictional immersion creates mnemonic links that are extremely stable between the representations induced by the fictional device and the actual stimuli apprehended in the background. It is as though the actual context, not thematized for the moment, was nonetheless registered in the form of an "attached file" that from now on will stay indissolubly linked to the virtual universe in question.

But we have to go further. Even though the degree of fictional immersion is always inversely proportional to the attention accorded to the actual perceptive environment (with the exception of course of the perceptions that are the vector of the immersion), this does not imply a cut between the world of mimetic stimuli and the repertory of mental representations that are issued by our past interactions with actual reality. Quite the contrary: the mimemes would remain radically opaque if they were not permanently coupled with the mnemonic traces of our real experiences. This signifies, notably and trivially, that every reactivation of mimemes can only be founded on the repertory of representations of which the receiver disposes, on his "world." In a more general way, taking up again the terminology of Quine introduced in the preceding chapter, there can be mimetic reactivation only inasmuch as the spreading of the qualities that work as a gate for the mimetic recognition with the receiver are not too different from those in whose frame the creator has created his mimemes. In other words, given mimemes are divisible by immersion only to the extent that the individuals that have access to them live in divided "realities" (i.e., in representations of the real). The division is doubtless never complete, because the "worlds" of any two individuals do not ever coincide entirely (for this to be so, the two individuals would have to be not only genetically identical but in addition have had exactly identical experiences). On the other hand, the absence of all division is not quite as rare, because the spreadings of qualities coincide enough from one human being to another for there to be a possibility of division, for example, at the level of visible mimemes.

— Fictional immersion is a homeostatic activity; that is, it regulates itself with the help of retroactive loops: in the imaginative self-stimulation it nourishes itself on the expectations that it creates; in the interactive ludic feints it entertains itself through a dynamic of turns of roles and of words; finally, in a situation of reception it is revived by the tension that exists between the always incomplete character of the imaginative reactivation and the (supposed) completeness of the fictional universe proposed. Thus the attraction, during our childhood, of fictional games that stretch without end: interrupted in the evening to be taken up again the next morning, certain of these games colonize the whole of the summer vacation in such a manner that when fall returns the children who come back from the most exotic voyage are not always the children one thinks they are — hence also the later taste for endless sagas and Romanesque cycles (like *La comédie humaine* and Trollope's Chronicles of Barsetshire), for the feuilletons (written or televised) that do not end, for film continuations (from *A Nightmare on Elm Street* 1–5, waiting for *Freddy n*), and hence still, as Proust notes, the feeling of vexation when all is ended: "We would have so much wanted that the book continue, and, if this were impossible, to have other information on all these characters."[60] On the side of the creator, the capacity that fictional immersion has to extend itself manifests itself in multiple forms. In the case of the fictional tale, for example, the indexing of the end of the story on the destiny of a character or a group of characters leaves the extra players pending a destiny of their own. In this sense every end is also a potential beginning. If *Un roi sans divertissement* closes with Langlois' suicide, it is because this character is "led . . . to the end of his destiny." But Delphine, who has just been a witness of this suicide, is not at the end of her destiny. Hence the temptation to make the dynamic of fiction start up again: "If you make so much of waiting for Delphine to arrive at the edge of the slaughter with her fine little shoes, if you make so much of trying to describe her, turning up her skirts above the blood and brains of Langlois as at the edge of a puddle, you will see that Delphine is going to live. So you haven't finished."[61] Also, the narrator of *Noé* (in this case Giono himself) decides to separate himself from "here." His "here" is of course not the Manosque of 1947 but "the land where I just lived underneath the snow from 1843 to almost 1920," that is, the universe of *Un roi sans divertissement*, which still haunts him to the point that he addresses its characters in taking up again in his account an exclamation that Shatov addresses to Nikolay Stavrogin in *The Possessed*: "But why am I condemned to believe in you always?"[62]

— The representations lived in a state of fictional immersion are in general saturated from the affective point of view. This affective investment plays at several levels. In the situation of reception there is first the "basso continuo" of the aesthetic appreciation, since the consummation of canonical fictions inserts itself in general in aesthetic conducts.[63] As for the tonality of this appreciation, it varies according to the index of satisfaction inherent in the activity of mimetic reactivation itself. It thus in fact depends directly on the good functioning of the fictional immersion. This level of affective investment is clearly not specific to the situations of fictional immersion: it is a simple effect of their aesthetic function and also finds itself again in the nonmimetic arts. It is thus necessary to distinguish it from the affective participation induced by the fictional mimemes as mimemes, that is, as much as they simulate real constellations. The first thing that comes to mind when one thinks of these phenomena of affective engagement is the affective empathy — positive or negative — with the characters. Plato had already noted that the auditors of poets "associate themselves with the expressed emotions."[64] And Proust speaks of "these beings to whom one had given more of one's attention and of one's tenderness than to the people of one's own life, not daring always to admit to what point one loved them, . . . these people for whom one had panted and sobbed."[65] In the tales of fiction, the theater, or the cinema the importance of this dynamic of affective empathy with the characters is not due to chance: for the process of immersion to be able to function, it is necessary that the characters and their destiny interest us, and to do this they must start resonating with our real affective investments. The fact that the basic affects mobilized by narrative and dramatic fictions are about the same everywhere and in all periods and that we manage with such a disconcerting facility to immerse ourselves in fictional universes that belong to cultural traditions different from our own shows at the same time that the fundamental human affects are universal and that their repertory is rather restricted.

It is nonetheless advisable to distinguish this empathy with the characters from the general question of the affective investment of mimetic representations, of which it constitutes only a specific form. For one thing, there exist fictions without characters: a painted landscape — for example, a *locus amoenus* — is apt to provoke an affective reaction as strong as an act of empathy with a novel character. This is not strange, it being given that in our real life the perceptive world is never a neutral world but is always strongly structured by our emotions. In a more general manner, in the case of visual fictions it is our look itself that is saturated by emotions: very often immersion is engaged there not as much through our empathy with what is represented (even if it is a person) as through our identification with a subject that sees, that looks, that is in the position of a witness (or, sometimes, of a voyeur). It is in this sense, for example, that Metz has linked the posture of the cinema spectator to the scopic drive—thus to the pleasure of seeing—more than to the identification with the hero or heroine. And, in a close view, David Freedberg has been able to show that from the point of view of mimetic immersion, the pious images and the pornographic labels function largely in the same manner (even though in different contexts and with largely different aims).[66] In both cases it is the look that makes the representation alive, providing of course that this representation is of a person or of a factual constellation that in reality would provoke a strong affective reaction.[67] In other words, the power of the mimeme as inductor of immersion nourishes itself in large part from the affective reaction provoked by the mimed reality, resulting in the very important fact that this power does not depend only on the mimetic "fidelity"—or rather on its richness in terms of representational factors—but quite as much on the affective charge linked to what is represented. The two dynamics are no doubt in relation of complementarity: the stronger the affective charge induced by what is represented, the less the mimeme has to be "faithful"; and, in the reverse, the more the mimeme is faithful, the less the affective charge of the represented object has to be large.

If we wanted to develop a true phenomenology of fictional immersion, each of these points would merit a more elaborate analysis. It would be necessary in addition to take into account a certain number of other aspects. But my aim here has been simply to draw attention to the tangible reality of the fact and to its central function in the fictional device. Also, rather than expand further on this aspect of things, I would like to concentrate on a few problems that should allow us to go a little further in the comprehension of its modalities of function. It seems to me that there are three points that merit reflection: the relation between immersion, the effects of lure, and the beliefs. There is a distinction between immersion in the situation of fictional production and immersion in the situation of reception — a distinction that is important in order to understand the difference not only between fictional games and fictional works but also, in the artistic domain, between the projective immersion of the artist and the reactivating immersion of the public. There is also the question of the relation between immersion and "identification," or rather the one of the necessity to distinguish between the two problems, it being given that the immersion can take multiple forms: according to the vectors of immersion (i.e., the types of ludic feint), it invests different postures of immersion. This last problem leads in fact directly to the comparative analysis of the different fictional devices. I will limit myself here to showing the irreducibility of the notion of immersion to that of psychological identification, since we often pretend that the specificity of our attitude faced with a fiction resides in our identification with the "characters."

The necessity to come back once again to the relations between lure and immersion is due to the fact that, even as I noted that the functioning of the fictional device implied the efficacity of a semblance, I nonetheless opposed the lure to fiction (e.g., in the analysis of *Marbot*). On the one hand, if the fictional variant of mimetic immersion consists in that the representative posture in it is caused by stimuli that mime an actualization of such and such of our modes of canonical access to the world when actually they do not constitute such an actualization, it follows that every fictional immersion implies the efficacity of a *semblance*. On the other hand, in making an allusion to the moments of total immersion in the cinema and in taking up again the notion of *perceptive transfer* proposed by Metz, I have distinguished this effect of preattentional lure from the pragmatic frame of the ludic feint and the beliefs linked to that frame. It is thus important to distinguish between the state of fictional immersion and the assumption of a belief. This distinction is in fact a distinction between two levels of treatment of information. Immersion accedes to representations *before* they are translated into beliefs. Their translation into beliefs homologous with those that would be "normally" induced by representations fictionally mimed is blocked at a superior cognitive level, that of conscious attention, informed by the fact that the stimuli take over from a mimetic self-stimulation or from a shared ludic feint. Thus, the situation of fictional immersion characterizes itself by the conjoined existence of preattentional mimetic lures and a concomitant neutralization of these lures by a blockage of their effects at the level of conscious attention.

The existence of this neutralization, which limits the specificity of the fictional immersion with respect to the "illusions" in the common sense of the term, manifests itself mainly through its momentary failures, like the situation where the lure operates with such force that it induces a short reactive loop that short-circuits the instance of conscious control. This is the case in the cinema of the perceptive transfers identified by Metz. In fact, these transfers correspond to short reactive loops, that is, to situations where the interaction between perception and reaction is entirely located at a preattentional level. This explains why the sketched motor reactions are generally reflexes of protection: such reactions would risk being inefficacious if they were obliged to transit first by an instance of conscious control. The subsequent blockage of the reflex is due to the fact that the access to consciousness of the sketched motor sequence reactivates the fact that we know that the stimuli that have induced it are mimemes: the illusion is neutralized and the motor reflex interrupted. Thus, if the existence of such moments of confusion between reality and semblance is remarkable, their relative rarity and their extreme brevity are also worthy of reflection, for this illustrates well the power of the conscious control that is exercised in the name of the pragmatic frame of the ludic feint. Or, to say it differently, the perceptive transfers show on the contrary that the situation of ludic feint blocks the group of reactive loops that are *long* (i.e., those that are under the control of conscious attention) and that are constitutive of our "normal" interactions with the world. It is by the efficacity of this blockage due to the (conscious) belief that we find ourselves in a fictional frame that allows us to let the preattentional lures that induce the representational or perceptive posture indispensable for immersion to operate without risk.

The state of immersion is therefore a divided mental state or, to take up again an expression of Iouri Lotman, a "biplanar behavior."[68] This hypothesis opposes that of Ernst Gombrich, who, on the contrary, thinks that the two states exclude each other: according to him, when we look at an image, we see either the thing represented or the imaged support, but we are never able to see the two conjointly.[69] It must be noted that he illustrates his thesis with the help of a situation that has nothing to do with the question of immersion. The example—borrowed from Jastrow and already used by Wittgenstein—is famous: it is a drawing that can be viewed either as a representation of a rabbit or as a representation of a duck. This situation is unable to strengthen his thesis, because it does not illustrate the problem of the divided ("biplanar") state—fictional immersion versus representational conscience—but that of the dilemma between two representations—or two mimetic identifications—equally possible though incompatible. It thus does not show the impossibility of seeing at the same time what is represented and the medium that represents but the one of identifying the same representation jointly in two different manners, or to serve oneself at the same moment of a unique mimetic beginning for two different acts of immersion. This does not prove that Gombrich's thesis is false. In fact, contrary to appearances, it is not incompatible with the analysis in terms of divided mental states. For Gombrich limits himself to affirming that one cannot see at the same time the represented object and the medium, which seems plausible, it being understood that the two perceptive constructions differ profoundly from each other. But this impossibility is not incompatible with the possibility of *seeing* the represented object while *knowing* that one sees a mimeme. For the two theses to be compatible, it is sufficient to distinguish between the preattentional aspects of the perceptive immersion and the level of beliefs.

If we make this distinction, we are no longer obliged to fall back on the solution proposed by Gombrich, which consists roughly in supposing that we oscillate between two states, the one where we see what is represented and the one where we see, for example, the picture: "Kenneth Clark, ... observing a large canvas of Velázquez, ... looked to see what happened in the instant when, backing up, he saw the layers of color transform themselves into a transfigured vision of the real. But whatever he dared to do, approaching or moving away, he could not, in the same instant, make the two visions coincide, and he felt incapable because of this fact to answer the question which he had asked himself: to know how this work had been realized."[70] Of course, situations of this type are legion, but they do not correspond to the divided state characteristic of fictional immersion. Gombrich describes a dynamic of oscillation between two perceptive attentions, the one accorded to representational content and the one directed to the means of representation. In the case of fictional immersion, on the other hand, the duality is internal at the level of the representational content: this content is apprehended in the frame of a "biplanar" mental state characterized by a schism between preattentional treatment and attentional treatment of the representations. The situation of fictional immersion could in fact be compared to the one in which we find ourselves when we are victims of a perceptive illusion all the while knowing that it is a matter of an illusion.

In fact, a perceptive illusion in the technical sense of the term (i.e., an illusion that results from an error of the preattentional perceptive modules) continues to be operative even when I am perfectly conscious of the fact that it is a matter of an illusion, that is, when I am able to hinder it from transforming itself into a (erroneous) perceptive belief.[71] Even though I am unable to avoid having my perceptive apparatus be the victim of the illusion, from the moment that I know that it is a matter of an illusion, I will not treat the preattentional lure in the same manner in which I would treat the "truthful" perception whose place it takes. In the case of fictional immersion, I know as it were by definition—that is, by the simple fact of the accord of the shared ludic feint—that I have to do with a semblance. This is enough to block the passage of lived mimemes in a state of immersion to the mental module that, in the absence of this pragmatic "motor brake," would treat them as the representations that they limit themselves to imitate. The question of knowing if the fictional immersion implies lures or illusions thus finds a double answer: it presupposes the efficacity of lures of a preattentional nature, but it excludes every state of illusion at the level of consciousness and beliefs. From the moment that a mimeme induces false beliefs, from the moment that our consciousness itself is lured, we are no longer in a state of fictional immersion but in an illusion in the common sense of the term. But at the same time we are no longer in the field of fiction.

If we admit the hypothesis of a distinction between the level of immersion and that of beliefs, we escape from two major difficulties. For one thing, we have no need to redouble the world of our propositional beliefs concerning what is the case and what is not the case in a world of "fictional beliefs"; for my part, at least, I do not see very well how we could define the local status in other than negative terms. For another thing, this hypothesis allows us to render account not only of the perceptive transfer (and, more generally, the representational transfer) but also of the parts of affective transfer. The difficulties that result from the absence of taking into account this distinction can be illustrated by certain aspects of the conception of Kendall Walton.[72] His theory of make-believe ends in fact with a sort of ontological dualism founded on a redoubling of all our serious attitudes faced with a world of fictional attitudes: he speaks in that way of fictional propositions, of the fact of being afraid fictionally, of the fact of sympathizing fictionally, and so on. The first problem with such an analysis is that it does not teach us much about the status of facts thus characterized: what we would want to know is what a fictional truth is or what "to entertain an attitude fictionally" means. Walton answers by saying that it is a matter of "doing-as-if," but insofar as the description in terms of fictional propositions or attitudes was to precisely explain in what consists the situation of "doing-as-if," it does not advance us a great deal.

A second aspect seems to me more important: according to Walton, all the effects induced by a fiction concern the attitude of "doing-as-if." He refuses thus to consider that a spectator of cinema can feel true fears, a thesis that seems to me denied by the existence of perceptive transfers. In the same way, to describe the emotive reactions of a reader or spectator by saying that he sympathizes fictionally, that he is fictionally sad, and so on, thus that he only feels quasi emotions, does not seem to me convincing from the psychological viewpoint.[73] The spectator "good public" (to take up again an expression of Metz) who sheds tears on the occasion of such and such a scene in *Titanic* does not shed fictional tears, nor does he shed them fictionally: he sheds real tears, the same he would perhaps shed when he is at a funeral, and he sheds them really, in the sense that he is really sad. Simply, here again the reaction concerns a preattentional transfer, of an affective nature this time around: he does not cry because he thinks that he really assists at the real separation of the large-hearted hero and his beautiful woman but because the represented affective constellation induces a preattentional affective raptus. The situation is, moreover, not limited to fictional contexts: the affective reactions provoked by representations largely escape our conscious control. This explains without a doubt why the capacity of fictional situations — or of dreams — to color our affective life persists sometimes long after our exit from the state of immersion to such a degree that we can really speak of an effect of contamination (without a pejorative nuance). These effects of contamination are particularly strong with children (and thus with all veritable amateurs of fiction). Many children react with real fears when we tell them (or read to them) fictions that depict ghosts or bandits. And these fears persists after the end of the tale, shown by the fact that they are often reactivated by anguishing situations of "real" life, such as the fear of darkness (the very type of a diffuse anguish, without a precise object, that the lived situation in fictional immersion comes to fill and to concretize).

It goes without saying that I do not mean here that fictional devices are not able to arrange simulations of emotions. This seems to be notably the case when we place ourselves at the level of the creation of mimemes. The example that we generally give is that of the actor. An actor who simulates a reaction of anger is certainly not angry in the way he can be angry after the end of the play if the audience sanctions his acting with whistles: when he is onstage, he limits himself to simulating anger. In fact, if this description is not false, it seems that it is only partial. With the professional actor, as in the lived theater studied by Leiris, the conscious simulation is in general only a willful beginning of which the aim is to induce a state of mimetic (actantial, in the present case) immersion — an immersion in which affective reactions on the preattentional level have a part as well. Certainly, the part of conscious simulation and of preattentional empathy varies according to the mimes, for, as Aristotle notes, "poetry belongs to beings well gifted or born to delirium: the first model easily, the others learn reading from themselves."[74] But even if the proportion between the two attitudes is variable from one individual to another, the two are always implied: the actor must at the same time know how to "modelize himself" and be capable of "stepping out of himself."

In fact, by means of this question we touch on our second problem, that of the difference between the dynamic of the creative fictional immersion and the one that rules the reception of fictions. On the one hand, in the case of the creator of fiction, immersion can only be the result of a self-affection: the creator of a fiction creates himself the beginnings susceptible of putting him in a situation of immersion. The receptor, on the other hand, finds himself faced with beginnings already constituted in which it is enough for him to "slide," to "let himself be taken." Let us take a very simple case. On the one hand, a child who plays with a doll must begin by producing mimemes susceptible of functioning as an initial beginning capable of putting him in a situation of immersion; this initial production can only be an act of conscious simulation. On the other hand, if the initial production functions correctly, the essence of the mimemes that it will produce later will be the result of the dynamic of fictional immersion, that is, will be issued by facts containing preattentional lures. Having begun by miming consciously a tearful mother in front of her child, the child playing with a doll will end by really crying and by living the scene of mourning in a situation of affective transfer, all the while knowing that he is playing with a doll. In the same way the actor, if he begins by simulating consciously an angry person, can in many cases produce convincing mimemes (i.e., mimemes susceptible to inducing a process of fictional immersion with the spectator) only as much as the initial beginnings allow him to enter the skin of the character and thus to draw profit from the specific effects of the immersion and notably from the preattentional empathy.[75]

Without a doubt it happens often in a creative situation that we have to restart the dynamic of immersion by "nourishing" it with a few conscious simulations, hence its relatively discontinuous character compared to the reactivating immersion. The difference is not astonishing: the receiver of a fiction engages himself (in principle) in a preexisting fictional universe whose force of immersion has been optimized, while the creator (whether it be the child who is playing or the artist) invents little by little the universe in which he immerses himself. It is normal that the blockages of the dynamic of immersion are more frequent in the second case than in the first. We can observe some discontinuities of the same type in interactive fictional games: the risk of entropy increases with the number of players, which necessitates the repeated recourse to fantasy negotiations; in what concerns the roles, the conventional function of certain accessories are imperfect from the mimetic point of view (e.g., "we will say that this rock is the police station"), the sequences of actions, and the global fictional context.[76] But this difference changes nothing of the identity of the processes of immersion considered in themselves. Simply, the conditions of immersion are more easily united in a situation of reception than in a situation of creation.

Up until now I have treated immersion as if it were a matter of a unique given. We will see in the next chapter that things are more complex. If this complexity usually goes unnoticed, it is because we have a tendency to reduce the notion of immersion to that of identification. Yet, just as the affective reactions provoked by a fiction are irreducible to empathy with the characters, immersion does not necessarily pass by a process of identification with the characters. Thus, in the cinema the vector of immersion is not the psychological identification with one or some character(s) but the assumption of a perceptive attitude. At the most one could say with Metz that the cinema spectator identifies with himself: "The spectator, on the whole, identifies with himself . . . as a pure act of perception (like waking up, like alert): like a condition of possibility of the perceived."[77] But in fact I doubt that the notion of identification (may it be under the form of self-identification) is suited to describe this type of immersion: it seems to me more correct to say that the spectator adopts the perceptive posture; that is, the cinematographic mimeme induces him to adopt the attitude that would be "normally" his if the mimetic stimuli were in reality what they only imitate. As for the notion of identification, it seems to me that we should reserve it for describing the situations in which the universe of immersion is constituted by a subjective interiority: it is thus that the actress identifies with Antigone, the child identifies with a thief, or the reader of a narrative fiction identifies himself, possibly, with the narrator (i.e., he adopts the posture of the narrator as the vector of immersion). The result is the necessity, to which I already referred, of distinguishing the psychological identification as operator of immersion from the affective empathy induced by the fictional universe.

This last is one of the effects of immersion insofar as it leads us to activate in our relation to the fictional world the repertory of attitudes that is ours in the reality of everyday life. Yet the affective (positive or negative) empathy is a constant element of this repertory of attitudes. It is thus not at all a property that would be particular to immersion. On the other hand, the fact that fictions are capable of activating it is an index of the efficacity of mimemes and thus of immersion. Let us take a concrete example. A cinematographic fiction is a quasi-perceptive semblance that induces an effect of immersion with the spectators, since it causes them to adopt in a certain measure the perceptive posture that is theirs in everyday life. But when I go to see a film, what interests me is the universe to which I have access thanks to this effect of immersion: I want "to see a story." In other words, what is at the center of my interest is that to which I have access thanks to mimetic immersion, that is, the fictional modelization of a group of actions, of events, of feelings, and so on. What is at the base of the confusion between the two aspects of fiction is, first, that they are inseparable. To say it briefly, even if I have to come back to it later: the fictional model can only be (re)activated by a mimetic immersion.[78] I don't want to suggest by this that the only approach that allows us to *learn* things about a work of fiction is mimetic immersion. Second, a fiction only *functions* as fiction insofar as it is interiorized through a process of mimetic immersion. When in school the pupils are supposed to analyze a passage from *The Stranger*, the mental attitude one asks them to adopt is *not* that of mimetic immersion but the analytic posture of someone who wants to identify the manner in which Camus structures his fictional universe. This is without a doubt a thing of great usefulness, although it is necessary that the fictional universe of the work be assimilated first, which means that the tale has first to be read on the mode of fictional immersion and thus on the mode of the pleasure—and the profit—taken in the dimension of "What does it tell?" This condition is, unfortunately, less and less fulfilled, since the fictional culture of today's young people is only marginally literary. It is in this way that one has to teach literary fiction like a dead language, for to accede to a work of fiction one must enter the created work (conceived as a mimetic model), and to enter this universe there exists no other way than fictional immersion.

5. Fictional Modelization: Fiction and Reference

If immersion plays a central role in fiction, the fact remains that its status is that of a means: it allows us to accede to what constitutes the true finality of every fictional device, namely, the "fictional universe" (Thomas Pavel). To say it differently, its role is to activate and to reactivate a process of fictional mimetic modelization; and it does so by bringing us to adopt (to a certain point) the attitude (the mental disposition, representational, perceptive, or actantial) that would be ours if we found ourselves really in the situation of which the mimemes elaborate the semblance. It is thus important to distinguish between immersion and modeling, especially because the contemplators of fiction have always tried to reduce it to the fabrication of a semblance capable of inducing a dynamic of immersion and because its defenders have only tried to save it by trying to show that it was, on the contrary, incompatible with all dynamics concerning semblance or sham. There has been the tendency to reduce the notion of mimesis either to a procedure of imitation-*semblance* or, on the contrary, to a technique of representation, not including any "imitating" component.[79] In fact, what is generally considered as an opposition between two rival and incompatible conceptions of fiction should be interpreted as a simple distinction between two aspects of the fictional device: the means that it puts to work, namely, immersion, and the aim that is served by this means, namely, the access to fictional modeling of any states of facts (perceptive experience, actantial situation, narration of events, inner-worldly situation, etc.). Let us repeat it one last time: fiction certainly proceeds through preattentional lures, but its aim is not to lure us, to elaborate semblances or illusions; the lures it elaborates are simply the vector thanks to which it can attain its true aim, which is to bring us to engage ourselves in an activity of modeling, or, to say it more simply, to lead us to enter into fiction.

The confusion between the means and the aim of fiction does not suffice, however, to explain why we have so much difficulty recognizing its modeling value and thus the fact that it operates cognitively. It is due also to the manner with which we generally approach the problem of the relations between fiction and the other modalities of representation (perception, referential beliefs, abstract knowledge, reflection, etc.) and therefore the question of the manner in which fictional devices can relate to the reality in which we live. We have a tendency to want to reduce the first problem to that of the relation between fictional representation and referential assertion; as for the second, we think that the nerve of the question is in the difference of status between the fictional entities and the entity of physical reality. From this fact the analysis of fiction is brought back more or less to the one of the denotational status of fictional propositions (or the propositions supposed to be implied by fictional representations that, like cinematographic or pictorial fiction, have no propositional structure) and that of the ontological status of fictional entities.[80] This way of seeing has for a long time influenced the philosophical definitions of fiction proposed in the twentieth century. Most of these definitions, even if they take into account the existence of a pragmatic factor, situate themselves in fact in a firmly semantic frame; we have had to wait for the decisive contribution of Searle to begin to accept the idea that the definition itself of fiction could only be pragmatic and not semantic, in other words, that what distinguishes fiction from other representational modalities was essentially the fact that it implied a specific usage of representations. What characterizes fictional representation in a correct manner is not so much its logical status (which in fact can be of the most diverse sort) as the usage that one can make of it.

The point of departure common to all semantic definitions can be reconstructed in the following way: linguistic statements fill diverse functions; one of their functions is to refer to the world; this act of reference is realized through descriptive and declarative sentences; then, whereas from the linguistic point of view fictional discourse is also a descriptive discourse, it deviates nonetheless from referential discourse in that its sentences do not send us back to "real" references; it is thus necessary to define fictional discourse by the specificity of the denotational value of the referential terms. The "classical" answer to the problem put in those terms has consisted in defining fiction as zero denotation: the linguistic constituents that in factual discourse have a denotative value (definite descriptions, proper names, demonstrative deictics, etc.) are here denotationally empty. This was already the position of Gottlob Frege, for whom fictional statements have a meaning (*Sinn*) but not a denotation (*Bedeutung*): "When we listen, for example, to an epic poem, what fascinates us, outside the verbal euphony, is uniquely the meaning of the sentences as well as the images and the sentiments that are evoked by them. If we asked the question of truth, we would leave aside the aesthetic pleasure and would turn toward scientific observation."[81]

At first sight we might think that the distinction between thought and denotation succeeds in saving a space for fiction. But the impression is deceptive. According to Frege, the notion of "truth" means, in effect, "denotational truth" and, more precisely, "scientific truth," that is, a truth proved by strict procedures of experimental or conceptual validation. From the moment truth is identified with denotation, there will be no cognitive space that will be fiction's own, since in the absence of a denotational dimension the meaning seems to lose what alone would be susceptible of "holding" it. This point has been underlined by Jacques Bouveresse, who notes that we cannot see how there could still be a specific modality of donation of reference when there is no longer a reference.[82] Also, the semantic definitions of fiction ulterior to Frege could be seen as so many attempts to get out of this deadlock. The proposed solutions have been numerous, but they can be divided roughly into three groups.

The most radical solution, which was favored by all those who accepted the verificationist rigorism à la Rudolf Carnap, has consisted in keeping the Fregean idea of a strict identity between truth and denotation but in being free from the problem of the distinction between meaning and reference by reducing the field of the propositions endowed with meaning to those that satisfy the denotational criterion. At the same time, fictional propositions can be only pseudopropositions, hence it fatally follows that fiction could not be a cognitive operator. The most famous example of a definition of this type has been the emotivist theory of Ogden and Richards, who maintained that literary statements, from the fact of their fictional character, are pseudopropositions expressing subjective attitudes and having a purely emotive function.[83] This thesis has the advantage of clarity. It pays for this advantage by its so manifestly faulty character that it has never convinced many people: whatever the status of fictional statements, their grammar is certainly not that of statements expressing emotions and more widely subjective attitudes. Also, even if the zero denotation is a necessary requisite of fictional statements, it could not be a sufficient condition, for if such were the case, every false utterance and every lie would be fictional statements.[84] A definition that is incapable of distinguishing fiction from error and from lie is of no utility. Finally, to suppose that the denotational zero is a necessary condition of fictional statements does not advance us a great deal, for the fictional tales in which all utterances are utterances with zero denotation are extremely rare. Thus, the historical novel draws a large part of its attraction from the way it inserts utterances of denotational force in utterances with zero denotation that constitute the global frame of the tale. This indicates that the question of the status of fiction should be asked at another level than that of the ultimate elements (propositions or others) that constitute it — a point we will find again further on.

The problems encountered by noncognitive definitions of fiction have led philosophers to look for a different solution that is susceptible of saving the thesis of the denotational zero even as it arranges a place for fiction at the interior of a referentialist semantic. The solution has consisted of widening the notion of reference in such a fashion that the literal denotational relation would be only a subrelation of it. In nontechnical forms this conception has been defended by numerous critics, but it is without contest Nelson Goodman who has elaborated the formulation that is the most ambitious and the most precise from a logical point of view. As this theory has been exposed several times in recent years, I will limit myself here to summing it up in a succinct fashion without entering into the technical details. Goodman, while maintaining the idea that fictional discourse is a discourse with zero literal denotation, widens the notion of reference by including in it for one thing the metaphoric denotation, for another modes of nondenotational reference. Thus, an assertion that is of zero denotation when it is read literally can become real (i.e., can possess a referential force) when it is read metaphorically: as Don Quixote does not exist, every assertion on his subject is literally false, but, taken metaphorically, the proper name in question applies with accuracy to a large number of men; the same thing can be said of quixotic actions. In addition, in fictional texts the absence of literal denotation incites the reader to activate those other types of referential relation that are exemplification and expression. One will thus say that *Remembrance of Things Past* exemplifies a narrative structure in a loop: the end of the tale engages the beginning of the narration, since the book closes with the decision of the hero, Marcel, to write the book the reader has just read. What is more, this structure expresses (i.e., exemplifies metaphorically) a certain type of relation between art and time: the fact that the end of the book rejoins its beginning is a metaphor of the Proustian belief according to which the work of art abolishes time. In other words, according to Goodman, the intrinsic literary characteristics as well as the expressive values belong to the referential structure of the symbolic systems in the same way as denotation: that a work has no denotation, thus that it is fictional, does not hinder it from having a referential dimension.

The big advantage of this Goodmanian definition is that it allows us to maintain the thesis of the absence of the literal denotational force of fictional utterances while granting them a referential force without being obliged to resort to some mystical theory of artistic meaning. Its disadvantage resides in the fact that in evacuating the question of the literal denotation it evacuates at the same time the "as if" of fiction: it bypasses the problem more than resolving it.[85] Certainly, every amateur of fiction brings a great deal of attention to the metaphorical denotation, to the literal exemplification (thus to the formal properties of works), and to the expression (i.e., the figural interpretation), since the aspect reality under which the universe of fiction presents itself is indissociable from this universe. For all that, these characteristics would not be for us a satisfactory definition of fiction. For one thing, according to Goodman's theory itself, the attention given to this type of referentiality is not specific to our relation to fiction: it concerns more widely the symptoms of aesthetic relation, thus an attitude that we can adopt with regard to any kind of object. More fundamentally, every interesting definition must first notice the fact that fictions are (re)presentations of worlds, and therefore their aspect is that of a representation in the most canonical sense of the term. This does not signify that the question of the aesthetic attitude has no importance to understand how fiction acts but only that in its case the object on which the aesthetic attention carries is the fictional universe created.[86] In what concerns the question of the status of that universe Goodman limits himself to taking up again the thesis of the zero denotation; that is, all things considered, he only gives us a negative definition of fiction.

The defenders of the thesis of the (literal) denotational zero all start from the hypothesis — entirely wise, it seems to me — that there exists only one reality, which is the (physical) world in which we live. They think in addition, just as wisely, that we would make reference only to things that existed, hence the conclusion that a sentence can be denotational only if it chooses entities that are a part of this physical world. The third type of semantic definition of fiction that will detain me here and that is also the most recent accepts the second hypothesis but questions the first, that is, the ontological bias. Its defenders, while they see in fiction a cognitive operator, don't think that we have to on account of this widen the notion of reference (to integrate in it semiotic relations other than literal denotation): they propose, on the contrary, to widen the domain of "things" to which we can make reference. This implies of course a displacement of the question of the functional status of the propositions toward that of the ontological status of the entities. The proposition to widen the referential field is founded generally on a particular philosophical interpretation of modal logic, an interpretation that became famous under the denomination "logic of possible worlds."

Conceived as pure technique of calculation on propositions, the modal logic of course does not interest itself in the question of fiction: its project is the one, quite different, of a formulation of propositions (and of deductive propositional chains), including modal operators ("it is possible that," "it is necessary that," "it is impossible that") and counterfactual ones (if x were the case, then y). But it is easy to understand that under the philosophical form of the theory of possible worlds it has interested the critics and philosophers in search of a semantic definition of fiction. It seems in fact much more welcoming to fiction than are the physicalist semantics. For instance, in its frame a counterfactual proposition, rather than being declared empty denotatively, will be supposed to refer to a possible world, that is, an alternative of the actual world in a structure of more general ontological interpretation of which that one is only one of the members (though a privileged member, at least in Kripke's theory). We see the advantage that a semantic definition of fiction can hope for from such a very generous ontology: if reality is not limited to the actual world but includes also possible worlds, then fictional worlds themselves accede to a proper subsistence — at least if we succeed in showing that the status of fictional universes is the same as that of possible worlds. Moreover, the twentieth-century theoreticians of fiction have not been the first to try to draw profit from this possibility. The theory of possible worlds has in fact its origin in Leibniz (more precisely, in his thesis of "the infinity of possible Universes in the Idea of God"), and certain critics of the eighteenth century had already adapted it to the problem of fiction.[87] This was the case with two critics important in Germany, Johann Jakob Breitinger and Johann Jakob Bodmer. The last one, elaborating his poetics in the frame of the philosophy of Christian von Wolff, affirmed, for example, that poetic creation "prefers always to borrow the substance of its imitation from the possible world rather than from the present world."[88]

The numerous contemporary critics and philosophers who define fiction in the frame of the theory of possible worlds — for example, Dijk, Lewis, Winner, Martinez-Bonati, Parsons, Wolterstorff, and Dolezel — on the whole only take up this idea again.[89] In fact, even if their formulations are more technical than those of Bodmer or Breitinger, at bottom they agree with the thesis defended by them, namely, with the idea according to which fictional statements refer to alternative realities. The strong points of this type of definition are obvious. For one thing, this definition allows us to escape a purely negative conception of fiction. For another thing, the notion of "fictional world" has the advantage of drawing attention to the undeniable fact that the fictional device does not limit itself to an addition of fictional statements (the fictionality of the whole being quite simply the sum of these individual fictional statement) but gives birth to a universe that is "like" the actual universe and in which we are immersed "like" we are in this actual universe.

But the fictional device pays an expensive price for these advantages. First, it is obliged to found itself on an ontology of which one sees badly how it could be legitimized in other than theological terms (as it was effectively in Leibniz). But this is a problem that, fortunately, need not hold us back here. The true difficulty (from the point of view of a comprehension of fiction) is due to the fact that the identification between possible world and fictional universe poses a problem — as the defenders of the thesis have shown themselves. David Lewis, Robert Howell, and others have thus observed that fictional worlds do not obey the rules that rule possible worlds.[90] For one thing, these last are identified in the frame of a constraining interpretation, whereas fictions are created freely, or at least without any procedure of formally strict constraint. For example, the logic of possible worlds excludes contradictory entities (like a squared circle), whereas such constraints do not exist in the case of fiction. For another thing, here again in contrast to possible worlds, fictional worlds are incomplete (hence the fact that one would, e.g., not know how to answer the question of how many children Lady Macbeth had), and certain of them at least, such as the fictional worlds with multiple internal focalizations (e.g., *Rashômon* by Akira Kurosawa), are semantically not homogeneous.[91] Briefly, the notion of a fictional world could not be reduced to the logical notion of a possible world. This does not signify that it is inoperative but simply that its interest does not lie in the function that it pretended to fill, namely, to give us a semantic definition of fiction that would be compatible with the constraints of semantic logics.

Whatever the advantages and disadvantages of different semantic definitions, they share three inconveniences that make them of no great help in understanding how fiction functions. The first inconvenience has been perfectly summed up by Arthur Danto: "Why, whichever of these theories is true, we, as readers, should have the slightest interest in Don Quixote if what it is about is an unactualized thin man in a region of being I would have no reason to know about save for the interventions of semantical theory; or if it were about the x that quixotizes (there being none) or a set of possible worlds other than my own, or primarily about nothing but secondarily about such things as a set of engravings by Gustav Doré?"[92] In other words, semantic theories are incapable of explaining why we are interested in fictions; they also have a tendency to reduce the status of fictional representations to that of verbal fiction. This is because they are not ever truly liberated from the frame in which they are born, that of an interrogation on what distinguishes the propositions concerned with nonexisting entities from those having reference. Goodman's theory seems to be an exception, since it presents itself explicitly as a general theory of symbolic systems and since it distinguishes notably between verbal description and depiction. But his fundamental hypothesis, according to which our relation to reality would pass exclusively through a group of symbolic systems culturally constituted, seems to me to rest on an abusive extrapolation starting from the linguistic model reduced to its logical framework. In such a conception — purely conventional — of the processes of representation there would be no place for facts of a mimetic order.[93] The more we distance ourselves from the verbal domain, the less easy the Goodmanian theory is to apply. Thus, the cinema is practically absent from his analyses.[94] That Goodman has accorded so little attention to it seems to me linked to the fact that his method of analysis has hardly any tools for understanding its functioning, because the specificity of the cinema (inasmuch as it is a fictional device) can only pass through the steps in the analysis that refuse from the beginning to take seriously the problem of representation by resemblance. If it is only because of the existence of perceptive transfers, the cinema does not allow an escape from the question of immersion, thus that of the mimemes as well as the ones of imitation and of analogical resemblance — many factors of which Goodman strove to deny the pertinence.

The second inconvenience of the semantic definitions of fiction is that in the most favorable hypothesis they succeed in expressing a condition necessary to fiction but prove themselves to be incapable of bringing out a sufficient condition. In fact, so as not to find themselves with a theory incapable of making a difference between fiction, lie, and error, they are all obliged to introduce surreptitiously a pragmatic condition. Frege already noted that in fiction we do not look for the same thing as we do in science, a way of saying that what fundamentally distinguishes the two domains does not concern semantics but our intentional attitude. Goodman also declares that, in the case of fiction, the fact that the inscriptions are empty results from "an *explicit stipulation* that the character has no concordance."[95] Nicholas Wolterstorff, even as he develops his theory of fiction in the frame of a semantic of possible worlds, ends up by noting: "The essence of fiction consists not in the nature of the states, neither of affairs indicated, nor in the truth or falsity of those states of affairs. It likes in the mood-stance taken up. . . . It is not necessary to a work of fiction that the states of affairs indicated be false, or that the author believe them to be false. He may in fact believe them all to be true, and they may all *be* true. What makes him a fictioneer none the less is that he nothing affirmeth but something presenteth."[96] All that comes back to conceding that fiction will not be defined on the semantic level. However, none of the authors in question has drawn this conclusion.

Among the philosophers, John Searle is, at least to my knowledge, the one who should be credited with having operated in a most resolute manner the change of perspective that imposed itself, that is, to have replaced the semantic problematic with a pragmatic definition. If "The Logical Status of Fictional Discourse" has made so much ink flow since its appearance in 1974, it is precisely because Searle maintains in it without the least ambiguity that "no textual property, syntactical or semantic, will identify a text as a work of fiction and alone counts the illocutionary stance that an author takes toward it."[97] To be sure, his analysis limits itself to literary fictions, but his central notion of "shared feint" applies to fiction as such, and it is for him who takes it up to determine which are the types of feint that operate in the fictional devices that are not verbal.[98] We must nonetheless remark that even Searle dismisses from the beginning the questions of the "suspension of incredulity" and of "mimesis."[99] Yet the "horizontal conventions" of which he speaks in a somewhat mysterious manner are precisely linked to the suspension of incredulity, or at least to the problem to which this hypothesis wants to be an answer. (Even if this answer is insufficient, it has at least the advantage of having correctly identified the problem.) Moreover, from the moment we define fiction in terms of feint, we place ourselves at the same time on the terrain of the mimetic problematic. But whichever way we decide these detailed points, the decisive advantage of pragmatic definitions, and that of Searle in particular, resides in the fact that they show the question of the denotation of fictional statements and of the ontological status of fictional entities to be, if not pointless, at least secondary. For, to take up again a formulation of Genette, what characterizes fiction is that it is "beyond true or false"; that is, it brackets the question itself of the referential value and of the ontological status of the representations that it induces.[100] This does not signify that the problem of the denotation of fictional statements and that of the ontological status of fictional entities are pointless interrogations. But it is a matter of properly philosophical interrogations, in the sense where, rather than to refer to important questions for the comprehension of fictional devices, they testify to the fact that philosophy has a problem with fiction.

It is perhaps not unnecessary to add that I in no sense want to suggest with this that the existence of fiction is an argument in favor of the inadequation of functional epistemology and of physical ontology. It could very well happen, alas (or had we better say, fortunately?), that there exists only one reality, namely, the physical reality in which we are born and in which we die.[101] The same way, despite the present triumph of conventionalism, I have the weakness to continue to think that truth is not a question of consensus, and to be true a statement must satisfy the conditions of this reality of which we are a part. Simply, the functions of the mental and symbolic representations are not all of a functional nature, and the question of the status of fictional devices concerns epistemology and ontology only in a marginal manner. This is not astonishing if it is true that, to take up once again the formulation of Winnicott, fiction characterizes itself by the fact that "there is here an accord ... on account of which we would never ask the question:

'This thing—did you conceive it, or did one present it to you from outside?' The important thing is that no decision is awaited on this point. The question itself has not been formulated."

It would be wrong to conclude in addition from the discussion devoted to semantic definitions that the question of the links that fiction entertains with nonfictional reality is without interest. But as soon as we admit that the distinction between fiction and nonfiction is pragmatic in order, it is no longer pertinent to put the problem of the relations between fictional representation and the referential function of signs (linguistic or other), or that of the difference of status between fictional entities and the entities that really exist, at the center of the investigation: the fact that fiction is instituted thanks to a shared feint removes a large part of their importance, since anyway the one who enters into a fictional device will not engage himself in a referential questioning in the logical sense of the term. Then, before asking ourselves the question of the relations of fiction with reality, we have to first ask ourselves what kind of reality fiction itself *is*. In fact, as a result of concentrating on its relation with reality we risk forgetting that fiction is also a reality and thus an integrating part of reality. In other words, the essential question is not that of the relations that fiction maintains *with* reality; it is more a matter of seeing how it operates *in* reality, that is, in our lives.

The general answer to this last question is already known to us: the mode of operation of fiction (in all its forms) is that of mimetic modeling. In this regard it has at least three different modes of being: all fictions exist in the form of mental contents; certain ones among them exist as well in the form of physically incarnated human actions or of publicly accessible representations (words, written texts, fixed images, cinematographic flow, resonant documents, etc.). The mental mode of being of fiction, besides the fact that it constitutes a form of specific realization of the fictional device (in the form of daydreams and, more widely, of imaginative activity), is at the basis of the two others. This follows directly from the fact that fiction is a pragmatic reality and, more precisely, that it necessitates the institution of a specific mental attitude (that of imaginative self-stimulation or, in the case of public fictions, that of divided feint). A human activity or a publicly accessible representation is a mode of being of fiction only as much as it is coupled to the adequate mental attitude. To say it in different terms: fiction rests on a specific intentional attitude; or, as Searle seems to me to have shown in a convincing manner, only mental states can have the intrinsic propriety to be intention facts (this is the reason why fiction qualifies the intentionality of public representations of "derived intentionality").[102] Of course, if every fiction exists (at least) as mental content, the contrary is not true: only mental contents (and, more widely, mental states) are fictional, delimited by the pragmatic frame of an imaginative self-stimulation or of a shared feint, and they are lived (or experimented) on the mode of fictional immersion.

From the moment we no longer accept the semantic definitions of fiction, the central question is clearly of knowing in what consists the specificity of fictional modeling. In order to give the means of answering it, I will first synthesize briefly the general elements that we have been able to gather to this point. I will take as my starting point the most general distinction that we have met, the one between nomological and mimetic models.[103] The first do not interest us really, if not insofar as they permit to bring to light by contrast the specificity of mimetic modeling. It seems to me that the difference between the two types of modeling is situated at the level of their cognitive constraints. The nomological models should satisfy a condition of generalizing homology; that is, the model should be applicable as such to an indefinite number of concrete cases. That is the reason why they take more or less the form of a law or an abstract rule. The mimetic models, on the contrary, are reinstantiations (either actual or, most often, virtual) of what they represent. This signifies that they have no generalizing dimension. Considered under the angle of the processes of learning, they are in fact a subgroup of what we sometimes call "instance learning."[104] Or, to take up again a Goodmanian category that, it seems to me, can be applied here *cum grano salis*, a mimetic model is an exemplification of what it represents.

The situation complicates itself, however, since the field of mimetic models subdivides itself into two subtypes that differ strongly from each other. We had met this distinction when we discussed the facts of mental mimetic self-stimulation. I had insisted there on the necessity for the child to arrive at tracing a frontier between self-stimulations that submit to the constraint of homology and imaginative self-stimulations that do not submit to this constraint. The distinction can be generalized for all the manifestations of the mimetic modeling; that is, we must distinguish between the mimetic-homologous models on one side and the fictional models on the other. The mimetic-homologous modeling has zones of intersection at the same time with the nomological models and with the fictional models. With the first it shares its cognitive constraints: the relation between the model and what is modelized must be of a homological nature — it must maintain the local structural equivalences. However, as we have seen, the mimetic homology distinguishes itself from the nomological models by the fact that it has not the form of a general rule or of a law distilled by abstraction but consists of an exemplification (real or virtual) of what it represents. One can express the same thing in saying (as certain authors do) that in the mimetic model the rule — or, better, the structure — remains inserted in the example and will not be separated from it. The point of intersection of the mimetic-homologous modeling with the fictional modeling consists of the trivial fact that both of them are founded on a relation of similitude between the model and what is modelized and that they operate by immersion. This mode of operation is a direct consequence of the fact that the structure is not detachable from the modelizing exemplification: the function of model of a mimetic representation is accessible only through a reactivation of the exemplification itself. As for the essential point on which the mimetic-homologous modeling distinguishes itself from fictional modeling, we have also already met it: the fictional models are not submitted to the constraint of global and local homology but to a very much weaker constraint, that of global analogy. This idea, according to which fiction would be linked by links of (global) analogy to reality, is a traditional idea, but it seems to me inherently correct. Still, it is necessary to try to see what it covers exactly.

But before applying myself to this task and to fix the ideas, it is perhaps not useless to close this (very brief) exercise in the typology of relations of modeling with a little table that sums up the essential distinctions we have met up to this point (see table 1). To point to the cognitive constraints of fictional modeling with the term *global analogy* entails a small risk of ambiguity. This is due to the fact that the mimetic modeling as such exploits a relation of analogy as vector that permits us to link the mimeme with what it aims for as representation. In the present context, however, the pertinent pair is not that of the analogical and the "conventional" (in the sense in which the relation that links a word with what it represents is a purely conventional relation) but that of analogy and homology. In biology one thus distinguishes this way between evolutive homology and evolutive analogy: resemblances (e.g., morphological) between two species are qualified as homologous when they are due to the same causes (according to the principle same causes : same result); however, when a (morphological) resemblance is the result of different causes having acted on the two species, one speaks of simple evolutive analogy. The distinction between mimetic-homologous modeling and fictional modeling is linked to a difference of the same type. In a mimetic-homologous model the representation has the properties it has because the state of fact that it modelizes has the properties it has: the properties of the model correspond to the properties of what it represents, and this at the local as well as the global level. The condition of local correspondence "all over" must be fulfilled because — as we have seen with the study of learning by observation — it alone can guarantee the structural homology. In the case of a projective mimetic model (e.g., in the case of an invention, technical or other, where the model precedes the modelized object) the causal relation is of course reversed: a representation (mentally or publicly accessible) is a projective model of a given state of fact inasmuch as this state of fact has the properties it has because the model has the properties it has.[105] But in both cases there is a causal relation: the conditions of homology demand that one of the two poles possesses the properties (local and global) n' because the other possesses the properties (local and global) n.

It is not the same thing in fictional modeling. Its conditions of satisfaction don't demand that the relation between the local properties of a fictional model and what it modelizes be that of a causal dependency. To say it more simply, in order for a mimetic model to have a value of fictional modeling, it is not necessary that it owe the local properties that it has to the fact that somewhere in the world there are states of facts that have the properties they have. Of course, it is possible that there are effectively such states of facts, but when such a relation of correspondence exists, it is not pertinent as epistemic relation. The emperor Hadrian has surely had a part of the properties that the fiction of Marguerite Yourcenar attributes to him, but among the conditions of satisfaction that the *Memoirs of Hadrian* must fulfill to be a fictional modeling, the one

Table 1

TYPES OF MODELS	NOMOLOGICAL	MIMETIC	
		Mimetic homologous	Fictional
Cognitive constraints	Generalizing homology	Homology by real reinstantiation or mental simulation	Global analogy
Mode of acquisition	Rational calculation	Mimetic immersion	Fictional immersion
Examples	Mathematical and numerical models	Apprenticeship by observation	Games of feint, daydreams, artistic fiction

does not figure that demands that the possession by the emperor Hadrian of some properties be the cause of the traits attributed to the *character* of Hadrian, even if the imitation of such a causal relation is an element of the vector of mimetic immersion of the ludic feint proposed by Yourcenar.[106] It is different in the case of a factual biography: here the condition of essential satisfaction is that if the model attributes such and such properties to Hadrian, this attribution must be caused by the fact that the emperor possessed the qualities in question. The same differences can be observed on the level of the projective modeling. The fact that *2001: A Space Odyssey* is a fiction does not forbid that in the future one could construct a space station corresponding point for point to that of the film or develop an organizer who has the properties of Hal, but that one does this or not does not take away any pertinence from the film as a fictional modeling. On the other hand, a virtual mimetic simulation of a space station is a homologous project model only insofar as the station effectively constructed will have the properties that it will have because the model has the properties that it has.

To say that the condition that must fulfill a fictional modeling is that of the global analogy comes back in fact to saying it must be such that we are able to accede to it by helping ourselves to mental (representational) competences that are those we dispose of in order to represent reality and, more precisely, those that we would put to work if the fictional universe were the universe in which we live. It must be noted that this constraint is *not* a convention that would result from a pragmatic accord: it is a matter of a direct consequence of the fact that we do not dispose of a representational competence that would be specifically reserved for fictions.[107] In order to accede to a fictional modeling, the only competences of which we can help ourselves are those of which we help ourselves otherwise. A fictional universe on which these competences would have no grip would not be a fictional universe because it would be no representation. At the same time (and in this sense one has to qualify what I have said about the nonpertinence of the referential question), a fictional model is de facto always a modeling of the real universe. In effect, the representational competences that are ours are those of the representation of the reality of which we are a part, since they have been selected by this reality itself in a process of permanent interaction. We can certainly form models asserting nonexistent entities, we can even invent the most fantastic universes, but in all cases these entities and these universes will be variants conforming to what signifies for us "to be a reality," because our representational competences are always already relative to the reality that has selected them and in which we live. Said differently, we cannot separate the specificity of our fictional competences from the specificity of the type of "reality" that we are able to represent, whether it is according to the homologous *or* the analogical modalities.

To say that fictional modeling distinguishes itself from homologous modeling in that it would represent an "unreal," "nonexistent," and so on university thus cannot mean that it has representational contents statutorily different from those that we thematize in homologous representations. Like homologous modeling, fiction *is* a thematization of reality according to this or that of its modalities of manifestation. If we are absolutely attached to the notion of "unreality," we can thus at the most apply it to the activity of modeling itself in that it situates itself in the frame of shared feint, which institutes a logic of the "as if."[108] In this sense the notion of "fictional universe," if it is a convenient shortcut, should not be taken literally: if we wanted to go to the bottom of things, we should not say that fictional modeling distinguishes itself from homologous models because it presents a *fictional universe* but rather because it is a *fictive model* of the "factual" universe; that is, it distinguishes itself from it by the type of relation (analogous vs. homologous) much more than by the point of anchorage. The fact that fiction is "beyond the true and the false" and that it puts into parentheses the referential question such as it poses itself in the frame of homologous models does not hinder the fictional models from yielding to reality (and are therefore referential in this sense, which is that of global analogy), since for human beings there is no representational model except as it relates to that which our representational acts are capable of relating to, that is, to what stands up to reality in the most general (and the most generic) sense of the term.

The fact that the cognitive constraints of fictional models are uniquely the ones of our representational competence as such explains why we can say that in the fictional universe the principle of internal coherence replaces the principle of functional relation. In fact, what we call internal coherence is nothing less than the conformity of local relations between fictional elements with inherent constraints of representation (these constraints being, according to the case, those of visual perception, of the logic of actions, of narration, etc.). But we also see by this that the principle of internal coherence is not veritably *opposed* to the principle of reference. If we wanted to formulate the situation in a paradoxical manner, we could say that the principle of coherence is what, in the fictional field, subsists of the principle of reference, because it corresponds to the constituent constraint of representability as such, constraint that rules the constitution itself of a relation of "aboutness" that is intelligible for human beings and thus that rules the formal conditions of referentiality as such. The difference between the two modalities is thus not that of a reciprocal exclusion but rather that which distinguishes the generic constraints of representability as such from the stricter constraints that rule the usage of our representational competences in the frame of a relation of homology.

This having been said, the simple constraint of coherence is effectively a very liberal constraint, as the shimmering diversity of the fictional universes created by human beings shows well. This signifies that we must distinguish between the representational coherence as a condition of possibility of fictional modeling and the coherence such as it is often put forward as a principle of critical evaluation in the domain of mimetic arts, for example, the Aristotelian idea according to which a fictional tale should represent unified action, or again the modern variant according to which it should obey a structure going from an initial to a final equilibrium, passing through a situation of disequilibrium not corresponding to constraints of representational intelligibility but to a particular ideal (even if it is shared by the larger number) of what should be a *successful* fiction. Thus, the fact that a tale is finished without ending with a reestablishment of equilibrium, or that it does not obey the hermeneutical schema of the "discordant concordance," which, according to Paul Ricoeur, would be the normative basis of every Occidental tale, does not in any way restore its aptitude to function as a fictional modeling. Rainer Rochlitz has most pertinently objected to the valorization of the "reestablished consonance" that it makes an impasse to an important part of modern literary fiction, which "is not necessarily structured according to the model of the plot."[109] If the constraints of fictional modeling, however, are those of representative intelligibility, then its conditions of existence are fulfilled from the moment that this intelligibility is guaranteed. As these conditions of intelligibility are not a specific property of fiction but are presupposed by it inasmuch as it is a mode of elaboration of representations, the minimal conditions that a fictional device must fulfill are, quite simply, those that structure the manner in which we represent reality to ourselves. A fiction is coherent from the moment it is in accord with these conditions.

In the domain of narrative this point has been emphasized by Claude Bremond. He insists, notably, on the necessity of distinguishing between the logic of actantially possible conditions and the effective structurations of narratives. The actantially possible conditions correspond to the constraints of representability of an action, but at the interior of these constraints the tellers have a liberty of movement that is limited only by the preferences (more or less stable or changing) of the public for such and such type of plot (each plot corresponding to a particular combination of the actantially possible conditions). In addition, he reminds us that the possible actantial conditions are those of effective action (insofar as they are intentional structures) before being those of fictional tales that propose to represent actions. He notes thus that the logic of a tale does not consist in structuring a sort of event or action "in itself," which would be a kind of crude fact: "What is told is not in its intimate texture, a complex of events and of roles organized according to laws foreign to those of narration, but a different tale that has already been put in the form of roles, 'enrolled,' the tissue of the narratable." To say it differently, the conditions of representability "of human acting and suffering" that rule the thematization of every (human) event "inasmuch as it is posed by the consciousness that thinks" are at the same time the conditions of possibility of the fictional narrative modelization.[110] The logic of acting and suffering is in fact always already a logic of the tale, and the conditions of emergence of a narrative fictional universe (there exist also nonnarrative universes) are united as soon as the mimemes are structured in conformity with this logic. To say it still more simply, to be able to invent or to comprehend a fictional narration, it is sufficient that we are able to undertake intentional actions, to understand the events that affect us according to the modality of suffering—and to distinguish this double field from the domain of quite as innumerable facts of which the intelligibility does not concern this (double) modality. Yet even if, according to cultures, the ages of life, individual beliefs, and contexts, the field of facts that is structured according to the logic of acting and suffering is variable, every human being is endowed with the competence necessary to apply this logic.[111] At the same time, every human being is able to invent, to understand, to repeat, or to transform narrative *fictions*, the only supplementary condition that he must fulfill being that he is also capable of adopting an attitude of shared ludic feint.

The analysis that precedes seems to me to confirm the idea according to which the difference between mimetic-homologous and fictional modeling depends neither on the utilized representation materials nor on the functional status of the basic bricks that form the elements of construction of the model. When a novelist creates a fictional universe, he does not use exclusively, perhaps not even in the majority of cases, representational materials invented ad hoc; he reutilizes materials deposited in his memory in the long range, he possibly takes notes to fix perceptive experiences that he has occasion to make, he records lived situations, he documents himself in books the content of which is altogether factual (books of history, scientific books, etc.). If we were to take the trouble (but the game is not worth the candle) to analyze the denotational force of individual statements of which a fictional tale is composed, we would no doubt find that a large part of them, far from being pure inventions, are very honest denotative statements.

What holds for the fictional tale holds also for cinematographic fiction. If we would break up a western to separate the signals corresponding to intramodal facts from those having an existence only as engendered fictionally, we would find that a large part of the filmic stimuli have in fact an extremely trite denotational force: most of the animated beings and the inanimate objects that are present in a film also lead a real existence outside the fiction; it is the same with landscapes (if the film takes in natural scenery) and so forth. In the case of landscapes we cannot even say that they are valid not in themselves but only as elements of a fictional universe: the Colorado River is valid as the Colorado River, Death Valley is valid as Death Valley, just as the New York of the films of Woody Allen is the real New York. It is true that the *characters* of the fictions are in general (but not necessarily) unreal entities. But the peculiarities that are attributed to them, the situations in which they find themselves, and so on, often correspond to real proprieties of real persons and to real situations recorded in the memory of the author. From this, the answer to the question of knowing whether they are fictive because they are related to a fictive character or if they have a reference because they correspond to peculiarities effectively existent depends only on the ontological perspective we adopt. For example, if we adopt an ontology à la Alexius Meinong that displaces the ontological question from the entities to the proprieties of these entities, we can say with Terence Parsons that the statements that predict these proprieties have an altogether normal referential value (since the proprieties themselves that are attributed to fictional entities are almost always proprieties that we can discover in the real world).[112] In any case, as François Jost notes for cinema, "fiction can contain elements or proprieties of the real . . . without for all that being a documentary." And he very justly recalls that the statement is also valid in the inverse sense: a documentary can "contain constitutive procedures of fiction (e.g., a continuity of looks) without for all that concerning fiction."[113]

This double statement is valid for every fiction and follows directly from the fact that the fictional device cannot be defined semantically but only at the pragmatic level. Insofar as it depends on the frame of shared ludic feint, the fictional character of a representation is an emergent propriety of the *global* model; that is, it is a matter of a propriety that could not be reduced to — or deduced from — the summation of the denotational character and not of the local elements that this model combines. This state of fact is perfectly summed up by Genette when he says that in fiction "the whole . . . is more fictive than each of its parts."[114] By this characteristic the fictional modeling distinguishes itself strongly from the homologous modeling: in the last mentioned, the cognitive value of the global model is indissociable from the value of truth of the elements that compose it. The functional value of a homologous mimetic model thus is not an emergent propriety. This is due to the fact that homologous mimetic models are a part of what Jerry Fodor calls the isotropic systems, that is, systems in which the cognitive value of a single element (of a single statement) and the value of truth of the global system of which this element is a part vary in a strictly concomitant manner.[115] Fiction, in contrast, is not isotropic in the sense that its status is not reducible to — or deducible from — the summation of values of truth of the elements of which it is composed but depends on a condition that belongs only to the model in its globality, which imposes particular constraints on the manner in which it can enter into relation with our other representations.

Of course, the usages of the fictional devices are multiple, just as the manner in which we can be led to approach them is largely unforeseeable. Nevertheless, all these usages share at least one negative condition: a fictional modelization is not destined to be utilized as a representation with referential function (in contrast with homologous models with a descriptive function) or as a practical scenario (in contrast with projective homologous models) or as an axiological injunction (in contrast with prescriptive models) — and this even if certain of the representations of which it is composed can perfectly be not empty denotationally, can exemplify livable practical scenarios or proposed axiological rules borrowed from the norms that are normal in our lives. And if such is not their usage, it is simply because they would not be able to fulfill it because of the liberality of their cognitive constraints.

One can also analyze the situation in terms of inference. Thus, according to David Lewis, the specificity of fictional representations resides in the fact that they induce a blockage of the inferences to which we would deliver ourselves if, instead of moving ourselves in a (propositional) universe induced by mimemes, we find ourselves in the simulated universe: if in the real universe a Mr. X lives at 221b Baker Street, and if in addition it is true that 221b Baker Street is a bank, then one can infer that Mr. X lives in a bank; on the other hand, if we replace Mr. X with Sherlock Holmes, the inference is no longer valid, given that the two occurrences of the expression "221b Baker Street" are not part of the same universe of semantic interpretation.[116] This does not mean that fiction characterizes itself by a complete blockage of inferences. Thus, as Wolterstorff has underlined with reason, all the inferences implied by fictional statements are lawful.[117] In fact, for a group of mimemes to be able to give birth to a fictional universe, the receiver must surrender to an incessant inferential activity, exactly as he must do in reality. One might thus be tempted to conclude from this that all mixed inferences are blocked, that is, those that would result from the logical conjunction of a statement linked to the fictional universe and from the statement linked to the "real" universe. In fact, I think that one must distinguish according to the direction of the chain of inferences. If all the inferences that go from the fictional universe toward the real universe seem to be blocked, this is not true in the reverse direction. The first are blocked because they would end at a contamination of our beliefs concerning what is and what is not the case for fictional representations. In fact, this is only a specific form of a problem approached already on three occasions: when I analyzed ludic feint, when I studied the genesis of fictional self-stimulation, and when I discussed oneiric mimesis—that of the necessity of a "motor brake," susceptible of hindering the mimemes from ending at reactive loops, at erroneous beliefs, at phenomena of self-deception, or (in the case of dreams) at motor discharges. But the example of Sherlock Holmes illustrates in fact the reverse contamination, and, contrary to appearances, it corresponds to no general rule. For example, the novels of Conan Doyle include many references to London geography that, contrary to the case of Sherlock Holmes's address, are susceptible to give space to inferential chains not only valid but, in certain cases, indispensable to the understanding of the tale. The example given by Lewis has this that is peculiar to it: the inference ends at a conclusion that enters into a conflict with the fictional universe (the reader knows that Holmes does not live in a bank). It could thus be that in the case of inferential direction, which goes from the real to the fictional universe, only the inferences susceptible of entering into conflict with the fictional world are blocked.

We can, moreover, note that most of the amateurs of fiction judge conflicts of this kind severely. I have a friend, a great lover of westerns and epics, whose overly keen eyesight spies immediately every trace of an airplane in the sky, every electric pole that sticks out from behind a hill, every tarred road on the horizon — all of which immediately disqualifies a film for him. Danto gives an example of the same type: "A friend makes his novel start with a description going *up* Fifth Avenue (which is one-way north–south) by car; I am incapable of reading further: we cannot necessarily have confidence in a man whose sense of reality is so weak concerning the more delicate psychic facts to which an author of novels is supposed to be faithful."[118]

There would undoubtedly be still much more to say about the particularities of fictional modelization. But it seems to me that the preceding analysis answers in its essentials the first unresolved question at the end of the previous chapter. In what can the fictional universe be a cognitive vector if it exists only as a mental representation (even if the latter is realized in representational supports publicly accessible)? It remains for me in principle to answer the second question. Even if ludic feint and fictional modelization are cognitive operators for him who elaborates this feint and this model (in the sense in which, e.g., fictional games of children are comportmental experimentations that play a role in the process of acculturation), does the same thing happen for the receiver of a fiction, since this one, it would seem, elaborates no mimeme? In fact, in the light of what we have learned about the mimetic inversion, the answer to this question is very simple. Since in a mimetic model the rule (or the underlying structure) is not detachable from its instantiation, the only manner to have access to it passes through the reactivation of the mimetic immersion itself. The phenomenological description of fictional inversion has shown that the same thing happens in its case, in this sense, that creative and receiving immersions are only two different modalities of the same dynamic. In this sense, our second question was not really a question.

The analysis of mimetic modeling that I have just proposed must, however, still be completed on one point, the one that concerns the relations between the model and the manner in which we have access to it. We must remember that our access to the fictional world always goes through the aspectuality under which it is presented, aspectuality that is inserted in the specific modalities of the mimetic beginning that induces the representational attitude.[119] For example, when I read *La vie de Marianne* (The Life of Marianne, 1731–41), I have access to the fictional universe only to the extent that I reactivate the ludic feint of the author, Marivaux, that is, to the extent that I adopt the posture that would be mine if a person named Marianne told me her life, unless I identify fictively with Marianne herself telling her story (the two types of immersion are in fact compatible with a homodiegetic fiction). This statement has a general value: every fictional universe is a "perspective" universe. In this sense, if it was important earlier to distinguish between immersion and modelization, it is quite as important to insist on the fact that, even though distinct, they are indissociable: the fictional universe is never accessible only through the specific aspectuality of the representational feint that gives us access to it. If it is clearly true that it is the "content" that makes us interested in fiction, it is quite as true that this content only gives itself through a particular "form" from which it is not detachable. Even though one must distinguish the two aspects for reason of analysis, they are indissociable from the point of view of the functioning of the fictional device. Thus the fictional universe of *La vie de Marianne* does not exist as pure content but uniquely, inasmuch as it is induced through a specific modality of immersion, the one of a ludic feint of an autobiographical tale.

It is understood that aspectuality is not a specificity of fictional representations: every representation is perspectivic. The only thing that is specific to fiction is the fact that in its case aspectuality is not detachable from the presented universe. It is a matter here of a consequence of the fact that the fictional universe does not exist except as a representation. The nonfictional representations are, however, always points of view on realities that exist independently of the activity that elaborates a representation of it. From this fact we can detach what is aimed for from the aspect under which it is aimed for. And even if it is true that this detachment can only be achieved through the replacement of one perspective with another, the simple fact that we are able to continue to aim for the same thing while changing aspectuality is the sign that what is aimed for exists independently of the representation that is proposed by it. It is different for fictional universes, since these are *created* by the aspectual posture itself, which we must mimetically reactivate to be able to accede to it. For this reason, the content and the form cannot be dissociated in fiction.

In addition, the fact that mimetic immersion passes through the reactivation of an aspectual posture—in the case of *La vie de Marianne* of a "formal mimesis" of the autobiographical narrative act and its modalities—shows that the level of the mimetic beginning is itself a cognitive operator. In acceding to the fictional universe of Marivaux, thanks to the proper aspectuality of his illocutory feint, I exercise myself ludically at a narrative role that is at the same time a manner of facing life. I make my own, I experiment, I face—a singular fashion in which to situate oneself in relation to events. I slip into a particular narrative respiration that exemplifies a type of mental inflection no less individual and of which the most remarkable characteristic is perhaps the fashion that it has to cut short every existential emphasis—an attitude that is admirably summed up by the fall that closes the brief presentation of the history of Marianne made by the (fictive) editor: "This is the life of Marianne; it is like this that she calls herself at the beginning of her story; she afterward takes the title of countess; she speaks to one of her friends whose name is a blank, and then this is all." That to which I accede mimetically through the particular modalities of Marianne's narrative voice is the story of a life that narrates itself on this minor mode of "and then this is all." And this mode incarnates itself in the most concrete manner in the narratological and stylistic characteristics of Marivaux's text. These traits called formal thus appear not only as being cognitive vectors of the same rank as the represented contents but also as being inseparable from them. And what is valid for fictional narrative is valid also for the other fictional forms. For instance, when I look at a film, my look slips into the quasi-perceptive experience that the fictional universe establishes. This aspectuality proper to the eye of the camera is itself a cognitive operator, this time at the level of perceptive experience. Fiction is thus always an affair of content and form at the same time.

4

Some Fictional Devices

1. Games, Daydreams, and Art

The little child enters into the world of fictions through games (gestural and verbal) and daydreams. These activities—whether they are interactive fictions with adults or the child's comrades, solitary games with mimetic beginnings (dolls, tiny cars, etc.), or the imaginary scene of his mental theater—form the nucleus of his fictional competence. It is thus thanks to them that he will later be able to draw profit and pleasure from artistic fictions, indeed, create them himself. Insofar as these ludic and imaginative activities are an integral part of the psychological development of the child and necessitate no particular cultural learning, we can suppose that they exist everywhere. In other words, fictional competence seems not to be a cultural convention but a universal psychological given, a basic modality of human intentionality.

This is certainly the status of mental self-stimulation, at least if we accept the results of works in psychopathology and of developmental psychology, which show that this type of activity corresponds to a specific functional modality of the human spirit. The fact that everywhere children devote themselves to fictional games indirectly confirms the accuracy of the hypothesis, insofar as imaginative self-stimulation is indissociable from every fictional game. Thus, the idea, so widespread today, according to which the distinction between fictional devices and real beliefs would not be a general given but a cultural variant, seems to me erroneous. It owes no doubt a lot of its apparent plausibility to the fact that we confuse two questions, the one of knowing, if the distinction between the situations of shared ludic feint and those in which the "serious" beliefs are elaborated is an anthropological given, and the one of the culturally variable distribution of the representational contents between these two camps. But this last question, which concerns the semantic of representations and more widely beliefs, has strictly nothing to do with the first, which concerns their pragmatic status.[1]

Certainly, insofar as the field itself of fiction is instituted in an interactive way, that is, through the relations between the child and the adults, its *contents* integrate from the beginning elements that are characteristic of the society in which the child grows up. In fact, if the representative *competences* of which I dispose are really mine, I am only for a tiny part at the origin of the *contents* of my representations. This is a corollary of the fact that the first learnings (and thus the representations that guide those learnings) result only partially from empirical groupings by trial and error and are effected for a large part by the assimilation (mimetic but evidently also verbal) of public representations already elaborated. The essence of our individual cultural repertory is not due to our proper efforts, but it is interiorized in the form of behavioral structures and of "evident" beliefs that we assimilate in a global manner by virtue of the principle of the division of intellectual work, which is one of the most remarkable traits of human culture.[2] The representational materials from which we elaborate our mental self-stimulations and our public fictions are thus always for a large part the ones that are current in the society to which we belong. The same thing applies to a part of the principles of organization of these contents: each culture makes preferential choices from among the multiplicity of types of organization that are compatible with the minimal constraints of representational intelligibility, constraints that are those of our species. These choices are mounted in the representational contents that they structure and are thus transmitted at the same time as they. In this fashion, even the most solitary fictional activity is never solipsistic: elaborated with the help of representational materials that for a large part belong to the established cultural repertory, it is from the beginning a (partially) shared reality. The fact that it is, so to speak, always possible to translate imaginative self-stimulations, even if they are the most private, into collective games or artistic fictions is a direct consequence of this shared character of a large part of mental representations. (The same thing applies, by the way, to the contents of our dreams.)[3]

We must still specify that if the contents of our fictional activities are fundamentally those that are current in the society in which we live, this does not signify that they are necessarily different from one culture to another or even that they are incommensurable. The question of the cultural variability of representations in general and of fictions in particular should not be treated as an article of faith. It is a matter of a simple question of fact, and although it surpasses by far the means of investigation of which I dispose, I must say a few words about it, insofar as the incidental remarks on some mimetic arts, remarks that will constitute the essence of the present chapter, have meaning only if one places them back in the frame of this problem.

In what concerns fictional games, we are in the right to await a large intercultural stability. This is due to the fact that on one side they imply the mastery of a very complex intentional competence, but on another side this competence is acquired from an early age.

To say it in a different way, the complexity of the fictional device is such that if it were a matter of a specific cultural dimension, thus of an exogenous acquisition that the little child borrows from the cultural world in which he grows up, he would in fact be capable of mastering it at a precocious age. As I already noted, the situation is not without the ability to remind us of the acquisition of language: if the learning of language could not draw profit from a "prewired" mental structure, that is, if the child were obliged to acquire his linguistic expertise (and notably his grammatical and illocutory competence) solely thanks to an inferential activity starting from the linguistic occurrences that he is led to hear, he would be manifestly incapable of learning to speak as fast as he does.

Unfortunately, with some exceptions, anthropologists are not sufficiently interested in the fictional games of children (it is the same thing regarding oneiric facts) to be able to test in a conclusive manner the universalist hypothesis. But the exemplary study by Goldman and Emmison, to which I have referred already several times, shows at the least that this competence is the same in two societies that are separated in every other way, our own and that of the Hulis of Papua New Guinea. The analysis of the two authors reveals in fact that the way in which the "sociodramatic games" of the Huli children take place corresponds in every way to the ludic feints practiced by Occidental children: the children engage spontaneously in the fictional activity; they use markers (verbal and other) to limit the practical frame of the fictional universe and to separate the feinted interactions from the field of their real interactions; the activities they mime are those that are significant in the life of adults; they travel unceasingly, and without a problem, between mimetic immersion and the pragmatic frame of the ludic feint; they utilize a sort of prescriptive didascaly or prompts to give instructions to other players concerning the action in which they ought to engage and concerning the words they ought to speak; from time to time the game is suspended to leave room for negotiations concerning the future development of the imaginary program and notably of the explicit fantasy proposals; the passage of acts of intrafictional language to the prescription of scenes and to the suggestions of the fictional program is generally signaled in tonality or in tone of voice; and so on.[4] As I already said, it would no doubt be difficult to find two social universes more distant one from the other than the society of the Hulis and our own. The fact that the fictional universes are, in spite of this, constructed in the same manner by the children of the two societies thus speaks strongly in favor of the validity of the universalist hypothesis. At a more "intuitive" level, whoever has been able to see (whether in reality or even simply in documentaries) African or Asian children play can only draw the same conclusion, even if the case of the Hulis constitutes a stronger argument, since it is a matter of a society that until recently had practically no contact with the "modern" world.

In a certain way the ludic fictional activities of children are also always "arts," at least if one takes this term in its literal sense, that is, designating the regulated putting to work of a productive competence of objects and events. We could besides very easily imagine — even though in fact I don't know if this possibility has been realized anywhere — societies in which the *only* fictional activities would be the games of childhood. In any case, it seems that the different human communities do not all accord the same place to mimetic arts, whether in social life or at the interior of the more restrained field of artistic activities. Still, this problem of the effective role of artistic activities should be distinguished from that of their social legitimacy. In the societies that distinguish between learned and vernacular cultures, fiction in fact often encounters problems of social legitimacy that hardly teach us anything in a reliable manner about the effective role that it fulfills. This deficit of fiction's social legitimacy seems often to be linked to the fact that it rests on a competence shared by everyone and that it activates a mode of reception also accessible to everyone, hence the difficulty of making of it a mark of social "distinction."

Other factors can enter the game, for example, religious reasons. In premodern Christian Europe (up until about the eighteenth century) the lack of legitimacy of fictional tales (often excluded from poetic arts and denounced for their harmful influence, notably on women) and, above all, the theater was due essentially to suspicions of a religious nature. In China, where, as Yolaine Escande reminds us, the well-read culture excluded fiction and imagination from literature, the reason was no doubt quite different.[5] In fact, Buddhism—the only religion in the strong sense of the term that classical China has known—has been a very fruitful source of tales of all kinds. One of the reasons for the exclusion of fiction seems rather to have been the "social snobbism" of the well-read (this same snobbism led them to postulate a natural distinction between the pictorial art that they practiced and that of the professionals). François Jullien has examined another, more conceptual reason: on the one hand, Chinese classical culture did not think of art through a mimetic conception; on the other hand, if one excepts the Taoist "heterodoxy," Chinese culture did not accord a place to the imagination and to the extraordinary.[6] But, as in Europe, this absence of social legitimacy cannot serve as a criterion for measuring the effective role of fiction in the life of people. In fact, the vernacular Chinese culture is rich in fantastic tales and, more generally, in works of fiction. Besides, during the dynasties of Ming and Qing, the well-read people, despite their "official" scorn for fiction, played a decisive role in the development of the theater and Romanesque tales.

In any case, whatever cultural differences existed in earlier periods, the present globalization of technological culture has changed the deal, because this globalization is also that of audiovisual fictional devices invented in the Occident. And manifestly, the love of fiction has spread in a fair way to most people, as the global success of American cinema shows. We are sometimes tempted to explain this phenomenon in terms of cultural imperialism. But, after all, no one is forced to see films. If everywhere in the world people hasten to see *Jurassic Park* and *Titanic*, it is no doubt because these films please them. We may not share in this taste, but it shows at least that an interest in fiction can be easily awakened in each one of us, whatever our cultural origin. A still more decisive argument is the ease with which the most diverse cultures have gotten hold of the cinematographic device to develop their own audiovisual fictions, that is, those that correspond to their traditional tastes and that produce situations that they are very fond of (let us think, e.g., of Indian, Egyptian, Japanese, Chinese, Brazilian, or African cinema). Briefly, it seems that the taste for "referential illusion" is a "voluntary servitude" shared by the common mortal . . .

There are evidently large differences between the fictional games of children and fictions in the artistic sense of the term, if only because the two types of activity register in very different social contexts. Already Aristotle had distinguished between several causes of fiction, among them the anthropological predisposition to imitation and what one could call the cultural selection of the most successful imitations. The first is enough to explain the fictional games of childhood. But we have to take into account the second to understand the historical evolution of mimetic arts, their transformations quite as much as their growing multiplication. Only cultural selection, diverse according to places and period, of the most successful imitations is capable of explaining how mimetic arts have been able to develop as distinctive realities. Without a doubt we must add to it a second factor (linked to the principle of cultural selection). It concerns the mode of reproduction of the fictional devices. Childish culture is a culture of horizontal, not vertical, transmission; that is, apart from exceptions, it is not the adults who transmit the ludic traditions of their own childhood to their offspring: the transmission takes place inside the group of children, the adults transmitting their ludic culture to the younger ones in admitting them to their games (it is a matter of an example of cultural learning by mimetic immersion). Quite as much as the psychological anchoring of the development of fictional competence, this horizontal transmission plays without a doubt a role in the eminently "conservative" character of the fictional activities of children, the level of production included.

However, the arts (mimetic or other) reproduce themselves in general by vertical transmission; that is, their cycle of reproduction is the one of generations, precisely the one that rules the whole of the transmissions of adult society. The difference between the two modes of reproduction is not only the one between short and long cycles but also the one between continuous recycling and hereditary transmission. The continuous recycling that characterizes the reproduction of childish ludic practices hinders every crystallization of a past state, which is susceptible to detaching itself from the present practice and which could thus become the object of a work (even if it were ludic) led on that state, whether to reactivate or to transform it. However, the vertical transmission by "generational" heritage lengthens the reproductive cycle; it introduces at the same time a relative temporal discontinuity between the practices of yesterday and those of today, for example, between the tales of old men and those of the young, between the art of the masters and that of the disciples. From this fact activities recrystallize with each generation, and these crystallizations — in our case, the large fictional forms — become the issue of a conscious and finalized evolution (at the level of the individuals who engage in it).

Of course, the specific forms that this evolution takes are indissociable from the other aspects of the social reproduction. For example, an oral culture reproduces itself differently from a written culture, and this difference concerns also the domain of fictions and in the first place that of verbal fictions: we have often noted that the idea itself of a stable work has no application in a culture of oral transmission. The same way, a society in which the social legitimation of the technical expertise rests on learning by mimetic immersion reproduces itself differently from a society where knowledge is legitimized as a reflexive and theorized knowledge (which is the case in an industrial society): in our days, painting is no longer learned in the studio but in school, which implies a very particular mode of transmission of mimetic figurations (for as much as such a transmission is still considered as a finality, which seems no longer to be the case). We could not overestimate the importance that multiple factors of this type have on the development itself of the arts (mimetic and other). Besides, the fact that a practice is sensible to other aspects of social life is an index of its crystallization — and thus of its importance. The degree of (notably institutional) crystallization is even directly proportional to this sensibility, for it is synonymous with social visibility, and only what is visible can become the issue of a conscious (harmonious or conflictual) interaction with the other aspects of life.

Since the object of this book is not to propose a history of fictional forms, I will limit myself to giving a single example of the multiplicity of factors that we would have to take into account if we wanted to take up such a task. I will take the case of fictional works that specifically address children. As a general rule, fictional works for children are created not by children but by adults. Also, their evolution registers in a vertical transmission and a cycle of reproduction whose unity is generational. This is true not only for the creation of works but also for their reception: with the exception of some rare works that have acquired the status of classics (e.g., Jules Verne and *Bécassine* in France, Karl May and Wilhelm Busch in

Germany, etc.), fictional works for children renew themselves from one generation to the other; that is, children have other readings and see other films than their parents did when they were young. However, the form of these works is in general adapted from adult forms: thus, only societies that have developed dramatic fictions for adults seem to know theatrical forms specially aimed at children, whether they are plays with marionettes or with actors.

It is thus not astonishing that works for children share with those for adults an extreme sensibility to the changes that affect the conditions of existence and of reproduction of the global society. For example, the growth of picture books for children is conceivable only in the frame of development of printing (engraving); this form of fiction for children, which seems to us so "natural," was unknown during the largest part of human evolution. The same way, verbal (written) fiction for children could only develop in a substantial manner after the mass education of the population, this condition applying indifferently to stories meant to be read to children by adults and to those accessible to children as they learn to read. Another factor that plays a very large role is the one of technological inventions. Since the end of World War II the development of vinyl disks and then of cassettes resulted in the relative decline of reading aloud done by adults or older children to the profit of solitary listening to prerecorded stories: a fiction told by a mother, a father, an older sister or brother, or a grandparent has characteristics of existential intimacy and closeness that the recorded voice of a stranger would not have (even though that voice could have other qualities that perhaps are lacking in familiar voices). More recently, the exponential growth of televised fictions (cartoons, series for children) accessible for the youngest as well as the development of thematic chains specially meant for children has led to an even more considerable change: verbal fictions that, up to this point, despite books of images and cartoons, had been at the center of artistic fictions aimed at children have begun to lose that role at the expense of audiovisual fictions. It is possible that this change is irreversible, since the present development of digital fictions can only reinforce the relative decline of verbal fictions.

Nonetheless, all these profound transformations at the level of the modes of access to fictional universes are counterbalanced by an often astonishing continuity at the level of directing themes that structure fictional universes. For example, from the point of scenarios, of sources of interest, of conflicts of production, of psychological tensions exemplified, of atmosphere, and so on, the distance between the oral tales of yesterday and certain video games is less than it would seem. These two forms of fiction, so distant in time, share moreover still another remarkable trait. We know that tales have become a properly childish literature only at a fairly recent period. For a long time they addressed instead the entire domestic community (e.g., during wakes), each age bracket being able to find its own spot. This explains their hermeneutic complexity: a good tale could be assimilated and appreciated at multiple levels of comprehension. Most of the video games address also a public indifferent from the point of view of age, and one of the criteria of their success (or of their failure) resides precisely in the capacity they have (or do not have) to awaken the interest of different ages: the worldwide success of *Myst* is certainly linked for a large part to the fact that the fictional universe that the players can "engender" is susceptible to deploying itself on different levels of complexity, adapted to different ages.

We can broaden the double statement of the formal variety and of the thematic constancy to the mimetic arts in general. We underline often, with reason, the great historical and cultural diversity of fictional forms. But when we look at the fictional universes generated or, rather, at the questions that are debated in these universes, we are struck by the fact that, beyond the superficial thematic differences, the problematics are often the same, whatever the cultural domain or historical period. This point has been strongly underlined by Thomas Pavel for the domain of verbal fiction: "Everywhere and always, we find thematic wholes more or less complete, including our principal worries, social and existential. Birth, love, death, success and failure, power and its loss, revolutions and wars, the production and the distribution of goods, the social status and morality, the sacred and the profane, the comic themes of inadaptation and of isolation, the compensating fantasies, etc., traverse the whole history of fiction, from the most ancient myths to contemporary literature. Changes in taste and interest modify this inventory only marginally."[7] This astonishing historical and transcultural stability of the "imaginary anthropology" developed by fictional representations is a supplementary index of the tight link that fictional activities have with human existence in its most fundamental manifestations.[8] It shows at the same time that the (psychological and affective) existential conditions of the human condition perhaps differ less from one society and from one period to another than we sometimes think.

But if reality is one, the manners in which we live it, in which we experience it, are as numerous as the modalities under which we can relate to it. This dynamic is found also in the domain of fictions. Whether we accede to the universe of *Lolita* through Nabokov's novel or Kubrick's film, it is always to the facts and gestures of some more or less commendable persons that we are introduced, that is, to an analogical modeling of a group of events of which, if they were real, the place of occurrence could only be what we call "reality" (past, present, or future, terrestrial or not, it matters little). This relationship does not depend on the type of fiction, and it does not vary according to the historical or cultural proximity of the mimed facts. It is constitutive of the fictional device itself, since it is born as ludic imitation of what is lived, acted, perceived, and so on, as being real.

But the modalities according to which we accede to reality are multiple and irreducible to one another. Insofar as fiction produces mimemes of these modalities (of which it serves itself as mimetic beginnings), this same multiplicity will find itself again at the level of fictional devices. It is thus important to recognize that fiction possesses very different modes of being according to the symbolic supports in which it incarnates itself: verbal narration, plays, mime, radio fiction, cartoons, paintings, photography (sometimes), films, animation, installations (in the plastic arts), multimedia, systems of virtual reality . . . And these differences are not "simple" formal differences. By virtue of the indissociable character of the fictional universe and of the aspectuality through which it comes into existence, the differences at the level of modalities of immersion (and thus of the type of ludic feint) translate themselves by fictional experiences that are irreducible one to the other. When I read *Lolita*, my experience is very different from the one that I make when I see the film adapted from that novel. And these two experiences could not be translated one into the other, even if the two works "tell the same story." The modes of intelligibility of the two fictional devices are in fact not the same. In the first case, our access to the work is of a verbal nature, whereas in the second case it is of a visual (and, more broadly, perceptive) nature. These differences, irreducible, are simply the "ludic" equivalent of the irreducibility of the different aspectualities thanks to which we have access to "real reality." To have someone tell an event to us is not the same thing as to see (to perceive) the event taking place.[9] And it is because these aspectual perspectives are irreducible one to the other in real life that they are also irreducible one to the other at the level of their usage as mimetic vectors.

2. Vectors and Postures of Immersion

On the one hand, all fictions have in common the same intentional structure (the one of shared ludic feint), the same type of operation (it is a matter of mimetic cognitive operators), the same cognitive constraints (the existence of a relation of global analogy between the model and what is modelized), and the same type of universe (the fictional universe is an analogue of what with one title or another is considered as being "real"). On the other hand, they distinguish themselves by the manner in which they permit us to accede to that universe and thus also by the aspectuality of the represented universe, that is, by the modality according to which the fictional universe takes shape in the process of mimetic immersion.

It is thus important to have at least an approximate idea of the most important fictional devices and of what differentiates them. Clearly, I don't offer to establish a typology of mimetic arts. It will be a matter only of seeing in what measure the analyses developed to this point are susceptible of making us understand better according to which modalities certain of the most important mimetic arts put to work specific fictional devices. It is thus these devices that will detain me rather than the arts that they serve. Neither does my enumeration pretend to be exhaustive. Finally, my allocation of this or that mimetic art to this or that fictional device will have to be taken *cum grano salis* for reasons that we will meet a little further on.

For my analysis I will use two notions: immersion vectors and immersion postures. Immersion vectors are ludic feints, ludic beginnings, that the creators utilize to give birth to a fictional universe and that permit the receivers to reactivate this universe mimetically. An immersion vector is in some way the key of access thanks to which we can enter into that universe. Immersion postures are the perspectives, the immersion scenes that the vectors assign to us. They determine the aspectuality or the particular modality with which the universe manifests itself to us from the fact that we enter it thanks to a key of access, a specific immersion vector. There exist multiple immersion postures, and to each one corresponds an immersion vector, thus a type of imitation-semblance, of particular mimetic beginning. In dividing up the immersion postures along an axis that goes from purely mental immersion (the one that is induced by a fictional tale) to immersion in an inner-worldly situation (the one of the theater actor or, according to a somewhat different modality, of someone who "enters" into a system of virtual reality), we can distinguish approximately (and subject to inventory) seven different devices. For each of the devices I will indicate the type(s) of mimetic art that, again approximately, seem to make the most important use of them. Finally, to simplify the description I will limit myself to the mimetic immersion in a receptive situation. But to the degree that, except for one complication of which I will take account, there is a strict equivalence between the modality of the situation of creative immersion and that of the situation of corresponding receptive immersion, this restriction does not have consequences.

The first fictional immersion vector we meet on the axis that goes from the imaginative interiority toward the physical incarnation is the ludic feint of mental acts. The immersion posture created by this vector is that of subjective interiority. Let us take the famous "autonomous monologue" of Molly that closes James Joyce's *Ulysses*.[10] Its immersion vector is a feint of mental acts, since the text simulates a flux of (verbal) conscience. Our mimetic reactivation of the thoughts that Molly daydreams in her bed assigns to us our own mental life as immersion posture: we think the thoughts of Molly. It is advisable to note that these thoughts have to be only verbal thoughts for the simple reason that "the verbal mimesis can only be mimesis of the verb."[11] We see by this how the choice of an immersion vector commands the aspectuality under which we can have access to a fictional universe. Thus, we will see that cinema, from the fact of the specificity of its immersion vector, is able to mime not only verbal thoughts (from the moment that it integrates elements of verbal mimesis) but also a mental imaginer (it does not deprive itself of it; see the oneiric scenes of Buñuel).[12] Even though homodiegetic literary fictions exist that are entirely constructed with the help of immersion vectors of simulation of mental states, the majority of tales that have recourse to it make it vary with other vectors. The fact that we can find it also in heterodiegetic fictions, thus precisely in Joyce's *Ulysses*, shows that the distinction of the immersion vectors that are verbal in nature does not necessarily superpose that of the great narrative divisions.

The second immersion vector is that of the illocutory feint, that is, the feint of acts of language. For the essential, the feigned acts are acts of descriptive language, since most of the fictions that have recourse to language are narrative, but nothing forbids the preparation of a verbal fiction that would consist wholly in the feint of declarative or interrogative acts of language. The immersion posture that corresponds to the feint of descriptive acts of language is that of "natural narration." We access the fictional universe through the voice and more broadly through the perspective of a narrator who pretends to tell us real facts, such as the one who begins his tale with these words: "Lucien Leuwen had been excluded from the polytechnical school for taking a walk, a day that he was on duty, like all his comrades: it was at the period of one of the famous days of June, April, or February 1832 or 1834." This modality to the fictional universe is typically that of heterodiegetic fiction, although the situation complicates itself when there is internal focalization, that is, when the narration adopts the point of view of a character who thus constitutes himself as a "fictive I- origin" (Käte Hamburger) of the mimetic universe.[13]

The third immersion vector is that of the substitution of narrative identity. We find it in a part of homodiegetic fiction, more precisely, in all the texts where the feint situates itself uphill from the acts of language at the level of the figure of the narrator, as is the case in a fictional autobiography. The posture of immersion that corresponds to this vector is again the one of "natural narration," with this difference that the accent displaces itself from the narrative act toward the identity of the narrator. The posture of immersion induced by a substitution of narrative identity is very different from the one induced by a feint of mental acts, even if both phenomena concern the homodiegetic perspective (even if it is inserted in a heterodiegetic tale, as in Joyce). This confirms the hypothesis that the differences pertinent to the level of techniques of immersion don't always superimpose big narrative divisions, a question to which I will return later.

The fourth immersion vector makes us pass purely mental mimetic reactivations induced by verbal mimemes to the domain of mimemes that concern the perceptive access of the world. The correct analysis of vectors of fictional immersion utilized by mimetic arts exploiting analogical representations poses a particular problem insofar as, uphill from the question of their fictional character or not, graphic images and photographs are always already mimemes and thus are always already interiorized by a process if mimetic immersion, hence the difficulty of making the part between what concerns mimetic immersion indissociable from the mimetic support and what concerns properly fictional immersion inasmuch as this one serves itself of mimetic support in the frame of a divided ludic feint. But I prefer to approach this question later on. At the point where we are, it is enough to bring out the distinction of principle that separates the homologous mimemes from the fictional mimemes. The vector of immersion that is utilized by the fictions that serve themselves of graphic or photographic support is the feint of a homologous visual representation. In other words, the situation of shared ludic feint leads us to treat a fictional visual representation "as if" it were a homologous and thus denotational visual representation. However (and this is one of the reasons for the difficulty that we have separating well the situations of fiction from the situations of homologous mimesis in the domain of painting and of photography), the posture of fictional immersion is exactly the same as in the case of a homologous visual mimeme: it is a matter of a perceptive immersion.[14]

The fifth vector of immersion distinguishes itself from the fourth uniquely (as one might say!) in that it has for support the moving rather than the fixed image. It is the vector through which the cinema and all the fictional techniques that serve themselves of the mobile image act. Here again, the fictional mimesis redoubles a mimetic process constitutive of the imaged flux itself, in this case the perceptive (visual but also in general auditory) immersion. The pertinent fictional immersion vector is the shared ludic feint that makes us treat the imaged flux as though it were caused by what it gives to see (which is clearly the case in the documentary): we treat what we see as though we see it because it took place, when in reality it took place only for us to see it. The camera has not registered such and such an action because it happened, but the action happened for the camera to be able to give it to see according to the modality of the shared ludic feint. It must be noted that the fictional immersion vector remains fundamentally the same, whether it is a matter of an effective filmic registration, of a cartoon, or of a film constructed with the help of synthetic images: this is explained by the fact that the perceptive immersion is induced by the phenomenology of the imaged flux rather than by the relation of print. From the point of view of their fictional functioning, there is no great difference between *Bambi* and *Babe*, even though the first is a cartoon and the second is a "real" film. It explains also the ease with which we accept mixed filmic universes that combine the two media, following the example of *Who Killed Roger Rabbit?*

This point is important, for it illustrates the gulf that separates the situation of shared ludic feint from that of serious feint: a serious feint serving itself of an imaged flux can only be efficacious as long as it "turns aside" indexical (cinematographic) images, for what is important is not that it deceives our perceptive mechanism (at a preattentional level), it is necessary that it leads us to maintain erroneous beliefs, in this case, the belief that it gives us to see real events. To arrive there, preattentional lures not only do not suffice but are finally superfluous. It is rather necessary that it draws profit from what formerly, concerning photography, I proposed to call the knowledge of *archē*: the (serious) feint has to lead us to believe that we are faced with a print and thus with a photograph or a film.[15] It is not the same in the frame of a ludic feint: forasmuch as a cartoon or images of synthesis are able to induce the same immersion posture as a film, they will do just as well. I clearly don't want to say by this that they are interchangeable, notably because a film can no doubt develop preattentional perceptive lures that are more powerful than cartoons because of its recourse to hypernormal lures. But this does not change anything at bottom. In what concerns the immersion posture induced by this vector, it is a matter, as in the case of graphic images and photographs, of a perceptive immersion. The two are nonetheless distinguished in that in the case of fixed images the immersion is purely visual and not saturated by the mimeme, whereas in the cinema it is mimetically saturated and (at least since the invention of talkies) at the same time visual and auditory. In the case of a cinematographic fiction, I immerse myself in a perceptive flux, in a perceptive *experience* in the full sense of the term. However, in the case of fixed images, the visual beginning that is not saturated (not only from the fact of the absence of movement at the interior of the visual cone but also because of the immobility of this cone itself) demands an active intervention of my imagination for the immersion to accede to the duration and the mobility of a true visual mimeme. For lack of being thus vivified imaginarily, "the beings that painting engenders stand up as though they were living, but when one interrogates them, they remain frozen in a solemn pose and keep silent."[16]

The sixth fictional device uses the simulation of inner-worldly elements as immersion vector. It thus invests a real space that it peoples with physically real persons but by equipping this real space and these real persons with a mimetic function. This is evidently the situation that prevails in the theater. It is important to note that the immersion vector here is *not* the simulation of a perceptive flux but a simulation of events. Even though the space of the scene is a fictional space, and even though the scenery is mimemes, this fictional universe occupies the physical space—it includes physical objects and, of course, is peopled by real human beings. The spectator in the theater is in a situation that resembles the one described by Giono, except that in the theater the two universes that superimpose each other (that of reality and that of fiction) both occupy the same space, namely, the real space. If the immersion vector of the theater is not constituted by the simulation of a perceptive flux, it follows that the immersion posture of the spectator is not the one of a pluriperceptive experience. In the theater I don't immerse myself in a mimeme that simulates a perceptive experience but in events and actions. Certainly, it is through perceptive acts that I come to be acquainted with these actions and events, but it is not these acts that constitute the mimetic immersion vector: they are all that is most real. The immersion vector is not constituted by the fact of *seeing* and *hearing* events but by the fact of *attending* events.

To say it differently, the ludic feint does not invest a quasi-perceptive mimeme but the events themselves. Of course, cinematographic fiction also demands real perceptive acts from the spectator, but these real acts only give him access to the luminous traces on the screen. However, in order to have access to the mimetic universe and thus also to the fictional universe (in the case where the cinematographic mimeme *is* fictional), he must immerse himself in the perceptive experience imitated by these luminous traces. The part of the spectator that charged itself with "looking at the film" is sitting in an armchair and focalizes his look on the screen, but the part of him that "sees the story"—the one that is in a situation, whether of mimetic immersion (in the case of a documentary) or of fictional immersion (in the case of a fictional film)—is stuck to the artifactual retina of the camera, his look being focused by and through the quasi-perceptive focalization of the filmic field.[17] In the theater the spectator really perceives the physical events that are real, and nonetheless fictional physical events that happen in the tridimensional real, and nonetheless fictional space, and he perceives them through the aspectuality of his own real perceptive acts and not through a quasi-perceptive mimeme (put to the service of a shared ludic feint). Besides, he can freely decide to focalize his visual attention on such and such a character, on such and such a part of the scene, which shows well that his access to the fictive universe does not pass by a mimesis of perceptive acts. In the case of cinema, we can accede to the fictional universe only through the perceptive aspectuality mimed by the camera: when the film director shows only one character, I have no means to see the others, hence the importance of the dialectic in the field versus outside the field that does not exist in the theater.[18]

But at the same time, like the cinema spectator, the theater spectator is excluded from the events that unroll before him, at least as much as the contract of shared ludic feint "forbids" him to intervene as "actor." There remains thus to understand the specificity of his immersion posture compared to the perceptive one of the cinema spectator. I am not very sure of the correctness of my hypothesis, but it seems to me that the real posture to which the immersion posture of the public in the theater approaches most closely is that of an observer. (This would explain perhaps why the antique chorus, which represented in some way the spectator inside the universe of fiction, could not intervene in the action but could only comment on it.) The fictional immersion posture typical of the theater would thus ludically imitate a posture that is far from being rare in everyday life: this goes from the child who assists, powerless, at the quarrels of its parents, to the citizen who assists, powerless, at the drift of his country, passing the amused spectator of the involuntary comic qualities of everyday life, the more or less shameful witness of a quarrel in the street, or the disenchanted observer of life's spectacle, and who, come back from everything, sees in reality as such only a spectacle full of sound and fury. These comparisons are worth what they are worth, but they permit us to understand that the fictional "engagement" of the theater spectator is without a doubt situated at a different level from the cinema spectator. As Christian Metz has noted, the cinema spectator *reduces himself* to a perceptive subject: he is nothing but perception. His reactional "interface" with the fictional universe is situated at the level of perceptive modalities: he is first and above all fulfilled, pacified, dumbfounded, disconcerted, immunized, attacked, and so on by what is discovered or, rather, by what imposes itself on his perception.

It is not the same with the theater spectator. There are no perceptive transfers in the theater and for a reason (because there is no perceptive simulation), and the point of mental passage that makes us pass from the real context to the fictional universe is situated in a way at a higher cognitive level than perceptive acts (since, contrary to what happens in the cinema, the perceptive treatment is not part of the fictional universe). The privileged reactional interface is situated at the level of more "developed" intentional attitudes, upstream from the reactions induced by the perceptive act itself: it will be a matter, for example, of feelings of embarrassment, shame, enthusiasm, pride, anger, respect, and so on — in other words, the type of reaction that we are susceptible of feeling when we assist at real events. (An event is more than a simple series of perceptions.) This does not signify that there are no zones of intersection between the two situations. The most manifest is the one of reactions that escape conscious control, for example, those due to affective empathy, like tears, or else the reactions of released tension, like laughter. The same way these differences at the level of the reactions linked to the specificity of the immersion vectors don't at all prevent the cognitive treatments of a more elevated level from following largely the same tracks in the two types of fiction, since the created fictional universes are in both cases modelizations of inner-worldly situations. Concretely, the understanding of a fiction film clearly also demands that the quasi perceptions that constitute the interface between the real context and the fictional universe are interpreted in terms of events. Thus, they will serve also as complex intentional reactions of the type I enumerated concerning the theater. But this does not prevent the zone of immediate contact from not being the same in the two cases and thus the reactions at the base not being part of the same class of intentional mental states.

I will terminate this enumeration with the seventh and last fictional device, the one in which the immersion vector resides in a substitution of physical identity. It thus implies at the same time a personifying identification and an actantial mimesis. We perhaps will remember the secular debate, going back to Aristotle, to know what is most important in a play, the characters or the actions. In fact, he who says substitution of *physical* identity says exteriorization: it can thus only be actantial (even if the majority of these acts are possibly acts of language).[19] Personification and actantial mimesis thus go together: characters can become publicly accessible only through actions (even if they are purely verbal); the events on their side can only be constituted into actions as much as they relate to a subject endowed with intentionality (and thus with interiority). The immersion posture that corresponds to this mimetic vector is that of the subjective mental and behavioral identification. We will without a doubt already have noted that this vector and this posture are those of fictional games. It is thus normal that in the domain of mimetic arts we find them again under the form of the actor's art. As the classical mimetic arts are built on the distinction between the creative and the receptive pole, this immersion vector is in fact only used by the creators of fictional devices without a receptive pole corresponding to it—this is how it constitutes an exception to the rule of the correspondence between creative and receptive immersion.

Like the children who play, the actors of theater and cinema (ludically) feign a substitution of actantial identity. It clearly goes differently with the spectators: the spectators of a play or of a film don't immerse themselves mimetically in another actantial identity but in a perceptive (cinema) or eventful (theater) mimeme. In effect, if they are spectators, it is precisely because they are excluded from the action (and from the game). The great interest of digital fictions—if one accepts considering them, if not as a constituted art, at least as a potential art—is due to the fact that they change this deal that until now was indissociable from the mimetic arts. In fact, in the games of adventure of the *Tomb Raider* type, I immerse myself fictionally in an acting subjectivity, since Lara Croft executes actions that I make her execute, in such a way that I can adapt the exclamation of Flaubert and exclaim: "Lara Croft is myself!" The devices of virtual reality—at least forasmuch as it is licit to extrapolate from their embryonic state—concern the same logic still more

Table 2

	First device	Second device	Third device	Fourth device
Vector of immersion	Simulation of verbal mental acts	Simulation of illocutory acts	Substitution of narrative identity	Simulation of homologous mimetic representations
Posture of immersion	Verbal subjective interiority	Natural narration	Natural narration	Visual perception

	Fifth device	Sixth device	Seventh device
Vector of immersion	Simulation of quasi-perceptive mimemes	Simulation of events	Substitution of physical identity
Posture of immersion	Pluriperceptive experience	Position of observer	Actantial allosubjective identification

clearly, since the immersion vector in it is constituted by the feint of a real situational constellation in which the player finds himself projected thanks to mimetic beginnings that fictionally translate the direction of his (real) look, which executes fictively the actions that correspond to the movements of his arm and that make him do fictional displacements (in a virtual environment) corresponding to the real movements of his legs (the player "displaces" himself on a moving walkway that annuls the consequences of his movements in the real space and that thus acts like a "motor brake" preventing the fictional actions from having consequences in reality). The player that immerses himself in a device of virtual reality is thus in a situation close to that of a player of a "traditional" fictional game, with this difference: he moves in a largely unforeseeable "reality" that he discovers only little by little.

As I have said, this enumeration does not pretend to be exhaustive, and whatever I have promoted concerning the relations between the diverse fictional devices and such and such mimetic art should be taken *cum grano salis*. Table 2 is thus to be consumed with restraint.

The elementary analysis that I have just proposed has a number of limitations. Thus, and in contrast to what is indicated by the table, it can happen that the same fictional device is compatible with different vectors (and thus postures) of immersion as soon as these vectors help themselves to the same semiotic support. I said, for example, that heterodiegetic fiction passed through the vector of feint of acts of descriptive language and that we apprehend the fictional universe through the voice and more widely through the perspective of a narrator. But, in fact, the immersion posture of natural narration is distributed between two immersion vectors, the simulation of illocutory acts and the substitution of narrative identity, and the two immersion vectors are compatible with the fictional tale in the third person *and* the homodiegetic tale. It seems to me that this possibility is the sign that, from the point of view of fictional logic, the distinction between the second and third device is no doubt a simple difference in accentuation. In fact, as Gérard Genette has shown, the simulation of illocutory acts that characterizes heterodiegetic fiction automatically implies a nonidentity between author and narrator.[20] This signifies that this type of feint is also always the place of a narrative substitution of identity, even if, with the difference of what happens in homodiegetic fiction (where the author feigns to be a character-narrator), the substitution concerns the extradiegetic narrative.[21] This seems to me to confirm the hypothesis formulated above, namely, that the differences between narrative immersion vectors don't superimpose on the great narrative divisions.

Another point that I have neglected concerns the fact that every narrative act poses two poles: a narrator and an addressee. It follows from this that the reader can, according to the case, figure as addressee or as narrator. Whatever his choice, he will clearly have to reactivate the vector of feint of acts of language or that of the substitution of narrative identity because these vectors alone permit him to enter the fictional universe. He does have the possibility, however, either to let the narrative voice resonate as a voice that addresses him, or to pose himself as narrative voice, or finally—and this is no doubt the most common situation—to oscillate between the two poles. The choice that he makes is no doubt influenced among other things by the narrative style of the text. One can suppose, for example, that a tale that puts the accent on the narrative act rather than on the narrated events will have a tendency to induce an identification with the narrative voice. But it is not possible to exclude the intervention of idiosyncrasies: someone who likes to tell stories or who has the whims of a narrator will no doubt slide into the skin of the narrator, but a person who adores being told stories will instead adopt the position of the addressee.

Another limitation of my analysis concerns the cinema. First, I have taken account only of its visual aspect and not of its verbal aspect, that is, dialogues. This does not carry consequences for silent films, which, despite the intertitles or the presence of a talker, make us carry the main weight of their intelligibility on visually accessible modalities of their actantial logic.[22] But most films are "talking," and their intelligibility depends as much on the dialogues as on the images (as we can easily realize when we look at a film the language of which is unknown to us and that is not subtitled). However, it seems to me that the taking into account of words changes nothing essential in the immersion vector, which remains that of a perceptive experience in the sense that the words themselves are a part of the pluriperceptive field in which the spectator immerses himself. Except for exceptions (*off* voices), the language in the talking cinema does not replace the narrative function of the cartoon (or of the talker): in giving the characters the possibility to explain the situations and the relations in which they move, it allows cinematographic fiction to do without narration in the technical sense of the term.[23]

Another aspect of which I did not take account is the fact that the perceptive feint that establishes the cinematographic fiction can take at least two forms, that of an "objective" perceptive field and that of a subjective perceptive field, this last subdividing itself into two different types according to whether the field is exogenous (sensible perception) or endogenous (mental images, e.g., memories or fantasies). In effect, many of the cinematographic fictions make plans (or entire scenes) filmed in subjective camera alternate with "objective" sequences. In the first case, the spectator sees what the character sees, which means that the feint is one of an *intrafictional* perceptive act. The spectator projects himself, so to speak, into the perceptive experience of the character. In the second case, a filmed plan according to objective mode, rather than project himself into the perception of "another," he interjects an impersonal perceptive experience; it is, moreover, because it is impersonal, because its point of view is still unoccupied, that he can make it his own. It would thus be advisable to subdivide the posture of pluriperspective experience into two modalities, a subjective modality and an objective modality. In the first case, the spectator sees the world through the mental acts, in this case perceptive, of a character; that is, he immerses himself in a perceptive experience that is involved in the fictional universe. In the second case, the immersion posture that he is meant to invest is that of someone who perceives the fictive action from the outside.[24] As has often been noted, this distinction is the cinematographic equivalent of the distinction between internal and external focalization in the heterodiegetic tale.

The variability of the modalities of immersion posture is one of the most important factors of the cognitive richness of artistic fictions, since it permits the creation of fictional universes with multiple perspectives (or points of access). It is the more remarkable that this aptitude exists since childhood, as is shown, for example, by the solitary fictional games with multiple roles during which the child passes from one personification to another, indeed alternates between actantial incarnation and narrative posture, that is, changes in fact the vector of immersion in the course of the same game. The same variability can be observed in *collective* fictional games. In the case of the games of Huli children, the oscillation between different immersion vectors is particularly striking: the children simulate a situation of narration (the narrative sceances *bi te*) at the same time as they mime characters in such a way that "the speakers have simultaneously the double identity of fictional actant and narrator."[25]

The rest of this chapter will be devoted to the discussion of some problems relative to the particular fictional devices that I have just distinguished: verbal fiction, the theater, arts of static visual mimesis (figurative painting, photography), cinema, and digital fictions. As I have already said, this list is far from exhaustive. Among the fictional devices not taken into account is, notably, the opera. The reason for its absence is its complexity. The inseparability of the fictional diegesis, of singing and music, makes it a device that is difficult to analyze. This applies mainly to the musical component, in which it is very difficult to make the past of the purely formal elements, of the indexical value of certain constructions, of the mimetic value of certain sequences, and of values of expressivity.[26] A serious study of all these questions would surpass the object of this work — and, I might as well admit it, of my competences. In fact, what will follow will be more a succession of incidental reflections — of very unequal importance and length — regarding diverse questions than a study in good and due form of the specific characteristics of the mimetic arts approached. They should nonetheless permit us to see if the sometimes laborious hypotheses that I have erected to this point are susceptible or not to helping us understand a little better what is the point of fiction in the mimetic arts. They will give us in any case the occasion to experience anew the limitations of the classification that I have just sketched in this section.

3. The Fictional Tale

Of all the fictional devices, the most amply studied are without contest those of narrative verbal fiction (heterodiegetic and homodiegetic). It even seems to me that this is the domain where literary studies have shown that they could develop methods specifically adapted to their object and capable of producing cumulative knowledge. This explains perhaps why those who study other forms of fiction are so frequently inspired by works concentrating on verbal narrative, often with success, sometimes — for a reason I will indicate further on — with more mixed results. In any case, the complexity and diversity of the problems approached by the studies devoted to fictional narrative as well as the sophistication of the methods employed are such that a general analysis like the one I here propose would hardly seem truly relevant to it. So I will limit myself to two incidental reflections.

The first point concerns a general question, ardently debated in the past (and which reappears sometimes in our own day): the relationship between literary fiction and mimesis. Does literary fiction "imitate" life? The naive answer to this question is affirmative. We can object that, in the technical sense of the term *imitation*, a text can imitate only other texts. Sometimes this perfectly valid objection gives rise to an interpretation that seems less valid. It happens, for example, that we identify the naive position with what we call the "referential illusion" and that we interpret the technical objection as though it demonstrated that in fictional texts the relation of "aboutness" would leave space for relations that are purely intertextual. In fact, this interpretation of the objection to the naive conception shares with the latter the same incapacity to distinguish between imitation as a means of immersion and modelizing mimesis. This confusion, which goes back at least to the Renaissance, has falsified the majority of the discussions devoted to the question of knowing whether literary fiction is mimetic or not. Since the debate has been surrounded by all the possible and imaginable ideological positions, its issue has been completely lost. We are left with a false alternative, one that enjoins us to choose between the idea according to which narrative fiction would be a reflection, a reproduction of reality, and the inverse thesis that sees on the contrary a sort of construction that is enough in itself and that holds links only with other fictional constructions.[27] It is enough in fact to accept the idea that imitation and modeling are two defining aspects of every fiction, and thus also of literary fiction, for the debate to liquidate itself. It is understood that the only things that a writer can imitate in the technical sense of the term are of course verbal facts, and the strongest justification of the pragmatic definition of fictional narrative as verbal feint resides in the fact that it has clearly established this fact. But one can very well say that "narrative fiction imitates life," if one understands thereby that it elaborates modeling of situations and actions or that the reader, reading it, imagines the described situations and the narrated actions. Because the finality of verbal fiction (whether it is narrative or dramatic), like that of any fiction, the same as the true criterion of its success and of its failure, resides in the creation of a model of the universe. Imitation-semblance is only the mimetic beginning that allows us to enter that universe, but in the last instance it is always the plausibility (for a given reader) of fictional modeling that decides the pleasure that he takes in his reading and the profit he can draw from it.

In the form of the debate around "verisimilitude," the question of the relationship between imitation and modeling has often been identified with the one of the efficacy of the operators of mimetic immersion: at the same time, modeling, that is, the representational nature of fiction, has been reduced to the "effect of the real" conceived as illusion — and thus with generally negative connotations. Certainly, the question of mimetic beginnings is important, and the studies devoted to "effects of the real" have fully displayed the complexity of the operators of mimetic immersion, notably in realist and naturalist fiction. But the criterion of verisimilitude and, more generally, the one concerning plausibility, possibility, the conceivable, and so on, find their basic foundation at the level of the elaborated fictional universe; that is, they not only concern the efficacy of mimetic beginnings but are linked to the validity of the fictional model (for a given reader) and thus to the possibility (or impossibility) in which he finds himself to weave links of global analogy between this model and what reality is for him.

The second point on which the analyses developed here could perhaps throw some light is rather more technical as well as more interesting. I have defined fiction as shared ludic feint. To the degree to which this definition lays claim to be valid for all fictional devices, it should clearly apply also to fictional narrative. Now, in the domain of the analysis of narrative, there exist in fact two competing conceptions that separate precisely on this question. According to the first, developed notably by John Searle and Gérard Genette and which I implicitly adopted in my study of the vectors of fictional immersion, all fictional narrative, whether it be heterodiegetic or homodiegetic, rests on a feint. To be sure, it is not the same in both cases: thus, Searle distinguishes between the narrative in the third person (heterodiegetic), where the author feigns to make true assertions, and the narrative in the first person (homodiegetic), where he feigns being someone else making true assertions.[28] Contrary to what certain lazy interpretations of the pragmatic definition of narrative fiction suppose, this definition therefore does not affirm that *every* verbal fiction rests on a feint of serious language acts: in the strict sense of the word, the thesis is valid only for heterodiegetic fiction. Homodiegetic fiction assuredly also rests on a feint, but rather than concerning the narrative act itself, it concerns the identity of the narrator. I nonetheless remind the reader that, analyzed in the perspective of mimetic immersion, the difference between the two does not seem to me absolute: heterodiegetic fiction mobilizes also, at least potentially, the vector of immersion of the substitution of narrative identity.

The competing conception, developed by Käte Hamburger (and particularly accepted by Dorrit Cohn), denies that fiction implies a feint. Hamburger proposes in fact a radical distinction between two types of ludic (not factual) uses of language: fiction and feint. According to her, in the verbal domain only the heterodiegetic narrative, the drama, and the narrative ballad belong to fiction.[29] Taken to its central core, her conception affirms that fiction implies no feint, in the sense that it imitates no serious discourse; that is, to mention again the terms introduced here, it does not have recourse to a mimetic beginning of a narrative type. It constitutes rather what we could describe as an autonomous presenting structure, without a narrator and constructed entirely through "the fictive I-origins," which are the characters. The homodiegetic narrative, on the contrary, concerns feint in the sense that it imitates "statements of reality." In other words, as soon as there are facts of formal mimesis, we find ourselves in the domain of feint. Inversely, if heterodiegetic narrative does not belong to feint, it is clearly necessary that every element of formal mimeticism (i.e., of imitation of factual narrations) be absent from it.

This double constraint explains why all the linguistic indices of fictionality studied by Hamburger and others (notably, Roland Harweg and Ann Banfield) are at the same time supposed to be incompatible with the typical traits of feigned narratives and thus with the procedures of formal mimesis. The fictionality of a narrative in the third person is inversely proportional to the traces of formal mimeticism that are found there. I rapidly recall the best-known indices.[30]

— The application to persons other than the narrator of the narrative of verbs that describe interior processes (to think, reflect, believe, feel, hope, etc.). Outside fiction these verbs apply above all to the first person, since we have access only to our own interiority.

— The use of free indirect discourse and interior monologue. By different techniques we end up with the same result as in the first case: the characters are seen from the inside.

— The anaphoric utilization without antecedent (e.g., Hemingway often introduces his characters directly by a personal pronoun).

— The utilization of verbs of situation (to get up, go, be seated, enter, etc.) in statements referring to events distant in time or to occurrences left relatively indeterminate. The beginning of *The Wild Ass's Skin* presents a good example of this technique: "*Toward the end* of the month of October 1829, a young man *entered* the Palais Royal at the instant the gambling houses opened."[31] In a factual narrative a statement of this kind would not seem plausible, the use of a verb of situation not suited to the vague character of the determination of the situation.

— The massive uses of dialogues, especially when they are meant to have taken place at a moment distant from the moment in which the narrative is told.

— The use of spatial deictics indexed to third parties, and especially the combination of temporal deictics with the preterite and the pluperfect. In factual discourse spatial deictics ("here," "there," etc.) cannot be used except if they refer to the speaker ("I"), whereas in fictional narrative they often refer to the third person ("He went under the trees: here it was cooler"); in the same way, it is only in fictional discourse that a temporal deictic like "today" can be combined with the preterite ("Today it was cooler") or "yesterday" with the pluperfect ("Yesterday it had been cold").

—The detemporalization of the preterite: according to Hamburger, in a (heterodiegetic) narrative the "preterite" no longer has the grammatical function to designate the past, as proved notably by the ungrammatical use of temporal deictics. The fictional character forms itself as a fictional I-origin here and now that "reduces to nothingness the imperfective significance of the verbs that serve to describe it." In that sense the heterodiegetic fictive narrative is atemporal in such a way that the "epic preterite" is in a certain manner the signature of fictionality in the domain of narrative.[32]

As Hamburger herself agrees, this is a matter of indices of fictionality rather than strict criteria. For one thing, the fact is that factual narratives sometimes have recourse to certain of these techniques. Historians since classical antiquity have commonly used verbs of propositional attitude to characterize the intentional states of third persons. Likewise, they have resorted to dialogues. Here, for example, is how Suetonius describes the last moments of the emperor Dominitian (I italicize the lexemes, which, according to Hamburger, are indices of fictionality):

> On the eve of his death, when one offered him truffles, he ordered that one reserve them for the next day, adding: "If however I am allowed to eat them," then, turning to his neighbors, he declared that "the next day the moon would stain like blood in the Aquarius and an event would happen that this world would speak of in the entire universe." Toward the middle of the night *he felt such dread (it a est exterritus)* that he jumped out of bed.

. . . Since he scratched with such force a very inflamed wart which he had on his forehead, the blood began to flow and he said: "Please the Gods that this be all." Then, when he asked the hour, in lieu of the fifth *which he feared (quam metuebat)*, one announced to him intentionally the sixth. *Happy (laetum)* because of these two circumstances and *thinking the dancer over (His velut transacto iam peroculo) he hurried (festinantem) to leave in order to get dressed.*[33]

In addition, dialogues are very frequent in ethnographic essays, and that already before ethnographers used techniques of auditory recording (alone capable of legitimizing their use, if one accepts the constraints of the epistemological model of Hamburger). A still more revealing phenomenon seems to me to be present in the writings that more or less concern "new journalism," of procedures like the anaphoric use without antecedents, the free indirect style, and, more generally, the techniques of internal focalization. All these phenomena show that the relationship between fictional and factual narrative techniques is not a one-way street. This interpenetration, which leads the factual discourse to borrow formal devices from fictional discourse quite as much as the latter borrows them from factual discourse, is, moreover, a supplementary sign of the fact that the opposition between fictional and factual narrative should not be approached in terms of an empiricist epistemology but from a functional, therefore pragmatic, point of view.

Though certain indices of fictionality pointed to by Hamburger correspond to techniques used in the domain of factual narrative, there exist in reverse numerous heterodiegetic *nonfactual* narratives that not only stay away from the enumerated indices of fictionality but, on the contrary, have recourse to what one should logically call indices of "factuality." This is the case of all the devices that concern formal mimesis. For comprehensible reasons Hamburger is not interested in these devices. They in fact eliminate her "logical" distinction between fiction and feint. Unfortunately (for her theory), most heterodiegetic narratives considered as fictional use devices of this kind more or less importantly. For known reasons, the case of *Marbot* is no doubt not the best example, but it at least shows that a heterodiegetic fictional narrative can, as much as a homodiegetic fiction, feign statements of reality closely. But one need not look for an example that is so unrepresentative. Before the second half of the nineteenth century heterodiegetic narratives that systematically privilege internal focalization are practically nonexistent. Equally, one can hardly count the number of fictions in the third person that, at the level of the institution of the frame of ludic feint, mobilize the model of the historical or biographical narrative.

To be sure, fictional narratives with *strict* external focalization are rare, but one can say the same of strict internal focalization. In reality, most of the fictional narratives in the third person mix the two types of focalization, which should logically lead the defenders of the Hamburgerian hypothesis to maintain that most of the nonfactual narratives are a mixture of fiction and feint. In fact, one can go further: most heterodiegetic narratives, whatever they are (i.e., whether they are fictional *or* factual), mix the two perspectives. The reason for these facts is very general and has no particular link with the problem of fiction: our relations with others, the manner in which we see our fellow creatures, are never limited to behaviorist notations but always engage attributions of mental states. It is precisely because of this projective attribution that I have in front of me not simply a physical body that resembles me externally but another human being (or an animal, to the extent we attribute to it mental states and therefore classify it in the group of entities that concern the notion of "another"). In other words, far from being reserved for fiction, internal focalization is one of our most frequent interpretive strategies in real life.

In reverse, the hypothesis according to which homodiegetic narratives concern only the feint of statements of reality must be qualified. If it is true that certain narratives in the first person resort more heavily to formal mimesis than heterodiegetic narratives (with the stipulation, let us remember, that we limit ourselves to the heterodiegetic fiction of the nineteenth and twentieth centuries), this is not true for all of them. Philippe Lejeune has shown, for example, that autobiographical fiction often focalizes on the experience of the character, whereas factual autobiography generally privileges the voice of the narrator (functionally different from the character, even if the two coincide from the ontic point of view), and that the two genres are often distinguished on the stylistic level.[34] One of the reasons why the factual and the fictional variants of autobiography don't have the same source of focalization is perhaps the fact that fictional immersion (in the context of the creation of a fiction) has the tendency to transport the representative posture of the writer of the narrative from the narration of events toward the imagining activation of the narrated events. This point has been raised by Hamburger, even though she (wrongly) limits it to the heterodiegetic narrative: "In the creation of epic literature . . . the principal element is the mimetic impulse and not narrating per se as a particular attitude of consciousness."[35] It is true that Hamburger implies that it is an internal matter to "epic art," which is no doubt exaggerated. Nothing keeps an author from accenting, on the contrary, narration as an act (so Sterne, Diderot, certain variants of the *nouveau roman*, etc.). But it is without contest a matter of a "natural slope," induced by the posture of fictional immersion itself: when one adopts this posture, the narrative act is only the vector and not the aim of the mental activity. It goes without saying that studies of the type undertaken by Lejeune for autobiography should also be devoted to other pairs of texts, for example, fictional diary versus real diary, epistolary narrative versus real epistolary exchange, fictional confessions versus nonfictional confessions, and so on. As long as one stays within the frame of classical literature, it seems in addition that there is a general difference for all the pairs in question. It concerns the global narrative organization: the (classical) fictional variants of the homodiegetic genres are practically always guided tacitly by the Aristotelian actantial logic. This trait is absent or at least very much weakened in the corresponding nonludic genres. Notable exceptions are autobiographical narratives with the function of exempla. Thus, the Pietist confessions of the eighteenth century have in general a very strong teleological structuration, that of a progressive discovery of the truth and of religious authenticity—a model that will be found again in a "laicized" form in the bildungsroman (often in the form of heterodiegetic fictions). It is true that in modern literature this difference tends to diminish a little in favor of a strong mimesis, perhaps because many writers of homodiegetic fictions want to escape the Aristotelian actantial model in favor of more open and nonteleological forms.

Often we retain of the conception of Hamburger mainly the fact that she refuses the idea that heterodiegetic fiction has a narrator. To the letter, her theory may not appear plausible. But with the stipulation that we limit the range of her theory to narratives of internal focalization and that we distinguish between the narrative function (Hamburger does not deny the existence of such a function) and the narrator as a figure, her conception puts its finger on an important point: in the scheme of strict internal focalization there are no semantic marks that can be related to a *figure* of the narrator in the heterodiegetic sense of the term. But, as Genette has shown, a sentence or group of sentences that follows a scheme of strict internal focalization can be reformulated in the first person while maintaining its semantic equivalence. It seems to me that one can therefore consider passages with strict internal focalization to be indirect homodiegetic sequences and, more precisely, sequences that concern not the imitation of natural narration (in the form of substitution of narrative identity) but the imitation of mental states. We see again, then, the pertinence of the distinction between two vectors of immersion in the homodiegetic domain. The hypothesis of an indirect homodiegetic state agrees well in addition with the existence of free indirect discourse, which represents the interior speech of a person even as it transcribes it into the third person. The upholding of enunciation in the third person in a schema of strict internal focalization has perhaps particularly the function to render more fluid the passages from one perspective to another. To say it differently, the upholding of the third person can very well be considered as an index of the fact that the global structure of the text is the one of a narration; in the passages of strict internal focalization it would only mark the empty place of the narrative act, waiting for it to be assumed again by the passage to one of the multiple variants of mixed focalization between which the majority of heterodiegetic fictions don't cease to alternate. What Hamburger constructs as an opposition between fiction and feint can thus be understood more simply in terms of variable postures of immersion. When the narrative passes to internal focalization, the reader passes to the first posture of immersion that we analyzed: the one where he identifies with the subjective aspectuality with which the fictional universe is seen by the hero. During the reading of a passage in free indirect style, the reader simultaneously adopts two postures of immersion (like Huli children in their games), one of natural narration and one of mental identification in the interior of a character. When the text passes to external focalization, the reader adopts the posture of natural narration either because he identifies with the narrative voice or because he poses as the addressee of the narrative.

Certainly, this interpretation is only acceptable if one admits that (indirect) homodiegetic sequences can be inserted in a heterodiegetic structure. But the existence of such situations in the ludic games of children shows that these changes in postures of immersion play an integral role in fictional competence. There is therefore no reason to want to exclude them from artistic fictions. Reinterpreted in this perspective, the expression "fluctuating narrative functions," proposed by Hamburger, fits perfectly. In this sense the techniques of internal focalization and, notably, free indirect discourse prove the inventiveness of writers and their will to draw profit from the variability of the postures of immersion with a view to render their fictional universes more complex and more polyphonic, even if it is at the expense of epistemological rigor. But the contract of shared ludic feint has precisely as its effect to disqualify this rigor, since the fictional models have as their aim to maximize their modelizing power at the level of global analogy and not at the level of homology.

It seems to me that in reformulating in this way the problem of feint and of narration one can escape the massive and unlikely opposition between a nonnarrated fiction, on the one hand, and a nonfictional feint, on the other. All narrative fiction implies a shared ludic feint by virtue of which the author pretends to report events (the second device) or pretends to be someone else who either reports events (third device) or experiences certain mental states (first device). To each of these shared ludic feints corresponds a mimetic vector and a specific posture of immersion. But nothing demands that a whole work adopt from beginning to end the same vector of immersion and therefore concerns from beginning to end the same type of feint. All combinations are possible, and that because we have all learned since childhood to change postures of immersion in the course of our fictional explorations. The strict maintenance during a work of the constraints of the same vector of immersion — and thus the working out of a single type of formal mimesis — is only one of the multiple options that offer themselves to the novelist.

4. Theatrical Fiction

The situation of theatrical fiction is interesting because it in fact corresponds to three different fictional devices, according to whether one approaches it by way of the text, of the scenic representation, or of the game. We have not always taken enough account of this diversity. Thus, the game (which corresponds to the seventh fictional device) is almost always neglected in the theatrical theories, essentially, it seems to me, because they interest themselves exclusively in the theater as we know it. Except for exceptions, they evacuate everything that concerns ritual and ludic theatricality. However, in these contexts the distinction between actors and public does not correspond to theater in its canonical form. In ritual theatricality the distinction is only relative, insofar as the ritual productions arrange in general the possibility for the members of the assistance to enter the "game" in their turn: this process is especially frequent in the sceances of possession, where the mimetic contagion underlined by Plato often operates in full. In the ludic theatricality (e.g., children's games) the distinction between players and public is even in general quite simply nonexistent.

Contrary to theoreticians of the theater, anthropologists, for lack of profound interest in the games of children, accord a great deal of attention to ritual activities. Also, they have not missed drawing attention to their theatrical *fiction* and ritual theatricality. But this latter — the "lived theater" (Leiris) — is an unstable point of passage between theatrical fiction and ritual performances rather than a canonical figure of the first. In effect, contrary to that one, the lived theater, like ritual performances without personification, is finalized in view of its direct efficacity in real life. On the other hand, participation in a communal ritual in the true sense of the term is rarely left to the discretion of individuals: the one who does not participate in it places himself (or is placed) on the margin of the community. The interpretation of the status of theatrical fiction in the light of the model of dramatic interaction developed by Erving Goffman, Victor Turner, or Clifford Geertz does not seem to me less problematic.[36] Certainly, the interpretation of social interactions among individuals in terms of social roles and of dramatic sketches underlines important aspects of our social conducts. On the other hand, the reimportation of these categories in the domain of the reflection on the theater seems to me more problematic, because in transposing them on the level of social relations anthropologists precisely put in brackets the fictional status of theatrical interactions. The "roles" and the types of "social dramas" that they study concern social mimetism (the competence of the social "game" rests in fact on mimetic learning) but not ludic mimetism. This last implies a pragmatic unhooking that is nonexistent in what is described by the term *social roles*.

Thus, when Turner proposes to analyze the dynamic processes, according to which social conflicts are unwound and resolved in the interior of human communities, with the help of the model of "social drama," he underlines an important aspect of social life.[37] But when we apply his analysis to the theater, we risk underestimating the fact that as fictional device, thus as founded on a shared ludic feint, the social fact that the theater constitutes concerns the cooperative sphere and not the conflictual sphere.[38] In the same way we risk misjudging the radical difference of pragmatic status between an acted social role (in a real conflict) and a mimeme of that role (which is the case of the theatrical game), even if, as Nathalie

Heinich has shown, the fictional modeling puts at our disposition "roles" that we can reinject in social life, this is, that we can "play" (or refuse to "play").[39] Despite these reservations, the analyses of anthropologists have the great merit of having reintroduced the aspect of theatrical play into the considerations of theatrical fiction and thus of helping us understand that theater such as we know it is in reality the result of several different devices having each its proper logic.

The fair comprehension of the two other fictional devices that compete in theatrical fiction, namely, the text and the representation, has suffered much from the sterile opposition between those who pretend to reduce the theater to the text and those who, on the contrary, want to reduce it to scenic reality. One finds a particularly explicit form of this opposition in the Prague Linguistic Circle, which of all the currents of literary structuralism is without a doubt the one that has granted the greatest attention to the theater. Thus, according to Otakar Zich, defender of the scenocentrist thesis, the dramatic work exists "really only from the scenic realization," and the text is only an "imperfect and incomplete" substitute. Jiri Veltrusky, on the other hand, adopting a textocentric point of view, maintains that the text "predetermines" the scenic representation and constitutes a dramatic work in the full sense of the term.[40] In France it is without contest textocentrism that has been and stays the most widespread, perhaps because of the influence of the classical theory of theater, which accorded primacy to the text. It is the same thing, though at a lesser degree, in Germany, where the weight of the clearly textocentric conception defended by Weimar classicism (Goethe considered the tragedies of Shakespeare as literary masterpieces but as not stageable) has for a long time determined the categorization of dramatic art.[41]

In France all classical theoreticians of the theater have been textocentrists. Let us take the case of the Abbé d'Aubignac. At first sight he seems to defend a balanced conception that recognizes an equal place to the two fictional devices, since he writes: "The Dramatic Poem is made principally to be represented by people who do things similar to what those whom they represent could have done; and also to be read by people who, without seeing anything, have present in imagination by the force of verses, the persons and the actions that are introduced to it as though all things make themselves truly in the same fashion as they are written."[42] But in choosing the notion of "dramatic *poem*," he has in fact already taken a decision regarding the proper place of dramatic fiction: the text. Also, it is not astonishing to see him reduce dramatic fiction to the status of a specific modality of verbal fiction. According to him, theater distinguishes itself from narrative fiction uniquely in that "there are only the persons introduced by the Poet who speak without taking any part in it and in every Theatrical action it does not seem either that if the Actors were in truth those they represent."[43] François Prodromidès is undoubtedly right when he notes that the classical French theater implies the "necessary resolution" of the spectacular in the reading. This "textualist" reduction is very well summed up by La Ménardière, who indicates in passing the classical authority that legitimates this conception: "I estimate with Aristotle that a work is imperfect when by the only reading done in a cabinet it does not excite the passions in the mind of its auditors and that it does not agitate them to the point of making them tremble or extract tears from them."[44]

In the Anglophone countries it is in general the scenocentrist conception that prevails. One finds it, for example, in Nelson Goodman, who considers that, like music and contrary to literature, dramatic art is an art of two phases, the dramatic work existing fully only in the theatrical performance: "A dramatic or musical work does not exist except when it is executed."[45] Which means, expressed in Goodmanian terms, that, contrary to texts of other literary genres, the dramatic text has as concordances its executions rather than the objects to which it refers.[46] In deciding that the concordances of the dramatic text are its executions, Goodman takes a clearly scenocentric position that inscribes itself fully in the Anglophone tradition, for which dramatic art is "theater" before being "literature." (Shakespeare's apparent lack of interest in the printed editions of his works is symptomatic of his essentially theatrical conception of dramatic art, above all when one compares it with the importance that the French classicists have accorded to the editions of their works.)

As is the case in binary oppositions, the facts are partially right and thus partially wrong for both conceptions. In other words, the quarrel has no reason for being: dramatic fiction can exist at the same time as textual fictional device and as theatrical device, and each of these forms is a state that is sufficient onto itself. This signifies that the two opposite conceptions are indispensable to understanding the theater on the condition that we drop their pretension to describe the one and only legitimate state of theatrical fiction.

I will not come back here to the question of theater as scenic presentation, since I already analyzed it as paradigm of the sixth fictional device, namely, the simulation of events. On the other hand, I will spend a little time on the question of the immersion vector that is implemented when the theater is received as text. This is a point on which the analyses of the theoreticians of the French classical theater can be useful to us. If we put into parentheses their pretension to define the theatrical device as is, that is, their will to reduce the plurality of the theatrical fictional devices to the one that is implemented when the play is read (or written), their analyses deliver very well the functioning of the theatrical fiction in its textual state. The elements displayed by their analyses show that it is a matter of a particular variant of our vector number six, that is, of the simulation of inner-worldly events. The specificity of the *textual* theatrical device resides in the fact that the evenmental universe is activated in a virtual form, that is, on a purely mental level. D'Aubignac, in the passage already quoted, gives a perfect definition of this virtual variant of our sixth device: the readers, "without seeing anything, have present in imagination by force of verses, the persons and the actions that are introduced to it as though all things make themselves truly in the same fashion as they are written."

Certainly, at first sight it may seem strange that the same d'Aubignac expresses reluctance when it comes to using didascalias. We could have expected, on the contrary, to have him accord them great importance. In fact, inasmuch as they act like fantasy negotiations for the mental scene, they would seem to have to ease this presence to the imagination of the "persons and the actions that are introduced to it as though all things make themselves truly in the same fashion as they are written." The reason that d'Aubignac gives to justify his reluctance is interesting: "These Notes, *interrupting the reading*, interrupt the connection of the reasonings and of the passions; and *dividing the application of the spirit* of the Readers, *disperse the images* that they began to form by understanding of the verses, cool down their attention, and diminish their pleasure by much."[47] In other words, d'Aubignac thinks that the didascalias risk thwarting fictional immersion because they divide our attention. What we know of the facility with which even children can change attentional posture inclines us to think that his fear was groundless. His reluctance is nonetheless interesting: it shows not only that it is fictional immersion that is at the center of his conception but also that he treats the immersion of the reader as the virtual equivalent of the actual immersion induced by the scenic fictional device and not as the equivalent of narration. Prodromidès draws attention to another aspect of this equivalence in noting that in the theater there is "a double structural absence of the author: absent from the body of the work as a 'diegetic instance,' he is also absent from the spectacle . . . where the dramatic poem effectuates itself."[48] It could thus be that the position of d'Aubignac is linked to the fact that the didascalias introduce a narrative element and thus potentially a narrative voice that, in the purist perspective that he adopts, risks endangering the uniqueness of the virtual theatrical device. But it is not certain that the reader reads didascalias in the mode of narrative immersion. As I have suggested, he can just as well treat them as prescriptions — as fantasy negotiations — that allow him to construct the scene of his virtual theater.

In fact, it seems to me that the choice between the two attitudes depends largely on the type of didascalias. For example, the didascalias often invading from Wagner's operas lend themselves in general to a narrative immersion posture, indeed, seem to demand such a posture. I will take only one example borrowed from the beginning of *Die Walküre*. It is a matter of the entry onto the scene of Sieglinde, who discovers the presence of Siegmund, lying (as is suitable for a Germanic hero) on a bear skin: "Sieglinde comes in by the door which leads to the back room. According to the noise that she had heard, she believed her husband had come home: discovering a stranger stretched out before the hearth, her face expresses astonishment."[49] One could multiply the examples showing that the didascalias of Wagner very often have recourse to procedures of internal focalization, notably, to verbs of propositional attitude, to affective verbs, and so on. In a more general manner, his didascalias describe more the fictional universe (places, characters) than the manner in which this universe is represented. Of course, the producer can derive scenic prescriptions from these narrative descriptions, but, manifestly, Wagner wrote them in large part by adopting a posture of narrative immersion.

I do not think, however, that this possibility of narrativization of didascalias, and thus the possibility that when we read a play we can pass momentarily from a state of immersion into a virtual simulation of inner-worldly events to a posture of narrative immersion, necessitates the introduction of a special category, since in general these changes are only local and, above all, are only the counterpart, in the domain of the dramatic text, of a phenomenon in the obverse sense that is very widespread in the domain of narrative fiction. In fact, from the moment that a narrative fiction privileges dialogues over narrative passages, the posture of immersion of natural narration has a tendency to make room for the one that prevails when we read a play; that is, we provisionally neutralize the narrative aspectuality to adopt the immersion posture that corresponds to that of dramatic fiction. We must note that the passages in one direction or the other are all the easier as the *virtual* variant of the vector of immersion number six (the virtual immersion in an inner-worldly situation) and the narrative immersion have both the same support, namely, our imaginative activity.

To see in the theater as textual state the virtual variant of the sixth device does not, however, go by itself. Should we not rather assign to it the third device? The support of the textual state of theatrical fiction is in fact purely verbal. But if we accept the principle according to which words can only imitate words, it would seem that they cannot operate as simulation of inner-worldly events. Should one not describe the theatrical text rather as a particular variant of the substitution of narrative identity? The reader of a play would adopt the narrative identity of the characters, the difference with the homodiegetic tale residing simply in the fact that it changes identity constantly (in passing from one character to another). I have no decisive argument that would permit excluding the possibility of an analysis in these terms. After all, what I attempt to analyze here are the intentional or psychological attitudes, thus clearly plastic and malleable realities, of which the interpretation remains always quite hazardous. Nonetheless, it seems to me that one can give two arguments in favor of the hypothesis that I proposed.

The first argument is purely negative. The substitution of identity that characterizes homodiegetic fiction is of the narrative order: the feint is not simply enunciative but holds to the figure of the narrator. Yet the characters of the theatrical text are not narrators (even if it happens that they narrate things) but actors in interaction. Even if, when we accede to theatrical fiction at the textual level, these interactions reduce themselves to verbal interactions, it is a space of verbal interaction that is created and not a narrative posture. If we extend this reflection, it results in a second argument that allows us to comprehend how a purely verbal feint can nonetheless be an evenmental feint. If what is created when we read a play is a space of verbal interaction, then the verbal feint is in fact the feint of an evenmental interaction, even though the events are reduced to verbal events. And if in addition we admit that the didascalias are, in the majority of cases at least, read on the prescriptive mode (as prescribing imaginations of places and actions) rather than on a descriptive mode, then we see clearly how in fact this mentally simulated evenmental interaction is not necessarily limited to a verbal interaction but to a virtual simulation of inner-worldly events in the largest sense of the term. Simply, this simulation implies repeated passages between the situation of fictional immersion and the taking into account of *fantasy negations* that are of course outside the fictional universe.

Whether my interpretation is correct or not, it shows, if this were still needed, that my table of postural immersions has only an entirely relative value: we have to distribute theatrical fiction either between the third, the sixth, and the seventh device or between the sixth and the seventh, but in this last case we have to introduce the possibility of a purely virtual variant of the sixth vector. I should have all the more taken into account the possibility of such a duality, because in the case of the seventh device I have distinguished between two forms: an actual and a virtual form. (I had given the example of the devices of virtual reality.) But to complicate the situation a little more, the textual state of theatrical fiction can, at least in certain particular cases, cause a fictional immersion that passes by the virtual variant of this seventh device, that is, of the vector of the substitution of physical identity. When I read a dramatic text, I am not obliged to construct the dramatic universe on the model of a simulation of events offering themselves to an observer; at the limit, I can also identify myself in imagination with the hero or the heroine and reactivate the universe through the aspectuality of the virtual situation of physical identity. Certainly, to the degree where, contrarily to the real actor, I cannot count on the collaboration of other players susceptible to interact with my character, I must either multiply the virtual substitutions or, what is more economical, exclude the other characters from the attitude of mimetic immersion and treat their words according to the modality of fantasy negotiations. Thus, I can identify with Bérénice and construct the fictional universe "through her eyes," interrupting my process of immersion each time another character intervenes: "Let us go, Phenice. / Then Titus would say: O heavens, how unjust you are. / Return, return to the venerable Senate," and so on. I do not think that this is a particularly widespread posture of immersion or a very satisfying one. But there is at least one situation where it seems to impose itself, namely, that of the actor who learns his role, text in hand and without having anyone at his disposal to give him the reply; he must then, at the same time, immerse himself in his character and hold account of his interactions with the other characters.

In fact, what is at issue in these redoublings (actual/virtual) is not linked specifically to the theater. *Every* vector of immersion that helps itself to a physical vehicle can be redoubled by a purely virtual vector for the quite simple reason that we have always the possibility of elaborating a virtual (mental, imaginary) mimeme from an actual fact. For example, if instead of loving simply cinematographic fiction I also love the *art* of cinematographic fiction, the reading of a synopsis of a film can very well lead me to imagine not directly the represented events (a situation that meets the canonical posture of immersion of the reading of a theatrical text) but the filmic representation of these events: I imagine cinematographic plans, movements of the camera, and I accede to the fictional universe through the virtualized modality of the fifth immersion vector.

Despite all these complications, it seems to me permissible to continue to consider the three theatrical devices enumerated in the beginning as the prototypes of theatrical fiction. All the more complex situations of immersion that we have met correspond to contexts if not marginal, then at least rarer. I will thus conclude these remarks by summing up the essential traits of the three devices in question:

—The theater as game has the same pragmatic frame as the fictional games of children, of which the game of actors is the extension. In both cases the immersion vector is the one of the substitution of actantial identity and the immersion posture the one of an allosubjective identification (our seventh device). The difference is that in the theatrical art, in the canonical sense of the term, the interaction of actors is not the final goal: they play in front of and for a public, which introduces specific constraints that are not internal to the constitution of the fictional universe but result from the necessity of making this universe accessible to persons who do not participate in the game. In other words, part of the properly theatrical conventions are not constraints that result directly from the fictional device of the dramatic game but have been adjusted to ease the mimetic immersion of the spectators, such as the masks in the antique theater (or the Noh theater), the Italian scene, the development of hypernormal lures at the level of decorations and scenography, and many others.[50]

— At the level of textual incarnation of dramatic art, the immersion vector is that of a virtual simulation of inner-worldly events, the canonical immersion posture being the virtual variant of the posture of observer or witness. The essential difference between this posture and that of the actor consists in the fact that the reader imagines directly the evenmental universe of which the represented persons are only elements, whereas the actor imagines that same universe seen and acted through a character (the seventh device). But we have seen that the reader can also activate the vector that the actor utilizes, that of the substitution of actantial identity (singular or plural), with the difference that, in his case, it is virtual and not actual (physically incarnated).

— At the level of scenic representation, theater mobilizes the same immersion device as the reading of the dramatic text. The difference between the two is simply the one between the virtual and the actual. As soon as we admit that neither of the two fictional devices has the logical priority over the other, we can say indifferently either that the scenic realization is the actualization of the textual fiction or that the theatrical text is the virtualization of the scenic actuality. In reality, it is clearly always one or the other that is the case. We thus admit in general that the textual state of Shakespearean plays is posterior to their scenic state, which explains itself when we remember, on the one hand, that Shakespeare was first the head of a troupe and that the Elizabethan theater admitted in part improvisation; the scenic state of classical French tragedies, on the other hand, is an actualization of a preexisting textual state.[51]

5. Visual Representation and Fiction

The problem of fiction in the visual arts poses itself in a manner a little peculiar because since Plato we have lived on a syncretic conception of mimesis. According to the contexts, the term refers itself to fiction in the proper sense of the term or to the mimetic visual representation. Plato thus treats the literature of fiction and painting equally, as though the visual representation was in itself already fictional. For him painting is a semblance, and that in a double sense: for one thing, what it gives us to see is not there where it appears; for another, it gives only the appearance of the object and not its nature. By virtue of the first characteristic, it can oppose painting to perception, since in perception the object is effectively there where it appears to us. More precisely, the perception presupposes the presence of the object that it gives us to see, since it is caused by this object. It is not the same thing as a pictorial representation of an object. Painting is thus a semblance because it functions according to the modalities of the perception without fulfilling the causal conditions of a perceptive act. One can even say that its presence presupposes the absence of the object: the painted object would not be there where we see it (represented), for if it were there, its representation would not be there. But the second characteristic — founded on the pair "appearance versus being" — of painting paradoxically approaches perception. In fact, perception also gives us access only to the shades of reality and not to reality itself, that is, to the Ideas. By virtue of this second thesis, painting, even as it opposes itself to perception, does not situate itself any less in a hierarchy of the relations to truth in the interior of which perception itself is already only a deficient mode. It is this hierarchy that is illustrated by the famous example of the threefold bed: the real bed (that of the carpenter), the bed as it appears to us in perception and that imitates the real bed, and, finally, the bed as the pictorial semblance offers it to us and that imitates what already is only an imitation.

This idea of an intrinsic fictionality — or of an intrinsic illusionism — of the mimetic visual representations has not ceased to preoccupy Occidental thought to this day: it was taken up again, for example, on the subject of photography (it is enough to reread the texts of Baudelaire), then on the subject of cinema, and in our own days, as I indicated at the beginning of this work, it is the ground of a large part of the debates devoted to digital imagery.

In what concerns cinema the thesis has notably been defended by Christian Metz under the form of an assertion concerning the very ontology of the cinematographic device: "All film is a fiction film." This signifies that, according to him, we have to place on this side of the distinction between cinematographic fiction and documentary film a constitutive fictionality of the filmic device itself: "The proper of the cinema is not the imaginary that it can possibly represent, it is the one that it is from the start, the one that constitutes it as significant." It is thus not astonishing that Metz finds the Platonic vocabulary once again: *in* the cinema "the perceived is not really the object," it is only "its shadow, its ghost, its double, its reply in a new sort of mirror." But where Plato treated equally this constitutive "fictionality" of the mimetic devices and fiction in the current sense of the term, Metz distinguishes clearly between the two. He notes, for example, that the fictionality of the theater is not the same as the one that defines the cinematic device: when we are in the theater what we perceive is really there, but in the cinema "the actor, the 'decoration,' the words that we hear, everything is absent, everything is registered (like a mnemonic trace that would be like this immediately, without having been anything else before), and that remains true even if what is registered is not a story, and does not aim at a properly fictional illusion. For it is the signifier itself, and the whole of it, which is registered, which is absence."[52] According to this conception, the theater, contrarily to the cinema, is thus fictional forasmuch as it represents imaginary facts but not by virtue of the theatrical device itself.

Taken literally, the thesis maintained by Metz would lead to the absurd conclusion that *all* the representations — mimetic or not — are fictional. In effect, the criterion of fictionality on which it founds itself is the absence of the represented. But *every* representation characterizes itself by the absence of what it represents: this is even its function, since its utility depends on the fact that it can take the place of that of which it is the sign. To make of it the definitional trait of fiction would make all signs fictive, apart from those utilized by the academicians of Laputa in *Gulliver's Travels*: these illustrious scholars, having discovered that linguistic terms were on the whole only names for designating things, had decided that to converse they would utilize as signs the things themselves of which they wanted to talk. The first disadvantage of this criterion of fictionality is that it is too wide: if all the usage of signs implies a fiction, we don't see very well how we could still distinguish this fiction from the one that is implemented by the mimetic arts. The second disadvantage of this thesis is that the idea of "everything fictive" would not in any manner integrate itself with our common conception of fiction, since what defines the latter, namely, the notion of shared feint, is missing here.[53] If there is a fiction inherent to the image as such, then it is a fiction "from which we would not escape."[54] It would only operate without our knowledge, since, when we look, for example, at a documentary film or when we contemplate a photograph, we think, on the contrary, that we are outside the field of fiction. Such a situation is very far removed from the one that characterizes the fictional devices consciously utilized as such.

In fact, and this is the reason for which I linger so long on this point, when one reads the text of Metz more closely, one discovers, as Roger Odin has shown, that the thesis is undoubtedly more circumscribed. He seems to have wanted to say not that every mimetic representation *is* fictional but that it *becomes* fiction in proportion to its perceptive saturation; that is, it results from the relation between the richness of "what is given to perceive and the presence or absence of the perceived itself."[55] The larger the perceptive richness proper to the sign, the more the absence of what is represented induces a fictionalization of this sign, which perhaps explains why in his text Metz speaks only of the cinema and not of fixed images: "The fictivizing force of the cinema results from its raising perception massively, but to swing it in its own absence (which is nonetheless the only signifying object present)." Although this hypothesis is not explicitly proposed by Metz, his position seems to imply the idea of a kind of scale of fictivity of the representations founded on imitation. This scale would go from the most schematic painting to the systems of virtual reality that are the most saturated from the point of view of perceptive richness, passing through photography and the cinema.

If this is the true content of the thesis, it loses its paradoxical aspect. But at the same time it seems that it rests quite simply on a confusion between the question of mimetic immersion and that of fiction. More precisely, the facts described by Metz concern the distinction between partial and total immersion. But this distinction is linked to the one of preattentional lures and not to the one of fiction. It therefore could not be reduced to the one of an objective scale of perceptive richness. Certainly, we can suppose that there are thresholds beyond which a preattentional lure can no longer be blocked at the level of conscious cognitive treatment in such a manner that it results in a (wrong) perceptive belief. This is because of the trompe l'oeil—when it acts truly as perceptive illusion: "The spectator has not to make the first step of accepting the work as a *representation*. He is surprised and deceived from the first contact.

His perception dictates to him that what he has in front of his eyes is an integral part of his surrounding world and his reaction is not to accept what he knows to be only an illusion, but to touch in order to verify the reality."[56] Such conditions are in fact rarely united, if only because they demand that the trompe l'oeil integrate itself without a solution of continuity into a real environment. That signifies that the simple fact of framing an "illusionist" (in the ordinary sense of the term) representation already destroys the effect of trompe l'oeil. In fact, in most situations the distinction between partial and total immersion is underdetermined by the degree of mimeticism of the "feigned" stimuli. In other words, from the moment the force of the preattentional lures remains below a certain threshold, the degree of immersion is a contextual variable rather than a size measurable in terms of objective intensity of mimetic stimuli. The first spectators of the films of the Lumière brothers perhaps lived on the mode of total immersion a device of which, from an objective viewpoint, the richness in mimetic stimuli was much weaker than it is in the current cinema without even speaking of the devices of virtual reality. In fact, we have to take into account the effects of habituation, susceptible to resulting in a capacity of progressive distanciation. This habituation is very rapid, as the history of cinema precisely shows with its perpetual search of more powerful preattentional lures.[57]

The confusion between mimetic immersion and fiction is, however, only the consequence of a more profound confusion, the one between the plan of mimetic modelization as such and that of fictional modeling. It explains itself by the fact that the two devices operate by perceptive immersion. Thus, to get out of the confusion it is necessary to distinguish between the mimetic representation as such and the fictional usages of this representation.[58] In effect, as we have seen it in connection with multiple mimetic facts, the mimetic immersion is not a phenomenon specifically linked to fiction: it plays in every relation that operates by mimemes, for example, in learning by immersion—a process that has strictly no link with fiction. And it also has appeared that the characteristic trait of the fictional variant of mimetic immersion, thus what distinguishes it from immersion in homologous mimemes, is that it operates through mimetic beginnings that concern feint. In principle, there should thus not be confusion here: the fictional usage of mimetic representations imitates their homologous usage; but since this homologous usage is already that of mimetic device, the fictionalization implies the fictional imitation of a homologous mimesis. Or, to say it in immersion terms: in the cases of fictional usages of mimetic representations, fictional immersion is the immersion in a relation that is itself already of a mimetic order.

It is enough to compare this situation with the one that we find, for example, in verbal fiction in order for the situation to clarify. Like all fiction, verbal fiction implies the elaboration of mimetic beginnings susceptible to inducing the state of mimetic immersion. In the simplest case, for instance, that of imaginary autobiography, the mimetic beginning consists in a ("nonserious") mimesis of the conditions of enunciation of factual autobiography. But the imitated device, being verbal itself, does not itself possess the status of a mimetic representation. But in a pictorial fiction, for example, the picture of an imaginary landscape, the mimetic beginning rests on the ludic feint of a representation that itself is already of a mimetic order (the picture of a real landscape). The differences are laid out in table 3. It can be completed by table 4, which accounts for the immersion vectors concerned. (I arbitrarily limit the field of verbal fiction to a single immersion vector.)

It is enough to have in memory these different statuses of the supports of which the fictional devices serve themselves to understand that, despite appearances, the question of fiction poses itself in exactly the same terms in painting, in photography, and in the

Table 3

Semiotic support	Factual modelization	Fictional modelization
Mimetic representation	Mimetic immersion	Fictional immersion
Language	—	Fictional immersion

Table 4

Semiotic support	Factual modelization	Fictional modelization
Mimetic representation	Homologous mimemes	Imitation of homologous mimemes
Language	Illocutory acts	Imitation of illocutory acts

cinema than it does in the other fictional devices. What distinguishes the fictional usages of the mimetic visual representations from their nonfictional usages is the existence of a pragmatic frame of shared feint and the fact that we gain access to the modeling through this specific variant of mimetic immersion, which fictional immersion is. A mimetic representation is thus only fictional when it fulfills these two conditions.

The criterion of shared feint implies notably that the question of knowing if a representation is fictional would not be resolved at the simple level of denotation, this by virtue of a principle already met and that Arthur Danto has picked up in a proposition that has the advantage of brevity and clarity: "A fiction can include historical truths and a non-fiction historical lies without the two . . . transforming themselves into their respective contraries."[59] For example, a picture representing a unicorn (an animal that, I have been told, does not exist) will have a different status according to whether the painter believes he is representing an existing animal (which seems to have been the case in certain periods) or, on the contrary, conceives it as a ludic proposition representing a fabulous animal. In the first case the painting will not be fictional but will fall in the class of mimetic representations with homologous pretensions. In the second case it will be a matter of a fictional representation. In fact, even if I represent an entity of which everyone (including myself) believes or thinks that it does not exist, my representation is not automatically fictional: my intention could be, for example, to make visible *the manner in which everyone represents* this (non-existent) entity to themselves.

This having been said, the question of the frontier between homologous mimetic representation and fictional representation could not be limited to the problem of the status of represented entities. In the Occidental tradition, at least, the majority of paintings — the ones in any case that register closely or from a certain distance in the "naturalist" or "illusionist" project — do not limit themselves to proposing mimemes of entities but transform the pictorial surface itself into a mimeme of a definite space through the unity of a point of view and thus into the mimeme of a perceptive space. The painting, rather than limiting itself to mimetically presenting (existing or nonexisting) entities, mimes a *view of* these entities, in other words, invites the speaker to a quasi-perceptive immersion.

Here again, the fact that it invites such an immersion does not make it automatically into a fiction. The Dutch landscape paintings of the seventeenth century all invite a quasi-perceptive immersion. However, a great part of them are not fictions but mimemes of homologous function. And here again, what is important is not their more or less great effective exactitude but their pragmatic or functional status. For example, although *View of Delft* by Vermeer includes topographic inexactitudes (rectification of the irregularities of the roofs, showing evidence of the horizontal lines, etc.), it is not a fiction but a homologous view: the fact that the homology is only partial changes nothing; what matters is that the function of the painting is (or at least was at the period) one of a homologous imitation in the tradition of the topographic view.[60] However, the series of Poussin's paintings of the four seasons constitutes without a doubt a set of fictional works. Here again, the problem is independent of the question of knowing if such and such an element is or is not copied from nature. The decisive point is rather that one can suppose that Poussin's intention was not to give a homologous representation of a (profane or sacred) landscape but to mime such a view with a homologous function (thus to serve himself of it as an immersion vector) in order to elaborate a complex fictional modeling that combines the cyclical universe of the seasons with the vectorized universe of history. (Each season represents at the same time a biblical event: the representation of winter is thus at the same time a representation of the Flood.) We have to specify that if the paintings are fictional, it is not because they represent biblical episodes at the same time as climactic facts, thus that they combine a sacred reality with a profane reality or states of "mythic" facts with states of "real" facts, but uniquely because — or insofar as — Poussin invites the spectator to enter with him into the ludic space of a shared feint, that is, to pretend that he has found himself faced with a (homologous) mimeme of a view opening on the icy and nocturnal landscape of the Flood.[61] It goes without saying that distinctions of the same type need to be made in photography. There is for this reason a radical difference in status between a photomontage of which the aim is to produce false beliefs in those who contemplate it and a photomontage that is a fictional proposition.

We can also approach the difference through the problem of mimetic immersion. The reception of an "analogical" visual representation concerns in every case a process of mimetic immersion, since it draws profit from a relation of resemblance between our schemas of visual perception and representation. But since this mimetic immersion can have as object two types of modeling, whether it be a mimetic model founded on a relation of local and global analogy or a model founded simply on a relation of global analogy, the categorical frontier between the two domains is univocal. For example, a photograph that registers a field of battle is stored in our evenmental memory of the world, it results in reactions that provoke our access to unpublished information about the world, it brings about opinions on the world, and so forth. However, a fictional photographic reconstitution of a battlefield in the manner of the work of Jeff Wall, for example, is not stored in our evenmental memory. It is treated in the mode of a modeling that obeys a logic of analogy with real events of which it presents a semblance.[62] Likewise, we do not treat in the same fashion a pictorial portrait and a painting of genre, even if in many cases the persons represented in the painting of genre correspond to real persons. It is because we leave from the idea that a pictorial portrait concerns a homologous mimetic modeling, whereas a scene of genre concerns a fictional modeling. We can evidently be wrong, since certain painters paint imaginary portraits, and what we take for a scene of genre can in certain cases have been conceived as a homologous modeling of a live scene. The last eventuality concerns involuntary states of fiction, whereas the first would be, in the reverse, an involuntary state of "factuality." But these errors don't problematize the principal distinction: it is because the distinction exists that we can commit errors.

Throughout these remarks I have treated painting and photography as though they had the same status, which is of course not the case. Painting concerns iconic mimesis, whereas photography is a device that is at the same time iconic and indexical; that is, it is a part of the class of mimetic representations in which the representation is caused by what it represents. However, this difference at the level of the relation that the representation entertains with what it represents does not seem to me to affect profoundly the question of its fictionality, precisely because this last is not justifiable from a definition in semantic (or referential) terms. A photo, whether it has a fictional status or not, is *always* an imprint: its status of imprint is thus pragmatically inert. We must therefore distinguish between a fictional photo and a fictive photo, that is, the fiction of a photo. There exist pictorial fictions—certain hyperrealist paintings, for example—whose fictionality is induced by the fact that they feign (ludically) being photos. Of course, it is not a matter of photographic fictions but of pictorial fictions of photographic images. A photographic fiction must *be* a photograph: it accedes to fictionality not in ceasing to be a photograph but in serving itself of the homologous (or indexical) photographic mimesis like a mimetic vector put at the service of a fictional modelization. One cannot even say that a photo becomes fictional from the moment that the photographed situation has been provoked *to be* photographed: the great majority of photographic portraits are "posed portraits," in the sense that the represented situation has been created to be represented; this does not transform them, for all that, into fictions. A photographic portrait does not become fictional only from the moment when, by an explicit or implicit contract, it is admitted that the indexical relation has a simple function of mimetic beginning for the access to a universe that is worth on the mode of "as if," even if de facto this indexical relation cannot be also—because of the mode of material functioning the photographic device—a homologous modeling of what makes a function of support of the fictional universe: *United #228* by Cindy Sherman, which represents her as Judith (this is at least what I suppose), is also an imprint of Cindy Sherman. Simply, the frame of the shared feint that establishes the photo in a fictional universe puts (provisionally) in brackets this relation of imprint, it being understood that one of the attractions of the work of Sherman lies in the fact that she invites us in reality to oscillate ceaselessly between the posture of fictional immersion and the canonical "referentialist" attitude. The example of Sherman also shows that the fictional device of a work is not necessarily coextensive to the work as such — a fact that confirms the necessity to distinguish between fictional devices and mimetic arts.

If the distinction of principle between what is fictional and what is "factual" is not more complicated in the domain of (visual) mimetic representations than in the one of other mimetic arts, there remains that the problem to know *concretely* if we find ourselves faced with a fictional device or not is often much harder to resolve in the domain of mimetic representations, or rather in the one of fixed images (it is not, in effect, the same in the case of cinema). It is that the pragmatic frame in which the image is meant to be received remains there almost always in the implicit state in such a way that we can accede to it only through a more or less uncertain contextual reconstruction. It is thus not surprising that we find there many involuntary states of fictionality as well as of "factuality," the receiver deciding in function of his own idiosyncrasies or, more often, in function of the type of reception favored by his period or the environment in which he lives. For example, in the case of graphic images, our period systematically privileges a fictional reception, whereas at least up to the eighteenth century the "factual" reception seems to have been more widespread, with the exception of paintings representing mythical scenes: notably, most of the religious paintings were approached in a factual perspective, in the sense in which, for example, numerous portraits of saints were effectively treated like homologous portraits.[63] It is therefore probable that our manner of approaching the figurative paintings of the past often endows them with a fictionality that is uniquely attentional. In the reverse, in the case of photography and the fact of the indexical nature of the photographic imprint, we have a tendency to approach all images as homologous mimemes, which not only gives birth in certain cases to involuntary states of "factuality" but also, as François Soulages has shown in a convincing manner, hinders us from appreciating in the right way photographic practices that are sometimes very interesting.[64]

6. The Cinema

Contrary to what happens in the field of fixed images, the identification of the status (fiction vs. documentary) of a film practically never poses problems. The difference, it seems to me, is due to at least three reasons. In the first place the films projected in an auditorium are, with a few rare exceptions, all fiction films. This results in, even in the absence of all supplementary information, the spectator establishing a sort of equivalence between the fact of seeing a film in a theater and seeing a fiction. This reason has clearly no effect in the case of television. There a second factor enters, namely, the fact that the pragmatic centering of fictional films is particularly easy to identify, notably, at the level of the parafilmic elements, such as the title and the credits. For example, the simple presence in the credits of the film of the names of the actors is already enough to establish a fictional frame.

A third reason concerns what Käte Hamburger has called, in the domain of verbal fiction, "indices of fictionality." The fiction cinema has developed a whole set of specific mimetic techniques (notably, hypernormal lures) that, similar to the techniques of verbal fiction with internal focalization, function like very strong indices of fictionality for anyone familiar with cinematographic fictions. This last is interesting for another reason. Although from the pragmatic viewpoint cinematographic fiction has the status of a ludic feint of a homologous cinematographic mimeme (the registering of real facts), the history of fiction cinema knows only relatively few examples of films resting on the production of a formal mimesis of a documentary film. Fiction cinema has rather attached itself to perfecting the possibilities of intrinsic mimetic immersion to the cinematographic device *such as it is*, that is, everything that concerns perceptive immersion. The parallel with heterodiegetic fiction as it developed in the nineteenth and twentieth centuries imposes itself. With few exceptions, the latter has also only rarely tried to develop techniques of formal mimesis with respect to the discursive device of which it constitutes a ludic feint. As Hamburger, Cohn, and still others have shown, it has concentrated most on the complexification of the techniques of internal focalization. But, as I indicated in passing, the factual tale also has implemented at all times elements of internal focalization, this for the very general reason that, as soon as we interpret the behavior of an entity in an anthropomorphic perspective, we cannot *not* attribute to it mental states and thus to "see" it from the interior. In other words, except for a conscious and reflexive effort to avoid it, every tale includes elements of internal focalization. We can say that fiction with internal focalization has "overdeveloped" certain traits of the tale *such as it is*. In brief, modern verbal heterodiegetic fiction and cinematographic fiction have this in common: they have overdeveloped certain generic elements of the device they copy, up to the point of making of them "hypernormal lures" susceptible of reinforcing the mimetic immersion — even though it is evidently not the same type of lure in both cases.[65]

This particularity of cinematographic fiction accords well with the fact that it happens more often to documentary films to borrow fictional techniques than to fictions to imitate documentaries. Flaherty's *Nanook of the North* thus utilizes an entire battery of formal principles developed by cinematographic fiction — notably, at the level of its sequential organization, which is rather typical of fiction films. (Manifestly, certain of the actions that Nanook undertakes are overdetermined by the fact that they are destined to integrate themselves in the course of a "story.") This fact shows, however, once more that in the domain of analogical representations, the distinction between mimetic and fictional immersion is not located at the level of the immersion process itself but at the level of ulterior cognitive treatment of the interiorized universes in a state of immersion.

From the point of view of the conception of fiction that I have tried to defend, the most important question in the domain of cinematographic fiction is that of its "semiotic" status. Since the sixties and seventies we have often admitted like an evident truth that the cinematic device can (or should) be thought of with the help of categories perfected for analyzing language; that is, we treat the diegetic organization of the film as though it were a matter of a sort of discursive act. The thesis exists in two versions. According to the strong version, the structure of cinematographic work is strictly homologous to that of verbal discourse. According to the weak version, the cinematographic fiction is organized according to the same modalities as the verbal tale, which renders it accessible to the methods of analysis that proved their efficiency in the domain of the verbal tale. The weak version does not imply the strong version. One must thus analyze the versions separately.

The strong version of the thesis underlies all filmic analyses that use such notions as "filmic enunciation," "filmic enunciator," "cinematographic phrase," "illocutionary force of filmic propositions," and so on. Odin, for example, maintains that "the production of a [cinematographic] work constitutes an authentic illocutory act," referable to an "enunciator of the work" who must be distinguished from the enunciator of the fiction, the latter being "the Enunciator of the statements" (cinematographic, I suppose).[66] If the terms in the question are taken literally, the analysis is quite simply false. A cinematographic work is certainly not an illocutionary act, because for something to be an illocutionary act it must first be an act of language (verbal or not).[67] It is the same thing for the notions of enunciator, of statement, and so forth. To attempt to apply tools of analysis of this type to the cinematographic device, that is, to propose to analyze "the work that one does when one *reads* a film," is to take the wrong object.[68] To pose questions of this sort comes back in fact to asking what cinematographic fiction would be if, in lieu of being cinematographic, it were in fact propositional. It is exactly as if one asked oneself: "What would a man be if he were a woman?" or "What would God be if he were the Devil?" Of course, if cinematographic fiction were a propositional fact and, more specifically, a verbal fact, it would give itself to read, it would have an enunciator, it would be the implementation of acts of language, and so on. Unfortunately, we find that it is *not* of a linguistic nature but of a visual nature: "Films, like other types of images, are made to be seen."[69] To evacuate the difference comes back to giving oneself an imaginary object of analysis.

One could object that I caricature the thesis in question: no one maintains that cinematographic fiction *is* of a linguistic nature but only that its functioning is homologous to that of discourse, which justifies the transposed usage of linguistic categories. But, precisely, there is no such homology. The decisive fact that ruins the thesis has been very well displayed by Metz without him, it seems to me, drawing all the consequences from it; it is the existence of perceptive transfers. The fact that the vision of a film can include perceptive transfers is an experimental proof of the fact that it operates at the level of perception. If its reception implemented properly propositional competences or if it were derived from propositional competences, the preattentional lures that it would be susceptible to produce would be of a type very different from those that it really produces. To treat the cinematographic device as though it had a syntagmatic organization similar to language or as though its sequential structure were the transposition of a propositional structure (definable in terms of enunciation, acts of language, etc.) is quite simply to disregard the fundamental fact that we approach the filmic universe through a perceptive immersion in such a way that if we wanted to understand anything about it, it is from there we would have to start. The base of every comprehension of cinematographic fiction is a correct analysis of what happens at the level of perception (visual or audile) of the film.

"In fact, one will insist, we have yet to leave caricature. The terms of 'enunciation,' of 'acts of language,' are only metaphors. They indicated simply that a cinematographic fiction always tells a story, that it has thus a narrative structure. This justifies that one applies to it, metaphorically, categories that have proved useful in the domain of narration: if 'enunciation' makes you feel uncomfortable, you only have to speak of 'narration,' and if 'enunciator' gives you the hives, you are free to replace it by 'narrator.'" But precisely, to replace linguistic categories with narrative categories goes back to a change of problematic: as I have said, the second do not imply the first. This does not signify that there is no link between the two; simply, it could be that a part of narrative categories is applicable to cinematographic fiction without for all that being able to treat it as the visual equivalent of verbal narration. Which leads us to the weak version of the thesis exposed above.

I will take off from the fact that there is no doubt of the pertinence for the analysis of cinematographic fiction of a good number of distinctions elaborated by narratology. Thus, when we take the list of categories of analysis proposed by Genette we quickly discover that the problems linked with the distinction between the time of the story and the time of narration (questions of order, of speed, and, though to a lesser degree, of frequency), the question of modalities of focalization, or else the problem of narrative levels are of the same order in the domain of verbal narration and of cinematographic fiction.[70] How could it be otherwise, since cinematographic fiction "tells a story"? In fact, the entire problem turns around the meaning that one gives to this expression. It seems to me that in starting out from the correct observation that a film, like a narrative, "tells a story" and thus that we can analyze it partially with the help of categories that agree with narrative, we conclude too rapidly that cinematographic fiction is only a semiotic transposition of the structure of verbal narration. A hypothesis at the same time simpler and, to my mind, more plausible is to consider that the kinship between the two types of fiction is not due to the fact that the eventful structure of the film would be a transcoding of the narrative structure of the verbal narrative but to the fact that cinematographic fiction, like verbal fiction, organizes events leaving from a common foundation that is the one of actantial logic. This is coherent with the fact that the categories of narratology that are the most adapted to cinematographic fiction are those that concern either the relation between story (the real or supposed sequence of events) and narration (the manner in which the events are presented) or those that concern the temporal relations between the narrative act and the story.

One could thus propose the following hypothesis: the structure of the story is that of the logic of action; the narrative, conceived as a verbal act endorsed by a narrator, is one of the manners according to which one can *represent* this logic; likewise, the *narrative* act is one of the activities that allow one to structure this representation of actions. The case of the theater shows, if this were still necessary, that the fact of "narrating a story" does not need to be taken on by a narrator but can just as well be represented (in this case actantially) as a sequence of events.[71] Thus, the fact that a large number of narratological categories can be applied to cinematographic fiction does not imply that we need to conclude that film is a narrative in the technical sense of the term, that is, the representation of an actantial sequence taken charge of by an enunciator (narrator).[72] Nor is anything opposed to cinematographic fiction having recourse to the same types of relations between filmic representation and story as those utilized by narration (such as prolepses, analepses, anisochronies, etc.); in fact, we know well that cinema has borrowed many of the techniques from fictional narrative, just as fictional narrative has been inspired by certain techniques of organization developed by cinema. That certain manners of organizing (e.g., the relations between the time of the represented events and the time of representation) have been directly borrowed from narrative fiction (notably, prolepses and analepses) does not transform filmic representation into narration, because the same procedures (in any case, analepses) have been taken up again by certain forms of modern theater. None of these crossed influences implies that cinematographic fiction is a narrative in the technical sense of the term and thus that it is "narrated" by a narrator: they are explained quite simply by the fact that narrative fiction, like cinematographic representation, takes off from the same base, the logic of action and has the same aim: to construct convincing and interesting fictional representations of human action. But the manners in which they elaborate these representations and thus the manners according to which the receiver can approach them are different: narration to one side, perceptive mimemes to the other.

"To tell a story" therefore does not imply "to be a narration" in the technical sense of the phrase, that is, an act of language taken on by a narrator. And in this case the analysis of the construction of filmic action (and of its mode of reception) in terms of "enunciator," of "narrator," of "implicit author," of "implicit narrator," of "meganarrator," of "narrative message" does not correspond to anything real, except, of course, when the film *effectively* contains a narrative figure.[73] For if the narrator is not necessary to the construction of a cinematographic fiction, the latter is not incompatible for all that with such a figure: nothing forbids the introduction of a narrator, whether he takes charge of only a few scenes or the entire film. In all cases, it is clearly permissible to serve oneself of narrative categories that concern the specific determinations of the narrative instance; that is, one can — according to the situation — speak of a heterodiegetic or an intradiegetic narrator, of levels of narration, of metadiegetic narration, and so on. Still, it is suitable to distinguish these situations from those where a scene is presented as being the perceptive experience (sensible perception or mental image) of a character. This case of a figure, that of internal ocularization (Jost), is certainly related to the internal narrative focalization in the sense in which this one represents the universe through the subjectivity of character.[74] It does not, however, inscribe itself for all that in a narrative logic: it is a matter of a perceptive subjectivity and not a specific modeling of a tale. To come back to the role of narration in cinematographic fictions, it seems to me that the filmic states with a narrator are marked states with respect to the unmarked state that is the one of absence of all mediation of a narrative nature. It is by the way of this that the passage from a scene seen through the eyes of a character to a scene seen in a "normal" scheme does not signify that the spectator changes narrative focalization: he passes from an immersion in the perceptive (external or internal) mental states of a character to the one of immersion in an "objective" perceptive universe.

If (verbal) narrative fiction and cinematographic fiction are irreducible one to the other, it is quite simply because a verbal description of events (real or fictive) is not the same thing as a quasi-perceptive representation of these same events. All verbal representations of a chain of events or actions implies a narrative act, because to verbally present actions *is* to narrate these actions. In reverse, if in cinematographic fiction the narrative posture is the exception and not the rule, it is because the quasi-perceptive representation of a sequence of events is not a narrative act but consists of the fact of putting before the eyes (and the ears) of the spectator a sequence of events. The same way, if a verbal tale always implies a narrator, it is because there exists no verbal representation except endorsed by an enunciator. But the visual representation of a series of events has no need to be endorsed by a subject. Or else, if a fictional narrative always implies the existence of a narratorial feint, it is because, being of a verbal nature, it cannot simulate, as Genette has noted, only verbal acts and thus acts of language and thus an instance that expresses these acts. In the figurations that draw profit from a representation by imitation, the situation is very different; to represent actions, it is enough for them to divert a mimetic relation already existing, that is, to make it operate in the frame of a ludic feint according to a logic of semblance susceptible to induce a perceptive immersion. In brief, the canonical case of a cinematographic fiction is the visual representation of a sequence of actions, it being understood that this sequence could in addition be narrated verbally. From the moment that it is filmed, it gives itself to see and to hear like the perceptible accessible representation of a sequence of actions; from the moment it is narrated (in the technical sense of the term), it gives itself to read as uttered by a narrator. Certainly, in the case of a verbal fiction, as in that of a cinematographic fiction, we have to do with a fictional modeling of inner-worldly situations and, more precisely, a series of actions and events lived (in general) by human beings, a sequence constructed in such a manner that it is intelligible to a human receiver. But what distinguishes the two types of fiction are the vector and the posture of immersion: a feint of narrative acts in the first case, a feint of perceptive acts in the second.

Those who defend a strictly narrative conception of cinema often suppose that the only alternative resides in the theory of self-narration defended by Hamburger. Robert Burgoyne thus notes:

"Under the pretense that cinema is a visual rather than verbal means of expression, which does not assume a speaker or listener in the literal sense of the term, certain theoreticians maintain that it is not really necessary to assign a narrative source to the representation of the fictional world: the events of that one quite simply 'tell themselves,' according to the expression of Emile Benveniste."[75] In effect, we can well admit that the author or the authors of a film tell a story or that the film tells a story (in both cases in the common sense of the expression "to tell a story") without for all that having to conclude from this that the film is a narration and that, therefore, if one refuses the idea of a narrator, one is condemned to admit that it is a matter of a tale that tells itself. The logic of filmic comprehension is the one of perceptive access to actions, situations, and events. As for the question of knowing who is at the origin of what we see, the answer is simple: they are those who collaborated at the elaboration of the film, from the author of the script to the director and to the actors, the camera man, the sound engineer, the editor, and all the technical crew. They have mounted a certain number of plans and sequences in such a way that they are susceptible to being assimilated by the spectator on the mode of fictional immersion in an actantial universe lived according to perceptive modalities. But they remain outside the fictional universe and do not delegate there fictional representatives (implicit author, implicit narrator, etc.) for the simple reason that cinematographic action is not (except in very particular cases) a tale assumed by a narrator or, to say it differently, because cinematographic fiction is not a feint of acts of language but a feint of perceptive nature. It is thus not our competence in the domain of some narrative "great syntagmatic" (Metz) that permits us to understand a film. It is, on the contrary, our competence in the field of perceptive identification of events and of intentional comprehension of the logic of actions (of which our capacity to understand exchanged acts of language is a part) that allows us to interpret correctly the multiple conventions sorted out by the cinema in order to integrate these events and these actions in the sequence of a well (or badly) tied up story.

7. Digital Fictions

At the moment of presenting the current polemics concerning digital media, I left in suspense the question of knowing to what extent digital fictions are susceptible to being distinguished from "traditional" fictions. It is possible to answer it now: insofar as the definition of fiction is of a pragmatic order, thus as much as it corresponds to a specific intentional attitude and to a particular usage of representations, its status does not depend on the semiotic support utilized. As for the thesis according to which the digital media as such imply an "irrealization" of the world, the analysis of the distinction between mimetic devices and fictional devices shows that it confuses the problem of media with the question of their possible usage for producing ludic feints. Let us add that insofar as one utilizes digital supports in a mimetic aim, one can evidently also utilize them to produce lures or shams in the service of serious feints. But these problems do not concern the status of digital support itself. In order to make ourselves a correct idea of digital fictions, we thus have to first distinguish the question of support from the one of the fictional usage of that support. We must also get rid of a second ambiguity: the term *digital fiction* is used indifferently to designate the digital "incarnation" of any kind of fictional device (e.g., verbal or mimetic) and fictions that are properly digital, that is, those where the fictional device itself draws profit from the technical possibilities of digital support. It will evidently be uniquely the last ones that will retain me here.

I will try to show first in what sense digital fictions are effectively fictions in the canonical sense of the term, that is, in what sense they are in keeping with the definition of fiction as divided ludic feint and do not include a larger risk of "irrealization" of the world than predigital fictions. In order not to solicit again the poor Lara Croft, I will take the case of another electronic game that is all the rage at the moment when I write these lines (and that therefore risks being forgotten when you read them). I want to speak of the Tamagotchi, that little character who hops on a tiny screen and who is in fact the digital equivalent of dolls and other "traditional" stuffed animals. Since it is aimed at infantile clients, the Tamagotchi has not missed disturbing the pedagogues (it is true that pedagogues are always disturbed — this trait is a part of their definition): do not the children, as a result of their immersion in interactions with a purely "virtual" entity, risk losing contact with "reality," that is, confusing the rules of the "virtual" world with those of the "real" world?

We can note first that if such a risk exists (or existed), it would be (have been) neither more nor less great than in the case of a doll, a stuffed animal, or any other support for imaginative actions. Besides, the pedagogues of yesteryear have not missed suspecting predigital fictions, for example, the novel, even fictional games of children, of including risks of the same order. Without going back to the Émile of Rousseau, it is enough to remember that for the pedagogue Maria Montessori, for example, the imaginative game was a "pathological tendency of early childhood," a "defect of character" that pedagogues should discourage.[76] And the novelists of disenchantment have not failed to draw profit from this suspicion to distinguish their own enterprise from that of the marvelous Romanesque (e.g., Cervantes in *Don Quixote*) or the sentimental Romanesque (thus Flaubert in *Madame Bovary*).

Whatever the case may be, in the case of the Tamagotchi the risk of ontological confusion could not be greater than in the classical fictions for the simple reason that, contrary to those who like to make themselves afraid, it does not replace the animal of real company (or, of course, the sister or the brother) but the traditional stuffed animal or the doll, "beings" quite as fictional as it and of which it retakes the function. To speak of "virtual toy" only maintains the confusion: when a child plays with a "real" doll, he does not play with the object in porcelain, in wood, in plastic, or in plush that he holds in his hands but with the "virtual" (and, more precisely, fictional) being he imagines holding in his arms, in serving himself of the mimetic aspects of the material object as a fictional beginning. That in the case of the Tamagotchi the inducting stimulus is a character moving on a little screen, whereas in the case of a doll or a stuffed animal it is a matter of a tridimensional imitation of the body of a child or an animal, does not change anything about the fact that the function stays the same: the doll or the stuffed animal, altogether like the character on the screen, is a mimetic beginning for an activity of fictional modeling.

There is more: the only important trait by which the Tamagotchi distinguishes itself from the traditional doll or toy animal is that it makes less credible the thesis of the danger of "irrealization." In fact, far from liberating the child more from the "real" constraints than a material doll, it imposes more on him. And this is due precisely to the fact that it is a matter of a programmed toy: this characteristic in effect reduces singularly the diversity of the play of roles that one can play with it. In the case of a real doll, the limits of fictional games coincide with those of the child's imagination. In the case of the Tamagotchi, they coincide with those of the imagination (in this case rather worn) of the conceiver of the program. Also, more than a real doll, the Tamagotchi is susceptible to teaching the child that what characterizes reality — as opposed to the world of imagination — is what we are obliged to "do with it."

Certainly, in the present case the reality with which the child must count is the imagination of the conceiver. But the imagination, as much as it crystallizes itself in forms, is *also* a reality. In this sense, the virtual companion limits more the rule of the principle of pleasure than a "real" doll would know how to do: when the fellow is hungry, it is *necessary* to feed him; when he is ill, it is *necessary* to give him an injection. Not obeying these orders—which are those of the conceiver of the toy—diminishes the duration of its "virtual" life. And, contrary to what happens with a toy animal, we cannot change the rules of the game according to the needs of the moment. For example, we cannot decree that, since we no longer want to play, the Tamagotchi will no longer be hungry or sick. In fact, if we do not make the gestures required, the funny beast "dies." Besides, even if one takes care of it perfectly, it will end by dying, since its duration of life is determined by the internal clock of the processor. Said differently, the real behavior of the child (the fact to lean or not to lean on such and such a button) as well as the real constraints of the program elaborated by the conceiver have consequences at the level of the imaginary world and thus constrain strongly the imaginary games. When the child plays with a real doll these causal links are much more distended. To tear an arm or an eye off a real teddy bear certainly has consequences at the level of the imagined teddy bear, but we can always arrange ourselves to exclude the real handicap from the mimetic dynamic. It is not the same thing in the case of the constraints imposed by the programmer of the Tamagotchi, for he is the true master of the game. In brief, far from speaking in favor of the thesis of a fundamental rupture between predigital fictional games and "cybernetic" fictions, the Tamagotchi shows that digital fictional games quite naturally find their place in the domain "traditionally" reserved for ludic feints.

In general, we associate three principal characteristics with the digital media, characteristics that, it is understood, also play a big role in their fictional usage: multimedia, interactivity, and total immersion. The "multimediatic" aspect of digital fictions profits from the fact that the digital code is a universal and reversible semiotic support; it is universal, since any signal can be digitalized; it is reversible, since a digitalized signal can be retranslated into its analogical signal of origin.[77] In other words, the digital supports accede to a complete semiotic ubiquity, since they can encode indifferently linguistic, iconic, or phonic signs and then combine them. This combination allows us to regroup in a single work fictional techniques linked to different media, which, in principle at least, is susceptible to reinforcing its mimetic power. As for the interactive aspect of digital fictions, it is due to the fact that the digital matrix can be programmed with a view to simulating, for example, a perceptive and physical environment causally linked to the real actions of the receiver. The program can also simulate the existence of a person who takes over my proper actions; this is what happens in the case of adventure games where the player is represented at the interior of the fictional universe by a character who interacts with other characters. This "personifying" simulation can evidently be integrated in the simulation of a perceptive and physical environment, like in certain devices of "virtual reality" where the player has a virtual double who "strolls" in the fictional universe and can meet fictional characters. The digital fictional worlds can thus directly accede to a very strong consistency for him who engages in it, since he must occupy the place that the program orders him to and since he can act only in the frame of scenarios rendered possible by this same program: more than any other fiction, digital fiction behaves as though it were an independent universe, a "reality" imposing its proper constraints.

Finally, the digital simulation permits us to produce effects of immersion of an unknown efficacity until now. This is linked to the fact, first of all, that, thanks to the greater and greater power of the processes, it can perfect the hypernormal lures at the level of each of the mediatic supports taken individually. The development of the devices of virtual reality testify eloquently of this will to reach psychological states of total immersion. On the other hand, to the degree that it can combine freely different supports of information, it can profit from the mechanism of perceptive compensation, thanks to which the power of immersion of a given support pales beside the weakness of another.[78] In the systems of virtual reality, the tactile stimuli due to sensitive gloves come to compensate the (relative) lack of mimetic conviction of the images of synthesis actually available.

It is a matter here without contest of three central characteristics of digital fictions. None is absolutely specific to them. Thus, the synthesis of several types of signs in the same work (the creation of multimedia works) is not at all an invention of the digital period. The "traditional" arts are in fact far from being all "monomedia" devices.[79] Many are founded on the combination of several semiotic supports and thus relieve the multimedia: this has been the case, since immemorial times, of theater and of ballet; it is the case of opera, of which the "multimedia" character had even led Richard Wagner to see in it the work of total art, a grandiloquent ideal that resurges in our own day precisely in relation to digital arts; this is still the case, of course, of that more recent art that is the cinema; this is finally the case of a certain number of nondigital works in contemporary art, for example, of installations. Neither is interactivity an invention of the period of computers. At least it is not like this for all forms of interactivity. Such as it is employed in the literature devoted to digital techniques, the term refers in effect to two very different processes: for one thing, the causal interaction between a human subject and a simulated physical environment, for another, the communication between a human subject and the sham of an entity endowed with intentionality.

The first type of interactivity seems effectively to be an invention of the digital era: at least I know of no predigital fictional device that implements a process of this type. The second form (notably, the one of the Tamagotchi) never does anything except vary an old principle that is the base of many imaginative games, like the game with a doll. In the case of the doll, like the one of digital simulation, the interaction is in fact the fictional mimesis of a real interaction between two entities endowed with intentionality (e.g., a mother and her baby). Just as the child, in his imagination, endows his doll with a personality, the programmer endows his software with properties that mime intentional states of a conscious being.[80] The exacerbation of the effect of immersion is also not a specificity of digital fictions: the perfection of the effects of immersion that we search for in the devices of virtual reality only follows the development in the same direction that we have been able to observe at any time in the fictional devices of all orders.

On the other hand, there is no doubt that what draws attention to digital fictions — that is (let us remember once again), the fictions that, at the level of their device, themselves profit from the digital techniques — is that they implement jointly all the techniques formerly distributed between different fictional devices. Even if it is necessary to recall that the psychological degree of effective immersion obtained depends to a (great) extent on pragmatic factors (familiarity or not with a technique of given immersion) and that it is thus not a direct causal effect of the force of the imitated stimuli, it remains the case that from the point of view of the diversity of means that are at the disposal of the artist to create these affects of immersion the systems of virtual reality surpass by far everything that humanity has known to this day. Through the simulated interactivity of systems of virtual reality, the real subject is called to becoming himself a causal element in the interior of the fictional world: the virtual world that offers itself to it changes in agreement with the direction that he imprints on its real look; he can intervene himself in the imaginary universe and this thanks to virtual members that prolong (or represent) his real members and depend on them causally. This necessitates the clarification of technical devices much more complex than those utilized until then in fictions.

I must thus help myself to headphones with two screens, the superimposition of which permits the establishment of a virtual visual field in 3D. I must add to it a driver capable of adapting the perceptive visual field to the movements of my head. The sonorous immersion necessitates a true sound in relief (3D) that takes into account the reflection and the refraction of sounds according to the environment but also according to the position of my head with respect to the sonorous source. (I have to take account of the fact that when a sonorous source is in a lateral position, it will not have the same spectral characteristics for both of my ears, since in order to reach the ear opposed to the sonorous source the sonorous waves must traverse my head, a phenomenon of absorption that can be mathematically modelized with the help of what I call the "function of head transfer.") At the tactile level it is necessary to have data gloves capable of transmitting commands to the virtual hand, instructing it, for example, to grab a ball. These gloves must also be endowed with returns of effort (to displace a feather is not the same thing as to displace a ball in a game of ninepins) and multiple haptic returns capable of transmitting to my hand not only sensations of the form and volume of the touched object but also sensations of its mechanical or elastic properties, its temperature, and its texture as well as the sensation of either the sliding of the object or its firm hold.[81]

During the analysis of the vectors and postures of immersion I had treated the digital fictions in the frame of the seventh device, more precisely, as one of the variants of this device, that is, that of the allosubjective identification. This categorization seems to suit well actual digital games, where the player finds himself faced with a screen and where he identifies himself with a fictive character who displaces himself in the fictional world in accordance with the orders that the player gives him. It is not certain that the systems of virtual reality can be truly analyzed in the same terms. I had notably said that the player who immerses himself in a device of virtual reality is in a situation that approaches that of the "traditional" player, adding that, in opposition to the latter, he moves in a "reality" largely unpredictable that he discovers only little by little. This difference is an index that in reality the fictional device is no doubt not the same. Thus, in the case of the virtual player, the immersion posture is not truly that of an allosubjective identification: the fictional subject who moves in the virtual universe is in fact a double of the real player. The immersion vector is thus not that of a substitution of physical identity but that of a virtualization of the identity of the player. That one is not, contrary to the "traditional" player, the creator of the universe in which he immerses himself mimetically; he does not create the universe through his activity of mimetic immersion. The universe preexists, and if he can act in it, it is uniquely as much as he conforms to the constraints that this universe imposes on him, like those that reality imposes on us. The immersion posture that matters here is thus irreducible at the same time to the perceptive immersion (since the virtual reality in which I move depends in part on my own actions, which is not the case, e.g., with the perceptive immersion of the cinematographic device), to the immersion in a position of observer, and to the substitution of allosubjective identity. To render it justice, it would thus be necessary to add an eighth device to my classification: its vector would be the virtualization of identity of the player, and its immersion posture that of lived reality. This having been said, what I just described, rather than reflect the actual state of the fictional utilization of the systems of virtual reality, still corresponds largely to a simple vision of the future. In other words, for the moment the eighth device itself exists only in its virtual state.

But digital fictions distinguish themselves still on another point from traditional fictions, and this characteristic is already fully operative today. When I insisted on the fact that Lara Croft and the Tamagotchi were fictional characters that were indistinguishable from Don Quixote, from Julien Sorel, or from Droopy, I specified that I put provisionally in parentheses the fact that the two first ones were the characters in a game. But this constitutes a real difference, even if it does not concern the ontological status of the characters. At the same time, from the fact of the importance of the representational constraints that they impose on the receptor, the digital fictional games are closer to artistic fictions, that is, to the fictional *representation*, than traditional fictional games ever have been. From that point on they do not address themselves only to the ludic sense of the player but also to his aesthetic attention. They thus combine traits that are typical of games (notably, the aspect of competition and the agonistic spirit) with traits typical of works of fiction (the creation of universes). The characteristic that permits them to accede to this hybrid status is the fact that digital techniques permit the creation of a master work that proposes at the same time a fictional universe and programs an interactive reception. But from the moment when they address aesthetic attention as much as ludic spirit, it would seem that they fulfill the necessary condition to be recognized also as fictional *works*—with this difference that, while they are works, they nonetheless stay games. It is precisely here, it seems to me, that is situated the true newness of digital fictions: they are indifferent to the traditional division between fictional *games* and fictional *works*. Or, to say it differently, they reconcile fiction with its ludic origins.

Conclusion

To elaborate mental representations that one knows to be "wrong," to communicate to others informations that present themselves as if they bore on real things when they are simply invented, or else to interest oneself in tales, visual representations, or actions of which one knows that they are "semblances" — these are behaviors that, it seems, don't exist by themselves. This is at least the conviction of the antimimetic position. The hypothesis that led me here was that one has to suppose with Aristotle that, from the moment fiction exists, it owes its birth to "natural causes."[1] If, however, one admits that in the order of the living causality is functionally selective, then if fiction exists, it is probably because it fulfills a task in human life and, more precisely, in the economy of representations. According to Aristotle, I remind the reader, the first cause of the birth of mimesis is the fact that "to imitate is natural for human beings and manifests itself from childhood on." The principal aim of the argumentation developed here has been to try to bring out the functionally selective cause, susceptible to explaining *why* "to imitate is natural for human beings." Aristotle had indicated still another cause, more specifically responsible for the development of poetic *art*, namely, the cultural selection of the most successful imitations from the point of view of modeling as well as of its aspectuality: "Since we have a natural tendency to representation, and also to melody and to rhythm (for it is evident that meters are part of rhythms), the ones who from the start had the best natural disposition made progress little by little and gave birth to poetry from their improvisations."[2] In extrapolating from poetry to mimesis as such, we see that this cause is the one of diversification of fictional devices according to their semiotic supports as well as their historical development (thematic as well as formal). The question of historical evolution, though very important, is not part of the objective of the present inquiry. However, we have met the problem of the diversification of fictional devices, which is an integral part of the general problem of fiction.

Aristotle had, however, drawn attention to a supplementary point. If to imitate is natural to human being, this natural fact must translate itself into an impulse for action. It is thus a matter of understanding under what form the tendency to imitation manifests itself at the level of our psychic economy. We know the answer given in the *Poetics*: "All men take pleasure in imitations."[3] In other words, the direct psychological motivation that pushes us to devote ourselves to ludic mimetic activities is of a hedonistic order. That is a notion of which (this is the least we can say) we have not talked about much in these pages. However, pleasure plays a central role in our usages of fiction. It is even the only immanent criterion according to which we judge of the success or failure of a fictional work. Also, if the question of the pleasure taken in fictions has been absent until now, it was for the simple reason of method; before asking ourselves about the usages of fiction, it is necessary first to know what it is. Of course, to insist on the importance of (dis)pleasure as immanent regulator of fictional immersion does not tell us yet what type of pleasure is concerned. We should not, however, confuse the question of the immanent motivation that regulates the mimetic immersion with the problem of the functions of fiction. I think that in fact we should distinguish three questions: the one of the status of the fictional device, the one of its immanent function or aim, and the one of its possible transcendent functions.

The essence of this book has been devoted to the attempt to answer the first question, and it is thus not necessary to come back to it in detail here. The problem is of course not new: ever since there have existed theories devoted to fiction, we have never ceased asking if fiction could or could not have a cognitive significance. I hope to have succeeded in convincing the reader that the answer to the question can only be positive, that is, that fictions are effectively cognitive operators. But we have to agree on the meaning of this affirmation. It is not a matter of saying that the *function* of fictions is of a cognitive order. In fact, the question does not concern the usages of fiction — or their transcendent functions — but their intrinsic status: if the fictional device is a cognitive operator, it is because it corresponds to an activity of modeling and because every modeling *is* a cognitive operation.

This is particularly apparent in the domain of canonical fictions, since their relationship to the world is of the nature of representation and since the elaboration of a representation (as a mental process or publicly accessible operation) is by definition a cognitive operation.[4] But the analysis is just as valid for fictional games, since we have seen that *every* ludic imitation implies also an operation of mental modelization. The distinction between status (or mode of operation) and function (or finality) is hardly mysterious, as we can show in taking the example of visual perception. Perception is, statutorily, a cognitive operator, since it gives us access to the reality in which we live and since it transmits to us information on this reality. But, according to the contexts and the concerned objects, the functions that visual experience can fulfill in our life are very diverse. Their scale goes from the most detached scientific curiosity to the signal of most interested appetency through an indefinite number of intermediate functions, including the aesthetic function. The comparison between the two situations has not as its aim to suggest that the fictional devices have the same functional amplitude as visual perception but only that, in their case also, one must distinguish between the type of relation to the world that concerns them and the question of the transcendent functions that they are able to fulfill.

By "transcendent functions" I mean the whole of the relations that fictions are susceptible to entertaining with our other modes of being, or the whole of the manners in which they can interact with our "real" life. The question is thus that of the usages that we can make of fictional modeling, whether it is a matter of games or works of mimetic art. (Clearly, I do not want to say by this that the usages of the two types of fictional activity are the same but only that in the two cases it is necessary to distinguish between the mode of intrinsic operation and the usages.) The number of transcendent functions that fiction can fulfill is no doubt indefinite, and to approach it seriously would take another work. This holds for the collective functions of fiction, which can only be studied through circumstantiated empirical studies, as much as for the individual functions and, of course, the multiple interactions between these two functional levels.[5] I will limit myself to saying in a few words what seems to me to be the principal function of fiction on the individual plane and, more precisely, in the frame of the psychological development of the individual — a problem that has the advantage of not diverting us too much from the genetic perspective that I have favored here. In the main I would like to draw attention to the fact that one is not able to reduce the function of fiction — even if it is a matter of simple daydreams — to that of a compensation, of a corrective of reality, or of a propulsive discharge of a cathartic order. It seems to me in fact that such an approach misjudges the importance of fiction in the development of the child quite as much as in the life of the adult.

Freud has been the most influential defender of the thesis according to which the imaginative activity is (probably) born as compensatory activity. The ultimate origin of fictions would be more precisely in the fact that the baby, not enduring the absence of immediate satisfaction, would hallucinate the image of the gratifying object (the mother's breast). At the sequence of development this hallucinated image would become the source of a partial pulsational satisfaction. The little child would thus learn, for one thing, to postpone the true satisfaction of its urges and, for another, to give imaginary solutions to conflicts that cannot be resolved in reality. According to this conception, fiction thus fulfills a function of satisfaction of desires, the specific manner in which it fulfills it — namely, by an imaginative transposition — permitting the child to master conflicting and anguishing situations. The hypothesis no doubt enlightens one of the sources of fictional activity, just as it draws attention to one of the functions of affective order that it is capable of fulfilling not only in children but also in adults. There are without contest situations where fictions fulfill a compensatory function with respect to pressures of a disagreeable reality, and one of the merits of Freud is to have shown that this function is far from despicable. Equally, it happens to us to use fictional devices to exteriorize destructive or aggressive pulsions that the constraints of social life keep us from expressing "in reality" except to accept paying the price for them in that same reality. But like all monocausal theories, the explanation of fiction in terms of pulsional discharge elevates to origin and unique function what is probably but one causal element among others.

In a more specific manner, it is doubtful that the Freudian variant of the cathartic theory, that is, the thesis according to which the role of fiction would be to furnish us with the occasion for pulsional discharges that otherwise would have to be repressed, truly realizes the major function of fiction in the balance of our affects. It has been shown that when children are placed in a real situation that causes them to become aggressive and then afterward they are exposed to a fictional representation of aggressive behavior, all of the "guinea pigs" are far from reacting in the same manner to this mimetic stimulus. In reality the children demonstrate two opposite reactions: the children with little imagination (according to the criteria of diverse projective tests, notably, the Rorschach) react with an increase in aggressivity and have a tendency to proceed to action. The reason for this is that they know how to live the situations that they meet only at the behavioral level; that is, they are incapable of transposing them to an imaginative level. Inversely, imaginative children, that is, those who in normal life have a significant tendency to devote themselves to games of feint, to daydreams, to role-playing, and so on, demonstrate a drop in the level of aggressive exteriorization and a diminishment of the tendency to proceed to action.[6] In the first group the risk of training (here, the risk of passage to an act aroused by the representation of a violent action), of which Plato makes such a case, is not proportional to the effect of immersion or to the time a child spends devoting himself to imaginative activities: the experiences in question suggest that, very much to the contrary, it is *inversely* proportional to the development of the imaginative capacity. The result of the experiences is not more in agreement with the thesis of catharsis.

If the intrinsic effect of fiction were cathartic in nature, if it allowed us to "purge" ourselves of our passions, then the exposition to situations of imaginative aggressivity would result in a drop of aggressivity with *all* children. The fact that this is not the case and that with the children whose fictional competence is deficient we witness instead a passage to action seems to show that the principal effect of the imaginary competence on our affective balance does not reside in a discharge of aggressivity (or of any other pulsion) but holds to the fact that it allows us to pass from the treatment of a real situation, characterized by a great tension, to the posture of fictional immersion, which *in itself* is characterized by a lowering of psychological tension: it neutralizes in effect the direct reactional loops between the individual and reality and at the same time liberates him (momentarily) from the necessity of an adaptation in real time to the counterreactions of "reality" that are dissociable from every real interaction and, more particularly, from all affective expression. Attention and imaginative self-stimulation, whatever their content, allow the individual to put in a state of wakefulness the whole of the mechanisms of alertness that would be activated if, instead of elaborating fictional representations, he found himself confronted with the exogenous representations that they mime and if, instead of producing its affects in the mode of the ludic "as if," it exteriorized them effectively.[7] The problem of children who react by a process to action resides precisely in the fact that they have difficulties acceding to the state of fictional immersion and thus to the "as if," which seems to indicate that they have badly negotiated the developmental change resulting in the sedentarization of mental self-stimulations and the institution of the relation of shared ludic feint.[8] At the same time, the violent fictional representations that one proposes to them cannot play with them the same role that they play with the other children: instead of giving space to an imaginary recycling of aggression, they are directly reinjected in reactive loops.

It seems thus that what matters for the role of fictional devices in the affective psychic economy is not so much the content of the imaginary representation as the fact itself of a passage from a real context to a fictional context. One of the principal functions of fiction on the affective plane would thus be the fact that it allows us to reorganize the fantasmatic affections on a ludic terrain, to produce them, which gives us the possibility of experiencing them without being submerged by them. The effect of this fictional reelaboration is not meant to be that of a purge but rather that of a partial disidentification.[9] As François Flahault notes in relation to the fictional representation of "badness," from the moment where it is in a space of games that we assume our affects, we can appropriate them "as semblance": "We do not any more identify ourselves for good (i.e., without knowing it) with our grand limitations. We continue to be liked by it, but with the distance and disidentification that are introduced by the consciousness that fiction and game are not reality."[10] Regarding the identificatory adhesion to our own affects, which is one of the most constant traits of our mode of existence outside of fiction, the fictional immersion is thus, paradoxically, the place of a disidentification. This shows, one more time, to what point the interpretation of fictional immersion in terms of identification is reductive.

But the affective disidentification is only a particular form of a more general process, that is, of the order of a distantiation. Every fiction is the place of a distantiation caused by the process of fictional immersion. We have seen that one of its characteristic traits resides in the fact that it is a matter of a split mental state: it detaches us from ourselves, or, rather, it detaches us from our own proper representations, in that it produces them according to the mode of the "as if," thus introducing a distance from ourselves to ourselves. The affects are only one of the domains where this dynamic manifests itself: it applies quite as much to perceptions and memories. The same way, the fictional retreatment of the affects is only a particular form of recycling of representations that is the basis of fictional invention as such and that concerns perceptions and memories at least as much as affects.[11] This rejoins a more general fact noted at the time of the analysis of the ontogenesis of fictional competence, namely, that the institution of the territory of fiction facilitates the elaboration of a consistent membrane between the subjective and the objective world and that it thus plays an important role in this originary distantiation, which gives birth conjointly to the "self" and to "reality." In fact, in constructing imaginary worlds, the child discovers that the representations that he experiences divide themselves in two distinct classes; there is, on one side, the endogenous mental contents that are independent of his volitional acts and, on the other side, the representations of exogenous origin that impose themselves on him.

The mental activity by mimetic self-stimulation acts in some way in the manner of a chemical revealer; in this case the precipitate of the mimetic self-stimulation is none other than the whole of the representations of which the efficient cause is outside the conscious activity itself. In other words, these representations that impose themselves on the child are not only perceptions but also, to varying degrees, representations induced by affects, memories, or dreams. These last three types of mental contents, though of internal origin, are in fact exogenous if one considers them from the point of view of conscious activity, since it is a matter of representations undergone by consciousness. In that sense they resemble perceptions more than representations constructed by conscious self-stimulation. This is obvious where the dream is concerned, but it applies also, though to a lesser degree, to the mental contents induced by affective stimuli and memories: the irrepressible character of affective constellations and the fixity of memories make these two types of representations not really "ours" in the sense that we are susceptible to master them. This signifies that the more the little child exercises himself in constructing groups of representations that mime, in recycling them fictionally, exogenous representations (i.e., representations causally irreducible to their conscious manifestation), the more the part of the stimuli that later he will learn to call "reality" (the one of affects and memories included) crystallizes itself *in contrast* into an independent and autonomous universe — a universe that "is what it is" and that has the means of making him know it when he tries to see it other than what it is. This importance of imaginative activities for the development of the sense of realities has been strongly underlined by Singer: the delimitation of reality itself in young children may in part depend upon their capacity to engage themselves in make-believe play. "There is even the likelihood that fantasy as part of play situation helps the child establish the difference between what is direct sensory material and material from long-term memory. There are various suggestions in the research literature that persons more experienced in daydreaming can distinguish more effectively between their own illusions and actual externally derived sensory events."[12]

The forms that fiction takes in adult life never lose their bonds with that developmental function that was theirs during the first years of our life. In that sense the arts of fiction and thus also the mimetic arts, insofar as they are arts of fiction, are the place of a self-selection by the human species of the neotenic characteristics of its affective cognitive profile. Doing this, fiction gives us the possibility to continue to enrich, to remodel, to readapt all along our existence the original cognitive and affective base thanks to which we have acceded to person identity and to our being-in-the-world. According to a pious legend (philosophic, alas), the development of the human being would lead him from the original confusion of sentiments and affects toward the state of rational subject. Fiction, by its very existence, is evidence that all our life we remain indebted to a relation to the world—to existence, to use a somewhat solemn term—much more complex, diversified, and, all things considered, precarious. But it does more than witness this fact: it is one of the privileged places where this relation does not cease to be renegotiated, repaired, readapted, reequilibrated—in a permanent mental makeshift to which only our death will put an end.

All this fiction is able to do, and many another thing still—with one condition, however: it must please. This signifies that, whatever are its possible functions, it would only be able to fulfill them if it succeeds, first, in pleasing us *as fiction*. Briefly, to fulfill a transcendental function whatever it may be, fiction must first directly fulfill its immanent function. By "immanent function" of fiction I understand the autotelic function fulfilled by the fictional *experience*, that is, by our mimetic immersion in a fictional universe. My hypothesis is that fiction has only a single immanent function and that this function is of an aesthetic order. If this is the case, the question of knowing of what type is the pleasure provoked by mimesis has found its answer: it is a matter of aesthetic satisfaction.

Several types of arguments speak in favor of this hypothesis. There are, first, arguments of fact. As far as we know, in all cultures, from the moment an art functions as a fictional device, its social usage concerns what we call the aesthetic relation. This clearly does not signify that only fictional practices can have a "constituent" aesthetic function or, of course, that the arts of mimetic representation can have an aesthetic function only inasmuch as they are utilized as fictional devices. On the other hand, I think that we can maintain without a great risk to be mistaken that from the moment that a form of art or a representational support is utilized according to the fictional modality, it is always linked to an aesthetic aim. The question is not to know if all cultures that have developed fictional arts possess a specific category to think the aesthetic aim but if the social and individual usages of works recognized as fictional are the same as those we analyze with the help of the category *aesthetic relation*. We must ask ourselves questions: In what context are these works created and consumed? Is the decision to interest oneself in them or not left to the discretion of each individual, or does it correspond to a social constraint? Are the modalities according to which we relate to them free, or are they prescribed? It seems to me that if we asked these questions (and others of the same type), we would effectively discover that the immanent function of fictional works is aesthetic in nature—if we want to admit that there is aesthetic behavior as soon as we engage ourselves in a cognitive relation with things and that this relation is regulated by the degree of satisfaction (or displeasure) immanent to this relation.[13]

In the course of the phenomenological description of mimetic immersion, it appeared that it is a homeostatic process, that is, a process that regulates itself with the help of retroactive loops. I had notably made the remark that in imaginative self-stimulation the fictional immersion nourishes itself of the expectations that it creates for itself, that in the collective fictional games it maintains itself through the effect of upsurge of the dynamic of turns of role or of words, and that in a situation of reception it is renewed by the tension between the always incomplete character of the imaginative reactivation and the (supposed) completeness of the fictional universe proposed.[14] What was missing in this description was the factor susceptible of regulating this homeostasis and thus susceptible of deciding the renewal or, possibly, the interruption of the activity of immersion. If the immanent function of fictional immersion is of an aesthetic order, then the searched-for regulator is nothing but the degree of (dis)satisfaction immanent to the reactivation of mimetic modeling and thus the (dis)pleasure induced by aesthetic attention.

Another argument in favor of the aesthetic hypothesis results from the analysis itself of the fictional device and, more precisely, from the analysis of the pragmatic frame thanks to which it is instituted *as* a fictional device. This frame delimits a ludic space, and this as well at the level of imaginative self-stimulations as at the level of public fictional devices. The activity that invests this ludic space, however, is of a representative nature. Since fictions are representations (or in any case — if we take into account fictional games — always imply representations). A fiction is thus a game with representations or a ludic usage of representational activity. Now, the ludic activation of representational faculties corresponds to the definition itself of aesthetic relation. Kant considered that this was the most decisive trait of the aesthetic functioning of the "faculties of knowing." In taking the Kantian conception as vital lead, we can show that the parallelism is very profound. Thus, according to this conception, the aesthetic relation is more specifically a free game between imagination and understanding. The imagination, in the sense that Kant gives to that term, is the faculty of schematization (e.g., he says that imagination treats nature as a schema for Ideas), that is, in fact, what we called here the faculty of mental modeling. On the other hand, contrary to perception, imagination has not as a condition of satisfaction the effective presence of its object; it "is a faculty to intuit even without the presence of the object."[15] Or, to take up again the terms of Heidegger reading Kant, "The imagination can . . . be named, in two characteristic meanings, a forming faculty. Inasmuch as it is a faculty of intuition, it is formational since it procures (forms) an image (a view). Inasmuch as it is a faculty not ordered to the presence of an object of intuition, it achieves itself, that is to say creates and forms, the images."[16]

It must also be specified that among the different modalities of the faculty of imagination Kant distinguishes, there is the "poietic imagination" (*dichtende Einbildungskraft*). Now, the definition of the latter rejoins in fact the definition of fiction and more precisely of the imaginative self-stimulation: "The faculty of poietic imagination institutes [*stiftet*] a sort of relation to ourselves; although it is only a matter of appearances of internal meaning, they are formed in analogy with those of external meaning."[17] Briefly, under the form of poietic imagination, the Kantian imagination is a faculty of "fictionalization." As for understanding, we know that according to Kant it concerns the faculty of categorization. Now one of the most fundamental activities of categorization operated by understanding is the distinction between "the possibility and reality of things," that is, the distinction between what is simply thought and that to which a reality corresponds. Understanding is thus, among other things, the faculty that is responsible for the modeling of our representations, according to the type of objectivity (real object, simple possibility) that is posed by them. More concretely, understanding can, in the absence of all sensible intuition, pose the objects according to the simple modality of the possible, that is, as the "position of a thing relative to our concept," "since we can always think something, even if it does not exist."[18] In other words, understanding is, among other things, the place where the pragmatic distinction between what is posed as real and what is simply posed as possible institutes itself.

If we now admit, as Kant does, that the activities of schematization (which concerns imagination) and conceptual determination (which concerns understanding) are inseparable (since, still according to Kant, there exists no intellectual intuition), we see that the simple *game* of imagination and understanding according to their internal principles is capable of posing a universe that certainly exists only "relative to our concept" but that can nonetheless be schematized and thought. It is true that the modality of fictionality is not superposable to that of the possible and that the Kantian conception makes no room for ludic feint.[19] Still, what remains is that the idea of a representation constrained not by the causal laws that rule perceptive representation but by the constitutive conditions of our representative faculties limits conjointly the specificity of fictional modeling and that of aesthetic relation. There is thus effectively a very profound homology between the functioning of fictional devices and the type of mental activity that characterizes the aesthetic relation.

What are the relations between the aesthetic relation and the (possible) transcendental functions fulfilled by fictions? It seems to me that from the moment we admit that the aesthetic relation is the immanent function of fiction, that is, that it is constituent of fictional immersion such as it is, it appears that it is compatible with any transcendental function. I will take the example of the function of entertainment, since we often reproach fiction—at least its commonest forms—for being only entertainment.

The conception of entertainment that is the ground of this reproach is in general the Pascalian one of an occupation that turns us away from what should really occupy us (death, salvation). Obviously, nothing prohibits us from taking the term in the banal and less devaluing sense of relaxation, of pleasure, of hobby, and so on. But it does not matter, since the notion will serve me only as an example of a function susceptible of being, in certain contexts and for certain persons, the transcendent issue of the aesthetic function. Who has not said one day a phrase of the kind "I want (or I need) to amuse myself a little. Let's go see a movie!"? What is at stake in such sentences is not the immanent function of fictional immersion itself but the transcendent function that the receiver accords to this immersion and thus to aesthetic attention. The same way, the fact that I read a novel in order to entertain myself does not signify that my reading does not concern aesthetic attention but rather that I devote myself to the aesthetic relation *in order to* entertain myself. This at least is the manner in which I interpret the distinction that Gérard Genette establishes between the *function* of entertainment and its aesthetic *aim*.[20] If it is a matter of a distinction rather than an opposition, it is because the two facts concern two different levels: on one side, the type of activity aimed at by a work (in this case an attitude of aesthetic attention), on the other, the transcendent function (possibly) accorded by the receiver of this activity. To say it differently, the aesthetic attention accorded to a work of fiction is one of the multiple activities to which we sometimes happen to surrender *in order* to entertain ourselves. This does not mean to say that this *is* the function of fictional works or that this *is* the function of aesthetic activity but simply that it can happen that we plunge into a work of fiction, thus that we devote ourselves to an activity of the aesthetic type, because we want to entertain ourselves.

The distinction is also pertinent when we interrogate ourselves about the creation of works of fiction. A creator of fictions can very well want his fiction to fulfill a *function* of entertainment—maybe because he thinks (rightly or wrongly) that most people who are interested in fictions do it only and always to entertain themselves. But even if his only aim is that his work fulfill this function, he has nevertheless every interest in conceiving of it as an aesthetic aim, since for the receiver it is the aesthetic relation he entertains with fiction in the frame of the process of fictional immersion that will be the condition of satisfaction of the function of entertainment. Steven Spielberg wanted no doubt for the public to be amused while watching *Jurassic Park*, but still it was necessary that the public find pleasure in *looking at* the film, that is, in reactivating mimetically the fictional universe. Thus, whether it is a matter of the creation of fictions or their reception, a work can fulfill the function of entertainment in a satisfying manner only if it causes a satisfying aesthetic relationship. And what applies to the function of entertainment applies to any other transcendent function: a work of fiction can fulfill in a satisfying manner any transcendent function only if it pleases from the point of view of fictional immersion, that is, from the point of view of the specific form of aesthetic attention that is constituent of the functioning of fictional devices.

There remains to know if this description, if it applies to canonical fictions, fictional works, can also be extended to fictional games. It seems to me that the answer is affirmative: to the extent that every fictional game implies a modelization, it includes also a representational component; this representational component, this fictional universe lived on the mode of mimetic immersion, is regulated by the index of (dis)satisfaction that is inherent to its deployment itself; now a representational activity that is regulated in this fashion *is* an aesthetic activity. The fantasy negotiations of which I have spoken several times and that play such a big role in the interactive fictions of children have precisely for an aim to adapt continuously the fictional universe created ludically to the degree of (dis)satisfaction that it induces, hence their often repairing function. In reorienting the scenario, in completing the fictional furnishing of the universe, and so on, they aim to reestablish a degree of inherent satisfaction sufficient for the participants to be able to "continue the game." Of course, to say that the ludic fictional activity always includes an aesthetic component does not signify that it should be the only criterion that determines the renewal or the abandonment of the game. In the same way it is not necessary for it to constitute the motivation or the function of it: simply from the moment that there is mimetic immersion in a fictional universe there is aesthetic attention, since what counts is the specific aspectual coherence of that universe. It is not necessary to add that nothing in all this implies in any way that fictional games are works of art: the aesthetic relation defines a certain type of connection to objects that can themselves have diverse statuses.

There remains the case of digital fictions, of which I said that they combine ludic traits with typical traits of fictional works. They are evidently linked to the role-playing and more particularly to the fictional games of children. But whereas in the role-playing of children the fictional scripts are negotiated in real time by the players, in digital fictions they are fixed upstream, even if the structure has multiple choices and not, as in the theater, for example, an imposed plot. We have thus (whatever we think of their value, since it is a matter of fictional universes proposed to the appreciation of the public. But the newness of digital works is that the receiver is at the same time player (actor) and spectator: he thus adopts simultaneously a posture of ludic action and a posture of aesthetic attention; he contemplates and plays at the same time. Still, this manner of describing what happens introduces an artificial separation between the two aspects: in fact, the ludic activity, to the degree that it operates according to the mode of the "as if" in a fictional universe that gives itself jointly to discover and to transform, is itself aesthetically invested. That which concerns the relation of (dis)pleasure is not simply an attention (perceptive or other) but a simulated interactive dynamic, that is, accessible only inasmuch as it is acted fictionally, thus inasmuch as it is mediatized by fictional *representations*. It is the (subjective) quality of this dynamic, indissociably acting and attentional, that becomes the real object of a global appreciation of which the aesthetic appreciation is constitutively a part (from the fact that the acted universe is valid only inasmuch as it is a simulated — and thus appreciated — universe at the level of our mental representations). Certainly, one could retort that most of the digital fictions now in circulation do not draw profit from this possibility, even if it is inscribed in the fictional device that they put to work. For many readers this description risks thus being a reality that for the moment stays largely virtual. Maybe. But what distinguishes the virtual from the fictional is precisely that it can become actual. Which means — and this permits me to come full circle — that all hopes are permitted for Lara Croft.

Notes

INTRODUCTION

1. Cadoz, *Les réalités virtuelles*, 72.

2. See Lévy, *Qu'est-ce que le virtuel?* 13 ff.

3. Lévy, *Qu'est-ce que le virtuel?* 69, takes the birth of procedures of virtualization back to the birth of language; in fact, language is only the most complex and the latest of the systems of representation developed in the course of the evolution of species. Even the most primitive representational system already presupposes a modelization (and thus a virtualization) of the external world.

4. Aristotle *Poetics* 15.30, 242. Translator's note: the rest of this note has been left out; it deals with the 1980 translation into French of this passage by Roselyne Dupont-Roc and Jean Lallot.

5. Literature devoted to the question of the status of literary fiction is very abundant, but the most convincing approach remains that of Searle, *Sens et expression*, such as it is developed and amended by Genette, "Les actes de fiction." There are clearly numerous philosophical analyses devoted to fiction, notably, the texts of Bentham and the classical book of Vaihinger, *Die Philosophie des Als ob*. But generally (this is the case of the two cited authors), they bear on fiction as philosophical concept much more than on fiction as human conduct. Other works (e.g., Iser, *Das Fiktive und das Imaginäre*) announce general analyses of fiction but remain centered in literary fiction. A notable exception is the important work by Walton, *Mimesis as Make-Believe*.

1. WHO IS AFRAID OF IMITATION?

1. Aymé, "Le loup."

2. A false response to the question consists in saying that computer language distinguishes itself from other media of information because it is of a digital nature. This could make us believe that the other vehicles of information are on an analogic nature and that the binary codage is implied by the passage from the analogical to the digital. (In the present context "analogical" does not mean "mimetic": an analogical signal is a continuous signal, whereas a digital signal is discontinuous.) But the binary computer code is evidently *not* the only digi-

tal code that humans have developed. Natural languages, for instance, are also systems of digital signs, at least if the Saussurean hypothesis is correct, that is, if their ultimate elements, whether on the phonetic, the syntactic, or the semantic level, rest on the principle of differential opposition. The example of languages also shows that one must not confuse "digital" and "binary"; a digital system is not necessarily based on a binary opposition; that is, the ultimate elements are not necessarily two in number.

3. The Wittgensteinian thesis is often presented as evidence, but it is far from evident, among other things because it makes little of informations treated at a preattentional level that nonetheless form a part of my world, even if they are cognitively silent.

4. This *skiagraphia* is explicitly implicated by Plato in the *Republic* 10.602d, where he puts it in the same bag as the art of the charlatan (*goteia*) and other applications of magic (*thaumatopoia*).

5. Plato *Republic* 3.

6. Plato *Republic* 3.

7. Plato *Republic* 2. The notion of remedy (*pharmakon*) enters into at least two very different contexts: in the passage just cited it is the *lie* that is a remedy; elsewhere it is said that it is important to oppose a remedy to fiction as it acts in the manner of contagion. See Derrida, "La pharmacie de Platon," 71–198, for an overall analysis of the complex and ambivalent lexicological field (*pharmakon* is poison as much as remedy; the term designates elsewhere the color, the makeup, the perfume, and the herb) of this notion and its related terms (e.g., *pharmakos*, which designates the wizard but also the scapegoat). The texts of Plato don't utilize the totality of this semantic field, so that the value of a part of the analysis proposed by Derrida, "La pharmacie de Platon," depends on the validity of what it presupposes (explicitly assumed on 148–49): given that language is a "system," the terms present in a given discourse refer back to "all the other words of the lexical system," which means that there exist in any text "forces of hidden attraction linking a present word to an absent word," and these forces can only "weigh on the writing and on the reading of this text" (Derrida, "La pharmacie de Platon," 149).

8. Bertrand Tavernier remarks that instead of asking always the same question of the possible effect of training of violence represented fictionally (*A Clockwork Orange* by Stanley Kubrick, *Natural Born Killers* by Oliver Stone, or *Fresh Bait* by Tavernier himself), we would first have to ask the question of the capacity of training of reality itself and, by extension, of the referential representation of

this reality, for example, in the televised newspaper. He adds, summing up the situation perfectly (but it is a matter of a situation that has always been the one of fiction in our culture), "We could say that it is only creation, fiction, which becomes the generator of problems" (*Libération*, October 9, 1997, 37).

9. Augustine *De utilitate credendi*, cited by Veyne, *Les Grecs*, 147n44.

10. Millar insists on this autonomy of ludic feint in noting: "The feint of games of make-believe is not a disguise for another thing, nor an activity that aims to induce error: it is a matter of a thought in action . . . that uses real objects as accessories" (*The Psychology of Play*, 256).

11. On this object see 296–97.

12. Plato *Republic* 3.

13. Plato *Ion*, notably 532c–533c, 542.

14. Plato *Republic* 10.605c–d. A few lines farther on Plato notes that such a behavior is a behavior of women rather than of men. This idea (derogatory, of course) of a link between the effect of imaginary fictional immersion and feminine "nature" will be used many times in the course of the history of the fictional genres, notably, in the polemics against novelistic literature.

15. Plato *Republic* 10.605.

16. See Plato *Republic* 10.604e–605e. We are not far from the condemnation of "Hollywood" cinema, which is not astonishing if it is true that Greek theater is not an art of the elite but truly a "popular" art.

17. I take this distinction from Lacoue-Labarthe, *L'imitation des modernes*, 30. Though it is not formulated in these terms by Plato, it corresponds well with the relationship of *mimēsis* and *alētheia* — imitation and truth — in view of their relationship to Ideas.

18. This fact has been stressed by numerous authors, notably, Deleuze, *Logique du sens*; Derrida, "La pharmacie de Platon"; Lacoue-Labarthe, *L'imitation des modernes*; and, quite recently, Château, *L'héritage de l'art*.

19. Plato *Sophist* 266c.

20. See Plato *Sophist* 10.598d. In Plato's *Ion* the conclusive verdict is the same, applied not to painting but to the art of the rhapsode.

21. Plato *Sophist* 10.605.

22. See Plato *Republic* 10.598d.

23. I have some reluctance to use this notion, which seems to me to be for a nonnegotiable part a knowledgeable artifact. See Détienne, *L'invention de la mythologie*, 87–189 for the Greek genesis of the notion of *myth* as a category used to put at a distance all belief resisting analytical or empirical reduction.

Détienne also shows to what point the actual use of the notion by anthropology remains within the Greek model (190–242). For a discussion of the relation between myth and fiction see 124–28.

24. "Plasmata ton proteron," Xenophanis fragment 1, 22, in Diels and Kranz, *Die Fragmente der Vorsokratiker*, 1:128. See also Détienne, *L'invention de la mythologie*, 125.

25. On the subject of this distinction between an attentional and an intentional definition of art, which seems to me to apply beautifully to this case, see Genette, *Palimpsests*, 267.

26. According to Fusillo (1989), the first Greek novel of which we have traces, *Ninos and Semiramis*, would have originated in the second or first century BC (15n4).

27. One will find these two texts in Leiris (1996), which regroups the whole of his texts devoted to Africa.

28. See on this subject the introduction by Jean Jamin (esp. 36–48) and the presentation by Jacques Mercier (891–911) in Leiris (1996) of the study on the rites of possession — two excellent texts that replace the problematic in the context of the work of Leiris by studying its relations with the conceptions of Bataille as well as with Sartrean philosophy (in what concerns the question of bad faith).

29. Leiris (1996, 1049).

30. For this question see Leiris (1996, 1054).

31. See Leiris for a discussion of the question of placing fictional competence.

32. Aristotle *Poetics* 235.

33. See 165–66 for this second type of possibility.

2. MIMESIS

1. See, for example, the excellent lexicological study by Bouverot, "Un simulacre peut en dissimuler un autre," devoted to the term *simulacre*.

2. For these examples and others see Caillois, *Le mythe et l'homme*, 109–16, 133–36, or Baudonnière, *Le mimétisme*, 13–18.

3. For a summary of the most important experiments and for a selective bibliography see Eibl-Eibesfelt, *Die Biologie des menschlichen Verhaltens*, 88–92.

4. Byrne and Russon, "Learning by Imitation," 667–84.

5. Baudonnière, *Le mimétisme*, 45–47.

6. Sometimes the observation of simple material traces (e.g., pieces of coconut) of a past activity suffices to provoke an activity of the same type in the animal that perceives these indices. See Byrne and Russon, "Learning by Imitation," 668.

7. As far as I can judge, the two expressions refer to the same type of learning. The first puts forward the mode of acquisition (by observation and not by rational calculation or by trial and error), whereas the second draws attention to the fact that the mimemes are cognitive units of a social rather than an individual nature.

8. See Byrne and Russon, "Learning by Imitation," 667–84.

9. Mehler and Dupoux, *Naître humain*. See also Pinker, *L'instinct du langage*, notably 416–20.

10. Baudonnière, *Le mimétisme*, 52–54.

11. Miller and Dollard, *Social Learning and Imitation*, 195.

12. Ricoeur, *Temps et récit*, 1:90–91, maintains that the passage from the sphere of the action to that of the telling of this action is equivalent to the passage of a paradigmatic to a syntagmatic order, that of the putting into plot of the action. But in reality the hierarchical structure of actions is that of a sequential organization; that is, it always already concerns the "syntagmatic" order. We can understand Ricoeur's position only if we take into account his philosophical presuppositions. According to the program of hermeneutics, the world of life is in fact always in sufferance of its own comprehension and thus of an interpretive activity. In the field of action it is the tale that is meant to bring this interpretation: the tale alone gives meaning to action, and this by way of a plotting of events. But the conclusion holds only to the degree one dispossesses the intentional action of its own structurations to reduce it to pure events waiting for an intelligibility that would only be able to come to it from elsewhere. See on this subject Bremond, "Le rôle, l'intrigue et le récit."

13. Byrne and Russon, "Learning by Imitation," 671.

14. Byrne and Russon, "Learning by Imitation," 677.

15. On the subject of this standardization see Boyd and Richerson, "An Evolutionary Model."

16. Byrne and Russon, "Learning by Imitation," 675.

17. The term *model* is itself ambiguous, since it is used at the same time to denote what is imitated (as in the expression "a model of writing") and the result of imitation (as in the expression "a reduced model"). But this duality is precisely that of the cognitive mimeme: it is the result of an activity of imitation, but at the same time, from the functional point of view, it has itself the status of a virtual model that will be transposed into the real.

18. Edelman, *Biologie de la conscience*, 293.

19. See Cadoz, *Les réalités virtuelles*, 95–98.

20. The meaning given to the notion of *modeling* in mathematics is without a doubt not even reducible to the one of *simulation*. But this question surpasses my competences and, fortunately, my subject.

21. I beg the reader curious to know the (fascinating) facts that hide behind these passably opaque technical terms to consult Le Masson et al., "Dialogues entre neurones biologiques et artificiels," from which I extracted them.

22. For the analysis see Cadoz, *Les réalités virtuelles*, 95–98; the quote is on 96.

23. Cadoz, *Les réalités virtuelles*, 97. The usage of the term *fictive* does not seem to me a very happy one to describe the projective simulation (or certainly the cognitive canonical simulation).

24. It is of course a matter of an archclassical philosophical theme. For a recent formulation see, for example, Searle, *L'intentionnalité*, 142–71.

25. See Dennett, *Consciousness Explained*, 171–226.

26. See Block, "On a Confusion," for a discussion of the necessity of distinguishing between two activities of recognition: (1) the discovery of a formal resemblance between two entities and (2) the fact of recognizing an individual as being the same from one perceptive experience to the next.

27. Quine, *Ontological Relativity*, 121.

28. To be honest, I must admit that this example is fabricated and that I don't even know if the salmon and the shark frequent the same maritime regions. But it would be easy to find other examples, no doubt more convincing.

29. Quine, *Ontological Relativity*, 144.

30. Quine, *Ontological Relativity*, 140. Quine's hypothesis is strengthened by recent works approaching the question of mental representation in the frame of cognitive sciences. Thus, Edelman, "Representation," criticizes the analogical theory of knowledge according to which our representations would resemble objects represented, a theory that postulates a "first-order isomorphism" between representation and what is represented. He proposes to replace it with the hypothesis of a "second-order isomorphism," according to which there would be a correspondence between distant and close similarities, in the sense where the coefficients of similarity of distant stimuli (thus of objects) would be represented in the form of corresponding coefficients of similarity of the projections of these stimuli on a neuronal map, that is, in the close space constructed from the stimuli.

31. Quine, *Ontological Relativity*, 126.

32. Quine, *Ontological Relativity*, 134.

33. Baudonnière, *Le mimétisme*, distinguishes between mimetism and imitation, reserving this last term for behaviors that are intentional and selective. The second criterion does not seem pertinent to me for two reasons. For one thing, mimetisms — including the facts of phenotypical *mimicry* — are themselves selective, or at least become selective, since from the fact of the pressure of natural selection alone the efficacious mimemes can reproduce themselves. On the other hand, in what concerns the supposedly nonselective mimetisms, such as the neonatal reflexes that we met with already, their absence of selectivity makes us precisely doubt their mimetic character.

34. The functional mimetic causality is an extremely complex process. For instance, in what sense can one say that the design decorating the wings of a butterfly *imitates* the eyes of a bird of prey? The eyes of a bird of prey are evidently not the cause of the apparition of a relation of resemblance, which is due to a genetic mutation. On the other hand, the higher rate of survival and of reproduction of the mutant butterfly and of its descendants *is* linked causally to the birds of prey. In fact, the natural predators of butterflies avoid those that bear this design *because* they resemble the eyes of birds of prey and they are themselves the natural victims of these birds of prey. In this way what started as a simple relation of resemblance (without causal link between the facts linked by this relation) transforms itself as a result of natural selection into a relation of imitation, since the birds of prey (more precisely, the perceptual gestalt of their eyes) are the (indirect) cause of the progressive increase in the global genetic pool of the genes that encode the design resembling an eye of a bird of prey.

35. The selectivity of the mimetic relation does not oppose itself to the fact that the relation of resemblance is in many cases, and notably in the learning by observation, holistic.

36. See 79–80 and especially Escande, "La calligraphie chinoise," 129–76.

37. On the other hand, if he is a nonheretical Christian, he cannot push the will of imitation of Christ up to a will of identification, since that would lead him to want to become identical with God.

38. Coiffet, *Mondes imaginaires*, 79.

39. See Turing, "Computing Machinery."

40. This fact has also been underlined by Descombes, *La denrée mentale*, 156–68, in the framework of a fascinating discussion devoted to the virtues and limits of Turing's test.

41. Certainly, to the extent that the computer is programmed by a human

being, the functional lure is in the last instance the result of an intentional activity, contrarily to what happens, for example, in the case of phenotypical lures.

42. This point has been strongly underlined by Austin, "Feindre," 222, especially 218, who discusses in a detailed manner the different modalities according to which the fact of feigning to do at the same time excludes that one does but at the same time necessitates that what one does in reality resembles the original "in a characteristic fashion," indeed, implies a partial realization of it.

43. To simplify the situation I treat Aesop here as though he were effectively the real author of the anonymous collection of fables that one traditionally attributes to him, whereas this is no doubt not the case. See on this subject Schaeffer, "Aesopus auctor inventus." For an attempt at a general classification of the different modalities of imitation-reinstantiation in the artistic domain see Château, *L'héritage de l'art*.

44. See also Genette, who, giving as an example "the emphatic art of the actor," remarks that the act of simulation consists most often in "making tons of it" ("Les actes de fiction," 48n2). These exaggerations often have a function of perceptual compensation susceptible of favoring psychological immersion, as in the case of the hyperexpressive mimics of the actors of the silent film. In a more general manner, the usage of hypernormal lures in the domain of fiction explains itself without doubt by their function of triggers for immersion.

45. Genette, *Palimpsestes*, 90.

46. Genette, *Palimpsestes*, 92.

47. Escande, "La calligraphie chinoise," 135, 138, quoting Jiang Ji (eighteenth century).

48. Genette, "Les actes de fiction," 48.

49. Searle, *Sens et expression*, 115.

50. Ricoeur, as he also puts his accent on what is lower down, that is, on the "mimetic activity inasmuch as it produces something" (*Temps et récit*, 1:59), thus on representation, retains however also the relation uphill, that is, the one that links mimesis to what it imitates (this is what he calls "mimesis I"). Unfortunately, his decision to count as a negligible quantity the distinction between the diverse mimetic modes (narrative versus dramatic) forbids him a rigorous definition of "mimesis I."

51. On this last point see 128–29.

52. For an analysis of the effects of the invention of writing on the development of centralized static structures see Good, *Languages of Art*.

53. See Descombes, *La denrée mentale*. I do not share his thesis according to

which spirit must be placed "outside" and not "inside," that is, in the exchanges between persons and not in an internal flux of representations. In my opinion the opposition between mentalism and public usage of signs is a false dilemma. If the human species had not the mental capacity to elaborate, to stock, and to reactivate representations, it could not have developed public signs; in the reverse, if men had not developed systems of public signs, they would be incapable not only of communicating their mental representations but, moreover, of enriching them from one generation to the other and thus making of them a means of specific evolution.

54. I say "in a substantial manner" because there exist genetically fixed semiotic codes with many species (it is enough to think of the dance of bees). On the other hand, as all owners of domestic animals know, the individuals of certain species are altogether capable of inventing elementary signs ad hoc for communication with humans.

55. According to the naturalist perspective that I adopt, it is evident that mental representations themselves are a biological property among others of the human species. Culture does not oppose itself to nature but is itself a fact of biological evolution.

56. This is *not* a criticism of the verificationist ideal. The question of knowing which are the multiple functionalities of representation does not merge with those of the legitimate exigencies, which all representation must accept. Representation *wants itself* to be descriptive or analytical, which is the case with the present work.

57. In effect, the legitimation of fictional worlds by the theory of possible worlds, that is, by modal logic, also aims at "saving" fiction from the point of view of the *logical* definition of representation. Pavel, *Univers de la fiction*, showed that fictional worlds are *irreducible* to possible worlds of the modal logic in such a way that this latter would not be able to assure the operation of rescue that we expect of it. See also 181–82.

58. Millikan, "A Common Structure," 64. In the bibliography of her article we find the references to the experiments of which she only sums up the global result.

59. Danto, *Philosophical Disenfranchisement*, 130–35, is one of the rare present-day philosophers to defend the pertinence of the relation of resemblance. See also Currie, *Image and Mind*, 79–112.

60. Goodman (1990, 40) notes quite correctly that resemblance is not a sufficient condition for representation. But he goes further: refusing the idea itself

of a representation *by* resemblance, he excludes in fact the similarity of the representational relation and sees in it just a (fallacious) criterion of fidelity or correction.

61. For a balanced argument of the pertinence of the notion of analogy in the domain of visual representations see Bellour, *L'entre-images 2*, 10–18.

62. "To resemble" is therefore not here synonymous with "to be the same as" but rather with "looking like." In English the distinction is easier to make [translator's note: than in French]: "to look alike" is not the same thing as "to be alike."

63. In what concerns the problem of the "conditioning" of our sensual organs by the ecological constraints having exercised their pressures on hominization and thus the question of the biological specificity of our "cognitive niche" see, for example, Oeser, "Evolutionäre Wissenschaftstheorie." According to Vollmer, "Mesokosmos und objektive Erkenntnis," 47, this functional character of perception with respect to our particular ecological niche is responsible for its inadequation from the moment that the objects of investigation belong to dimensions of the real situated outside the "mesocosm" (i.e., of a universe notably defined by objectal sizes close to our own organism, by spatial dimensions adapted to our own speed of displacement, etc.) for which our cognitive apparatus has been selected by the biological evolution of our species. The result is our difficulties to "represent," for example, the atomic structure of matter, the macroscopic objects studied by astronomy, the scales of temporality of scientific cosmology without speaking of Einsteinian space-time or of the indeterminate relation between elementary corpuscles.

64. This does not signify that the question of knowing whether our vision of an object is correct or faithful is lacking in meaning, for to answer this question we can refer to other visual acts, to other perceptual modalities, or to other tools of knowledge (including artificial instruments). What makes no sense is to ask ourselves if the mode of visual knowledge as such resembles the object that it gives us to see.

65. In fact, in most situations it is a matter more precisely of mnemonic trace correlated to acts of seeing the object, or of the type of object, in question. This situation is only a particular case of the "isomorphism to the second degree" that, according to Edelman, defines the relation between representation and represented object. The mimetic theory of knowledge proposed by Aristotle and that one still finds in the Wittgenstein of the *Tractatus* rests, on the other hand, on the idea of an "isomorphism to the first degree" (see on this subject note 30 of the present chapter).

66. For a discussion of the intrinsically aspectual character of representation see Searle, *La redécouverte de l'esprit*, 216 ff.

67. Thus, Nelson Goodman notes: "The theory of representation-copy is thus condemned at its origin by its incapacity to specify what is to be copied" (1990, 37). He advances arguments of the same type to refute the idea (prohibited, notably, by Gombrich and by Gibson) according to which the constraints of the pictorial perspective would be isomorphous to those of human vision (39–46). His criticisms, in addition to not distinguishing clearly between "isomorphism of the first degree" and "isomorphism of the second degree," presuppose that the conception of representation by imitation rests on the idea of mathematical isomorphism, that is, on a point-by-point correspondence between two projective spaces, and that it excludes the existence of representational schemas that are culturally specific—which no one has ever sustained.

68. In fact, the functioning of any symbolic system necessitates the intervention of our capacities of categorization by similarity, from the simple fact that we should be capable of reidentifying the same sign through multiple occurrences. It is therefore futile to agitate the pennant of semiotic conventionalism in the hope of getting rid of similarity and its problems.

69. See Millikan, "A Common Structure," for bibliographical indications.

70. See Bandura, *Social Learning Theory*, 12.

71. See Shanks and St. John, "Characteristics," for a study of the modes of nonmediatized learning by rules.

72. The expression is unfortunate, since it seems to exclude the preattentional processes of the cognitive domain. That would be absurd, for, as the example of vision shows, these treatments in fact constitute the first stage of every cognitive process. But since it is a matter of the technical expression devoted to the designation of the facts that interests me here, I prefer to keep it. It is enough to remember that "cognitively not penetrable" means simply "not accessible to a descending cognitive treatment," that is, escaping all influence of a conscious cognitive state.

73. Miller and Dollard, *Social Learning and Imitation*, give innumerable examples of such mimetic learning, which they designate with the term *social learning*.

74. See Bandura, *Social Learning and Personality Development* and *Social Learning Theory*.

75. On the subject of the advantages in terms of natural selection of mimetic transmission on individual acquisition see the fundamental study by Boyd and Richerson, *Culture and the Evolutionary Process*.

76. Dawkins, *Le gène égoïste*, 257–62. The term *meme* is, of course, a contraction of the term *mimeme*.

77. Searle notes that the notion of *meme*, in treating the evolution of ideas on the same mode as the evolution of genes, does not take into account the fact that the explanation of the evolution of ideas through the process of imitation "necessitates the entire apparatus of the human consciousness and intentionality" (*The Mystery of Consciousness*, 105).

78. For a criticism of the phenomenological illusion see Place, "Is Consciousness a Brain Process?" See also 91–92.

79. For these problems see Shanks and St. John, "Characteristics," as well as Pylyshym, "Is Vision Continuous with Cognition?"

80. For an argued defense of the hypothesis of a dissociation between the most fundamental visual processes and the conscious cognitive treatments see Pylyshym, "Is Vision Continuous with Cognition?"

81. See 133–36.

82. Boyd and Richerson, *Culture and the Evolutionary Process*, 49–60.

83. Bandura, *Social Learning Theory*, 38.

84. Flinn and Alexander, "Culture Theory."

85. When the rituals for the preparation for the hunt are not idiosyncrasies but concern behaviors that are socially anchored, their function is very different: one can suppose that every socially sanctioned ritual fulfills functions for every member of the group and thus corresponds to an element of social psychology that is susceptible of playing a causal role in the success of any hunter (of this group). A ritual of which the function is to diminish an anguish shared among the entire group is clearly a part of the behavioral structure that the apprentice must assimilate: if he does not assimilate it, he exposes himself to a situation of anguish that risks endangering his success.

86. Wilson, *Sociobiology*, 141.

87. Darwin, *L'expression des émotions*, 65–66.

88. Thus, when we compare the phenotype of races of domesticated horses to the wild members of the horse family, for instance, the horse of Prjewalski, we discover that the first rests on a selection of traits that are typical for foals: legs excessively elongated, face slender, and so on. See, for example, Budiansky, *The Nature of Horses*.

89. See Wilson, *Sociobiology*, 226 ff.

90. Except in the domain of language learning by immersion, an aptitude that, alas, diminishes strongly after the end of childhood, as every adult learning a foreign language at the same time as his child cannot help experiencing.

3. FICTION

1. *Tauschung*, according to its context, signifies "deceit," "dupe," "mystification," "feint," or "a diversionary maneuver." See "Arbeitsprotokolle des Verfahrens Marbot," in Hildesheimer, *Das Ende der Fiktionen*, 145–46.

2. In what follows I take up again a part of the analyses presented in Schaeffer, "Loup, si on jouait au loup?" See Cohn, "Breaking the Code," reprinted with changes in Cohn, *The Distinction of Fiction*, 79–95, for an excellent analysis of the generic status of *Marbot* conducted in the perspective of a Hamburgerian conception of the fiction.

3. Cohn, "Breaking the Code," 302.

4. In this entire chapter, and so as not to weigh down the text too much, the terms *immersion* and *fictional immersion* designate what rigorously should be called *fictional mimetic immersion*. Although fictional immersion functions on the same mode as generic mimetic immersion, such as it operates, for example, in the frame of learning by imitation, it distinguishes itself, however, in that its potential consequences at the level of beliefs at the motor level, even at the actantial level, are neutralized by the pragmatic frame of shared feint—and this even when fictional immersion *is* actantial (like that of the actor). The difference between the two situations is thus not a difference in the process of immersion itself: it is due to the intervention of an external factor.

5. On the subject of the paratext, which designates the whole of the indices other than intratextual by which the author (or the editor) orients the reading of his text, see Genette, *Seuils*. For the "formal mimesis" see Glowinski, "Sur le roman." For a more detailed analysis of the fourth heading see Schaeffer, "Loup, si on jouait au loup?" and Cohn, "Breaking the Code."

6. "Was sagt Music aus," in Hildesheimer, *Das Ende der Fiktionen*, 59–60, 73.

7. Cohn, "Breaking the Code," 317, underlines also the decisive importance of this generic indication of paratextual in nature. She adds that, on the other hand, for the reader who already knows the real status of the book, the indication *Eine Biographie* ceases to be a subtitle with a pragmatic function and becomes a part of the title that then no longer reads *Marbot. Eine Biographie* but rather *Marbot: Eine Biographie*.

8. On the subject of the logical difference of these two roles of historical proper names see Descombes, *Grammaire d'objets en tous genres*, 251–80.

9. Cohn, "Breaking the Code," insists particularly on this aspect—the refusal of narratorial omniscience—that attests to the fact that the fiction of Hildesheimer opposes at every point the definition of fiction proposed by Hamburger.

10. Cohn, "Breaking the Code," 307.

11. Cohn, "Breaking the Code," 307.

12. On the subject of this notion see Genette (1987).

13. Searle, *Sens et expression*, 115. Austin, "Feindre," sees in the ludic feint a parasitical form of the serious feint, which brings him to dismiss it. This makes his analysis somewhat unilateral, when even the notion of a parasitical usage (which has no negative connotation but designates quite simply a type of intentional structure that can only exist on the basis of another from which it draws profit) would have without a doubt constituted an interesting point of departure for a study of genealogical relations between serious and ludic feint.

14. Riffaterre, *Fictional Truth*, 2, himself insists on this duality when he notes that a fiction always has to combine marks of fictionality with a convention of truth (i.e., signs of plausibility), bringing readers to react to the story as though it were true.

15. For a justification of the use of quotes see p. 27, note 23.

16. This is the reason for which the fact that even theologians sometimes feel themselves obliged to discuss the status of Christian beliefs in terms of "fiction" testifies in an eloquent fashion to the loss of credibility of those beliefs. To fall back on a defense in terms of "fiction" is not liable to arrange things. The approach resembles more a latent suicide. For an example of the tactic see Pannenberg, "Das Irreale des Glaubens."

17. Genette, "Les actes de fiction," 60.

18. The analysis by Goldman and Emmison of the fictional games of Huli children of Papua New Guinea shows that these games attain an intentional complexity that can compete with our most refined fictions; see "Fantasy and Double-Play."

19. Pavel, *Univers de la fiction*, 81.

20. See Goldman and Emmison, "Fantasy and Double-Play," 27–28.

21. See 86–88.

22. Sartre, *L'imaginaire*, 51, like all phenomenologists, has drawn attention to the fact that the representational conscience *as such* defines itself as the aim of an object. But he distinguishes between the significant conscience, which, even as it has an aim, would not be positional (it would become so only by being linked to an act of judgment), and the imaging conscience, which would always be positional, even if it does not assume its object exists. According to him, "to read on a sign 'office of the underchief' is to pose nothing." The sign aims for "a certain nature," but "on that nature, one affirms nothing, one limits oneself to

aiming at it" (51). It seems to me, on the contrary, that for most French speakers such a sign saturates the "nature" with multiple properties, though not the same, according to whether the reader of the sign is the chief, the underchief himself, some subordinate, a client, or a pest (the last two categories coinciding when the administrative magic changes the client into a "user"). The casual theory of signification, defended notably by Millikan in "A Common Structure," seems to me more pertinent than the Sartrean conception that no doubt gives too good a deal to the judicative activity in the referential functioning of language. The idea according to which to represent oneself as something is equivalent to posing it is already found in Frege, when he says that a fictional proper name can be assured of meaning only inasmuch as "it pretends to name" a real being (*Nachgelassene Schriften*, 134, quoted in Bouveresse, "Fait, fiction et diction," 16).

23. The usage of hyphens is a convention of writing proposed by Goodman (1990, 48) to mark the fact that the predicates in which fictional entities intervene are in fact invisible monadic predicates and not "honest predicates with two places." In *An Apology for Poetry* (1580) Philip Sidney had already drawn attention to one of these generic representational constraints that imposes itself on the creator of fictions, in this case, the constraint of singular identification and, notably, the necessity of naming the characters. Comparing the situation to the one of lawyers who invent fictive cases, he notes: "Representing men, they cannot leave them unnamed" (quoted in Enright and Chickera, *English Critical Texts*, 31). It is certainly a matter of a general constraint, that is, it imposes itself on every discourse that makes reference (really or fictionally) to particular men: the simple fact of introducing a singular reference in a sentence implies an act of individual identification (even if it is indefinite) and thus, at least implicitly, an act of nomination. (Insofar as every human being has a name, nomination is virtually present in the act of individual identification, even if the poet stays away from an effective nomination and limits himself to indefinite identifications of the kind "a man.")

24. See 39.

25. Roland Barthes, "En sortant du cinéma," 383–87, notes that the filmic image *is* a lure, which is certainly a hyperbolic thesis. Moreover, he interprets the effects of this lure in the frame of the Lacanian theory of the Imaginary before bringing its functioning closer to that of ideology—which is to make little of the situation of ludic feint. At the other extreme, Walton (*Mimesis as Make-Believe*) and Currie (*Image and Mind*) maintain that the situation of *make-believe* excludes the possibility itself that there are lures. But Currie studies

the problem only in relation to the question of the cinematographic *movement*. His refusal to take into account the eventuality of preattentional lures results essentially from the fact that he wants to demonstrate that the cinematographic movement is real and not illusionary. Whatever the status of the movement, the simple fact that we construct the cinematographic image like a whole of tridimensional precepts implies preattentional lures. In contrast, this does not signify, as Christian Metz, for example, maintains, that the cinematographic device as such is fictional. See 259–62.

26. See 258–70.

27. The existence of a module of treatment of the perception independent of the perceptual attention in itself, long discussed, has been confirmed by multiple recent works, notably, those devoted to the treatment of subliminal images (see, e.g., the report of the works of Stanslas Dehaene et al., conducted in the frame of the unity INSER 334, in [Anonymous], "Images subliminales"). For a general account of the present state of the question and an argument in favor of the cognitive impenetrability of the basic module of visual perception see Pylyshym, "Is Vision Continuous with Cognition?"

28. Metz, *Le signifiant imaginaire*, 124. The other term of the comparison is that of a state of hypnosis, which, by the way, one finds also in Barthes, "En sortant du cinéma," 383–84.

29. I evidently do not want to say that a *work* of fiction can't make of the situation of ludic feint itself a thematic element. This would be an absurd thesis, since this manner of proceeding corresponds to a venerable tradition of fictional literature — whether it is of the ironic romanesque novel in a Diderot or a Thomas Mann, for instance, of the theater in the theater, or the autoreferential "denunciation" of dramatic fiction, for example, with Pirandello, Annouilh, and many others. In a certain manner a self-denouncing fiction does nothing but reflect from within how the double attitude defines the shared ludic feint: mimetic immersion on one side, neutralization of its pragmatic effects on the other. As for the particular pleasure that we take from fictions of this type, it is maybe due to the fact itself of these repeated swingings between lure and conscious neutralization.

30. On the subject of the complex situation of the cinematographic fiction as such see 258–70 and 270–72.

31. See Genette, *Seuils*, notably 82, 86, 88, and 89–97.

32. Stern, "Engagements subjectifs," 32. I would like to thank Raymond Bellour for having drawn my attention to this important article. In what concerns

language see 51–52. For motor functions and especially for the visual perception and notably the distinction between "short" reactional loops, self-regulated and "preattentive," and the "long" systems, responsible for the construction of the conscious representations, see Bonnet, Ghiglione, and Richard, *Traité de psychologie cognitive*, especially 3–6, 17–74, and 160–62.

33. For a presentation of the different theories descended from "classical" psychology (notably Wallon, Piaget, and Janet) see, for example, Ey, *La conscience*, 290–366; for nondogmatic psychoanalytic conceptions see Winnicott, *Jeu et réalité*, 7–39, and Stern, *Le monde interpersonnel*.

34. Singer, *The Child's World of Make-Believe*, 194.

35. This fact makes inoperative every project of foundational pedagogy, like the one presented in Rousseau's *Émile*. In his theory the thesis of the purely sensitive nature of the baby legitimates directly the refusal of the imagination. Starting from the idea that "in the beginning of life, when memory and imagination are still inactive, the child is attentive only to what actually affects his senses," Rousseau concludes that "fantasy . . . is not in nature," and thus we must not accord it anything (*Oeuvres complètes*, 4:284, 290).

36. See 186–88 for a more concrete and thus less esoteric description of the distinction that seems to me central for understanding the specificity of imaginative modelization.

37. For a discussion of problems posed by the notion of self-deception and its relation with the Sartrean notion of "bad faith" see the studies assembled in Ames and Dissanayak, *Self and Deception*.

38. On all these questions see Flahault, "L'artiste créateur," 29–34.

39. See 30–31.

40. Metz, in very stimulating pages devoted to the relation between dream and cinematographic experience, sums up the difference perfectly: "The dreamer does not know that he dreams; the spectator of cinema knows that he is in the cinema" (*Le signifiant imaginaire*, 123).

41. Monique Gessain reports the following account gathered from a Bassari (a people living on the two sides of the frontier between Senegal and the Guinnies): "When endyuw [the soul] travels, you dream: you see what your endyuw sees" (Jouvet and Gessain, *Le grenier des rêves*, 88).

42. See Jouvet, *Le sommeil et le rêve*, 80.

43. Contrary to what Freud supposed, according to whom the dream was the guardian of sleep, it is rather sleep that is the guardian of dream in the sense that it is during the dream phases that access to the external world is most bolted and

that the threshold of waking is highest: from this fact, the system of endogenous self-stimulation functions practically in autarchy, a situation that is rarely realized in the domain of conscious fictional activities.

44. See Jouvet, *Le sommeil et le rêve*, 37–104, especially 88–89, for a more technical presentation of the zones of the brain and the groups of neurons concerned.

45. Jouvet, *Le sommeil et le rêve*, 92–94.

46. Jouvet, *Le sommeil et le rêve*, 53.

47. Currie, *Image and Mind*, 98, is thus wrong to move aside casually the comparison between dreams and the situation of fictional immersion.

48. Stern, "Engagements subjectifs," 39.

49. Winnicott, *Jeu et réalité*, 22–23.

50. Bessière, *Dire le littéraire*, 95.

51. Winnicott, *Jeu et réalité*, 19.

52. For "counter-game" see Mannoni, "La part du jeu," 124.

53. Heinich, *États de femme*, 333.

54. Metz, *Le signifiant imaginaire*, 143.

55. Proust, *Journées de lecture*, 161. This benevolent attitude toward childish reading gives its place to much more ambivalent judgment when it is a matter of reading at an adult age: possible introduction to spiritual life, it always risks transforming itself into an obstacle, almost that it tends to substitute itself "for the personal life of the spirit" (180).

56. Proust, *Journées de lecture*, 170.

57. See Giono, *Noé*, 622.

58. Giono, *Noé*, 616.

59. In fact, Proust goes further: what remains, according to him, are uniquely the circumstances of the reading and not the books. This conception explains itself if we remember that the ultimate aim of his text is not to celebrate reading (or fiction) but, on the contrary, to assign it a territory and a legitimacy all in all limited in the development of "spiritual life."

60. Proust, *Journées de lecture*, 171.

61. Giono, *Noé*, 611.

62. Giono, *Noé*, 613, 612. See also Robert Ricatte.

63. On this subject see 301–2.

64. Plato *Republic* 10.605c–d. See 22–23.

65. Proust, *Journées de lecture*, 170.

66. Although the frontiers are not always impermeable, Frey reports the

words of German mystic Margarethe Ebener, who tells how during the night she removed the image of Christ from her basket because the Child was not good ("*nicht züchtig*") and kept her from sleeping. She embraces him and talks to him. Then, pushing the game further, she nurses him, pressing him against her naked breasts. And there she is all impressed to feel "the human caress of his mouth" [*ein menschliches Beruhren seines Mundes*] (*Kunstwissenschaftliche Grundfragen*, 124).

67. See Freedberg, *The Power of Images*, especially 136–60, 317–44.

68. Lotman, *La structure du texte artistique*, 106.

69. Gombrich, *L'art et l'illusion*, 24–25. See Podro for a representation of the debate provoked by Gombrich's thesis.

70. Gombrich, *L'art et l'illusion*, 25.

71. This point, often underlined by psychologists, is also recalled by Currie, *Image and Mind*, 29.

72. See Walton, *Mimesis as Make-Believe*. The same thing is true of Currie, *Image and Mind*, whose conception, despite differences on certain point, agrees in essentials with that of Walton.

73. Tadié, "La fiction et ses usages," 124, no. 22, seems to accept Walton's thesis according to which the emotions are simply simulated or, as he says, imagined, but at the same time he suggests that the distinction between true emotion and imagined emotion is not a difference in nature but simply a difference in intensity. Currie, *Image and Mind*, also registers himself in a perspective close to Walton's, since he identifies empathy with a "mental simulation."

74. Aristotle *Poetics* 224.

75. I do not make absolute rules about it, since there are schools of actors that, on the contrary, insist on the conscious control and refusal of all immersion.

76. See Goldman and Emmison, "Fantasy and Double-Play," 49.

77. Metz, *Le signifiant imaginaire*, 69.

78. See 201–2.

79. In what concerns this last temptation see item 4 in the introduction.

80. In what follows I develop somewhat an analysis sketched in Ducrot and Schaeffer, *Nouveau dictionnaire encyclopédique*, 312–15. The interested reader will find there also a selective bibliography devoted to the philosophical treatment of fiction.

81. Frege, *Écrits logiques*, 109.

82. See Bouveresse, "Fait, fiction et diction," 16.

83. The works of Ogden and Richards are, however, far more interesting than

the emotivist thesis to which one too often reduces them. For an analysis of the complex though not always very coherent ideas of Richards see Shusterman, *Critique et poésie*, 47–54, 199–221.

84. Of course, we must not confuse the question of knowing if fictional statements have a value of truth with the one of knowing if one can express truths on their subject. As Terence Parsons notes, most people who express the statement "Pegasus is a winged horse" don't limit themselves to saying that this statement is true according to the myth but that it is true in an absolute manner: "It is a real truth concerning an unreal object" ("A Meinongian Analysis," 78).

85. The analysis of the theory of fiction by Goodman that I proposed in Schaeffer, "Nelson Goodman en poéticien," thus seems to me no longer satisfying.

86. It is a matter, on the contrary, of the immanent function of every fictional device. See 301–2.

87. Leibniz, *Philosophische Schriften*, 462.

88. Wolff quoted in Bodmer, *Critische Abhandlung*, 32.

89. The interested reader will find a selective bibliography of the definitions of fiction inspired by modal logic in Ducrot and Schaeffer, *Nouveau dictionnaire encyclopédique*, 315.

90. See Lewis, "Truth in Fiction"; Howell, "Fictional Objects."

91. On this last point see Dolezel, "Mimesis and Possible Worlds."

92. Danto, *Philosophical Disenfranchisement*, 144.

93. The conventionalism of Goodman accords well with his nominalist bias as well as with his adhesion to the psychological works by the school of Jerome Bruner. In effect, according to Bruner, the perceptive construction of reality obeys *grosso modo* the same logic as the scientific inquest: it is a matter of an inferential process (not conscious in the case of perception) proceeding by indices, hypotheses, verification, correction, and so on, hence the refusal of Bruner to distinguish between perception and thought by virtue of the hypothesis (put into question again by more recent works in the domain of the neuropathology of perception) that *all* the stages of the mental treatment of perceptions are accessible to descending processes (top-down) and thus susceptible to be influenced by conscious beliefs. For a discussion of the present state of the question see Pylyshym, "Is Vision Continuous with Cognition?"

94. Goodman, *Languages of Art*, 124, speaks of the "obsessive cadences and quasi-indescribable emotional and sensorial qualities" of *L'année dernière à Marienbad*—which, after all, may be a way of recognizing the proper effects of mimetic immersion.

95. Goodman, *Languages of Art*, 182, emphasis added.

96. Wolterstorff, *Works and Worlds of Art*, 234.

97. Searle, *Sens et expression*, 65.

98. Searle's analysis leaves a certain number of questions in suspense, by the way. See on this subject Genette, "Les actes de fiction," 41–63.

99. Searle, *Sens et expression*, 99.

100. Genette, "Les actes de fiction," 20. Fiction as I understand it here thus notably distinguishes itself from juridic fictions, which, according to the analysis of Yan Thomas, "*Fictio legis*," always presuppose "the certainty of the false," that is, they treat as facts what is contrary to facts. Fiction as shared ludic feint distinguishes itself also from "scientific fictions" in the sense of Jean-Marc Lévy-Leblond, for example, who identifies fiction with modelization: "In this sense, science, also effective with modelization, is fiction" (*Aux contraires*, 397). It seems to me that one has to distinguish between nomological modelization (and, more widely, modelization by homology) and fictional modelization. See on this subject 187–88.

101. This supposes that we admit that mental realities (and thus also social facts) are part of physical reality. This does *not* imply that they can only be described adequately through an action that would reduce to their microphysical or neurological level. At the same rank as the physical description of the subatomic particles, the mentalist description of mental facts is the description of an aspect, or a level, of the physical reality of which we are a part.

102. See Searle, *L'intentionnalité*, 19–20. According to Searle, *La construction*, chap. 1, the distinction between intrinsic and derived intentionality does not superimpose itself on the one between individual and collective intentionality: the first concerns the localization and the place of foundation of intentional facts, the second their form of expression.

103. See 56–57.

104. See Shanks and St. John, "Characteristics," who oppose learning by example to "rule learning." They note that in the first case the learning consists of the memorization of reactivable examples, whereas in the second case we abstract a rule from the occurrences of stimuli, this rule alone being stocked in the memory in the long term.

105. We can remark that the conditions of satisfaction of the projective homologous modelization are only one particular case of the conditions of satisfaction of intentional actions, such as they are analyzed, for example, by Searle: a physical event (e.g., to lift an arm) is an intentional action only inasmuch as this event

is caused by intention in action (or the previous intention) to lift an arm (see Searle, *L'intentionnalité*, 122–23).

106. This precision is not without importance, for it explains why we endure very badly the conflict between the fictional universe and the islands of factual referentiality that it integrates: these conflicts disrupt the mimetic immersion. See 201.

107. See 209–10 and 268–69.

108. See, for example, Herrnstein Smith, *On the Margins of Discourse*, 29, cited here after Genette, who notes that the fictivity of novels "is not to be looked for in the unreality of the characters and the events mentioned but in the unreality of the mention itself. . . . It is the act of reporting events, the act of describing characters and to refer to places that is fictive" ("Les actes de fiction," 81).

109. Rochlitz, "Sens et tradition," 154, 150.

110. Bremond, "Le rôle, l'intrigue et le récit," 68. See Bremond, *Logique de récit*, for what constitutes to this day the most important analysis of this problematic.

111. Bremond notes that all that is anthropomorphized becomes tellable according to the modalities of human acting and suffering. One finds here again in fact the question of the attribution of mental states of which the field of application is itself variable according to the ages of life, the cultures, and so on.

112. Certainly, as Rorty, "Is There a Problem," 85, remarks, such a recourse does not impose itself as long as one continues to treat semantic questions as epistemological problems. However, I will not follow Rorty when he spreads his critique to the verificationist program as such and proposes to replace the notions of reference and of truth by that of "talking about."

113. Jost, "Le feint du monde," 167.

114. Genette, "Les actes de fiction," 60.

115. Fodor, *La modularité de l'esprit*, 137–39, qualifies as isotropic system every system—that is, every modelization—in which all the knowledge already acquired is pertinent to the confirmation of a new hypothesis. He maintains, however, that the fixation of our beliefs (concerning what is the case and what is not the case) is an example of an isotropic system.

116. See Lewis, "Truth in Fiction."

117. Wolterstorff, "Worlds of Works of Art," 125.

118. Danto, *L'assujettissement philosophique de l'art*, 218.

119. It seems to me that this aspect of the mode of cognitive operation of fiction corresponds to what Ricoeur calls "*mimesis III*" (*Temps et récit*, 1:109

ff.). However, I don't see why the experience of time would necessarily be the central cognitive operator. Even if one limits oneself to narrative fictions, which is what Ricoeur does, a thesis of this kind is too restrictive.

4. SOME FICTIONAL DEVICES

1. See 124–25.

2. This idea of the division of cognitive work was advanced by Hilary Putnam (see, e.g., "Philosophers and Human Understanding," 186 ff.). He elaborates the notion essentially with respect to scientific knowledge, but it applies to the whole of human representations.

3. See on this subject the analyses of Descombes, *La denrée mentale*.

4. Goldman and Emmison, "Fantasy and Double-Play," 31.

5. Escande, "Littérature chinoise." See Levi, *La Chine romanesque*, for the role of fiction in China.

6. Jullien, "Limites à une conception mimétique" and "Naissance de l'imagination."

7. Pavel, *Univers de la fiction*, 186.

8. To take up again the expression proposed by Bremond and Pavel, *De Barthes à Balzac*, 197.

9. See 274–75.

10. See Cohn, *La transparence intérieure*, 245–300.

11. See Genette, *Figures III*, 185–86.

12. This does not mean, of course, that a fictional tale is incapable of presenting mental contents that are not verbal. But it can do it only through the voice of a narrator who reports these mental states, that is, through what Dorrit Cohn calls "psycho-narration"; he cannot mime these states himself. Cohn notes that the great advantage of psychonarration resides precisely in the fact that it is able to take into account "nonverbalized psychic movements" (*La transparence intérieure*, 63).

13. See 238–39.

14. The same thing also goes for cinema. On the subject of the distinction between quasi-perceptive mimemes and their fictional usage see 263–65.

15. See Schaeffer, *L'image précaire*, 41 ff.

16. Plato *Phaedrus* 275d.

17. This description is clearly unilateral, since it does not take into account the sonorous mimemes. It would be necessary in addition to distinguish these from the sound-band in its globality, since this one includes in general also a nonmimetic

element, music, that most of the time does not belong to the fictional universe itself but functions like an operator of affective empathy. See Jost, *L'oeil-caméra*, 37–59, for an analysis of the sonorous elements in the fiction cinema.

18. Of course, in the cinema I have a certain liberty to vary the point of focalization of my look *inside* the quasi-perceptive field, at least as the global frame of the field remains stable for a long enough time, that is, as long as it is a matter of a fixed plane. From the moment there are mobile planes, my look has a tendency to remain centered on the point of escape, because only this centering of the focalization permits me to integrate the transformations of the field in the continuity of a moving visual experience.

19. Without a doubt there exist intermediary cases, like that of fiction broadcast on the radio, where the physical incarnation is limited to the voice.

20. See Genette, "Les actes de fiction," 82–88.

21. In fact (as it emerges very well from the schemes proposed by Genette), the true difference between homodiegetic fiction and heterodiegetic fiction is located at the level of the relations between narrator and character: in the first case they coincide, whereas in the second case the narrator is not one of the characters of the diegetic universe.

22. See on this subject Gaudreault and Jost, *Le récit cinématographique*, 73–80.

23. See 274–75.

24. See on this subject Jost, *L'oeil-caméra*, 29–30, who opposes the "internal occularization" (the subjective camera) to the "zero occularization" (the objective camera). On the distinction between internal occularization (we see what the character sees) and internal focalization (we know what the character knows) see Gaudreault and Jost, *Le récit cinématographique*, 138–39.

25. Goldman and Emmison, "Fantasy and Double-Play," 29.

26. See, for example, Karbusicky, *Sinn und Bedeutung*.

27. For a criticism of this conception see Danto, *L'assujettissement philosophique de l'art*, 184–91.

28. See Searle, *Sens et expression*, 108, 112; Genette, "Les actes de fiction," 47–48, 62.

29. This precise formulation is necessary, since Hamburger considers that the cinema also belongs to the "logical domain of literary fiction" (*The Logic of Literature*, 229). For the moment I leave drama aside (see 246–47).

30. I make use here of my entry "Fiction" in Ducrot and Schaeffer, *Nouveau dictionnaire encyclopédique*, 318–20.

31. *The Wild Ass's Skin*, emphasis added.

32. For the study of these indices and their interpretation see Hamburger, *The Logic of Literature*, 55–194; Harweg, *Pronomina und Textkonstitution*; and Banfield, *Unspeakable Sentences*.

33. Suétone, *La vie des douze Césars*, 97.

34. Lejeune, *Moi aussi*, 25–26.

35. Hamburger, *The Logic of Literature*, 142.

36. Goffman, *La mise en scène de la vie quotidienne*; Turner, *Dramas, Fields and Metaphors*; and Geertz, *Negara*.

37. Turner, *Dramas, Fields and Metaphors*.

38. See Turner, *From Ritual to Theater*; Schechner, 168.

39. Heinich, *États de femme*, 338–39. Heinich includes a pertinent critique of the notion of role as model of description of the lived experience. For one thing, "to play a role" implies a detachment "of which the conditions are only exceptionally united"; for another, the notion "is often undergirded by an essentialist conception that, behind the superficiality and the contingency associated with the 'role,' presupposes the existence of an authentic 'self'" (339). In sum, the notion of "social role," at least if it is not handled with prudence, risks being the location of a double lack of understanding. From the point of view of fiction, it underestimates the specificity of the pragmatic unhooking that defines the fictional game; from the point of view of real interactions, it overestimates our "detachment," thus underestimates our lack "of hold on the elements of real life that compose the situations, and . . . the symbolic processes of occupation of places" (339).

40. See my entry "Enunciation théatrale" in Ducrot and Schaeffer, *Nouveau dictionnaire encyclopédique*, 612.

41. One finds this conception still with Käte Hamburger, for whom "the theatrical scene has no influence on the literary existence and the value of works" (*The Logic of Literature*, 199), a situation she opposes to that of the filmic transposition of these same works, which is supposed to result in a new work, precisely, the film. But this distinction has meaning only if we have decided in advance that the theatrical production of a play is not a work (which explains, e.g., that for her the theatrical scenery is *not* part of the theatrical work). Contrary to what Hamburger pretends, the "form created by the author, the drama writer, stays unaltered" not only in the case of the theatrical production but quite as much in the case of a cinematographic transposition.

42. Abbé d'Aubignac, *La pratique du théâtre* (1657), quoted by Prodromidès,

"Le théâtre de la lecture," 425. I have profited tremendously from this excellent article, which puts well into evidence the textualist bias of the theory of tragedy developed during the classical period.

43. See Prodromidès, "Le théâtre de la lecture," 425.

44. La Ménardière, *La poétique* (1639), 12, quoted by Prodromidès, "Le théâtre de la lecture," 424.

45. Goodman, *Of Mind and Other Matters*, 144. For a deeper discussion of Goodman's conception see Schaeffer, "Nelson Goodman en poéticien," 90.

46. In fact, Goodman's analysis is finer than I suppose here, since it takes account of the composite status of the text: "The text of a play, however, is composed of scores and scripts. The dialogue is in a quasi-notational system, having enunciation as concordants. This part of the text is a score and the executions which concord with it constitute the work. The scenic indications, the descriptions of the scenery, etc. are scripts in a language that obeys none of the semantic requisites of notationality and an execution determines in no single manner such a script or a class of coextensive scripts" (*Languages of Art*, 199).

47. D'Aubignac, quoted by Prodromidès, "Le théâtre de la lecture," 431, emphasis added.

48. Prodromidès, "Le théâtre de la lecture," 427.

49. Richard Wagner, *Die Walküre*, in Wagner, *Werke*, 2:75, my translation.

50. The problem of hypernormal lures would necessitate a chapter of its own, notably because they are not synonyms of naturalist imitation. They are always characterized by deformations, exaggerations that are exactly the contrary of what we expect in general from a naturalistic mimeme. It is in this frame that one would have to notably study the theatrical versification or the role of singing in the opera.

51. We must not confuse the question of the priority of one or the other fictional device with that of the publication of texts: in the classical theater the *editions* of texts generally follow their representation, which signifies that the public has access to the scenic state before disposing of the textual state.

52. Metz, *Le signifiant imaginaire*, 63, 64.

53. Jost, "Le feint du monde," 165. His criticism of the thesis of the intrinsic fictionality of cinema goes in the same direction as the one sketched here.

54. Odin, "Christian Metz et la fiction," 15.

55. Odin, "Christian Metz et la fiction," 10.

56. Milman, *Le trompe-l'oeil*, 7.

57. Gombrich, *L'art et l'illusion*, 87, notes the same thing concerning the

technique of the stereoscopic vision (in the cinema). He says very justly that the power of the "naturalist" effect depends essentially on a difference between expectation and experience. He seems, however, not to take into account the possibility that there can exist an absolute neurophysiological threshold beyond which this difference is not active.

58. For want of making the partition between the two plans, Odin, "Christian Metz et la fiction," though he starts out from an interesting analysis of the theories of Christian Metz, ends up with a true theoretical tetralogy that distinguishes between "fictivization 1" (representative mimemes), fictivization 2 (supposed to be due to the irrealization of the here and now of reality by its tale formation), fictivization 3 (fiction in the current sense of the term, i.e., the construction of an imaginary universe), without forgetting what he calls fictionalization 4, which, if I understood correctly, is a sort of result of the first three processes! In fact, only the third process concerns fiction.

59. Danto, *Philosophical Disenfranchisement*, 232.

60. See on this subject Broos et al., *De Rembrandt à Vermeer*, 355. The question to know whether the picture has been painted with the aid of a dark chamber is not the decisive criterion to know whether it is a matter of a fiction.

61. One could develop analogous considerations on the subject of the paintings united by Chrystèle Burgard and Baldine Saint-Girons in the exhibition *Le paysage et la question du sublime*.

62. See Soulages, *Esthétique de la photographie*, for a stimulating presentation of the multiple fictional devices susceptible to be developed in the frame of photography.

63. See on this subject Freedberg, *The Power of Images*.

64. Soulages, *Esthétique de la photographie*. Retrospectively, one of the weak points of Schaeffer, *L'image précaire*, seems to me to be the absence of his taking account of the fictional usages of photography. However, I do not share the hostility of François Soulages toward what he calls "the imperialist practice and the dogmatic ideology of realistic photography," of which the origin would be found in "a need to believe in a forever fixed and settled reality, to believe in the real" (*Esthétique de la photographie*, 94, 95).

65. This shows again the necessity of distinguishing between formal mimesis in the naturalist sense of the term and the hypernormal lures.

66. Odin, "Christian Metz et la fiction," 9–19. Casetti, "Les yeux dans les yeux," speaks also of "enunciator."

67. An illocutory act can be realized—that is, a propositional content and

attitude can be expressed — by other vehicles than language, for example, gestures and graphic codes.

68. Odin, "Christian Metz et la fiction," 15, emphasis added.

69. Currie, *Image and Mind*, 3. See also Deleuze, *L'image-temps*, 40.

70. Genette, *Figures III*, 67–273. To convince oneself of the pertinence of narratology on the question of modalities of focalization, it suffices to read the analyses of François Jost devoted to what he calls the occularization of its (complex) links with focalization. See Jost, *L'oeil-caméra*. On the final point see, for example, Gaudreault and Jost, *Le récit cinématographique*.

71. The fact that in the case of the cinema my perception is "constrained" by the quasi-perceptive flux of the filmic mimeme, which is clearly not the case in the theater, does not suffice to legitimate the thesis of a narrative instance, not even that of a "Great Imager." With certain exceptions, the cinema spectator does not see the film as something that someone shows him but as a perceptive flux that would be his own.

72. The excellent work of García Barrientos, *Drama y tiempo*, shows that a large part of the categories of narratology are also pertinent for theater. No one would conclude from this that theater is a narrative genre in the sense that there would be a "narrative instance."

73. For critics going in the same direction see Currie, *Image and Mind*, 225–80.

74. The two techniques are related but not identical. See, in this chapter, note 24.

75. Burgoyne, "Le narrateur au cinéma," 272–74.

76. Quoted by Singer, *The Child's World of Make-Believe*, 76.

77. See 7–12.

78. Coiffet, *Mondes imaginaires*, 40. For experiences demonstrating the possibility for sonorous stimuli to compensate the lack of immersion induced by images with weak definition see Negroponte, *L'homme numérique*, 159.

79. I take up again Schmuck's term (*Introduction au multimédia*, 6).

80. Of course, the digital support allows *also* the considerable development of the real interactions between human subjects, essentially by the intermediary of the Internet. But this question has strictly nothing to do with that of fictional interactivity (i.e., with the simulation by an algorithm causally linked to a perceiving subject or an intentional system), which one finds in video games or the systems of virtual reality. The exchanges on Internet are not simulated exchanges: they are real exchanges that distinguish themselves from other modes

of communication simply because the messages are in transit there and are locked there (temporarily) in digital form.

81. See Coiffet, *Mondes imaginaires*, 15–30.

CONCLUSION

1. "Poetic art as a whole seems to owe its origin to two causes [*aitiai*], both natural [*phusical*]" (Aristotle *Poetics* 4.48b.5). Aristotle of course deals only with poetic art, but he treats it as a modality of mimesis, and the causes that he enumerates have value for mimesis as such — with the exception of the "natural tendency . . . to melody and to rhythm," which, it is understood, concerns only the poetic variant of mimesis (but also this major nonmimetic art that is music).

2. Aristotle *Poetics* 48b.20–24.

3. Aristotle *Poetics* 48b.8–9. Translator's note: The rest of this note has been left out; it deals with the two causes that the French and English translations attribute to Aristotle for the reason men take pleasure in imitations.

4. Only a very restrictive conception of cognition — that is, its reduction to a direct perceptive relation with objects and physical facts — and a misunderstanding of the particularities of knowledge by mimetic immersion allow the opposition between fiction and knowledge. For an example of a restrictive interpretation of this type that limits the cognitive range of fiction to a function of recognition see Shusterman, "Fiction, connaissance, épistémologie."

5. See, for instance, the work Nathalie Heinich devotes to the representation of women in Occidental literary fiction (*États de femme*). For an anthropological study of the relations between fiction and individual and public imagination see Augé, *La guerre des rêves*.

6. For an account of these experiences see Ephraim Biblow *in* Singer, *The Child's World of Make-Believe*, 126–28.

7. On the general question of the relations between fiction and affect see Izard and Tomkins, "Affect and Behavior."

8. See 139–40.

9. See on this subject Mannoni (1985).

10. Flahault, *La méchanceté*, 67.

11. See 142–43, 196–98.

12. Singer, *The Child's World of Make-Believe*, 203.

13. For this definition of aesthetic behavior I allow myself to refer to my own *Les célibataires de l'art*, 163 ff.

14. See 158–60.

15. Kant, *Kritik der Urteilskraft*, 48, 137, 293.

16. Heidegger, *Kant et le problème*, 187.

17. Kant, *Kritik der Urteilskraft*, 312.

18. Kant, *Kritik der Urteilskraft*, 343.

19. See 182–83. However, as we just saw, it takes into account the other source of fiction, namely, imaginative self-stimulation.

20. Genette, *Palimpsests*, 164–65.

Bibliography

Ames, Roger T., and Wimal Dissanayak, eds. *Self and Deception: A Cross-Cultural Enquiry*. Albany: State University of New York Press, 1996.

[Anonymous]. "Images subliminales." *Pour la Science* (November 1998): 32.

Aristotle. *Poetics*. Trans. Ingram Bywater. New York: Modern Library, 1954.

Augé, Marc. *La guerre des rêves. Exercices d'ethno-fiction*. Librairie du XXe siècle. Paris: Éditions du Seuil, 1997.

Austin, John L. "Feindre." In *Écrits philosophiques*. Paris: Éditions du Seuil, 1994. 206–28.

Aymé, Marcel. "Le loup." In *Les contes bleus du chat perché*. Folio Junior, no. 433. Paris: Gallimard. 9–28.

Bandura, Albert. *Social Learning and Personality Development*. New York: Holt, 1963.

———. *Social Learning Theory*. Englewood Cliffs NJ: Prentice Hall, 1977.

Banfield, Ann. *Unspeakable Sentences*. London: Routledge and Kegan Paul, 1982.

Barthes, Roland. "En sortant du cinéma" (1975). In *Le bruissement de la langue*. Paris: Éditions du Seuil, 1984.

Baudonnière, Pierre-Marie. *Le mimétisme et l'imitation*. Dominos. Paris: Flammarion, 1997.

Bellour, Raymond. *L'entre-images 2: Mots, images*. Paris: Éditions POL, 1999.

Bessière, Jean. *Dire le littéraire. Points de vue théoriques*. Brussels: Pierre Mardaga, 1990.

———, ed. *Modernité. Fiction. Déconstruction*. Lettres modernes, 1994.

Block, Ned. "On a Confusion about a Function of Consciousness." *Behavioral and Brain Sciences* 18, no. 2 (1995): 227–87.

Bodmer, Johann Jakob. *Critische Abhandlung von dem Wunderbaren in der Poesie* (1740). Stuttgart: J. B. Metzlersche Verlagsbuchhandlung, 1966.

Bonnet, Claude, Rodolphe Ghiglione, and Jean-François Richard. *Traité de psychologie cognitive*. Vol. 1. Paris: Dunod, 1989.

Bouveresse, Jacques. "Fait, fiction et diction." *Les Cahiers du Musée national d'art moderne*, no. 41 (1992): 15–32.

Bouverot, Danielle. "Un simulacre peut en dissimuler un autre: le mot d'après Frantext." *Autrement Dire*, no. 6 (1989): 7–28.

Boyd, Robert, and Peter J. Richerson. *Culture and the Evolutionary Process.* Chicago: University of Chicago Press, 1985.

———. "An Evolutionary Model of Social Learning: The Effects of Spatial and Temporal Variation." In *Social Learning: Psychological and Biological Approaches*, ed. Thomas R. Zentall and Bennett G. Galef. Hillsdale NJ: Lawrence Erlbaum Associates, 1988. 29–48.

Bremond, Claude. *Logique de récit.* Paris: Éditions du Seuil, 1973.

———. "Le rôle, l'intrigue et le récit." In *Temps et récit de Paul Ricoeur en débat.* Paris: Éditions du Cerf, 1990. 57–71.

Bremond, Claude, and Thomas Pavel. *De Barthes à Balzac. Fictions d'une critique, critiques d'une fiction.* Paris: Albin Michel, 1998.

Broos, Ben, et al. *De Rembrandt à Vermeer.* The Hague: Éditions de la Fondation Johan Maurits van Nassau, 1986.

Budiansky, Stephen. *The Nature of Horses: Exploring Equine Evolution, Intelligence and Behavior.* New York: Simon and Schuster, 1997.

Burgard, Chrystèle, et al. *Le paysage et la question du sublime.* Réunion des musées nationaux, 1997.

Burgoyne, Robert. "Le narrateur au cinéma. Logique et pragmatique de la narration impersonnelle." *Poétique*, no. 87 (1991): 271–88.

Buxton, Richard. *La Grèce de l'imaginaire. Les contextes de la mythologie.* Paris: La Découverte, 1996.

Byrne, Richard W., and Anne E. Russon. "Learning by Imitation: A Hierarchical Approach." *Behavioral and Brain Sciences* 21, no. 5 (1998): 667–84.

Cadoz, Claude. *Les réalités virtuelles.* Dominos. Paris: Flammarion, 1994.

Caillois, Roger. *Les jeux et les hommes.* Paris: Gallimard, 1967.

———. *Le mythe et l'homme.* Paris: Gallimard, 1938.

Casetti, Francesco. "Les yeux dans les yeux." *Communications*, no. 38 (1983).

Château, Dominique. *L'héritage de l'art. Imitation, tradition et modernité.* Paris: L'Harmattan, 1998.

Cohn, Dorrit. "Breaking the Code of Fictional Biography." In *Traditions of Experiment from the Enlightenment to the Present. Essays in Honor of Peter Demetz*, ed. Nancy Kaiser and David E. Wellbery. Ann Arbor: University of Michigan Press, 1992. 301–19.

———. *The Distinction of Fiction.* Baltimore MD: Johns Hopkins University Press, 1999.

———. *La transparence intérieure*. Paris: Éditions du Seuil, 1981.

Coiffet, Philippe. *Mondes imaginaires*. Hermès, 1995.

Currie, Gregory. *Image and Mind: Film, Philosophy and Cognitive Science*. New York: Cambridge University Press, 1995.

———. *The Nature of Fiction*. New York: Cambridge University Press, 1990.

Danto, Arthur. *L'assujettissement philosophique de l'art*. Paris: Éditions du Seuil, 1993.

———. *The Philosophical Disenfranchisement of Art*. New York: Columbia University Press, 1985.

Darwin, Charles. *L'expression des émotions chez l'homme et les animaux* (1872). Paris: Éditions du CTHS, 1998.

Dawkins, Richard. *Le gène égoïste*. Trans. Laura Ovion. Paris: Éditions Odile Jacob, 1996.

———. "Hierarchical Organization: A Candidate Principle for Ethology." In *Growing Points in Ethology*, ed. Patrick P. G. Bateson and Robert A. Hinde. New York: Cambridge University Press, 1976.

Deleuze, Gilles. *L'image-temps*. Paris: Éditions de Minuit, 1985.

———. *Logique du sens*. Paris: Éditions de Minuit, 1969.

Dennett, Daniel C. *Consciousness Explained*. 1991; Harmondsworth: Penguin, 1993.

Derrida, Jacques. "La pharmacie de Platon." In *La dissémination*. Paris: Éditions du Seuil, 1972. 70–197.

Descombes, Vincent. *La denrée mentale*. Paris: Éditions de Minuit, 1995.

———. *Grammaire d'objets en tous genres*. Paris: Éditions de Minuit, 1983.

Détienne, Marcel. *L'invention de la mythologie*. Paris: Gallimard, 1981.

Diels, Hermann, and Walter Kranz. *Die Fragmente der Vorsokratiker* (1903). 3 vols. 11th ed. Zürich: Weidmannsche Verlagsbuchhandlung, 1964.

Dolezel, Lubomir. "Mimesis and Possible Worlds." *Poetics Today* 9, no. 3 (1988): 475–96.

Ducrot, Oswald, and Jean-Marie Schaeffer. *Nouveau dictionnaire encyclopédique des sciences du langage*. Paris: Éditions du Seuil, 1995.

Edelman, Gerald M. *Biologie de la conscience*. Points Odile Jacob. 1994.

Edelman, Shimon. "Representation Is Representation of Similarities." *Brain and Behavioral Sciences* 21, no. 4 (1998): 449–67.

Eibl-Eibesfelt, Irenäus. *Die Biologie des menschlichen Verhaltens. Grundriss der Humanethologie*. 3rd revised and expanded ed. Munich: Piper Verlag, 1995.

Elgin, Catherine Z. "Les fonctions de la fiction." *Les Cahiers du Musée national d'art moderne*, no. 64 (1992): 15–54.

Enright, D. J., and Ernst de Chickera. *English Critical Texts*. London: Oxford University Press, 1962.

Escande, Yolaine. "La calligraphie chinoise: une image de l'homme." *Cahiers Robinson*, no. 2 (1997): 129–76.

———. "Littérature chinoise et art lettré" (à paraître). 1999.

Ey, Henri. *La conscience*. Paris: PUF, 1968.

Flahault, François. "L'artiste créateur et le culte des restes." *Communications*, no. 64 (1997): 15–54.

———. *La méchanceté*. Paris: Descartes et Cie, 1998.

Flinn, M. V., and R. D. Alexander. "Culture Theory: The Developing Synthesis from Biology." *Human Ecology* 10 (1982): 383–400.

Fodor, Jerry. *La modularité de l'esprit. Esprit sur la psychologie des facultés*. Trans. Abel Gerschenfeld. Paris: Éditions de Minuit, 1986.

Freedberg, David. *The Power of Images: Studies in the History and Theory of Response*. Chicago: University of Chicago Press, 1989.

Frege, Gottlob. *Écrits logiques et philosophiques*. Paris: Éditions du Seuil, 1971.

———. *Nachgelassene Schriften*. Hamburg: Felix Meiner Verlag, 1969.

Frey, Dagobert. *Kunstwissenschaftliche Grundfragen. Prolegomena zu einer Kunstphilosophie*. 1946; Darmstadt: Wissenschaftliche Buchgesellschaft, 1992.

García Barrientos, José Luis. *Drama y tiempo*. Madrid: Biblioteca de Filologia Hispánica, Consejo Superior de Investigaciones Científicas, 1991.

Gaudreault, André, and François Jost, eds. *Le récit cinématographique (cinéma et récit II)*. Nathan, 1990.

Geertz, Clifford. *Negara: The Theatre State in Nineteenth-Century Bali*. Princeton NJ: Princeton University Press, 1980.

Genette, Gérard. "Les actes de fiction." In *Fiction et diction*. Paris: Éditions du Seuil, 1991.

———. *Figures III*. Paris: Éditions du Seuil, 1972.

———. *L'oeuvre de l'art*. Vol. 2, *La relation esthétique*. Paris: Éditions du Seuil, 1977.

———. *Palimpsestes*. Paris: Éditions du Seuil, 1982.

———. *Palimpsests*. Lincoln: University of Nebraska Press, 1997.

———. *Seuils*. Paris: Éditions du Seuil, 1987.

Giono, Jean. *Noé* (1947). In *Oeuvres romanesques complètes*. Vol. 3. La Bibliothèque de la Pléiade. Paris: Gallimard, 1974. 607–862.

Glowinski, Michal. "Sur le roman à la première personne." *Poétique*, no. 72 (1987): 497–506.

Goffman, Erving. *La mise en scène de la vie quotidienne*. Vol. 1, *La présentation de soi*. 1956; Paris: Éditions de Minuit, 1973.

Goldman, Laurence, and Michael Emmison. "Fantasy and Double-Play among Huli Children of Papoua New Guinea." *Text* 16, no. 1 (1996): 23–60.

Gombrich, Ernst. *L'art et l'illusion*. 1956; Paris: Gallimard, 1987.

Goodman, Nelson. *Languages of Art*. 1960; New York: Bobbs-Merrill Company, 1968.

———. *Of Mind and Other Matters*. Cambridge MA: Harvard University Press, 1984.

Goody, Jack. *La logique de l'écriture*. Paris: Armand Colin, 1986.

Hamburger, Käte. *The Logic of Literature*. 2nd rev. ed. Bloomington: Indiana University Press, 1993.

Harweg, Roland. *Pronomina und Textkonstitution*. Munich: Fink Verlag, 1968.

Heidegger, Martin. *Kant et le problème de la métaphysique* (1929). Tel. Paris: Gallimard, 1981.

Heinich, Nathalie. *États de femme: l'identité féminine dans la fiction occidentale*. Paris: Gallimard, 1996.

Henrich, Dieter, and Wolfgang Iser, eds. *Funktionen des Fiktiven (Poetik und Hermeneutik X)*. Munich: Wilhelm Fink Verlag, 1983.

Herrnstein Smith, Barbara. *On the Margins of Discourse*. Chicago: University of Chicago Press, 1978.

Hildesheimer, Wolfgang. *Das Ende der Fiktionen*. Frankfurt-am-Main: Suhrkamp Verlag, 1988.

———. *Marbot. Eine Biographie*. Frankfurt-am-Main: Suhrkamp Verlag, 1981.

———. *Mozart*. Frankfurt-am-Main: Suhrkamp Verlag, 1977.

———. *Sir Andrew Marbot*. Paris: Stock, 1984.

Howell, Robert. "Fictional Objects: How They Are and How They Are Not." *Poetics* 8 (1979): 129–78.

Iser, Wolfgang. *Das Fiktive und das Imaginäre. Perspektiven literarischer Anthropologie*. Frankfurt-am-Main: Suhrkamp, 1991.

Izard, Carrol E., and Jerome L. Tomkins. "Affect and Behavior: Anxiety as a Negative Affect." In *Anxiety and Behavior*, ed. Charles Spielberger. New York: Academic Press, 1966.

Jost, François. "Le feint du monde." *Réseaux*, nos. 72–73 (1995).

——. *L'oeil-caméra. Entre film et roman.* Lyon: Presses Universitaires de Lyon, 1987.

Jouvet, Michel. *Le château des songes.* Paris: Éditions Odile Jacob, 1992.

——. *Le sommeil et le rêve.* Paris: Éditions Odile Jacob, 1993.

Jouvet, Michel, and Monique Gessain. *Le grenier des rêves. Essai d'onirologie diachronique.* Paris: Éditions Odile Jacob, 1997.

Jullien, François. "Limites à une conception mimétique de l'oeuvre littéraire." *Extrême-Orient. Extrême Occident,* no. 3 (*Le rapport à la nature. Notes diverses*) (1983): 69–81.

——. "Naissance de 'l'imagination': essai de problématique au travers de la réflexion littéraire de la Chine et de l'Occident." *Extrême-Orient. Extrême Occident,* no. 7 (*Le réel. L'imaginaire*) (1985): 23–81.

Kant, Immanuel. *Kritik der Urteilskraft,* ed. Karl Vorlander. Hamburg: Verlag von Felix Meiner, 1963.

Karbusicky, Vladimir. *Sinn und Bedeutung in der Musik.* Darmstadt: Wissenschaftliche Buchgesellschaft, 1990.

Kuhns, Richard. "The Cultural Function of Fiction." In Henrich and Iser, *Funktionen des Fiktiven,* 55–66.

Lacoue-Labarthe, Philippe. *L'imitation des modernes.* Paris: Galilée, 1986.

Leibniz, Gottfried Wilhelm. *Philosophische Schriften.* Vol. 1. Darmstadt: Wissenschaftliche Buchgesellschaft, 1965.

Lejeune, Philippe. *Moi aussi.* Paris: Éditions du Seuil, 1986.

Le Masson, Gwendall, Arnaud Laflaquière, Thierry Bal, and Sylvie Le Masson. "Dialogues entre neurones biologiques et artificiels." *La Recherche,* no. 314 (1998): 34–37.

Levi, Jean. *La Chine romanesque: fictions d'Orient et d'Occident.* Paris: Éditions du Seuil, 1995.

Lévy, Pierre. *Qu'est-ce que le virtuel?* Paris: La Découverte, 1995.

Lévy-Leblond, Jean-Marc. *Aux contraires. L'exercice de la pensée et la pratique de la science.* Paris: Gallimard, 1996.

Lewis, David. "Truth in Fiction." *American Philosophical Quarterly* 15 (1978): 37–46.

Lorenz, Konrad, and Franz W. Wuketits, eds. *Die Evolution des Denkens.* Munich: Piper Verlag, 1983.

Lotman, Iouri. *La structure du texte artistique.* Paris: Gallimard, 1973.

Lütterfels, Wilhelm, ed. *Transzendentale oder evolutionäre Erkenntnistheorie.* Darmstadt: Wissenschaftliche Buchgesellschaft, 1987.

Lyons, William, ed. *Modern Philosophy of Mind*. London: J. M. Dent, 1995.

Mannoni, Octave. "L'illusion comique ou le théâtre du point de vue de l'imaginaire." In *Clefs pour l'imaginaire ou l'autre scène*. Paris: Éditions du Seuil, 1969. 161–83.

———. "La part du jeu." In *Un commencement qui n'en finit pas. Transfert, interprétation, théorie*. Paris: Éditions du Seuil, 1980. 121–33.

———. "Le théâtre et la folie." In *Clefs pour l'imaginaire ou l'Autre Scène*. Paris: Éditions du Seuil, 1969. 301–14.

Mehler, Jacques, and E. Dupoux. *Naître humain*. Paris: Éditions Odile Jacob, 1990.

Metz, Christian. *Le signifiant imaginaire. Psychanalyse et cinéma*. 10/18. Union Générale d'Éditions, 1977.

Millar, Susanna. *The Psychology of Play*. Harmondsworth: Penguin, 1968.

Miller, Neal E., and John Dollard. *Social Learning and Imitation*. 1941; New Haven CT: Yale University Press, 1962.

Millikan, Ruth G. "A Common Structure for Concepts of Individuals, Stuffs and Real Kinds: More Mama, More Milk and More Mouse." *Behavioral and Brain Sciences* 21, no. 1 (1998): 55–60.

Milman, Myriam. *Le trompe-l'oeil*. Paris: Skira, 1992.

Negroponte, Nicholas. *L'homme numérique*. Paris: Robert Laffont, 1995.

Odin, Roger. "Christian Metz et la fiction." *Semiotica* 112, nos. 1–2 (1996): 9–19.

Oeser, Erhard. "Evolutionäre Wissenschaftstheorie." In *Transzendentale oder evolutionäre Erkenntnistheorie*, ed. Wilhelm Lütterfels. Darmstadt: Wissenschaftliche Buchgesellschaft, 1987. 51–63.

Opie, Iona, and Peter Opie. *Children's Games in Street and Playground*. Oxford: Oxford University Press, 1962.

———. *The Lore and Language of School-Children*. Oxford: Oxford University Press, 1959.

Pannenberg, Wolfgang. "Das Irreale des Glaubens." In Henrich and Iser, *Funktionen des Fiktiven*, 27–34.

Parsons, Terence. "A Meinongian Analysis of Fictional Objects." *Grazer philosophische Studien* 1 (1974): 73–86.

Pavel, Thomas. *Univers de la fiction*. Poétique. Paris: Éditions du Seuil, 1988.

Pinker, Steven. *L'instinct du langage*. Trans. Marie-France Desjeux. Paris: Éditions Odile Jacob, 1999.

Place, U. T. "Is Consciousness a Brain Process?" (1956). In *Modern Philosophy of Mind*, ed. William Lyons. London: J. M. Dent, 1995. 106–16.

Plato. *Dialogues*. Trans. B. Jowett. New York: Random House, 1929.

———. *Republic*. Trans. Paul Shorey. Cambridge MA: Harvard University Press, 1994.

Prodromidès, François. "Le théâtre de la lecture. Texte et spectacle dans *La pratique du théâtre* de d'Aubignac." *Poétique*, no. 112 (1997): 423–43.

Proust, Marcel. *Journées de lecture* (1905). In *Contre Sainte-Beuve*. La Bibliothèque de la Pléiade. Paris: Gallimard, 1971. 160–94.

Putnam, Hilary. "Philosophers and Human Understanding." In *Philosophical Papers*. Vol. 3, *Realism and Reason*. New York: Cambridge University Press, 1983. 184–204.

Pylyshym, Zenon. "Is Vision Continuous with Cognition? The Case for Cognitive Impenetrability of Visual Perception." *Behavioral and Brain Sciences*, preprint, 1997.

Quine, Willard V. O. *Ontological Relativity and Other Essays*. New York: Columbia University Press, 1977.

Ricoeur, Paul. *Temps et récit*. 3 vols. Paris: Éditions du Seuil, 1983–85.

Riffaterre, Michael. *Fictional Truth*. Baltimore MD: Johns Hopkins University Press, 1990.

Rochlitz, Rainer. "Sens et tradition chez Paul Ricoeur." In *Temps et récit de Paul Ricoeur en débat*. Paris: Éditions du Cerf, 1990. 139–83.

Rorty, Richard. "Is There a Problem about Fictional Discourse?" In Henrich and Iser, *Funktionen des Fiktiven*. Munich: Wilhelm Fink Verlag, 1983. 67–93.

Rousseau, Jean-Jacques. *Oeuvres complètes*. Vol. 4, *Émile. Éducation. Morale. Botanique*. La Bibliothèque de la Pléiade. Paris: Gallimard, 1969.

Sartre, Jean-Paul. *L'imaginaire* (1940). Idées. Paris: Gallimard, 1968.

Schaeffer, Jean-Marie. "Aesopus auctor inventus." *Poétique*, no. 63 (1985): 345–64.

———. *Les célibataires de l'art. Pour une esthétique sans mythes*. Paris: Gallimard, 1996.

———. *L'image précaire. Du dispositif photographique*. Paris: Éditions du Seuil, 1987.

———. "Loup, si on jouait au loup?" In *Autrement dire. no. 6*. Nancy: Presses Universitaires de Nancy, 1989. 111–23.

————. "Nelson Goodman en poéticien." *Les Cahiers du Musée national d'art moderne*, no. 41 (1992): 85–97.

Schmuck, Claudine. *Introduction au multimédia. Technologies et marchés*. Saint-Denis La Plaine: Éditions Afnor, 1995.

Searle, John R. *La construction de la réalité sociale*. Paris: Gallimard, 1998.

————. *L'intentionnalité. Essai de philosophie des états mentaux*. Trans. Claude Pichevin. Paris: Éditions de Minuit, 1985.

————. *The Mystery of Consciousness*. London: Granta Books, 1997.

————. *La redécouverte de l'esprit*. Trans. Claudine Tiercelin. Paris: Gallimard, 1995.

————. *Sens et expression. Études de théorie des actes du langage*. 1979; Paris: Éditions de Minuit, 1982.

Shanks, David R., and Mark F. St. John. "Characteristics of Dissociable Human Learning Systems." *Behavioral and Brain Sciences* 17, no. 3 (1994): 367–447.

Shusterman, Ronald. *Critique et poésie selon I. A. Richards. De la confiance positiviste au relativisme naissant*. Bordeaux: Presses Universitaires de Bordeaux, 1988.

————. "Fiction, connaissance, épistémologie." *Poétique*, no. 104 (1995): 503–18.

Singer, Jerome L. *The Child's World of Make-Believe. Experimental Studies of Imaginative Play*. New York: Academic Press, 1973.

Soulages, François. *Esthétique de la photographie. La perte et le reste*. Paris: Nathan, 1998.

Spielberger, Charles, ed. *Anxiety and Behavior*. New York: Academic Press, 1966.

Stern, Daniel. "Engagements subjectifs: le point de vue de l'enfant." In *Le nourrisson et sa famille*. Lyon: Éditions Césura, 1990.

————. *Le monde interpersonnel du nourrisson*. Paris: PUF, 1989.

Suétone. *La vie des douze Césars*. Vol. 3. Trans. Henri Aillaud. Paris: Les Belles Lettres, 1957.

Tadié, Alexis. "La fiction et ses usages. Analyse pragmatique du concept de fiction." *Poétique*, no. 113 (1998): 111–25.

Thomas, Yan. "*Fictio legis*. L'empire de la fiction romaine et ses limites médiévales." *Droits*, no. 21 (1995): 17–63.

Tomkins, Silvan S. *Affect, Imagery, Consciousness*. Vols. 1 and 2. New York: Springer, 1962–63.

Trimpi, Wesley. "The Ancient Hypothesis of Fiction: An Essay on the Origins of Literary Theory." *Traditio: Studies in Ancient and Medieval History, Thought, and Religion* 27 (1974): 1–118.

Turing, Alan. "Computing Machinery and Intelligence." *Mind* 59 (1950): 433–60.

Turner, Victor. *Dramas, Fields and Metaphors*. Ithaca NY: Cornell University Press, 1974.

———. *From Ritual to Theater*. New York: Performing Arts Journal Press, 1982.

Veyne, Paul. *Les Grecs ont-ils cru à leurs mythes?* Paris: Éditions du Seuil, 1983.

Vollmer, Gerhard. "Mesokosmos und objektive Erkenntnis—Über Probleme die von der evolutionären Erkenntnistheorie gelöst warden." In *Die Evolution des Denkens*, ed. Konrad Lorenz and Franz W. Wuketits. Munich: Piper Verlag, 1983. 29–91.

Wagner, Richard. *Werke*. Vol. 2. Zürich: Stauffacher-Verlag, 1966.

Walton, Kendall L. "Comment on 'Apprécie la fiction.'" *Agone*, no. 14 (1995): 15–47.

———. *Mimesis as Make-Believe: On the Foundations of the Representational Arts*. Cambridge MA: Harvard University Press, 1990.

Wilson, E. O. *Sociobiology: The New Synthesis*. Cambridge MA: Harvard University Press, 1975.

Winnicott, D. W. *Jeu et réalité. L'espace potentiel*. Paris: Gallimard, 1975.

Wolterstorff, Nicholas. *Works and Worlds of Art*. Oxford: Clarendon Press, 1980.

———. "Worlds of Works of Art." *Journal of Aesthetics and Art Criticism* 35 (1976): 121–32.

Zentall, Thomas R., and Bennett G. Galef, eds. *Social Learning: Psychological and Biological Approaches*. Hillsdale NJ: Lawrence Erlbaum Associates, 1988.

Index

action: hierarchical structure of, 53, 313n12; and knowledge, 58–59; Plato on, 23; and reality, 38

actors, 89–90, 327n75; hypernormal lures by, 316n44; personification of characters by, 2, 83; simulation of emotion by, 169, 170; substitution of identity by, 228, 255

Aesop, 76, 78, 316n43

aesthetics: in cinema, 161; in digital fiction, 289, 308; and fictional universe, 179; as fiction's immanent function, 292–93, 294, 301–3, 305; in games, 307–8; involves both creation and reception, 306–7

affective empathy: in cinema, 161, 167–68, 172, 227; contamination of, 168; fictional immersion and, 159–61, 171–72; Plato and Proust on, 160

Alexander, R. D., 101–2

Allen, Woody: *Zelig*, 137

analogy: and fictional modeling, 57, 189, 245, 267; global, 189, 267; and homology, 189; mimesis as, 24–25; and reality, 91; and representation, 61, 272; and resemblance, 91, 183

Andersen, Hans Christian, 3

animals: dreams by, 148; and ludic feint, 105–6, 320n88; and ludic ritualization, 35; mimetic capacities of, xv–xvi; mimetic learning by, 101–2, 105; and observational priming, 48; similarity judgments by, 62, 63–64; use of lures by, 45; use of signs by, 317n54

Annouilh, Jean, 324n29

antimimeticism, xiv–xv, 3–7, 36, 291; of Plato, xiv–xv, 6, 15–22; on rupture between technological and traditional arts, 7–14

Apollodorus, 14

An Apology for Poetry (Sidney), 323n23

Aristotle: actantial logic of, 243; on fiction, xvii, 37–38, 57, 194, 211, 227, 291, 337n1; on mimesis, xvi, 34, 81, 292; on observational learning, 51; on poetry, 28, 169, 292, 337n1

art: definition of, 209; economic profitability of, 7; fictional games as, 307; and imitation, 5, 79; reproduction mode of, 212–13; social role and legitimacy, 42, 209; and technological changes, 7, 214–15; and time, 178; variety and constancy of, 215–16

aspectuality, 202–3, 220, 292; perceptive, 225, 332n18

Austin, John L., 316n42, 322n13
autobiography, 242, 243, 263
Aymé, Marcel, 1–2, 16, 31, 80–81

Babe, 222
Balzac, Honoré de: *La comédie humaine*, 115, 158; *The Wild Ass's Skin*, 238
Bambi, 222
Bandura, Albert, 101
Banfield, Ann, 238
Barthes, Roland, 323n25
Batman, 3
Baudelaire, Charles, 259
Baudonnière, Pierre-Marie, 52, 315n33
Bécassine, 213
behavior: hierarchical organization of, 53, 78; and imitation, 55, 71; and ludic feint, 149, 153; and modelization, 20–21, 310–11n8; and observational priming, 49–50, 51
beliefs: diversity of modalities of, 37; and fictional devices, 206; historical transformation of, 27–28; and immersion, 163, 165, 167; ludic feint and, 135–36; and perception, 87; and reality, 128; and representations, 163; theory of make-believe, 167
Benveniste, Emile, 279
Bérénice, 255
biography, 190–91. See also *Marbot: Eine Biographie*
The Birth of Tragedy from the Spirit of Music, (Nietzsche), 30
Block, Ned, 314n26
blockage mechanisms: in dreaming,

148–49; in fictional immersion, 39, 138–39, 163, 164, 166, 170; of inferences, 199–200
Bodmer, Johann Jakob, 180, 181
Bouveresse, Jacques, 176
Brecht, Bertold, 4
Breitinger, Johann Jakob, 180, 181
Bremond, Claude, 195, 330n111
Broch, Hermann: *The Death of Virgil*, 118
Bruner, Jerome, 328n93
Buddhism, 210
Buñuel, Luis, 220
Burgoyne, Robert, 278–79
Busch, Wilhelm, 213–14
Byrne, Richard, 53, 54, 79

Cadoz, Claude, ix, 57, 58
Camus, Albert: *The Stranger*, 172
Carnap, Rudolph, 176
catharsis theory, 34–35, 295, 296–97
Cervantes, Miguel de: *Don Quixote*, 281
children: fiction for, 213–14, 215; games of, xii, xviii, 126–27, 151–52, 205, 208–9, 233, 307, 322n18; and imagination, 295, 296–97; learning of reality by, 140–45, 300; and ludic feint, xvi, 153, 208; reaction to external stimuli by, 142–43, 325n35; role playing by, 308; and self-stimulation, 143–45, 151–52; social learning by, 97, 102–3
China, 210
cinema, 270–80; actantial logic in, 275–76; and affective empathy, 161, 167–68, 172, 227; antimimetic

criticisms of, 4, 7; compared to dreams, 155, 325n40; denotational force of, 197–98; feint in, 270, 271, 279; and fictional blockages, 200–201; fictionality of, 12, 137–38, 259, 272, 332n29; fictional universe in, 197–98, 204; fiction vs. documentary, 132, 137, 198, 270, 271–72; and globalization, 211; homologous character of, 272–73; hypernormal lures in, 132–33, 135, 223, 270, 271; and identification, 171; immersion vector and posture of, 222–23; internal focalization in, 271; linguistic categories in, 273–74; lures in, 132, 133, 262, 323–24n25; narrative character in, 275–78, 279, 336n71; nonillocutionary nature of, 272–73; paratext in, 138; and perceptive identification, 179–80, 224–25; perceptive immersion in, 183, 271, 274; perceptive transfer in, 167–68, 183, 273; quasi-perceptive flux of, 332n18, 336n71; semiotic status of, 272; sonorous mimes in, 331–32n17; spectators of, 155, 161, 167–68, 224–25, 226, 279; stereoscopic vision in, 335n57; subjective and objective camera in, 332n24; verbal and visual aspects of, 12–13, 231–32, 331–32n17

A Clockwork Orange (Kubrick), 310n8

cognition: division of work of, 206, 331n2; and fiction, 103–4, 179, 193, 201, 293, 300; of imitation, 53; ludic feint and, 104–5, 107–8,

201; and mimesis, 29–30, 36, 100–101; and modeling, 57; and myth, 28–29; and perception, 94, 293–94, 318n63; preattentional processes, 319n72; of reality, 91, 318n63; representation as, 293, 314n30; of resemblance, 66; restrictive definition of, 337n4; of similarity, 62, 67, 70, 94, 314n26; and simulation, 59, 99; through immersion, 96

Cohn, Dorrit, 237, 271, 331n12; on *Marbot,* 111, 118, 119–20

La comédie humaine (Balzac), 115, 158

Conan Doyle, Arthur, 200

conflict, ludic ritualization of, 35

consciousness: adaptive values of, 59; control of, 134, 135, 138, 142, 164; and defusion of lure, 134; evolution of, 59; and representation, 92–93, 299

constructionism, 66

contamination, mimetic: of affective reactions, 168; of historical world by fictional world, 117–18, 122; Plato on danger of, 18–20, 23–24, 36, 38–39; as type of knowledge, 29–30

culture: and cognition, 97–98; cyberculture, vii–xii; and fiction, xiii, 43–44, 125–26; and games, 205, 207–8; and mimetic arts, 211; mimetic learning's role in, 98, 102–3; and representations, 84, 85, 207; transcultural generalizations, 95; and visual representation, 95

focalization: external, 241, 244–45; internal, 220, 241, 242, 243–44, 245, 271

Fodor, Jerry, 198, 330n115

Freedberg, David, 161

Frege, Gottlob, 175, 176, 183

Fresh Bait (Tavernier), 310n9

Freud, Sigmund, 295, 325–26n43

Frey, Dagobert, 326–27n66

Fusillo, Massimo, 312n26

games, fictional: aesthetic character of, 307–8; blockage mechanisms in, 39; of children, 126–27, 151–52, 205, 208–9, 233, 307, 322n18; digital, 73–74, 287–88, 289; and fiction, xii, xviii, 211, 303; of Huli in Papua New Guinea, 208–9, 233, 244; imaginary, 283; immersion vector of, 228; intercultural stability of, 205, 207–8; and ludic feint, xii, 208; modelization in, 307; multiple personifications in, 233; Plato on, 16; and representation, 293, 307, 308; and self-stimulation, 205–6, 207. *See also* video games

García Barrientos, José Luis, 336n72

Gates, Bill, 7

Geertz, Clifford, 247

Genette, Gérard, 126, 185, 198, 236, 330n108; on function of entertainment, 305; on internal focalization, 243–44; on narrative in fiction, 274, 278; on simulation, 230, 316n44; on stylistic imitation, 78

Gessain, Moique, 325n41

Giono, Jean, 224; *Noé*, 154, 156, 157, 159; *Un roi sans divertissement*, 58, 159

globalization, 210–11

Glowinski, Michal, 82

Goethe, Johann Wolfgang von, 117, 248; *The Sorrows of Young Werther*, 16

Goffman, Erving, 247

Goldman, Laurence, 127, 208

Gombrich, Ernst, 12, 164, 165, 334–35n57

Goodman, Nelson, 183, 323n23, 328nn93–94; on denotational zero, 177, 178; on representation, 317–18n60, 319n67; scenocentric view of, 249–50, 334n46; on symbolic systems, 182–83

Greece, ancient, 14

Gulliver's Travels (Swift), 260

habituation, 262

hallucinations, 145, 146, 295

Hamburger, Käte, 332n29, 333n41; on distinction between feint and fiction, 120, 237, 238, 240–41, 244; on hetereodiegetic narrative, 242, 243, 245; on indices of fictionality, 220, 239, 270; on internal focalization, 220, 271

Harweg, Roland, 238

Heidegger, Martin, 303

Heinich, Nathalie, 152, 247–48, 333n39

Hemingway, Ernest, 238

Hildesheimer, Wolfgang, 109–11;

explanation of *Marbot* by, 110–11; introduces Marbot as character, 113; *Mozart*, 109. See also *Marbot: Eine Biographie*

history: and fiction, 29, 38, 58; fictional world's contamination of, 117–18, 122; historical novels, 177; representations of, 87

Hollywood, 6, 311n16

Homer, 23

Howell, Robert, 181

Huli tribe of Papua New Guinea, 127–28, 322n18; children's games of, 208–9, 233, 244

hypernormal lures, 77, 134–35, 316n44; in cinema, 270, 271; in digital fiction, 285; in film, 132–33, 135; in theater, 334n50

hypnosis, 324n28

illocutionary acts, 272–73, 335–36n67

illusion: antimimetic position on, xv, 5; and being, 13; and fictional immersion, 163, 166–67; perceptive, 101, 133–34, 166–67, 262; referential, 234–35; visual, 101, 261–62

imagination: autonomy of, 36; and categorization, 304; in children, 295, 296–97; as compensatory activity, 295; and digital fictions, 14, 281, 282–83; and fictional competence, 140; and fictional immersion, 154–55; Kant on, 303–4; Plato on, 296; and reality, x, 297, 300, 304; and representa-

tions, 88; and self-stimulation, 149–50, 152, 303; and simulation, xii, 99

imitation: Aristotle on, xvi, 38, 291–92; and art, 5, 79; behavioral, 21, 55, 71; and cinema, 183; cognitive function of, 53; definition of, 46–47; in digital games, 73–74; and feint, 55, 71, 72, 73, 74, 75–77, 80, 316n42; and fiction, 2, 234, 235; human predisposition to, xvi, xvii; and immersion, 32–33; and learning, 51–56, 70, 71, 79, 94, 95, 97, 98–105, 101; and lived incarnation, 33; and lures, 44–45, 47, 73, 131–32; mimetic, 5, 47–48, 60, 315n33; and modeling, xvii, 17, 38, 98–99, 235, 236, 313n17, 393; and myth, 28; and observational priming, 48–51; of painting, 71–72; Plato on, 15, 16–19, 22–30, 26, 38–39, 70, 311n14; and reality, viii, x, 38–39; and reinstantiation, 55–56, 75, 76–78, 80, 82; religion and, 30, 31; and representation, xiv, 69, 81–83, 89, 90, 93, 94, 95, 261, 278, 319n67; and resemblance, 48, 60–61, 69, 315n34; selective, 60–61; and semblance, 72, 78, 80, 82, 103, 104; and sham, 31, 42; and similarity, 61, 68; and simulation, 56, 73; social, 20–21; stylistic, 78–79, 80; surface vs. hierarchical, 102; and truth, 24, 311n17; verbal, 26; and what is imitated, 74, 76–77, 131. *See also* mimesis immersion, fictional mimetic: and affective empathy, 159–61, 170, 171–72; and beliefs, 163, 165, 167; blockage mechanisms in, 39, 138–39, 163, 164, 166, 170; in cathartic theory, 297; and cinema, 183, 271, 274; coexistence of environment and imagined world in, 156–58; in creation of fiction, 153–54, 159, 169, 170–71, 201; in digital fiction, 284–85, 286; as divided mental state, 164–66; and feint, 22, 158, 321; fictional and actual, 251; and generic immersion, 321n4; as homeostatic activity, 158–59, 302; and identification, 162, 171; and imitation, 32–33; interiorization through, 172; and knowledge, 37, 96; learning by, 213, 263; and lures, 40, 162–63, 166–67; mimetic/fictional distinction, 201, 261, 262–63, 272; and modeling, 20, 21, 98–99, 173–74, 202, 267; necessity of, 172–73; partial/total distinction, 261, 262; Plato on, 96, 153–54; pragmatic frame of, 122; quasi-perceptive, 222–24, 265, 332n18, 336n71; in reception of fiction, 153–54, 158, 159–60, 169, 170–71, 201; relations between inner-worldly perception and imaginative activity, 154–55, 278; in religious ritual, 31; and representation, 135, 161, 165, 266–67; and self-stimulation, 158, 302; and semblance, 108, 134, 163, 278; and simulation, 169, 253

immersion postures: actantial allosubjective identification, 228; defined, 218–19; natural narration, 220, 221, 230; pluriperceptive experience, 223–24; position of observer, 225–26, 257; subjective interiority, 219, 244; variability of, 232–33, 245–46; visual perception, 221–22

immersion vectors: defined, 218–19; simulation of events, 224–27, 250–51, 253, 254–55, 257; simulation of homologous mimetic representations, 221–22; simulation of illocutory acts, 220, 230, 231, 278; simulation of mental acts, 219–20, 230, 278; simulation of quasi-perceptive mimemes, 222–24; substitution of narrative identity, 221, 230, 231, 253–54; substitution of physical identity, 227–29, 254–55, 256, 257, 287–88; variability of, 245; virtual character of, 255–56

Indiana Jones, 3

inferences, 199–200

interiorization, 26, 172

internal coherence, 193–95

Ion (Plato), 23, 311n20

irrealization, 8, 280, 281, 282

Jamin, Jean, 312n28

Jansenism, 3

Jastrow, Joseph, 164

Jena romanticism, 3

Jost, François, 198, 277, 332n24, 336n71

Jouvet, Michel, 148
Joyce, James: *Ulysses*, 219, 221
Jullien, François, 210
Jurassic Park (Spielberg), 211, 306

Kandinsky, Wassily, 3
Kant, Immanuel, 303–4
knowledge: abstract, 52–53; and action, 58–59; and fiction, 337n4; hierarchy of, 24–26; and immersion, 37, 96; mimesis and, 29–30, 36, 70; Plato on, 23, 96; social, 27–28; visual, 92, 318n64. *See also* cognition; learning
Kripke, Saul, 180
Kubrick, Stanley, 310n8; *Lolita*, 216
Kurosawa, Akira: *Rashômon*, 182

Lacoue-Labarthe, Philippe, 311n17
La Fontaine, Jean, 76, 78, 80
Lallot, Jean, 81
La Ménardière, Hippolyte-Jules Pilet de, 249
language: binary, 8–9, 309–10n2; cinema and, 273–74; learning of, 52, 55, 69–70, 208, 320n90; and lures, 46; and perception, 88; referential and fictional, 175; and signs, 10, 83, 309–10n2
learning: by children, 97, 102–3, 140–45, 300; effects of training, 20–22, 310–11n8; by imitation, 70, 71, 79, 94, 95, 97, 98–105; instance, 188; of language, 52, 55, 69–70, 208, 320n90; ludic feints in, 104–5, 106–7; mimetic, 53–54, 95–97, 98, 101–3, 104–5, 206, 213,

263, 320n77; observational, 51–53, 60, 69, 313n7; by rational calculation, 97; to recognize similarities, 62–63; "rule learning," 329n104; social, 27–28, 51, 96–97, 102–3, 106–7, 313n7, 319n73; by trial and error, 97, 101, 206; by way of speech, 87. *See also* knowledge
Leibniz, Gottfried, 180, 181
Leiris, Michel, 146, 169, 246; "La possession et ses aspects théatraux chez les Éthiopiens de Gondar," 33
Lejeune, Philippe, 242–43
Lévy, Pierre, 309n3
Lévy-Bruhl, Lucien, 32
Lévy-Leblond, Jean-Marc, 329n100
Lewis, David, 181, 199, 200
Libération, vii–viii, x
lies: and fable, 81; and ludic feint, 21, 29; and myth, 18; Plato on, 17–18, 21, 310n7; truth and falsity in, 124
"The Logical Status of Fictional Discourse" (Searle), 184
Lolita, 216, 217
Lotman, Iouri, 106, 164
ludic feint: about, 123; animals and, xv–xvi, 105–6, 320n88; autonomy of, 22, 311n10; children and, xii, xvi, xviii, 153, 208; in cinema, 270, 271, 279; cognitive function of, 104–5, 107–8, 201; creates imaginary universe, 130–31; decouples mind and beliefs, 135–36; in digital fiction, 281, 283; and fiction, xii, 2, 29, 80, 127, 245, 324n29; as distinct from serious feint, 21, 76, 123–24, 131, 139, 145, 223, 322n13;

narrative literary fiction (*continued*)
213; self-narration theory, 278–79;
verbal feint in, 235
Natural Born Killers (Stone), 310n8
Nietzsche, Friedrich, 32; *The Birth of
Tragedy from the Spirit of Music,*
30
A Nightmare on Elm Street, 158
Ninos and Semiramis, 312n26

observational priming, 48–51, 68–69
occularization, 277, 336n71
Odin, Roger, 260–61, 272, 335n58
Ogden, Charles K., 176, 327–28n83
opera, 233, 252

painting: abstract, 4; in ancient
Greece, 14; antimimetic arguments on, 4, 6–7; and fictional
modeling, 267; fictional reception of, 269; as iconic mimesis,
267–68; imitation of, 71–72; and
perception, 258; representation in,
263–64, 265–66; as semblance,
xvii, 258–59
Papua New Guinea. *See* Huli tribe of
Papua New Guinea
paratext, 112, 114–16, 137, 138, 321n7
Parrhasius, 14
Parsons, Josh, 181
Parsons, Terence, 197–98, 328n84
Pavel, Thomas, 127, 173, 216, 317n57
perception: and belief, 87; and
cinema, 273, 274, 279–80, 336n71;
and cognition, 94, 293–94,
318n63; in digital fiction, 285;
and identification, 92, 94; and

illusion, 262; and imagination,
88, 303; inner-world, 156, 157;
learning from, 87; and painting,
258; and representation, 88, 92,
265, 318n63; saturation of, 261; of
signs, 92–93; and thought, 328n93
perceptive illusion, 101, 133–34,
166–67, 262
perceptive transfer, 133–34, 135,
163–64, 167–68, 183, 226–27
personification, 2, 83, 233
Phaedrus, 76, 78
philosophy, 28, 29, 36
photography: digital, 9, 11; factual
reception of, 269–70, 335n64;
feint in, 223, 268; mimetic techniques in, xvii, 4, 7, 12; representation in, 263–64, 266, 267–68
pictorial naturalism, 12
Pietists, 243
Pirandello, Luigi, 324n29
Plato, 160, 246, 259; antimimetic
position of, xiv–xv, xvii, 6, 14, 37,
310n4; conception of *mimēsis,*
15–30; on contagion of reality
by shams, 36, 38–39; distrust of
fiction, xiii, 3, 32, 296; on fictional
immersion, 96, 153–54; on imitation, 39, 70; on observational
learning, 51; on painting, 6, 258
Poetics (Aristotle), 28, 51, 81, 292
poetry, 4; Aristotle on, 28, 37–38,
169, 292, 337n1
The Possessed (Dostoyevsky), 159
possession, 34; rites of, 32–33, 145,
312n28
possible worlds theory, 179–82, 184

Poussin, Nicolas, 266
Prague Linguistic Circle, 248
Promomidès, François, 249, 251–52
Proust, Marcel, 160; *À la recherche du temps perdu*, 115; *Journées de lecture*, 154, 155, 156–57, 158–59, 326n55, 326n59; *Remembrance of Things Past*, 178
psycho-narration, 331n12
Putnam, Hilary, 331n2

quasi-perceptive immersion, 222–24, 265, 332n18, 336n71
Quine, Willard, 62–63, 64, 66, 67, 157, 314n30

radio, 332n19
Raeburn, Henry, 114
Rashômon (Kurosawa), 182
realism, 91
reality: and analogy, 91; beliefs and, 128; children's learning of, 140–45, 300; cognition of, 91, 318n63; divided, 158; and feint, 21–22, 38–39; and fiction, x, 20, 26–27, 38, 185–86, 187, 198, 242–43; and fictional universe, 117–18, 122; and games, 16; and imagination, x, 297, 300, 304; and imitation, viii, x, 38–39; mental-physical relationship of, 145, 185, 329n101; and modeling, 192–93; modes of accessing, 217; Plato on, 36, 38–39; and representation, 71, 72–73, 82–83, 91; and self, 140–45; and semblance, 75, 121, 164; and sham, 13–14, 36;

and signs, 182–83. *See also* virtual reality
referentiality, 128–29, 177, 178–79, 194, 234–35
reinstantiation, 55–56, 75, 76–78, 80, 82
religion: and fiction, 31, 124–25, 210, 322n16; and rise of ludic imitation, 30, 31
remedy, notion of, 310n7
Renaissance, 14, 235
representation: about term, 82–84; affective investment of, 130, 160–61; analogical, 61, 272; Aristotle on, 292; and aspectuality, 202–3; and beliefs, 163; and cognition, 293, 314n30; and culture, 84, 207; descriptive, 89; and digital fiction, 289, 307, 308; and dismissal, 86; and feint, 264–65; fictional, xi, xiii, 87, 126–27, 128–30, 174, 175, 179, 203, 260, 262, 265, 293, 303; homologous, 263, 265, 266; iconic, 130; and imagination, 88; and imitation, xiv, 69, 81–83, 89, 90, 93, 94, 95, 261, 278, 319n67; intelligibility of, 195; internal constitution of, 130; Kantian idea on, 304–5; mental, 83–86, 317n55; Metz theories on, 335n58; mimetic, 60, 262; and mimetic reactivation, 157–58; and modeling, 58, 190, 304; and perception, 88, 92, 265, 318n63; Plato on, 15; and preattentional lures, 261–62; and reality, 71, 72–73, 82–83, 91; referential, 128–29, 174; and rep-

children and, 141–42; in cinema, 272; in digital fiction, 284–85; in fiction, 82; and language, 10, 83, 309–10n2; and perception, 92–93; and reality, 182–83; and representation, 82, 83–84, 89–90, 91, 317n53, 322–23n22; and resemblance, 90

similarity: absolute and relative, 63–64; classifications of, 65–66; in everyday life, 61–62; human judgments on, 66–67; and imitation, 61, 68; recognition of, 62–63, 67, 70, 94, 314n26; and representation, 90, 93; and signs, 82, 89–90; by visual projection, 93

simulation: cognitive, 59, 99; digital, viii–ix, 284, 286; of emotion, 168–69, 327n73; fictive, 58, 314n23; formative role of, 37; and imagination, xii, 99; and imitation, 56, 73; and immersion, 169, 253; and modeling, 37, 56, 69; of possession, 33; and sham, 72–73; and social learning, 106–7

Singer, Jerome, 142, 300

skiagraphia, 310n4

snobbism, 210

social learning, 51, 71, 96–97, 102–3, 313n7, 319n73; and ludic simulation, 106–7; and observational priming, 49–50; transmission of, 27–28

social role, 247–48, 333n39

Socrates, 23

Sophist (Plato), 26

The Sorrows of Young Werther (Goethe), 16

Soulagles, François, 270, 335n64

Spielberg, Steven: *Jurassic Park,* 211, 306

Stern, David, 141

Sterne, Laurence, 242

Stone, Oliver, 310n8

The Stranger (Camus), 172

Suetonius, 239–40

symbolic commodities, 84–85, 316–17n53

Tadié, Alexis, 327n73

Tamagotchi, 281–82, 283

Tavernier, Bertrand, 310–11n8

technology, xii, 7, 214–15

television, 7, 12, 214–15

theater, 246–57; in ancient Greece, 14; development after Renaissance, 12; feint in, 254; fictionality devices, 137, 246, 259–60; as game, 246, 256–57; hypernormal lures in, 334n50; immersion vector and posture of, 224, 225, 226–27; "lived," 33, 34, 146; and narration, 254, 275, 336nn71–72; representation in, 248; ritual, 246–47; scenic level, 246, 248, 249–50, 257; social drama in, 247–48; spectators of, 225–27, 246, 256–57; textual level, 246, 248–49, 250, 333n41, 334n51

Thomas, Yan, 329n100

Tinbergen, Niko, 46–47

Titanic, 168, 211

Tomb Raider, vii, 228

In the Stages Series

To order or obtain more information on these or other University of Nebraska Press titles, visit www.nebraskapress.unl.edu.

CPSIA information can be obtained
at www.ICGtesting.com
Printed in the USA
LVHW111154120821
695152LV00009B/500/J